J2EE™ AntiPatterns

J2EE™ AntiPatterns

Bill Dudney
Stephen Asbury
Joseph K. Krozak
Kevin Wittkopf

WILEY
Wiley Publishing, Inc.

Publisher: Robert Ipsen
Vice President and Publisher: Joe Wikert
Executive Editor: Robert Elliot
Development Editor: Eileen Bien Calabro
Editorial Manager: Kathryn A. Malm
Media Development Specialist: Greg Stafford
Production Editor: Felicia Robinson
Text Design & Composition: Wiley Composition Services

Published by Wiley Publishing, Inc., Indianapolis, Indiana
Published simultaneously in Canada

Library of Congress Cataloging-in-Publication Data available from the publisher

ISBN: 0-471-14615-3

Printed in the United States of America

10 9 8 7 6 5 4 3 2 1

Contents

Acknowledgments

I would like to thank first and foremost Christ, for all He has done in my life to teach me to be more than I was and to inspire me to be more than I am. I would also like to thank my wonderful wife Sarah, without her support and love I'd be lost. And I'd also like to thank my great kids that keep life interesting. Andrew, Isaac, Anna, and Sophia; you are the definition of joy. I'd also like to thank my dad who always told me that I'd make the top of the hill if only I'd stand up, keep my feet on the foot pegs, and gas it on.

Thank you Jack Greenfield for forcing me to think outside the box. I'm a better thinker because of your prodding, Jack, thanks. I'd also like to thank John Crupi and Bill Brown for all their great feedback on the content of this book. It's a better book because of them. And finally I'd like to thank Eileen Bien Calabro for all her hard work on turning my gibberish into English and helping me to deliver a better book. I hope you learn as much from reading this book as I did in writing it.

—BD

Thanks to all the folks I work and have worked with for providing AntiPatterns, either knowingly or not. Immeasurable appreciation to my wife Cheryl; after 12 years of marriage, words cannot express my appreciation for her being my best friend and wife.

—SA

I would like to thank my Lord and savior Jesus Christ, without whom I would be eternally lost. I would also like to thank my darling wife Jennifer for her endless patience, love and support. I thank God for my beautiful daughter Kristina; sweetheart anything is possible if you put your mind and energy to it! I would also like to thank my wonderful brother Raymond, for all of his wisdom, and guidance. Finally, I would like to thank my Mother for all of her love, encouragement, and selfless sacrifices.

—JKK

I would like to dedicate this to the loves of my life. First, to my wife and best friend Catherine, for her constant love, support, and encouragement throughout this effort. I couldn't have done it without you! Also, to my two wonderful daughters, for their infectious energy and spirit.

I would like to thank all of my co-authors, for all their hard work and great contributions. I would especially like to thank Bill Dudney for inviting me in on this (no, really!) and for his hard work on many of the coordinating and review activities to make sure this all came together.

Also, I would like to thank all the people at Wiley Technical Publications, especially Eileen Bien Calabro, for their hard work, guidance and patience in my initial foray into writing.

—*KW*

Foreword

Psychologists say that doing the same thing over and over and expecting a different result is a form of insanity. This may also apply to software development. Unfortunately, we have repeated some of our designs so often that we don't realize they can be a source of some of our major problems. Herein lies the opportunity for AntiPatterns to educate us. An AntiPattern can be thought of as an expression of a bad practice in a formal template, in much the same way you would document a good practice, such as a Pattern. Thus an AntiPattern is a bad practice done so often that it is deemed worthy to be documented.

When a technology is introduced, many of us want to understand its details. This was especially true in the first three years of J2EE, as seen by the large number of "how to" J2EE books published. Many of these books put the specs in a language the rest of us could understand. However, as J2EE became more mature, and more developers understood the details and practiced applying them, J2EE design books began to emerge. These books didn't teach you about the technology per se, but focused more on how to design with the technology. This was the case with *Core J2EE Patterns*. We focused heavily on best practices in the form of Patterns.

This book can be used in many ways. It can confirm bad practices you've avoided. It can validate your belief that something was a bad practice. It can be used in design meetings to provide a vocabulary as to what not to do when designing a system. Or, if you're feeling feisty, you may use this book to overthrow that lead developer who always thinks his designs are so great (when everyone else, except management, knows they are not).

Many of you reading this book are well versed in J2EE. So, you may not read it as a "things to avoid" book, but rather as an "oops, I guess I shouldn't have done that" book. I'm pretty sure the authors understood this point, because they don't just tell you what you may have done wrong, but also explain how to fix it. This is what the authors achieve so nicely in this book.

There is lot of excellent information in *J2EE AntiPatterns*. The authors make it easy to understand the heart of an AntiPattern quickly. This is a key factor when you use this book as a design companion.

One last thing. Read the "Web Services AntiPatterns" chapter. With all the noise and confusion around Web Services, this will help you for years to come. Enjoy this book.

John Crupi
Coauthor *Core J2EE Patterns*
Distinguished Engineer, Sun Microsystems, Inc.
john.crupi@sun.com

Author Bios

Bill Dudney is a Java architect with Object Systems Group. He has been building J2EE applications and software for five years and has been doing distributed computing for almost 14 years. Bill has been using EJB since he was at InLine Software and the first public beta was released, and has built several J2EE applications as well as tools to help others do the same. He is the coauthor of *Jakarta Pitfalls: Time-Saving Solutions for Struts, Ant, JUnit,* and *Cactus* and *Mastering JavaServer Faces* (Wiley). You can reach him at j2eeantipatterns@yahoo.com.

Stephen Asbury has authored eight books on Web technology, covering topics that range from CGI, Perl, ASP, and Linux to Enterprise Java. He has authored numerous courses on Java, JavaScript, Active Server Pages, HTML, and just about everything else that Web programmers need to know. Stephen has also worked with most of the major enterprise application integration companies over the last five years, including Active Software (now WebMethods), Vitria Technology, and Tibco Software.

As a developer, Stephen has been involved with the design and development of systems ranging from some of the first Web applications that used Perl and CGI, to online training environments developed as both applets and JavaServer Pages (JSP), to development environments and infrastructure products, including a JSP engine and a Java Message Service (JMS) implementation. He is currently a senior engineering manager at Tibco Software Inc. where he is one of the lead architects developing new generations of enterprise development tools. Stephen lives in California with his beloved wife Cheryl.

Joseph K. Krozak is the vice president of technology development for Krozak Information Technologies, Inc, a leading supplier of advanced software solutions to Fortune 500 and mid-market companies. Joseph has over 15 years experience in the information technology industry, including 10 years of extensive experience building large, distributed-object-, and component-oriented systems. Joseph leads an innovative team of senior architects and developers who repeatedly break down barriers and enable success in their customers' information technology projects.

Kevin Wittkopf has been a software architect and developer for over 17 years, and has worked with object languages and technologies since 1988. Since 1996, he has been working with Java, Enterprise JavaBeans (EJB), and J2EE. He has acted as technical lead and mentor on many large-scale distributed object-oriented (OO) application projects, most recently focusing on enterprise integration, Web services, messaging, and service-based architecture. He holds degrees in mining engineering and computing science.

Kevin spends his free time creating electronic music, attending improv theatre, and spending as much time as possible with his lovely wife Catherine and two children.

Introduction

All too often delivered software is full of bugs and poorly performing processes. Unfortunately, it is often hard to figure out exactly what has gone wrong and what needs to be done to make things better. AntiPatterns lie at this juncture between problems and solutions.

This book provides practical advice on how to recognize bad code and design in J2EE and provides steps to making the code better. You will find AntiPatterns in J2EE with formal definitions of typical coding and design errors, as well as real-world examples of code that is stuck in AntiPatterns. For each AntiPattern, there is at least one refactoring and often more. Each will walk you through the process of making code better.

In designing and developing any application, we believe you should look at both positive (Patterns) and negative (AntiPatterns) examples of how an application might be built. We all want to build better software in better ways, learning from our own mistakes and those of others. For example, in a typical J2EE application, there are usually multiple tiers—the database tier housing the data for the application, the Enterprise JavaBean (EJB) tier interacting with the database and housing the business logic, and the Web tier, which provides the user interface. There are many opportunities to make mistakes in building across these different tiers. A typical mistake is to have the Web tier directly interact with entity EJBs. Applications written in this manner have serious performance problems. Over time, the Session Façade pattern [Alur, Crupi, Malks] has emerged as a means to avoid the poor performance for applications that are being written. However, applications that were written without the Façade still need to be fixed. Rather than throw out the code and start over, Chapter 9 has a refactoring called Façade that provides practical steps to take to fix the poor performance.

AntiPatterns in J2EE

J2EE as an architecture is very powerful and flexible. As with most other areas in life, to get something, we have to give something else up. In J2EE, we have achieved great power and flexibility but we had to give up simplicity.

The breadth of J2EE covers everything from database access to Web-based presentation. There are many different libraries—or parts—of J2EE that are themselves worthy of entire books. Figure Intro.1 shows some of the breadth of what is covered by J2EE.

The AntiPatterns covered in this book span most of the conceptual space of J2EE. There are AntiPatterns for almost every section of the J2EE API, including database access to using JavaServer Pages (JSPs).

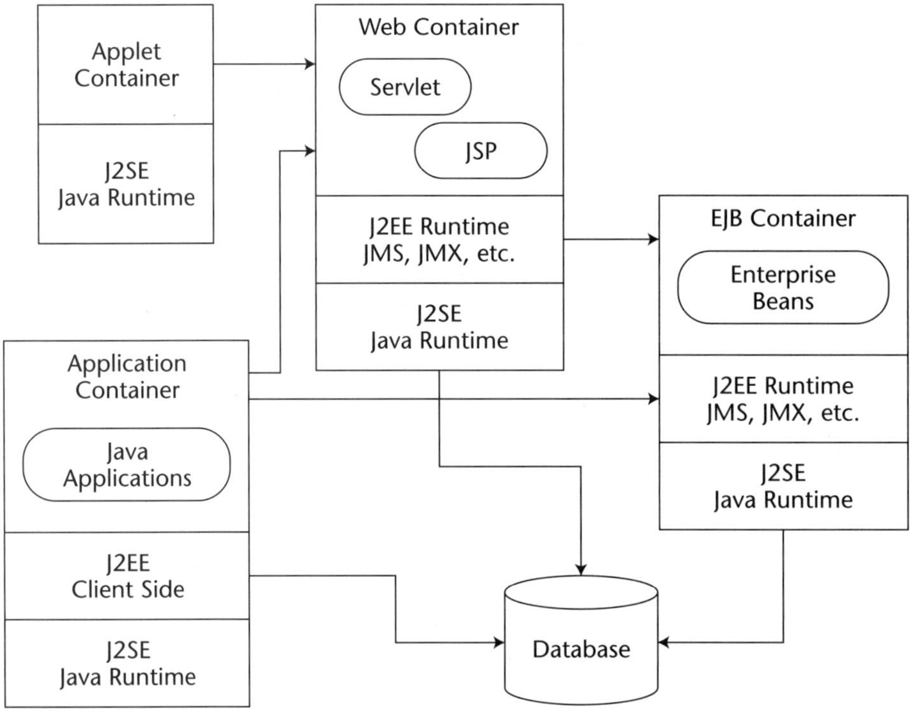

Figure Intro.1 J2EE overview

AntiPatterns

An AntiPattern is a repeated application of code or design that leads to a bad outcome. The outcome can be poor performance or hard-to-maintain code or even a complete failure of the project. AntiPatterns are a detailed or specific way to capture the code errors.

The AntiPatterns in this book are captured in a template. The template helps to ensure a formal, consistent definition so that the AntiPatterns are easier to learn. The template also provides a way to capture information about the AntiPattern from different perspectives. Some might recognize the AntiPattern in their code by the "Symptoms and Consequences," others from one of the "Typical Causes." The template is made up of two sections, a list of *Catalog* items that are short phrases or names, and more involved *Detail* items with items that go into more depth. The items are listed below.

Catalog Items

- **Also Known As.** This is one or more alternative name that can also be attached to the AntiPattern.
- **Most Frequent Scale.** This item documents the most likely area of an application that the AntiPattern is likely to appear.
- **Refactorings.** This item lists the appropriate refactorings that work the code or design out of the AntiPattern.
- **Refactored Solutions Type.** This item provides the kind of refactoring that can be applied to the AntiPattern.
- **Root Causes.** This item provides the root cause of the AntiPattern. Fix this, and the AntiPattern will be gone for good.
- **Unbalanced Forces.** This item captures the forces that are not balanced on the project. Usually when an AntiPattern is developed, there are forces that work with the root cause that realize the AntiPattern. Often, a balance cannot be struck between all forces.
- **Anecdotal Evidence.** This item captures quotes that are likely to be heard from developers or managers when a project is struck by the AntiPattern.

Detail Items

- **Background.** This section provides background and often personal examples of the AntiPattern at work. How the AntiPattern has affected various projects and other information about how it came up or was noticed is included here.
- **General Form.** This is the most likely way that the AntiPattern will manifest itself. This is a good place to look for information to help you identify if your application is trapped in an AntiPattern. This section will often include diagrams or code to make concrete the concepts discussed.
- **Symptoms and Consequences.** Symptoms are pain points in the development of an application that are good indicators of the AntiPattern. Consequences document the effect of not doing anything about the AntiPattern and letting it trouble your design and code.
- **Typical Causes.** This section documents concrete instances of the "Root Causes" and contains information about real-world, practical examples of what has caused the AntiPattern in projects in the past.
- **Known Exceptions.** An exception is a situation where having the AntiPattern does not adversely affect the project.
- **Refactorings.** This section contains details about how to apply the refactorings to this AntiPattern to most effectively remove the AntiPattern from your application.
- **Variations.** This section highlights significant examples that show how the AntiPattern varies from instance to instance.
- **Example.** This section contains an example to illustrate what code or design placed in the AntiPattern will look like.
- **Related Solutions.** This section contains references to other AntiPatterns that are typically encountered along with the AntiPattern, or refactorings that can be helpful in resolving the AntiPattern.

Refactoring

A refactoring is a disciplined means of transforming the implementation of code to make the design better without changing the externally visible behavior.

The key to successful refactoring is to have a good set of unit tests. A whole book could be written on the topic of unit testing, and many have been. The bottom line, however, is that you can never be sure that your refactoring has been successful, especially in not changing externally visible behavior, without a preexisting set of unit tests.

The refactorings in this book are also captured according to a template. In fact, the template owes much to Martin Fowler's well-regarded Refactorings book (Fowler 2000). As with the AntiPatterns, the refactoring template provides a means to standardize the refactorings so that they are easier to learn. The template is explained below.

- **Refactoring diagram.** Each contains a problem statement (a single sentence or phrase description of what is wrong with the code or design that needs to be fixed), a solution statement (a single-sentence or -phrase description of what needs to be done to fix the problem) and a diagram (a brief picture of what needs to be done to fix the problem). The latter contains either a snippet of code or a piece of a Unified Modeling Language (UML) design diagram that needs to be refactored, followed by a view at what the code or UML should look like after the refactoring is applied.
- **Motivation.** This section documents why the refactoring should be applied. This section typically contains a description of what consequences will be avoided or minimized if the refactoring is applied.
- **Mechanics.** This section describes the step-by-step process that will take the code from the current bad state to the better state.
- **Example.** The section contains an example of code or design that is affected by the AntiPattern. Each step is applied to the bad code or design until the refactoring is complete.

Why This Book?

There are a number of good books on how to start a fresh J2EE project, but none are much help in making your existing applications better. This book documents many of the common mistakes made while developing J2EE applications and provides help on how to refactor your way out of them. The goal is to help you become a better J2EE developer by illustrating what often goes wrong in application development as well as by providing tools to fix what has gone wrong. Refactorings provide practical advice on how to migrate the code away from the AntiPattern-laden design and implementation to a cleaner, more maintainable application. In other words, this is not a book about how to do J2EE design and development. Instead, this book is about the commonly made mistakes and how to correct them.

It is our hope and desire that you will learn at least a fraction of what we did from writing this book. In our years of experience in building J2EE applications, we have seen (and written) some horrible code and had equally bad results. In capturing some of the most common problems we have seen that your code will work better, quicker, and with less effort than it otherwise would and we hope that in learning from our mistakes you will become a better J2EE developer.

CHAPTER

1

Distribution and Scaling

The network is at the heart of any enterprise solution, large or small. J2EE is no exception; all J2EE solutions are built around the network. This means that J2EE developers will take on new problems and complexities as they move from the single application to the J2EE solution world.

As developers move from building small enterprise solutions to building large ones, they take on further architectural choices, complexities, and consequences, as well as solve new problems that didn't exist in the smaller world. In order to succeed in a distributed-networked world of J2EE, the first step is for the developers to understand the new environment in which they are working, and the differences between that environment and the smaller, non-networked one of which they are used to.

The best summary of the common misconceptions of distributed computing, and therefore J2EE programming, is the eight fallacies of distributed computing. I first heard about these fallacies from James Gosling at JavaOne in 2000. Gosling attributed them to Peter Deutsch. Although they are not widely known, these fallacies do a great job of summarizing the dangers that developers of distributed applications face. As a result, understanding the eight fallacies is of the utmost importance for all J2EE developers.

Fallacy 1: The network is reliable. One of the easiest assumptions to make in distributed computing is that the network will always be there. This simply isn't true. Networks are becoming more reliable, but due to the possibility of unexpected power failures and physical dangers, they cannot provide 100 percent availability. You simply can't expect the network to be 100 percent reliable.

Fallacy 2: Latency is zero. *Latency* is the time that it takes for messages to travel through the network. As most of us know, this value is not zero. Latency doesn't so much affect the amount of data you can send, but the delay in between sending and receiving data, so latency can have some interesting effects on your applications. For example, in some networking technologies, if a program A sends two messages to program B, it is possible that the messages will arrive out of order. More likely, you may have messages that travel a branched path, where the shorter path actually takes longer.

Fallacy 3: Bandwidth is infinite. Despite increasing network speeds, there are still limits to bandwidth; most homes are capped at 1.5 Mbps, most corporate networks at 100 Mbps. These limits can become important in mission-critical applications, since they limit the amount of data you pass around the network over time. The problem with bandwidth is that it is very hard to figure out where it all goes. Network protocols have some overhead, as do messaging implementations such as Java Message Service (JMS). Plus, there is background noise in an enterprise network caused by email, Web browsing, and file sharing.

Fallacy 4: The network is secure. Security can be a challenge for both administrators and users. These challenges include authentication, authorization, privacy, and data protection. If you are interested in security, you might start your study with the book *Secrets and Lies* by Bruce Schneier (Schneier 2002). Then, start working with experienced professionals. Keep in mind that security is not obtained by hiding algorithms and techniques; it is obtained by peer-reviewed solutions that don't depend on hiding the implementation to attain their goals.

Fallacy 5: Topology doesn't change. *Topology* is the physical connectivity of the computers. Failing hardware, handhelds, and laptops can change topology by removing computers, or paths through the network. New wireless technologies allow people to access your network from anywhere in the world. This makes developing applications a complex business, since wireless connections may be slow, they may go away and return, and they may have security issues. You need to think about providing customized interfaces for each type of client. These interfaces should reduce or increase functionality as needed to deal with the limitations of the client's bandwidth. You also have to think about clients connecting and disconnecting all the time, which can change your data architecture.

Fallacy 6: There is one administrator. Large companies have numerous system administrators. The same problem may be solved in different ways, and there are time and version differentials during software updates. Plan for administration and maintenance as much as possible during design time

Fallacy 7: Transport cost is zero. In a world were it costs money to move data, developers must be aware of the issues such as quality of service and speed versus price. Although most networks don't have a price per bit sent, at least not yet, there is still a cost. Buying bigger hardware and backup networks is expensive. If a solution can be designed in a way that provides the same functionality at a reduced total cost, do it. Don't rely on time as the only measure of a good choice; money must play a part as well. The business-savvy folks know this, but it is easy to get into a situation where you solve problems with money, not design. On the other hand, if you have the money and it will solve the problem quickly, go for it.

Fallacy 8: The network is homogeneous. Networks are a collection of technologies. Distributed applications have to deal with an alphabet soup of standards, such as TCP/IP (Transmission Control Protocol/Internet Protocol), HTTP (HyperText Transport Protocol), SOAP (Simple Object Access Protocol), CORBA (Common Object Request Broker Architecture), RMI (Remote Method Invocation), and others.

As you can imagine, these eight simple misunderstandings can generate a lot of problems and lead to many of the AntiPatterns in this chapter. Hopefully, by identifying and avoiding the AntiPatterns in this book, you will be able to overcome many of these problems and create truly distributed and scalable solutions.

The following AntiPatterns focus on the problems and mistakes that many developers make when building distributed, scalable solutions with J2EE. These AntiPatterns often grow out of the fallacies of distributed computing, but can also come from other sources such as time-to-market constraints. These AntiPatterns discuss some common misconceptions, often presented by nontechnical sources such as managers and analysts, which can mislead developers into choosing a suboptimal basic architecture for their solution.

All of these AntiPatterns represent architectural problems that may affect small elements of a solution or an entire network of J2EE applications. These are not problems with code that a single developer needs to look out for, rather they are architecture and design problems that the entire team needs to watch for and keep in mind throughout development.

Localizing Data. Localizing data is the process of putting data in a location that can only be accessed by a single element of your larger solution. For example, putting data in the static variables for a particular servlet results in the inability of servlets on other machines to access it. This AntiPattern often occurs when solutions are grown from small deployments to larger ones.

Misunderstanding Data Requirements. Poor planning and feature creep can lead to a situation where you are passing too much or too little data around the network.

Miscalculating Bandwidth Requirements. When bandwidth requirements are not realistically calculated, the final solution can end up having some major problems, mainly related to terrible performance. Sometimes bandwidth is miscalculated within a single solution. Sometimes it happens when multiple J2EE solutions are installed on one network.

Overworked Hubs. Hubs are rendezvous points in your J2EE application. These hubs may be database servers, JMS servers, EJB servers, and other applications that host or implement specific features you need. When a hub is overworked, it will begin to slow down and possibly fail.

The Man with the Axe. Failure is a part of life. Planning for failure is a key part of building a robust J2EE application.

Localizing Data

Also Known As: Simple Data Model, Data at the Nodes

Most Frequent Scale: Application, system

Refactorings: Plan for Scaling, Choose the Right Data Architecture

Refactored Solution Type: Process, role, architecture

Root Causes: Haste, feature creep

Unbalanced Forces: Time to market, individual/role responsibilities, unplanned features

Anecdotal Evidence: "We have too many copies of the data." "I need the data from this bean in that bean."

Background

Often the easiest implementation for a simple J2EE solution will place the data for that solution in the same location as the code that operates on the data. In the extreme, this could mean static variables, local files, and/or Entity Beans. Once data is localized, it may be hard to delocalize it. This makes your enterprise solution inherently limited in scale.

General Form

Localized data is found whenever a single node in an enterprise solution is storing its own data. Storing data locally isn't always wrong. The problems arise when data that is stored locally needs to be used somewhere else. For example, imagine that you are building a Web site for taking customer orders. Moreover, your initial customer base is small, so you write the solution with a set of servlets that stores customer data in files. This design might look like the one pictured in Figure 1.1.

Now, imagine that your customer base grows, or perhaps you open a previously internal Web application to your external customers. In either case, you have a lot more traffic than now than you did before, more than your Web server can handle. So you do the obvious thing; you buy more Web servers.

Now you have a problem, pictured in Figure 1.2. All your customer data is in files located on the first Web server. The other servers need to get to the data, but they can't; it is local to the first Web server.

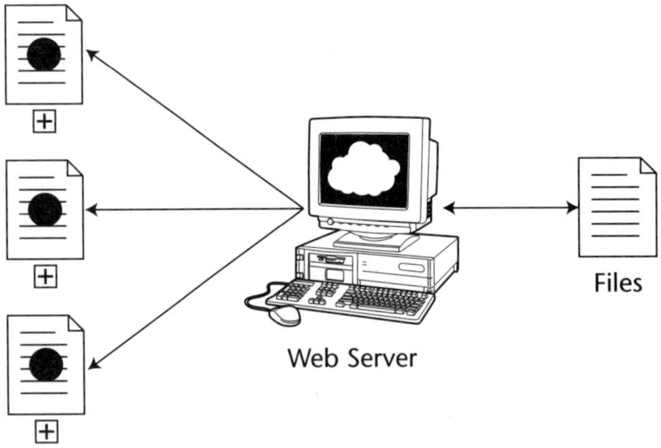

Figure 1.1 Early customer order site.

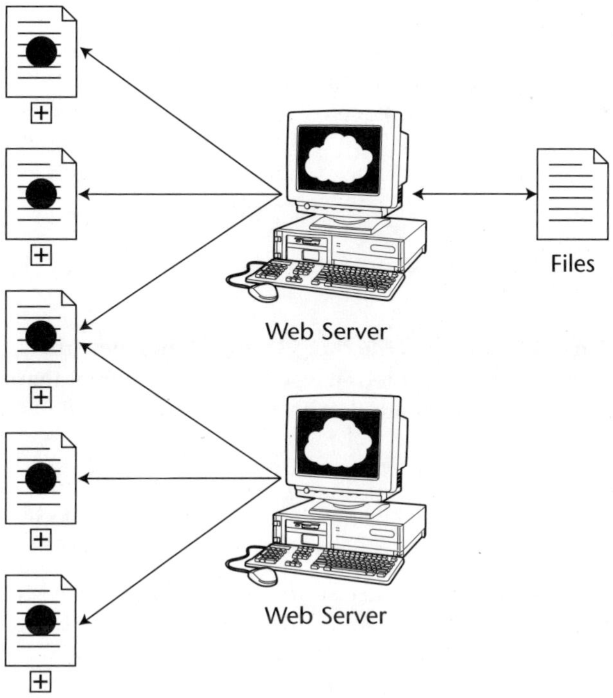

Figure 1.2 All the data is local (one server with data, two without).

Symptoms and Consequences

Local data is pretty easy to spot. You will be putting data in memory or files on a specific machine. The consequences are equally identifiable. You will not be able to get to the data you need.

- **You are storing data in static variables.** This is considered and documented as a bad thing for most J2EE technologies, like Enterprise JavaBeans (EJBs) and servlets, but is commonplace for custom applications that use JMS, RMI, or another communications protocol.
- **You are storing data in files on the local system.** While EJBs are not supposed to use the file libraries, servlets certainly do, as can other custom applications.
- **Data is only available to one machine.** Perhaps it is in an Entity Bean that is only available locally within the server.
- **You are storing data in a singleton.** This is similar to using a static variable, except that you have essentially hidden the data behind the singleton. However, the singleton itself is probably stored in a static variable, which should also be an indicator that something is wrong.

- **You may be going against document package restrictions**. For example, you are expressly not supposed to use the file application programming interfaces (APIs) in EJBs. A server might even prevent you from doing so, which could break your solution when you upgrade your server.

Typical Causes

Generally a solution that grows over time, rather than one that was built from scratch, causes this AntiPattern.

- **The solution is built over time**. Often, when the first version of an enterprise solution is built, it is prototyped or implemented in a smaller environment than the one it will ultimately be deployed in. As a result, local data may not be a problem in the development environment.
- **Localized data is easy to access.** Using localized data is often the easiest solution. Without the oversight of an enterprise-level architect, individual developers may take the easiest route to a solution despite its long-term negative effects.
- **Lack of experience.** Developers new to enterprise solutions, and large-scale deployments, may not have encountered problems with localized data before. They might think that they are applying good object-oriented techniques by encapsulating data, while not realizing that there are larger-scale concepts at work.

Known Exceptions

Localized data is not always wrong. Sometimes the solution you are building will work fine on top of the local file system, as in the example of a single-server Web site, or when using an in-memory static variable cache. The real issue is whether or not you have to scale access to the data. If the data is used for a local cache, possibly even a local cache of data from a shared location, then having the local data is the point, and not a problem. If the data is going to be part of an application that might grow, you need to rethink your solution.

Refactorings

Once you have localized data, the only thing to do is to get rid of it. This means picking a new data architecture and implementing it. The specific refactorings to apply to this AntiPattern are Plan for Scaling, and Choose the Right Data Architecture, both found in this chapter.

To avoid the problem from the beginning, you should think about how your solution will scale to the enterprise from the very beginning. This doesn't mean building every application with an *n*-tiered model to support scaling. You just need to think, "How big can my design scale?" If the answer is, "Big enough that if I had to go bigger, I would have plenty of money to rewrite it," then your solution is good enough.

Variations

You might decide to add tiers to your application as a way of changing the data architecture. Adding tiers, or new levels to the solution, can take the form of databases, servlets, JMS servers, and other middleware that separates functionality into multiple components. Adding tiers is basically changing the data architecture from a functional perspective. By changing the data architecture, you may be improving your solutions scalability.

Example

You can fix the Localized Data AntiPattern by changing your data architecture. As an example, let's go back to the case of a single Web application being moved to a multi-Web-server installation. Originally, all of the customer data was on one Web server, stored in files. While you can copy it, as pictured in Figure 1.3, if one server handles the same customers as another, you may end up with data that is out of sync. You might even corrupt your data if two servlets from different servers perform mutually exclusive operations on the customer data before their files are synchronized.

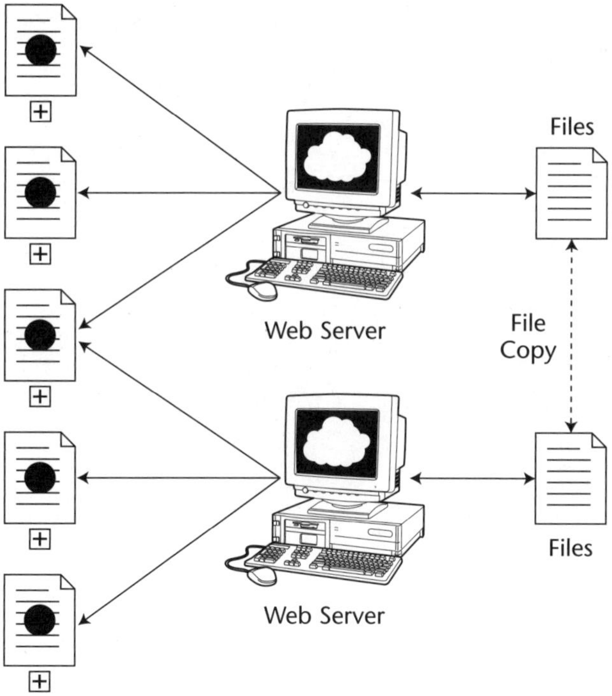

Figure 1.3 Synchronizing files.

You might realize that synchronization has problems and decide to share the files and do file locking. In this design, pictured in Figure 1.4, each Web server works off the same files, via file sharing. To prevent corruption, you can lock the files to protect them from simultaneous access.

This last step demonstrates the basic idea of changing the data architecture; you have to move the data away from a single server to a shared location. If you are familiar with relational databases, you might notice that this idea of file sharing and locking gets pretty close to what you use a relational database for. So, the next step in the solution is to move up to a formal database, pictured in Figure 1.5. This will include the locking, but also add transactional support to your solution.

As you can see, changing the data architecture can be an iterative process where you start with one solution and move towards a heavier, yet more scalable solution. In a large enterprise situation, you might even have to scale your database solution to include multiple databases, which just goes to show that there isn't one silver bullet solution. Any solution may have localized data that has to be refactored.

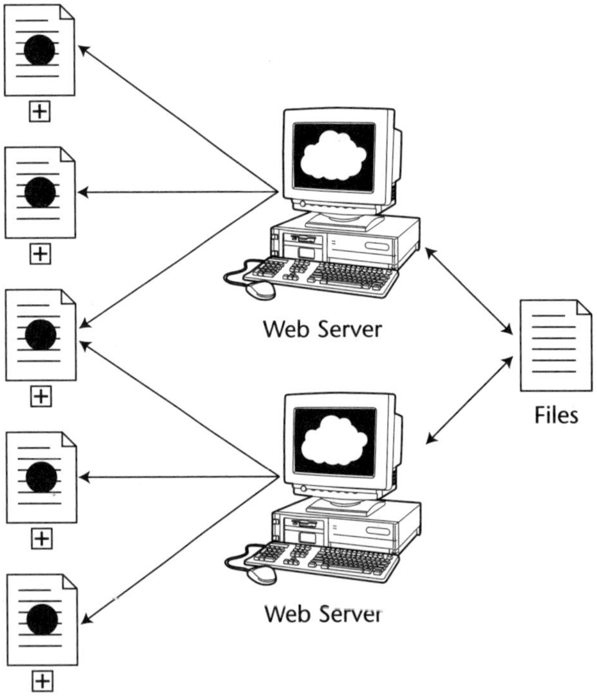

Figure 1.4 Sharing files.

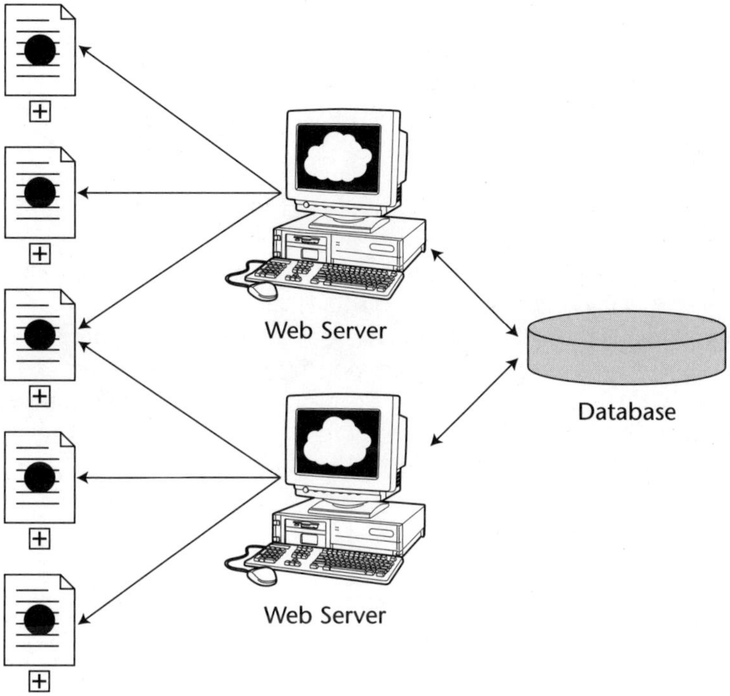

Figure 1.5 Using a database.

Related Solutions

Localizing data is very similar to the next AntiPattern in this chapter, called Misunderstanding Data Requirements. Misunderstood requirements can lead to localized data and other problems such as underestimating bandwidth requirements, and the approaches to resolving it are similar.

AntiPattern

Misunderstanding Data Requirements

Also Known As: Big Data, Bad Data, Too Much Data

Most Frequent Scale: Application, system

Refactorings: Plan for Scaling, Choose the Right Data Architecture

Refactored Solution Type: Process, role, architecture

Root Causes: Designing by prototype, growing a solution instead of designing it, feature creep

Unbalanced Forces: Time to market, individual/role responsibilities, unplanned features

Anecdotal Evidence: "The deployed system is much slower than the development system." "The system can't handle enough throughput."

Background

Often, your initial designs don't take into account realistic data. During design, it is easier to get a handle on simple records than complex, multivalued records, so designers will often think in terms of the simplified records. This AntiPattern, Misunderstanding Data Requirements, can affect the final solution in terms of both the size of data and the performance requirements for parsing and operating on it. Basically, if you don't know what the data will really look like, your design is based on invalid assumptions. These incorrect assumptions can then affect your entire distributed solution by changing the amount of network bandwidth used, causing you to underestimate the time it takes for each endpoint to do its work, or causing some other effect.

General Form

Misunderstood data requirements can take many forms, but there are two main ones. First, developers might use small data sets for development because they are easy to manage, but upon deployment, the real data sets may be much larger. This can result in bad performance on the network and in specific applications.

The second situation manifests when more data is passed around the network than is actually needed. For example, suppose that a customer service application represents customer data in an XML file. Moreover, that XML file contains all of the information about a customer. Now, suppose that one step in your J2EE application needs to confirm that a customer number is valid, and that you implement this check in an EJB. Do you need to pass the entire customer record, possibly over a megabyte of data to the EJB? The answer is no; you can just pass the customer number. But if you choose the wrong application design, you may have to pass the entire record to every node in the solution.

Symptoms and Consequences

Often, misunderstood data requirements don't affect a prototype or test installation. They come into play when you really deploy your solution. The following issues are important to look for.

- **Parts of your solution may end up getting more data than they need.** If that data is in Extensible Markup Language (XML), that may mean that more time is spent parsing and rendering the XML than is truly necessary. If the data is in a JMS, CORBA, or RMI message, the parsing and rendering time is hidden by the protocol but the time is still there, and still wasted on unused data.
- **Big, unexpected changes in performance from the test environment to the deployment.** This can indicate that you misunderstood the data, most likely indicating that the size changed noticeably.
- **If you overestimate data requirements you will get the inverse effect.** You may have way more available bandwidth or processing power than you need. This can lead to a higher project cost than was actually necessary.

Typical Causes

Generally, misunderstood requirements are caused by bad design, like the following issues.

- **Bad data architecture.** When you create a data architecture that relies on messages carrying all of the data, you will often send more data than each node in the architecture needs.
- **Bad planning or research.** If you don't talk to the actual users to gather data requirements, you might not estimate data sizes correctly and might end up with a solution that expects small data chunks when it will really see large ones, or vice versa.

Known Exceptions

Misunderstood data requirements are not acceptable, but the symptoms of misunderstood data requirements can arise when you create the same situations on purpose. For example, it's okay if you send too much data to one part of an application just to be sure that it gets to the next part. Or you might know that the data sizes will change at deployment and have planned for it, even though the data sizes you use during testing are much smaller. Ultimately, you need to understand the data, but you may plan in some of the same symptoms you would get if you didn't.

Refactorings

There are a couple ways to fix the problem of the Misunderstanding Data Requirements AntiPattern. Fundamentally, the solution is to understand the data requirements. To do this, you have to make realistic bandwidth calculations, which requires realistic data calculations. Second, you have to look at what information each part of a distributed application really needs. Then you have to pick the right data architecture from these requirements. The refactorings to apply are Plan for Scaling, and Choose the Right Data Architecture, both found in this chapter.

Variations

The main variation of the Misunderstanding Data Requirements AntiPattern is overestimating data rather than underestimating it. Or in the case of passing too much data, passing too little data. This can occur when you try to optimize too early, and end up in the situation where an endpoint in the solution needs more data than you initially thought.

Example

If we take the example in the general form, in which customer information is stored in XML files and we need to validate the customer number using an EJB to encapsulate the validation process, then the obvious solution is to not require that the EJB get the entire customer record. This means that any part of the application that needs to validate the customer number must get the number, call the EJB, receive the results, and use those results appropriately. If you want to have a piece of the application that makes a decision on how to proceed based on the validation, that piece can take the full XML, extract the number, validate it, and proceed accordingly. The important part is that the EJB for validating the number doesn't have to deal with the full record. This does mean that that EJB can't pass data to other EJBs or servlets that require more information than just the customer number. If you need the validation EJB to pass more data to one of its service providers, you must design the EJB interface to take the additional data with a request so that it can include that data in the messages it sends.

Related Solutions

Misunderstood data requirements can easily grow out of the Localizing Data AntiPattern and can easily lead to the Miscalculating Bandwidth Requirements AntiPattern, which are also found in this chapter. These three AntiPatterns are tightly linked and have similar solutions. When misunderstood data leads to miscalculated bandwidth requirements, it can become the underlying cause of a performance failure.

Miscalculating Bandwidth Requirements

Also Known As: Network Slowdowns, Low Transaction Rates

Most Frequent Scale: System

Refactorings: Plan Realistic Network Requirements, Plan for Scaling, Use Specialized Networks, Choose the Right Data Architecture

Refactored Solution Type: Process, architecture

Root Causes: Using example data, rarely a true representation of the actual data that will need to be processed, particularly in size. Similarly, data rates are often mimicked for the initial testing at much lower requirement levels.

Unbalanced Forces: Creating a solution in a development environment that is truly representative. Taking the time to evaluate the actual requirements, not just sketch out a simple solution.

Anecdotal Evidence: "Why did the network slow down when we deployed the solution?" "How come the development system can handle more messages per second than the deployed machine when the deployment machine has more powerful hardware?"

Background

Perhaps one of the biggest issues with the Misunderstooding Data AntiPattern is the Miscalculating Bandwidth Requirements AntiPattern. For example, if you think that all of your JMS messages will be 1 KB and they are really 100 KB, you are going to use 100 times the network capacity than you planned. Often a development group might be given a requirement of *x* number of transactions per second, where *x* is small, such as 5. But, the size of the data being passed around may be very large, such as 50 MB. So, the actual bandwidth requirement is 250 Mbps which is beyond the abilities of the basic Ethernet card, and probably beyond the processing power of a small to midsize server.

General Form

The Miscalculating Bandwidth Requirements AntiPattern generally appears when the size of the data that is sent between nodes or tiers in a solution is large. For example, an order management solution that passes data about the orders in XML files might look like the solution pictured in Figure 1.6. If the orders are small, say under 100 KB, then a typical Ethernet system, with 10 Mbps, can certainly handle tens of these orders each second.

Let's say that the only requirement is that we need to handle a single order each second. Our 100-KB orders will certainly fit inside our network's existing bandwidth, even if we assume that all the machines are on the same local area network (LAN).

In this example, there are five nodes that have to process each order. Further, we would expect that each node takes some amount of time to do its work. So let's estimate that each node takes some fraction of a second to process the data. Now, there might be several orders moving between nodes at one time, as pictured in Figure 1.7.

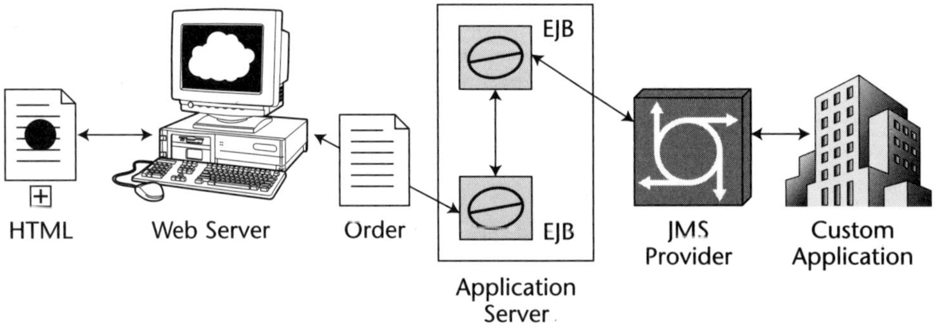

Figure 1.6 Sample order management solution (with five nodes).

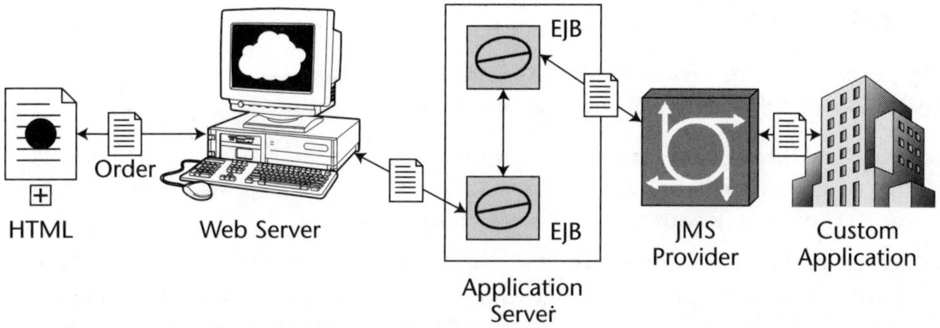

Figure 1.7 Multiple orders in the system.

We are still meeting our requirement, and assuming that we have small, 100-KB messages, so we are probably still okay. But what if the orders are bigger? Suppose that the orders are really patient records, or include graphics, or historical data, as these enterprise messages often do. So, now the records are 1 MB or even more. The solution in Figure 1.6 has turned into the one in Figure 1.8.

Our bandwidth is starting to get into trouble. Each message is now a noticeable percentage of a normal Ethernet network. Filling up the network will slow the overall performance of the application and all others distributed on the same network.

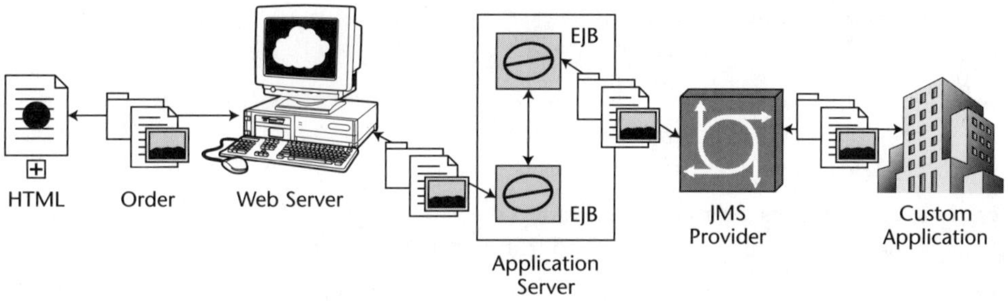

Figure 1.8 Big orders in the system.

Symptoms and Consequences

Look for the following issues to identify bandwidth issues. Note that these may not appear until the final deployment if you don't test in an equivalent situation.

- **Message throughput, or transaction times are very high when bandwidth is limited or overwhelmed.** This can lead to message backup, which may require quiet times to allow the systems to catch up.
- **When messages can't be delivered, they might be lost.** This can even happen on systems that support persistent store and forward methods. One example of this, which I have seen in practice, occurs when the persistence mechanism runs out of space. Even a 2-GB file size limit can be a problem if the messaging infrastructure is asked to store more than 2 GB of messages. With 5-MB messages, this is unlikely, but it is possible with larger messages. Lost messages are a terrible symptom of overwhelmed bandwidth and can cause dire consequences with lost data.
- **A single application that has very high bandwidth requirements might affect other applications on the network**. This causes a rippling effect, where each application is degraded due to no fault of its own.

Typical Causes

Generally, bandwidth issues arise from poor planning. Look for the following issues during your design process:

- **Unexpected message sizes**. During design, if the developers thought that messages would be 100 KB and they turn out to really be 1 MB, there is likely to be a problem.
- **Unexpected message volumes**. Often designers can make a good guess at average message volume, but forget to think about peak volume.
- **Not planning for multiple hops.** When given the requirements that a system has to handle a single 1-MB message per second, most designers will say, "No problem." But if you consider a system that is going to take five or ten network hops, that 1 MB turns into 5 or 10 MB.
- **Not planning for hubs**. Systems that use a JMS server, Web server, process automation engine, or some other hub may wind up with more network hops than an initial design might show. For example, in a process automation design, each step in a business process will often result in a network call and response, rather than a single call. This doubles the number of messages, although not necessarily the bandwidth requirements, since one direction doesn't necessarily use the same size messages as the other.
- **Overworked networks**. When a J2EE solution is installed on an existing network, there is already traffic flying around. If that traffic is taxing the network, implementing a new solution in combination with all the existing ones may overload the network.

- **Overworked machines.** Installing numerous J2EE services on one machine means that a single network card may be forced to deal with all of the network bandwidth requirements. This single card becomes a choke point that must be reevaluated.
- **Not planning for latency**. Network messages take time to get from one place to another. You may encounter situations where machine A sends messages to machines B and C, and machine B sends a message to machine C after it receives the messages from A. But because of the network layout, the message from A to B to C gets there before the message going from A to C directly. Timing can play a key role in your application.

Known Exceptions

This AntiPattern is never acceptable, but it may not be applicable for simple solutions on fast networks. This is where planning is important. If you are building a small departmental solution with reasonably small messages on a 100-Mbps network, your requirements may be far below the available bandwidth. Also, developers lucky enough to have gigabit networks for their deployments are more insulated than a developer on a smaller department-sized network.

Refactorings

The first solution to bandwidth problems is to perform reliable bandwidth analysis at design time. Ask questions like, "How big is the biggest message or document?" and, "What does the peak message traffic look like?" By getting a broader picture ahead of time, you can solve the problem before deployment.

The other solutions to bandwidth problems are split between design time and deploy time. If you think you have a large data requirement, you should think about the data architecture you are using. Could the customer data go into a database, thus reducing network traffic? Also, could each node only retrieve what it needed, rather than get the entire order document?

You can also add hardware to the situation. Build special networks for subsets of the solution or buy a faster network. Both of these are valid solutions and may be required for very large problems that simply push the boundaries of network technology. But in many cases, you can use architecture to solve the bandwidth problem. The specific refactorings to apply to this AntiPattern are Plan Realistic Network Requirements, Plan for Scaling, Use Specialized Networks, and Choose the Right Data Architecture, all found in this chapter.

Variations

The main variation on the single network hog is a group of applications that combine to create a high bandwidth requirement.

Example

Let's take the order management system example in Figure 1.6. Suppose that our orders are just too big, and there are too many for the network to support. We might fix this by revamping the system to use a database to store order data. In this case, the first node in the system would store data in the database. Other nodes, as pictured in Figure 1.9, would grab only the data they needed from the database, thus reducing the overall traffic requirements. Note there are still messages being sent from one node to the next, but these can be very small notification messages instead of larger, bandwidth-hogging data messages.

Keep in mind that when we redesign the data architecture, we might be adding network hops. In this case, we are replacing one network hop from one node to the next with three network hops, one from the node to the next to say go, and two to get the data from the database. If the total requirements of these three hops exceed the original one, we have made the problem worse, not better. For example, if the original hop would have been 1 MB of bandwidth, but the new set of hops is 1.5 MB, we have added network traffic.

Related Solutions

Another possible solution is to look at store and forward methodology as a way to control the times that messages flow through the system. For example, you might optimize for order entry during the day, while optimizing for order processing at night.

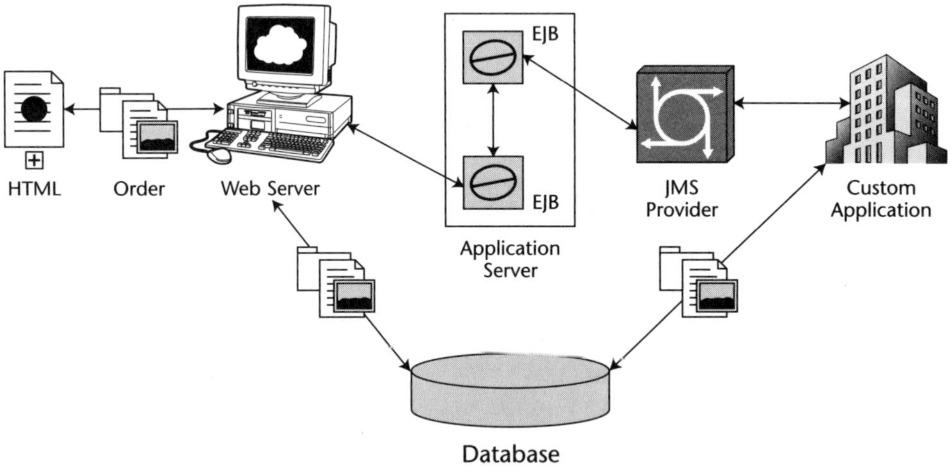

Figure 1.9 Refactored order management system.

AntiPattern

Overworked Hubs

Also Known As: Not Planning for Scale, Chokepoints

Most Frequent Scale: System

Refactorings: Partition Data and Work, Plan for Scaling, Throw Hardware at the Problem

Refactored Solution Type: Software, technology, architecture

Root Causes: Systems that implement rendezvous points in J2EE; hidden hubs

Unbalanced Forces: Requirements changing or demand growing

Anecdotal Evidence: "The database is slowing everything down." "The application server is not working correctly."

Background

Many enterprise solutions rely on a hub-and-spoke architecture. This means that one piece of software is acting as a hub for data or processing destined for other software in the solution. These hubs are often hidden or overused. Overuse can lead to overall system performance problems. For example, a database or rules engine will often be a hub. As a result, it must be taken into account for all performance and scalability requirements.

Often hubs represent bandwidth hogs, so the architecting you do to identify your bandwidth requirements will also help you identify the hubs. In order to create scalable hubs, you may need to architect your solutions from the beginning with that scaling in mind. This means that the biggest task, from the start, is finding your hubs. Once you know them, you can plan for how they can grow.

General Form

An Overworked Hubs AntiPattern will generally take one of two forms. Drawing a picture that shows the various connections in your J2EE solution can identify the first form, where a single component or machine has a very large number of connections to it. In this case, connections mean two machines or applications talking to each other. It is very important when drawing this picture that you don't leave out any network hops. You must capture the exact path of data across the network.

For example, in Figure 1.10 there is a J2EE solution with several machines and applications. We have even included the router in the picture to show that it, too, can be thought of as a hub. Notice that the database has a lot of connections, while the JMS server doesn't. Seeing a picture like this should draw your attention to the database and the possibility that it is going to be or has become overworked.

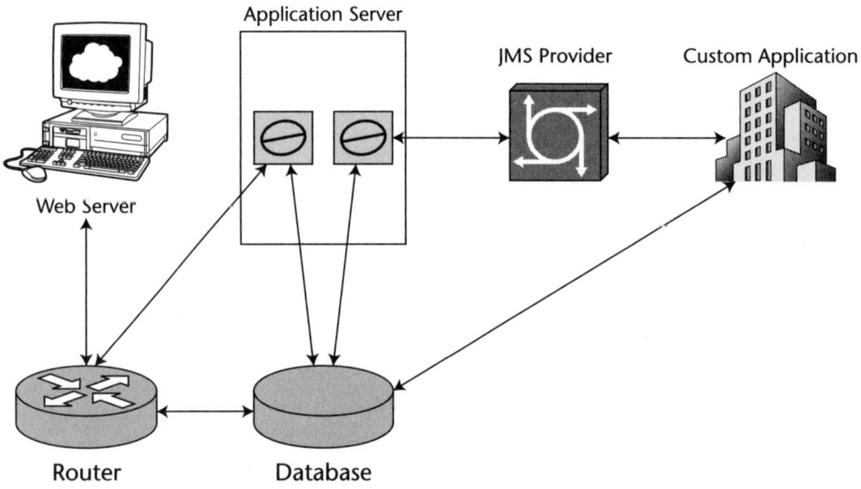

Figure 1.10 Finding hubs.

The second form of an Overworked Hubs AntiPattern can be found when you add bandwidth information to the network picture. If we updated Figure 1.10 with this information, it might look like Figure 1.11 or Figure 1.12. In the first version, the database is still a suspect since it is requiring a lot more bandwidth than the other nodes. In the second figure, the bandwidth requirements have changed, and now the JMS server looks like it is more at risk of overwork than the database server.

As you may have surmised from the examples, this second form of an overworked hub occurs when a single node has to process a lot of data. The node may not have a lot of connections, but its data requirements may be so high that even a few connections can overload it.

Symptoms and Consequences

Hubs are too important to mess up. Look for the following symptoms in your deployment to avoid the resulting consequences:

- **When a hub is overworked it may slow the system down.** It might even start to slow down the machine itself as the operating system "thrashes" as a result of requiring too much memory and having to save data to disk too often.
- **An overworked hub can lose data if it is not transactionally sound.** Even a hub that supports transactions could be at risk of losing data if it is so overworked that it breaks down the operating system's standard behaviors by causing system crashes or the exhaustion of disk space.

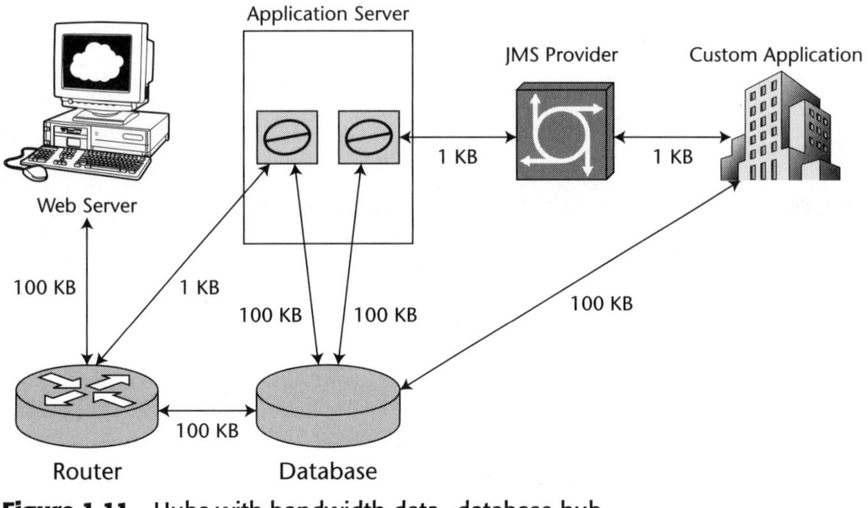

Figure 1.11 Hubs with bandwidth data—database hub.

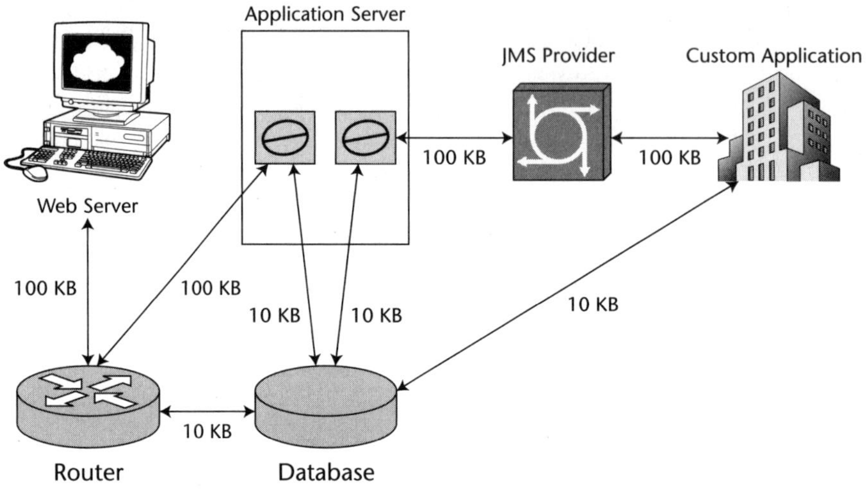

Figure 1.12 Hubs with bandwidth data—JMS hub.

- **When a single hub is overworked, the endpoints that connect to it may begin to show slow message delivery or dropped messages.** This can put a strain on the endpoint, which could cause it to lose data. For example, this could happen if a Java Connector Architecture (JCA) connector is pushing data to a JMS server and the JMS server is strained. The JCA connector may not be able to process requests while it waits for each message to make it to the JMS server. This could result in lost events or late events coming from the external system.
- **Overworked hubs that deal with real-time user input.** These may create a bad user experience by slowing down the user's perceived response times.

Typical Causes

Generally, problems at hubs can appear at any time in the process. The following causes are examples of these different time frames. For example, budget constraints can happen early in a project, while changing requirements happen later.

- **Changing requirements.** When a system is put into operation the hardware and architecture may be more than able to support the daily requirements. However, if more customers, transactions, or requests are added to the system, some machines that have been acting as hubs may be unable to keep up with the new requirements.
- **Budget constraints.** Sometimes the scalable solution may involve hardware or software that is more expensive. A poorly planned or highly constrained budget could result in the purchase of less than ideal technology support, which could lead to overworked hubs.

- **Adding new clients**. Companies that buy software that inherently creates hubs—such as messaging, database, application, and Web servers—are likely to reuse them for multiple applications. This is a perfectly reasonable plan under the right circumstances. However, as new uses are found for existing software and hardware, and new clients are added to the hub, there may come a point where the current implementation of the hub is not able to handle the new clients.
- **Hidden hubs**. Sometimes a hub isn't even recognized at design time. For example, a router that will come into play during the final deployment may be missing from the development or test environment. If the router is there, it may not be under the same load in the test case as it will be in the deployment case. This can lead to hubs that are actually going to be overworked in the actual solution that are not identified until too late.

Known Exceptions

It is never okay to have an overworked hub. But that doesn't mean that you shouldn't have hubs at all. It just means that you have to plan for them. Some architects try to create completely distributed solutions with few or no hubs. This approach may avoid overworking a single machine, but it creates two undesirable side effects. First, total distribution is likely to create much higher and possibly less-controlled bandwidth requirements. Second, systems that are highly distributed are harder to maintain and back up. So, while you can have a system with three endpoints all talking directly to one another, you may not want 300 endpoints doing the same thing. With many endpoints, it is easier to design, manage, and administer the system if you add hubs to focus the connections.

Refactorings

There are a number of ways to deal with the Overworked Hubs AntiPattern. The first thing you can do is to avoid the problem during design time. This requires really planning for scale and looking at realistic bandwidth requirements. You should also draw network diagrams to look for hidden hubs.

The second thing you can do is to fix the problem when it arises. There are a couple ways to do this. First, you can add hubs. Adding hubs may require some architectural changes. Generally, hubs are added transparently or nontransparently. In either case, you can think of adding hubs as load balancing since you are distributing the work or data load across several machines.

Nontransparently adding hubs will often involve partitioning data. This means that the work and data from one subset all go to one hub, and the work and data for another subset all go to another hub. An example might be storing North American data in one database and European data in another. The big problem with partitioning data is that if you didn't plan for it from the beginning, you may end up with mixed data in the first database, since it was getting all the data for a while. Partitioning data is perhaps the most common form of nontransparent load balancing. This means that you are balancing the load between multiple hubs, but there is some knowledge of the data or work going into the balancing decisions.

You can add hubs transparently when you have the special situation where all hubs are equal. This might be the case on a Web server for example, where all the servers might have the same Web site. In this case, you may be able to add hubs and load balance across the set. When hubs are equivalent, you can do transparent load balancing, which means that you can just add hubs all day long to fix the problem.

When all of your hubs are equal, you throw hardware at the problem, which is perhaps the easiest solution. It may or may not cost more to use this technique than the other, but in a lot of situations, it can be done with little rearchitecting. Where redesigning costs time, hardware costs money. If the redesigning is quick, the time is less costly than the hardware. If the redesign takes a long time, it may exceed the cost of new hardware.

Neither throwing hardware at a problem nor adding hubs has to be purely reactionary. These fixes can be part of the original plans. For example, the development machine might be a single CPU PC with the express plan to make it a multiple process PC at deployment.

The refactorings to apply to this AntiPattern are Partition Data and Work, Plan for Scaling, and Throw Hardware at the Problem, all found in this chapter.

Variations

One variation of an Overworked Hubs AntiPattern is a database or external system connection that only allows single-threaded access. This connection might not support sufficient response times and appear to be an overworked hub in your final solution.

Example

Let's look at the examples in Figure 1.11 and 1.12. Both have potentially overworked hubs. The first has a database with several clients; the second shows a JMS server with a large bandwidth requirement. Taking the database example first, we need to add support for more clients to the database node. There are two ways to do this. First, we could just use a bigger machine. That might work and could be easy to implement. The second thing we could do is partition the work. Depending on our database vendor, we might be able to use some kind of built-in load balancing, as pictured in Figure 1.13.

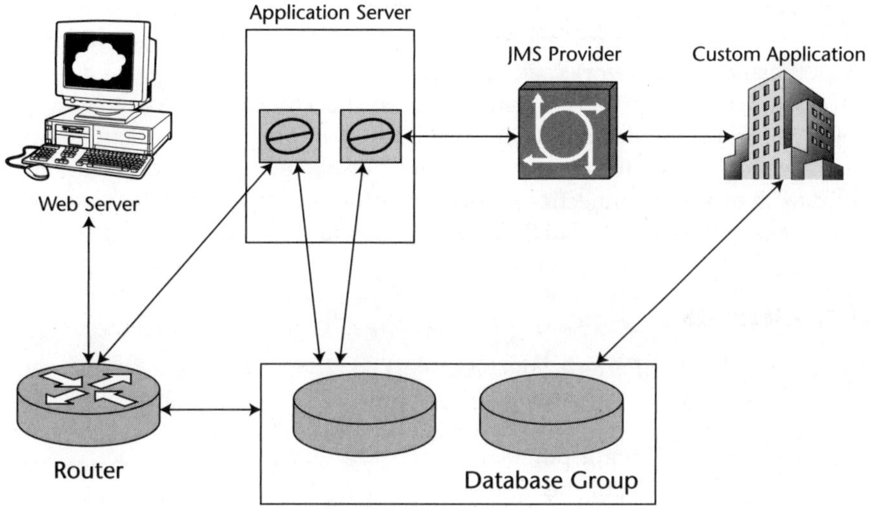

Figure 1.13 Load-balanced database.

If the vendor doesn't provide load balancing, we could partition data. This could require rearchitecting the solution and possibly adding a hub that does less work, making it able to handle the same number of connections as the original database. This solution is pictured in Figure 1.14.

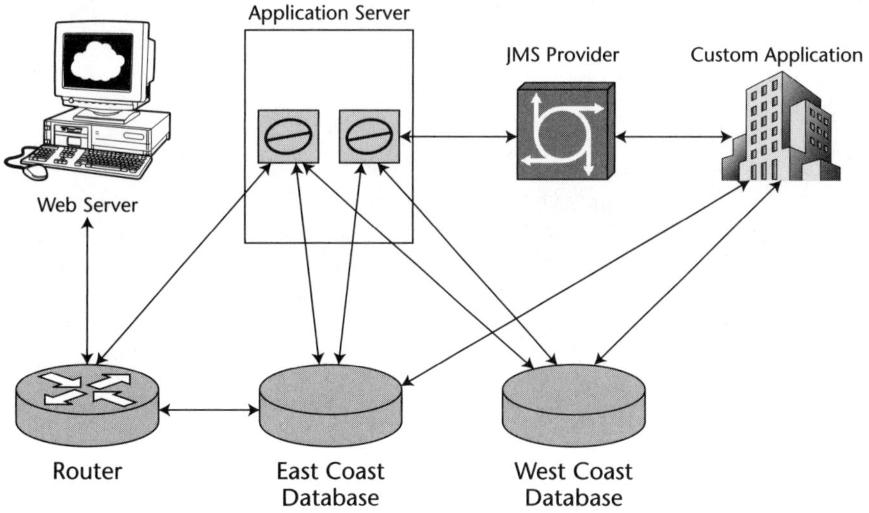

Figure 1.14 Partitioning data.

The second example has an overworked JMS server. We can attack this server with the same techniques: first, a bigger machine, then, load balancing if the server supports it. If neither of those solutions works, we can then try to partition the messages. This might involve setting up Java Naming and Directory Interface (JNDI), so that some clients get one JMS server, while other clients get a different one. Repartitioning a JMS server with preexisting data and connections could cause a few main problems. First, you may have to change the connection information for existing clients. Second, you may have messages in the JMS queues that are stored in the wrong server.

Related Solutions

As with most of the J2EE AntiPatterns, the Overworked Hubs AntiPattern is related to most of the other AntiPatterns. Some specific tight links exist between hubs and bandwidth requirements and hubs and dislocated data. In both of those situations, the data or the bandwidth is often related to a hub. Similarly, overworking a hub often involves placing high bandwidth or data requirements on it.

The Man with the Axe

Also Known As: Network Outages, The Guy with the Backhoe

Most Frequent Scale: Enterprise, system, application

Refactorings: Be Paranoid, Plan Ahead

Refactored Solution Type: Process, technology

Root Causes: Poor planning, unexpected problems, crazy people

Unbalanced Forces: Money, the world at large

Anecdotal Evidence: "The network is down." "Our site is offline."

Background

Every once in a while you hear a horror story about network downtime. Two horror stories pop into my head. The first happened in Grand Rapids, Michigan, while I was teaching a class. Things were going well when suddenly all of the power went out. We looked out the window, and there was a man with a backhoe cutting the main power line to the building, which housed the data center. The second story happened in San Jose, California. Someone took a backhoe to a main fiber-optic line that belonged to the phone company. It took days to hand-splice the thousands of fibers back together. Both stories are testament to the fact that network programming has risks that go beyond those of single computer programming, and you have to plan for them. I like to motivate myself by thinking of a person with an axe who likes to cut network, and other, cables.

General Form

The man with the axe's job is to break your network. He may do it a number of ways: He might kill the power supply; he might break a network connection; he might decide to crush a router or install a bad software patch on it. He is unpredictable, but the one thing that is consistent in all of this madman's actions is that he will take down at least one of the components in your network solution.

Symptoms and Consequences

Network failure is pretty devastating when it happens, so the symptoms, such as the following two, should be easy to spot.

- **The application stops working.** Network failures can stop the application from working. If a key database is down or offline, then the entire application may be unavailable.
- **A machine is not reachable.** This can indicate a problem in the network or at that machine. Either way, you may have serious repercussions at the application level.

Typical Causes

There are several problems that qualify as "men with axes." Here are a few:

- **People with backhoes.** There isn't much you can do to prevent someone from taking a backhoe to your power line. There are a couple of things you can do to avoid this, such as creating redundant lines, but even these extreme preparations may not succeed.
- **Failing hardware**. Hardware can fail. Perhaps a hard drive crashes, or a power supply dies, or some memory goes bad. In any case, hardware is reliable but not infallible.

- **Bad software.** Often new software, or even software currently running, may have problems. When this happens it can take one piece of your J2EE solution out of commission.
- **Overworked resources.** Sometimes everything is fine, except the amount of available resources. For example, a disk may become full on your database server. This can lead to massive problems, even though no one component can really be blamed.
- **Crackers.** Bad people don't have to have an axe. They can have a computer or a network of computers. These people can break single machines, break groups of machines, or just bog down your network.

Known Exceptions

While there is no perfect solution, you can certainly restrict your planning to the level of consequences that a failure would bring. For example, if you are an Internet service provider that charges people for making their Web site available, then you need to have very high reliability. But if you are just putting up a personal Web site with pictures of your kids, you don't need to pay for the same reliability that an online store requires.

Refactorings

The two applicable refactorings – both found in this chapter – are Be Paranoid and Plan Ahead. You have to plan for and assume failure. You have to be paranoid. You have to look at your system and analyze it for failure points. You also have to think about how important a failure is to determine the amount of work it is worth to try and avoid failures. Once you have an idea of the problem areas and their importance, you can apply numerous solutions, such as load balancing, fault tolerance, backup networks, and generally throwing hardware at the problem. You may also rethink your data architecture in light of possible failure points.

Another part of planning for failure is to think about how you will deal with upgrades in general. If you have a plan for upgrading a system, you can use that same plan to fix a problem with the system. For example, if you build in administrative messages that shut down the various system components, you can send these messages on a network failure, perhaps from both sides of the broken connection, to avoid a message backup in the senders, and timeouts on the receivers in your J2EE solution.

Variations

The number of ways things can fail is endless. You have to analyze each piece of your solution and ask, "How can this fail, and how much do I care if it does?"

You might encounter a situation where you have an intermittent failure. This is the worst kind since it can be hard to track down. Look for the same issues as those in this

AntiPattern, as well as situations caused by overloaded machines from message backups and similar problems from the other AntiPatterns in this chapter.

Example

When Netscape was building one of their first buildings, they had two network access links. These links were on opposite sides of the building and were managed by different phone companies. The reasoning behind this was that it is safer to have two companies because if a backhoe hits one, it shouldn't hit the other one on the other side of the building. This struck me as great planning on Netscape's part.

Another great example of paranoid planning and simply planning ahead comes from one of NASA's Mars missions. An error occurred in the application code on the rover while it was on Mars. But WindRiver Systems, having a great deal of experience with real-time systems, had planned for that type of error and had included support for dynamically updating the code. Not only were the programmers able to leverage the tools provided by WindRiver's experience, they were also able to use an important, but little-used, feature to fix the problem. Now, if programming across the solar system isn't an example of distribution, I don't know what is.

Related Solutions

The way you deal with failure is tied to the way you plan your hubs. Hubs are an intricate part of your solution, which makes them very high-risk failure points. Look at your hubs when analyzing your solution for failures. When a hub fails, it affects a lot of other components. Therefore, they are likely to be the worst failure points. Luckily, in the case of Enterprise JavaBeans, JMS, and other J2EE server technologies, the server providers try hard to help reduce the likelihood of failure.

Refactorings

Avoiding and eliminating AntiPatterns in distributed-scalable systems is mainly a matter of planning ahead. This involves choosing the right architecture, partitioning data, planning for scale, and other architectural decisions, as well as being a bit paranoid throughout your planning, keeping in mind the fallacies of distributed computing, and, when all else fails, throwing hardware at your problem. For example, managing your bandwidth requires that you plan realistic network requirements, but also that you choose the right data architecture. This breadth of knowledge and technique is a direct outgrowth of the compound nature of J2EE solutions. J2EE solutions often contain messaging applications, Web pages, Enterprise JavaBeans, and legacy code all on different computers and possibly on different platforms. As a result, each element will bring new issues to bear, as will the combination of elements. As a result, building a good distributed, scalable solution requires that you apply all of the refactorings listed below in one form or another.

Plan Ahead. When building a J2EE solution, think about issues in distribution before they come up. One way to help with this is to plan for some standard life-cycle issues from the start. These life-cycle issues include how you are going to fix bugs and upgrade software.

Choose the Right Data Architecture. There are different data designs. You can build hub and spoke, random distributions, centralized data stores, distributed data stores, and all sorts of combinations of these. Pick the right one for each job.

Partition Data and Work. When there is too much data, sometimes you need to organize it. Generally, data is organized along a particular axis, like time or location. In very large data sets, you might organize data several ways or on multiple axes.

Plan for Scaling (Enterprise-Scale OO). Encapsulation, abstraction, inheritance, and polymorphism are the key components of object-oriented programming. J2EE is about taking these concepts to a larger scale. Where objects encapsulate data and implementation, Enterprise JavaBeans encapsulate data and implementations into Session and Entity Beans. Both Enterprise Beans and other objects abstract concepts. JMS creates a polymorphic relationship between sender and receiver, where one sender may talk to many receivers who are not well known to the sender.

Plan Realistic Network Requirements. Why is my email so slow? Didn't we just install the new customer service application? When you plan the network requirements for an application you have to look at realistic data requirements and realistic traffic patterns. Not planning accurately can result in unexpected network performance consequences.

Use Specialized Networks. Add bandwidth by adding networks. Using small, specialized networks allows you to add bandwidth inexpensively and control bandwidth interactions between network applications.

Be Paranoid. If there is one good thing you can say about paranoid people, they are always ready for the worst. When planning distributed applications, you have to be paranoid. You have to think about possible failures far more than you do in single-computer applications.

Throw Hardware at the Problem. When all else fails, throw hardware at the problem. Some problems are easily solved with bigger hardware. Some are only solved with more hardware or an expensive redesign. Throwing hardware at problems is a tried-and-true solution to many scaling problems.

Plan Ahead

You built your solution over time, and there are performance and complexity issues.

Plan ahead, looking at data and network architecture as a core piece of the design.

Figure 1.15 Before refactoring.

Figure 1.16 After refactoring.

Motivation

If a problem arises in your running system, you may have to install a fix of some sort. Upgrading your system can be painful, taking a lot of time and manpower, if you haven't planned for it. However, if you have already thought about how you will upgrade your system, you can likely use this same mechanism to install the fix. Similarly, if you plan in system monitoring, you can use that monitoring to discover bugs and resource problems. For example, you might be monitoring network traffic or throughput, and in the process notice that one machine is slowing down. Further checks might identify an almost full hard disk.

Mechanics

Planning for scale involves the following four steps:

1. *Look at in-memory data*. When you have to upgrade or fix a particular system, you will loose all of the data it has in memory. Therefore, you need to have a mechanism for saving that data. For example, if you have data in an Entity EJB, it should be persisted before the application server is shut down. While the application should help with this, you need to make sure that shutting down the application server properly is part of the upgrading process.
2. *Evaluate message persistence*. Another important area where data can be persisted is inside messages on the network. Most JMS servers support various levels of persistence, via durable subscribers. These persistent messages will be safe if the JMS server is taken offline, but nondurable messages won't be. Also, you need to make sure that your subscribers register correctly on startup so no messages are lost.
3. *Analyze the effect of shutting down applications*. When one application is offline, it may have an effect on other applications. For example, turning off the JMS server will stop all message traffic, just as turning off the Web server could stop all user input. Mapping out the cause and effects between applications is important because you can use this information to determine the shutdown and startup order of the entire J2EE installation.
4. *Think about adding administrative signals*. One way to plan in upgrades is to have administrative signals that are part of your design. These signals might start when the administrator fills in a particular form on the Web site. The servlet that processes that form could send a JMS message to the associated Message Beans that a shutdown is going to occur. Likewise, a special Message Bean might be listening for the signal and notify the other types of Enterprise JavaBeans and other custom software. Each component can react to the administrative signal by cleaning up any in-memory data and closing out open requests. Once all of the components are ready, the system can be shutdown smoothly.

Example

Imagine that you have a system like the one pictured in Figure 1.17. In this example, there is a Web server hosting set of JSPs, along with EJBs to back the JSPs with logic and data. The EJBs talk to a legacy system via JMS and a custom application. For the purposes of the example, let's assume that the legacy system is restricted to single-thread access, so it can only process one message at a time.

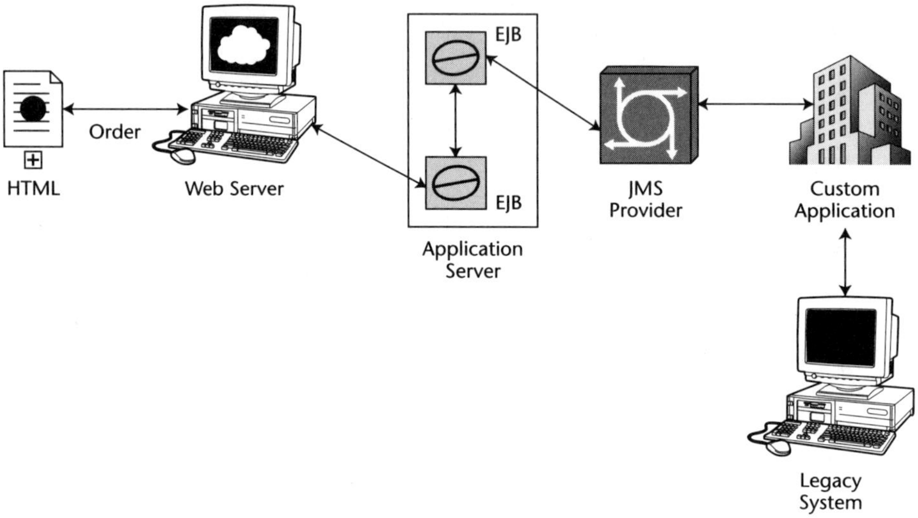

Figure 1.17 Planning ahead.

Step 1 is to look at the data. In this case, we have the information sent by the user to the JSP. This goes to the EJB and from there into the legacy system. There is little data sitting around the system. Second, we look at the messages. These are sent from the EJB to the legacy system. If we make them persistent, this improves the code that talks to the legacy system, but we don't have to. Third, we look at shutting down the Web server, which is probably not going to affect the other components since they don't depend on it for anything except input. Shutting down the application server, however, will kill the user interface since the JSPs won't have anything to talk to. Therefore, you should plan to shut down the Web applications before the application server, and restore them in the opposite order. The legacy connector can be safely shut down if the messages to it are persistent. However, the subscriber for the legacy connector must be registered before the application server is launched; otherwise, the messages from the EJBs will be lost.

The legacy connector needs to finish handling its current message before it is shut down. If the legacy system supports transactions, we might be able to avoid this requirement. Otherwise, we will need to have some sort of administrative signal to tell the legacy connector to stop processing messages.

As you can see, even in a simple example, there are a number of dependencies to consider. By planning ahead, and writing scripts or processes for shutting down and upgrading the system, you can capture these dependencies safely.

Choose the Right Data Architecture

You are sending more data around the network than you need to.

Refactor your design to optimize the network architecture.

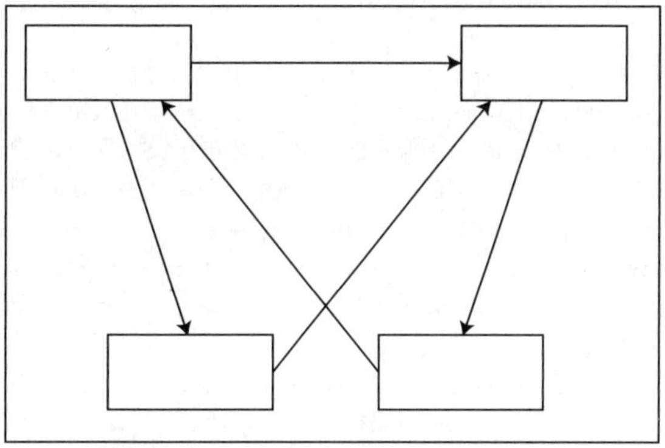

Figure 1.18 Before refactoring.

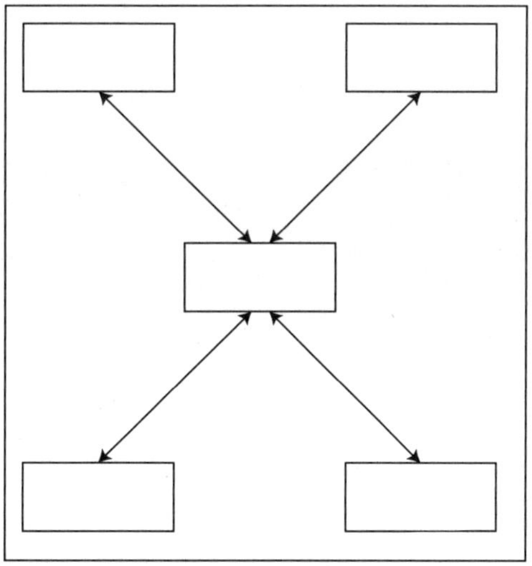

Figure 1.19 After refactoring.

Motivation

The way you organize your data flow has a big effect on your overall solution. There are three main data architectures. First, you can pass data between applications in messages. When you pass the data in the messages, you are passing everything to each node or application in your solution.

The second standard architecture is the database style design. In this design, each endpoint gets the minimum information in a message that tells it to go and get everything else it needs from a central database.

The third standard architecture is to use a central server of some kind to store most of the data, and to have it pass data as needed to the other applications. This design will have different messages flowing around the network, and will require the central server to have some smarts so that it will be able to filter information as needed. It will also require the central broker to store information between messages.

The first architecture is common when you have just a few network hops, perhaps only one or two. The second is common when there are a lot of pieces sharing data. The last is found in most business process automation solutions.

That said, you also have to keep in mind that these architectures are just common patterns, but they can apply at numerous scales. So the "Data in a Central Controller" design can be used at a small scale, or a large scale. For example, you might use it to implement a servlet, as pictured in Figure 1.20. In this case, the servlet is the central controller and is using the EJBs for services to get new data to pass to the next EJB. Data is persisted in memory between network calls.

Solving your distribution and scaling problems will require you to pick the right architecture at each level of your J2EE solution.

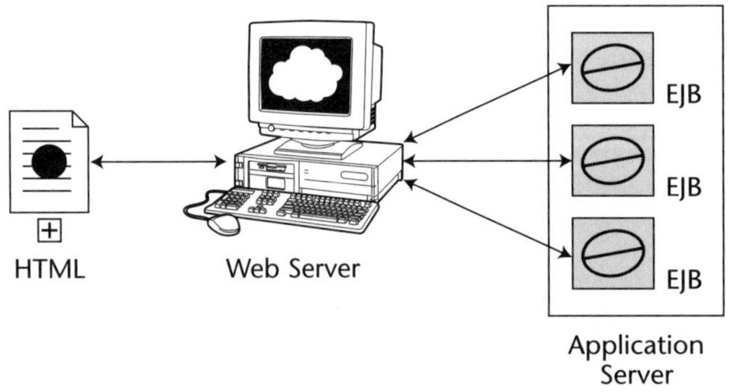

Figure 1.20 Servlet as central controller.

Mechanics

Complete the following steps to help identify the right architecture for your solution:

1. *List data requirements.* Look at each part of a J2EE solution and determine what data it needs. For example, what information does your addCustomer Web service require? Capture this information first so that you can use it to determine the right model to use.
2. *Map out data dependencies.* Once you know what each element of the solution needs, figure out where that data comes from. Who calls the addCustomer Web service? Where does it get the information it needs?
3. *Look for hubs that can capture and hold temporary data.* JMS servers with durable subscribers are storing data, and you can use this to your advantage. If you are using a business process or rules engine of some kind, does it perform a set of steps and keep data in memory between the steps? Do you have custom code that runs the solution? All of these applications can be temporary data stores.
4. *Look for your permanent data stores.* These are things like a relational database or file. Anywhere that you store data over time is a potential permanent data store.
5. *Analyze performance requirements.* Putting data in messages reduces network hops, so it can make a solution fast, but it also increases your bandwidth. Using a database can increase or reduce traffic, depending on how much data each part of an application needs.
6. *Assign your central controllers.* Once you have the data you need, this is the easiest first step in your design decisions. Look at the hubs you captured in the previous steps. The ones that capture processes of some kind are pretty much built to be central controllers. The application elements that these controllers talk to can receive the minimum data required to perform their work.
7. *Look for places where you have already persisted the data.* In a lot of cases, you will want to store data in your persistent storage as part of your design. If you are going to do that anyway, use it in the rest of the design. If the customer info goes to the database, then is used to validate other information, which means that the other application elements can just get it from the database. You don't have to pass it around. At this point, you will start mixing architectures, since your controllers may be using the database for some of their data.
8. *Look for places that message-based data works efficiently.* There are two times when message-based data is a great idea. The first is when you want to do notifications or synchronizations and you can trust the JMS server to hold the notification until you can process it. The second is when you have low data requirements and high performance requirements. By using messages to hold the data, you minimize network hops. If the messages are small, that means you can send a lot of them over the network in a short amount of time.
9. *Connect the remaining pieces.* If you have any application elements left that still need data and don't have it. Look at your flow and figure out where these elements should get the data they need.

Example

Let's look at two examples. The first is a simple servlet that uses two EJBs to do some work for it. Clearly, we have a central controller, the servlet, which passes data to the EJBs. Working through our checklist, the data is moving from the servlet to the EJBs. The servlet is essentially a hub between the user and the EJB back end. There are no permanent data stores, and the servlet works well as a central controller. In this case, the checklist is longer than we needed to design the solution, but it asks the questions we need to answer.

Now let's think about something more complex. A set of servlets and JSPs provide the user interface for a customer support application. This application is required to store its data in a database. The data is being passed from the JSPs to the EJBs to the database. The application implements a number of business processes, so they need to have access to the data. The EJBs need access to the data that is coming from the JSPs and going into the database. In this example, the EJBs are clearly hubs for doing work. The database is also a hub for the data.

First, let's look at the network diagram. The network connections and flow would look something like Figure 1.21.

We have data moving from the servlet to EJBs, but also from EJBs to a database and other EJBs. Assuming that the customer records are 1 MB and that you get 1 a second, you need to have network bandwidth that supports 1 Mbps from the JSPs to the EJBs to the database. This is within the realm of normal Ethernet, even for these semilarge records.

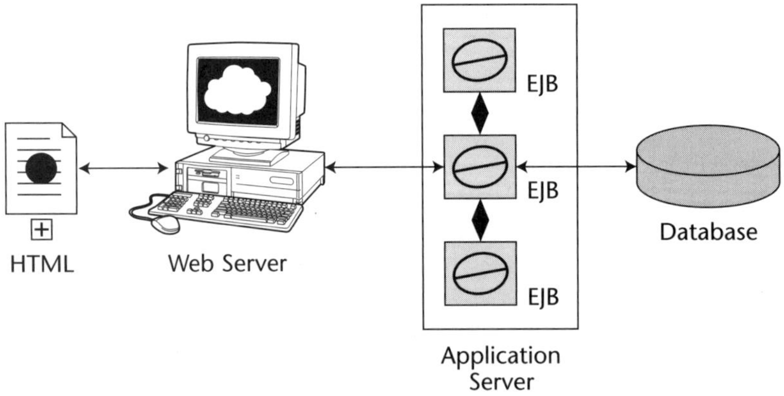

Figure 1.21 A more complex example.

Next, you must assign your controllers. In this case, the role of controller moves to the EJB that implements each business process. That EJB then uses the database as a central store for data, and makes calls to other EJBs that may also get data from the database as necessary.

Next, look for already persisted data. If we use some Entity Beans for caching we might be able to improve data flow by caching customer data in the application server. These Entity Beans would be responsible for moving the data down to the database. If we use Session Beans only, then we pretty much have transient data everywhere except the database itself.

You should also look for messaging opportunities. None really exist in this example, except possibly from the JSP to the EJB, but given the real-time requirements on most JSPs, we probably want to use Remote Method Invocation (RMI) or the Inter-Orb Inter-Operability Protocol (IIOP). This leads us to Step 9: "Connect the Remaining Pieces." The JSP-to-EJB transmission can use RMI, and the JDBC driver you pick will proscribe the EJB-to-database connection. Hopefully that driver will use TCP/IP connections.

Ultimately, your goal is to choose the optimal architecture of your J2EE solution. You may break the solution into smaller pieces that rely on different architectures to meet their specific needs, and tie these together using a larger pattern to meet the overall needs of your solution.

Partition Data and Work

Your data model is overwhelming and complex, or your work is all done at one place.

Look for ways to partition the data and work. Break it on logical boundaries such as time and geography.

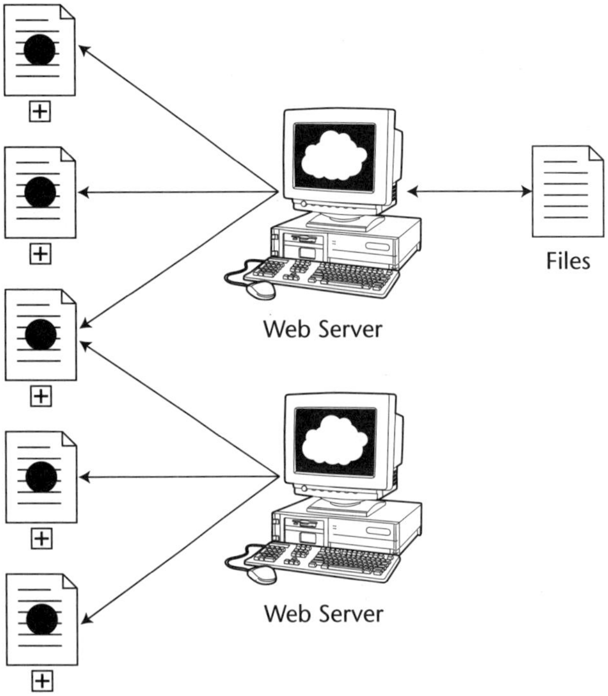

Figure 1.22 Before refactoring.

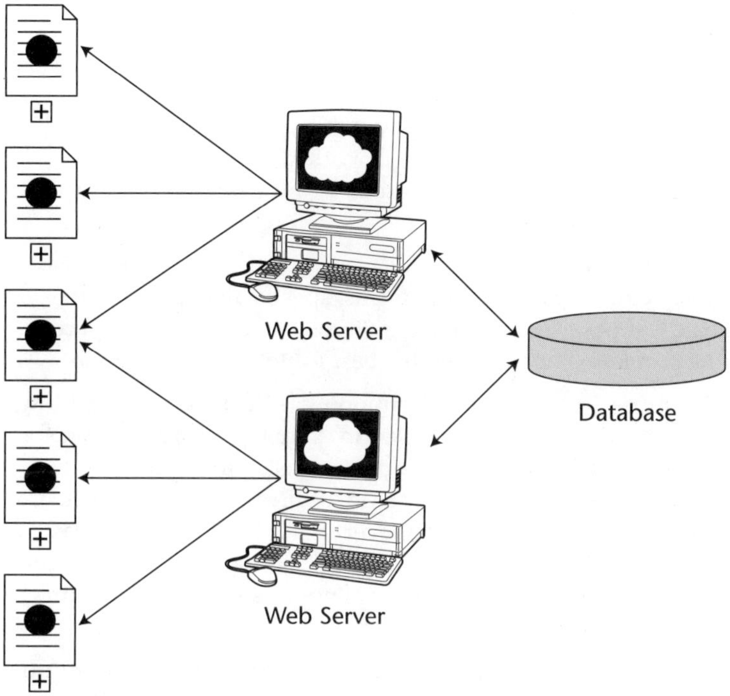

Figure 1.23 After refactoring.

Motivation

In a large project, there may be too much data to send through a single processor or database. We might call this data or processor overload. While databases scale to the very large, the price of scaling might be cost-prohibitive. Processing time, on the other hand, is more bound by the applications being used and their fundamental structure. Process automation, for example, has some fundamental architecture issues that may make it hard to scale on a single machine.

Sometimes, you can solve the problem of data overload or processor performance using transparent load balancing. In this case, the application runs on multiple computers with little or no knowledge of the different providers implemented or accessed by the clients.

When transparent load balancing isn't an option, you may have to partition. This uses the same principle as load balancing — multiple computers doing the same work — except that you build in knowledge at the client level to manage the splitting up of the work. You may also need to do partitioning because of bandwidth requirements, which is necessitated by the desire to use special networks, or because of geographic limitations. For example, if you were sending data from Asia to North America using a very-low-bandwidth connection, you would want to process the data as much as possible on either side of the connection before sending it through. Using special networks is a powerful refactoring that can be used to solve several types of problems, so we will discuss it separately.

Mechanics

Follow these steps to partition your data or work:

1. *Identify the overloaded application.* Generally, you would partition data or work because one of the hubs in your solution is overworked. If the hub is a data storage application, you may want to partition data. If the hub were a processor, you would partition the work.
2. *Determine if you can scale the application directly.* Can you add hardware or use transparent load balancing? Many J2EE platforms, specifically application servers and databases, support load balancing. If you can use this transparent means of fixing the problem, it is probably the best route.
3. *Look for an attribute, or axis, to partition on.* Partitioning is the process of splitting the work and data up into manageable chunks. To do that, you can take one of two routes. If the work is basic, you might be able to just split the data up randomly. More likely, you need to pick some metric for breaking up the work or data. For example, you might determine that everything from the East Coast goes in one database, and everything from the West Coast goes in another. You can do the same thing with work; all data processing for a region could happen on a machine in that region.
4. *Think about partitioning in time.* You may be able to partition work by time, optimizing for one type of operation during the day and another at night. This is like the old batch-processing concept, but it works in situations where you have an overwhelming number of orders during the day and nothing to do at night. For example, if your company does most of its sales during the day, and the people restocking work during the day, it is reasonable to store data for Monday on Monday, process the data on Monday night, and have the restockers look at it Tuesday morning. While this isn't real time, it is probably the reality of your process anyway, and it reduces the strain on your solution during the daylight hours.
5. *Find the job foreman.* Splitting up data and work requires that someone do the actual splitting. Does each client of the database know about the split? Can you use JNDI to find different connection information for different clients based on their login? You want scheduling work to be as simple as possible and preferably not too distributed and hard to manage.
6. *Analyze the implications.* Partitioning data has some very obvious implications. If all the East Coast data is in one place and all the West Coast data is in another, you have to go to two places if you want to query the entire database. Similarly, what if someone moves—do you move his or her data? These implications may send you back to Step 3, leading you to pick a different partitioning criterion.
7. *Look at existing data.* Existing data is the real bane of partitioning. If you currently have all of your data in one database, and you start splitting it by state, then what happens to the existing data? You have to copy it over. What if the

existing data is in the form of messages in a durable subscribers queue? Now, you need to process the messages in some way before you can partition. Partitioning your data after deployment can be a major hassle, which is why it is probably easier just to upgrade whenever possible. In other words, once you have a running system, you probably don't want to start partitioning work in a way that you didn't plan for. It is likely to be easier and cheaper just to solve any performance problems with hardware.

8. *Plan ahead*. When you start any project, you may want to think about building in partitioning data. For example, you might add a simple field to every message that is always the same by default, but that you can use later for partitioning. Of course, Planning Ahead is an entire refactoring in itself, but it is always worth mentioning.

Example

Rather than focus on one example, let's look at a number of different partitioning solutions. First, we have the example mentioned earlier: You have too much data for your database, so you partition it by geographic region. This breaks up the data load for each server.

Following the refactoring steps, you have identified the overloaded application as the database. Suppose that you can't scale the database, for the purposes of the argument. If you could scale the database server itself, then you could solve the problem that way. Once you determine that you can't scale, you find a partition attribute; in this case we picked geographic location. Then, we need to assign a job foreman. If the data is coming from Entity EJBs, then those beans might manage the partitioning. Otherwise, you might create Session Beans to do the partitioning. You want to minimize the surface area for code that deals with partitioning to make it easier to maintain. With the new design, you need to look at the existing data. Do you move it to the new databases or keep it in a legacy database? Either technique works. Finally, think about whether or not you will have to go through this again, and if so, how you can plan ahead for another partitioning. Planning ahead is another place where you want to minimize code so that you can change things as needed with the least possible effort.

Second, suppose that you are sending JMS messages all around the globe. Do you want to send them all to the same JMS server in L.A.? Probably not. Instead, you might distribute JMS servers in regionally centralized locations. Many JMS vendors will allow you do this in a way that the servers forward messages transparently as necessary. Even if the servers don't, you can create that solution by hand. Moreover, by distributing your messaging provider, you can improve local performance and plan a little paranoia into your solutions, something I highly recommend. So both of these examples are data-related partitions; in one the database holds the data, while in the other the JMS server holds the data.

You might also store, or rather access, data in Entity Beans. This data is subject to the same issues as using a database, in that you may want to localize it to geographic areas where the programs using it are located. You might also run into issues with your performance that suggests that you should use partitioning.

Entity Beans are actually a great tool in this case. You can use JNDI to reconfigure where different clients get their beans, making it easier to partition the data than it would be in the database directly.

Work can also be partitioned. Sessions Beans are generally pretty easy to partition since they are stateless. Custom applications can be easy as well, or very hard, depending on their design. If you use JMS, you might think about using topics more than queues when sending messages to custom code, even for single-subscriber situations. This will allow you to add clients if necessary to handle messages.

Plan for Scaling (Enterprise-Scale Object Orientation)

You have a large library for performing shared operations in your various applications.

Organize reusable code into reusable network components such as EJBs, JMS clients, and servlets.

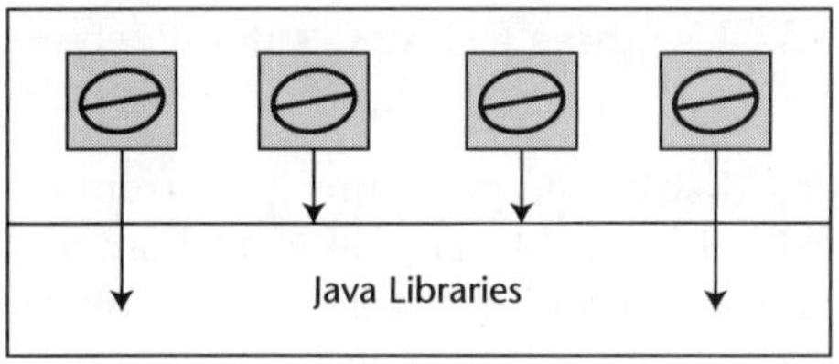

Figure 1.24 Before refactoring.

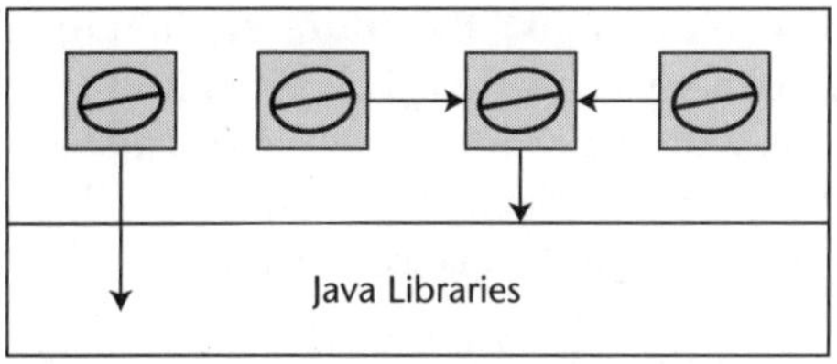

Figure 1.25 After refactoring.

Motivation

One of the biggest benefits of object-oriented programming (OOP) is that it helps you manage complexity. Objects can encapsulate implementations that involve numerous other objects. Inheritance can be used to create interface terms for a multitude of specific implementations. J2EE and all enterprise programming technologies have some of the same concepts. In particular, the more you can abstract and encapsulate the components of your solution, the more able you will be to scale your solution as needed.

Mechanics

Planning for scaling is not a step-by-step process. Use these techniques iteratively to improve your design.

1. *Organize work into tiers.* During the nineties, distributed programs grew from client/server, to three-tier, to *n*-tier. Basically this meant that you went from a client and server application, to a client and server and database, to a combination of clients and servers and databases. Think of these tiers as a part of your encapsulation process. Put work at one "tier" and keep it there. Assign responsibilities to each level of the solution and provide a strong interface on top of them.
2. *Leverage JNDI and dynamic discovery.* JNDI allows you to look up resources by a name or key. This type of indirection is similar to the separation of interface and implementation provided by OOP. Build the clients so that they have as little knowledge of the server as possible. If you can, make the addresses that the client uses dynamic so that you can change them as needed. This will allow you to plug in new server implementations without changing the client, just as polymorphism allows you to plug in new objects in place of others. This technique applies to Web Services as well as the other J2EE service mechanisms such as EJB and JMS.
3. *Use EJBs and JMS destinations to hide work.* You can think of an EJB as an interface to an unspecified amount of work. The same is true of a JMS destination, since it takes a message, and somehow the message is processed and a reply is sent. Any technology that goes over the network has the opportunity to work as an encapsulator for hiding implementation; try to use and document them this way.

Example

Imagine that you are building a customer entry application. The users will submit new customer information to the system via a Web interface. As a prototype, you create a servlet that accesses the database to add the customer data and accesses the network to validate the customer's credit card information.

In order to plan for scaling, you want to break apart behaviors using good OOP techniques. But, you want to use enterprise OOP so that reusability is handled via the network, not libraries. In our example, this means that you want to take the database code and move it to either session EJBs or entity EJBs. You would also move the credit card validation to a session EJB. This allows you to reuse both of these functions as needed from other servlets. It also minimizes the code of the customer entry servlet to allow it to focus on the specific tasks it is designed for. This design also organizes the work into tiers, Step 1 of the refactoring, and leverages EJBs, Step 3 in the refactoring. The remaining step is to be sure to leverage JNDI.

To go a step farther, you might replace the servlet with a set of JSPs, then develop custom tags to provide access to your EJBs, especially the credit card validation one. With these tags, you have created an even more formal encapsulation of the EJBs and made them reusable for any JSP developer with minimal documentation.

Plan Realistic Network Requirements

You are facing network performance problems in deployment that weren't there during testing.

The data for the deployed application may be very different from the data in tests. Plan realistic data from the beginning to avoid problems upon deployment.

Figure 1.26 Before refactoring.

Figure 1.27 After refactoring.

Motivation

It is easy to forget about the network when building a J2EE application. You know it is there, but JNDI, JMS, IIOP, and RMI make it so easy to build distributed programs that you can forget what these different technologies really mean. While this has implications across your solutions, one major implication of using any distributed program is that it uses network bandwidth. You have to plan realistically for this bandwidth usage.

Mechanics

Use the following techniques to build a realistic network plan:

1. *Build a realistic network map.* Write down every network component and every connection. Don't forget round trips for request-reply messages. These may happen at EJBs, JMS calls, RMI, IIOP, HTTP, and basically any network communication.
2. *Determine data sizes.* Use your data requirements to figure out the actual data sizes on messages, over time, as an average, and at the peak. Include request sizes and reply sizes. Sometimes, people forget the reply part of the messages, which might be the biggest part. For example, a database query may be very small, and the results very large. Sometimes people forget the small side of the request-reply, so they might capture the database results as a size, not the query itself. You want to get all the data requirements for the network.

3. *Look at the effect of time.* Do the requirements change over time? Is it busier at one part of the day?
4. *Analyze technology requirements.* Many technologies add data to the messages. JMS has an envelope, HTTP has a header, IIOP has a wrapper, and other technologies have their additional requirements. These requirements are usually small, but think about them, and make some estimates.
5. *Estimate latency times.* Messages on the network take time. Messages that store and forward, like JMS or mail, can take additional time. Similarly, messages that trigger other messages may result in time spent in the triggering application. All of these latency times can affect the overall performance and behavior of your J2EE solution.
6. *Identify unnecessary network hops.* Are there places where you are making network calls when you don't have to? Could data go into a message instead of being loaded from a database? Just as you did for data architectures, look at how to minimize network hops. These two elements, data and hops, combine to create the total bandwidth picture.

Example

One of the common mistakes I have seen in business process automation scenarios is people forgetting that the automation engine is a part of the installation. So, they send lots of data to every element of the solution, when they could store it in the automation engine. Moreover, they forget that each message is getting a round trip, coming from the engine to the element and going back to the engine. This round trip can double your bandwidth usage in some cases, and can greatly effect the final performance of your solution. By planning in the round trips and actual message traffic, you will create a more accurate picture of the overall traffic requirements.

Planning round trips is Step 1, in this example, of the refactoring. The next step is to make sure that you determine realistic data sizes. Perhaps even minimize the data in each message by leveraging the automation engine's memory. Step 3 is to double-check your assumptions over time. Is the process using more bandwidth in the morning or at night? You might want to plan for that.

Given the good network map, you can look at the technology issues. Do you have latency or transport overhead? Are you making unnecessary network hops? The automation engine may require round trips, but that isn't necessarily bad. It does mean that you want to leverage the automation engine's memory so that you don't move more data than necessary on the network. It also means that you want to check that the work you do per call is maximized to pay for the cost of the round trip.

Use Specialized Networks

Your network is overloaded.

Create specialized networks for specific functionality.

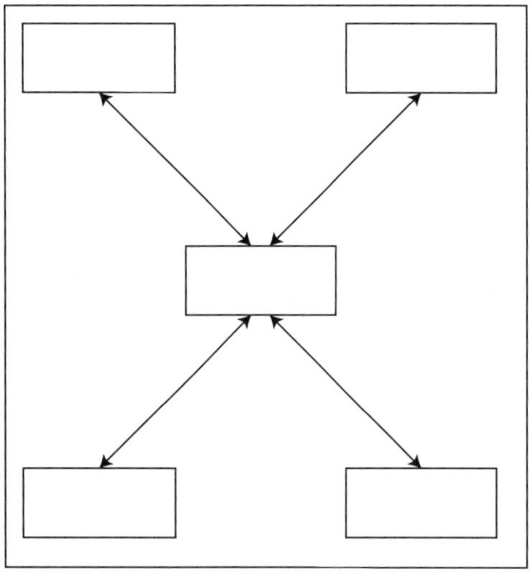

Figure 1.28 Before refactoring.

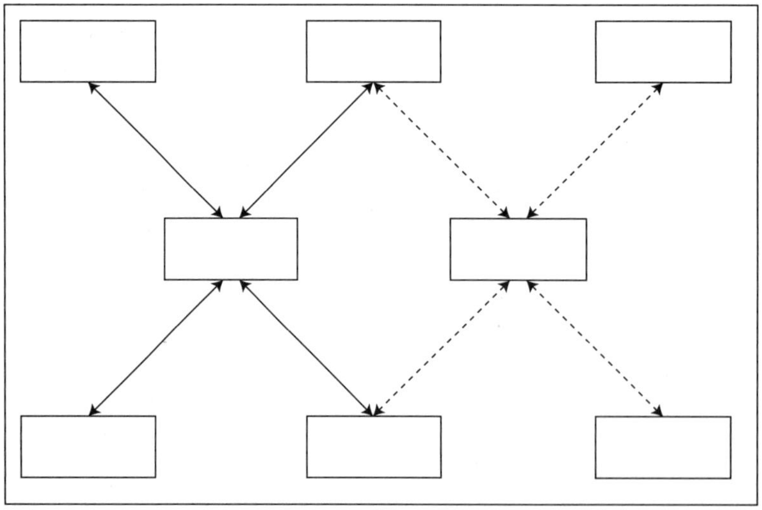

Figure 1.29 After refactoring.

Motivation

Sometimes you have a bandwidth problem that can't be solved by upgrading the existing network. Or, perhaps you have a security issue that requires that certain machines not be available to the public. In both cases, you can use separate networks to solve your problem. Since this isn't a security book, let's focus on the bandwidth problem. Let's say that you are a small department, without the budget for an optical multigigabit network. You have a J2EE application that needs to send data between a number of applications, and the data is bigger than the 100 Mbps you have on your current Ethernet. Break the network into several pieces; each piece will have 100 Mbps available.

Mechanics

In order to identify opportunities to use this refactoring, perform the following steps:

1. *Identify network bottlenecks.* Find the places where you are having trouble supporting your bandwidth requirements.
2. *Look for clusters of machines that work together.* This is similar to the garbage collection process that the JVM carries out. Look for closed graphs of machines that you might be able to "cut free" from the rest of the network.
3. *Analyze security requirements.* See if you can use the security requirements to your advantage. Routers and firewalls may already create custom networks; see if you can use these.
4. *Talk to your network administrator.* Before doing any network tinkering, consult the network administrator to make sure that there isn't another solution, and that you have the permissions you need to get the job done.

Example

Suppose that you have a very high-traffic Web site. You are getting lots of requests on your servers, tying up a lot of your bandwidth.

Step 1 of the refactoring is to identify this as a bottleneck. These servers connect to you application server to do work, and the application server uses a database server to store data. You might put two network cards in the Web servers, one pointing out, and one pointing in. Now, you have done Step 2, identified the clusters that work together and can move on to security. Breaking up the network would not only add a firewall capability to the Web servers themselves, it would allow you to separate the data traffic between the application components, the servlets, EJBS, and the database, and the user interface traffic to the Web site. By creating separate networks for the user traffic and the application traffic, you can control security, performance, and other network characteristics independently. As always, discuss all network changes with the administrator.

Be Paranoid

You have three pagers and are called at night to fix problems.

Be more paranoid at the beginning. Plan for failure and build in reasonable solutions for it.

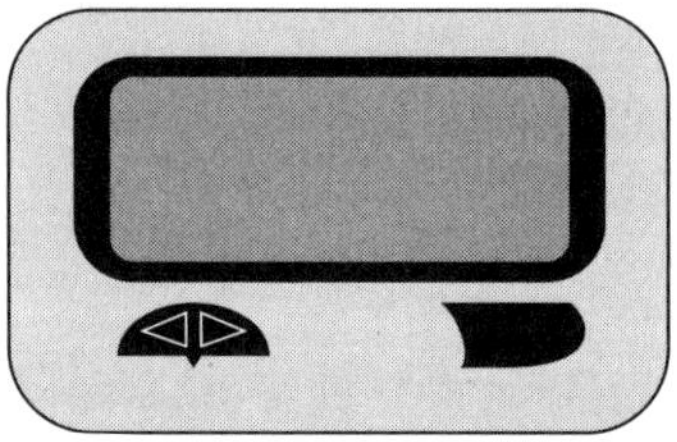

Figure 1.30 Before refactoring.

Figure 1.31 After refactoring.

Motivation

Risk and failure are issues we have to deal with all the time. Enterprise architects and J2EE developers need to keep a bit of paranoia around to help them plan for potential failures and risks. Many of the projects J2EE is used for put millions of dollars at stake, both during development and while they are running. You can't deploy these applications and not be ready for the consequences of failure.

Mechanics

Being paranoid is a full-time job; make sure you aren't forgetting to:

1. *Analyze network connections.* Look at all of your network connections and think about what would happen if they were lost or severed.
2. *Analyze data storage.* How much disk space is available on the persistent servers such as JMS, the database, and so on? This is an important value to track since running out of disk space can be a massive problem. If you run out of disk space on a storage server, you can't store any more data. This can result in lost

data and could bring your application to a halt.

3. *Build in monitoring*. The more monitoring and tracking you build into the system, the better able you will be to handle problems that arise and catch other problems before they occur.
4. *Perform standard risk analysis*. Identify the risks and the costs associated with reducing the risk or allowing the failure. If you have a really big installation or project, you might consider bringing in a professional risk analyst to help you with this.
5. *Identify your highest risks*. If you are an ISP, consider having multiple main network lines. If you are running the data center for your company, consider a backup generator or at least an uninterruptible power supply (UPS). Look for the things that can hurt you the most and protect them.
6. *Plan for recovery*. Create plans for what to do if something fails. Don't wait for the failure to happen to deal with it, especially for very big failures, like a power outage.

Example

Some great examples of paranoia in action are Netscape's multiple network links, RAID (redundant array of independent [or inexpensive] disks) arrays, and UPSs. Banks often use systems that have duplicate hardware for everything, including the central processing unit (CPU), to handle hardware failures at any place. Many application servers can be run in fault-tolerant mode, where one server takes over if another fails. All of these actions address Steps 1 and 2 of the refactoring, looking at data and network connections. Often planning for failure means including redundancy. Sometimes it is just having a plan for what to do.

Given these redundant systems, you can ride out a failure, but you also want to build in monitoring to notify you of problems. Otherwise, you may find that your backup died after your main resource because you never replaced the main resource on a failure (such as having one disk in a raid go bad, then another, before you get the first one replaced).

When I was working at a small startup company, we found it cheaper to build our own PCs than to buy them from name-brand vendors. We didn't have any support, so we had to deal with the failures, but we had a plan. When a failure occurred, we went to Fry's, bought the part that broke, and installed it. We had some downtime, but it was worth the cost savings that resulted from not buying name brands. For us, Steps 4 through 6 said that we would rather fix the problem ourselves than depend on an outside source. We realized there was risk, but planned to deal with it in a responsible way.

Throw Hardware at the Problem

You have performance problems.

Buy more boxes and throw hardware at the problem.

Figure 1.32 Before refactoring.

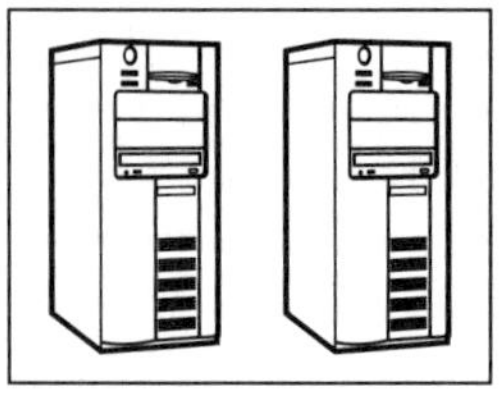

Figure 1.33 After refactoring.

Motivation

Sometimes you just can't get the performance you want from the hardware you have. When this happens, you just have to buy new hardware. The real question, when throwing hardware at a problem, is cost. Can you be smart with your design so that you can throw cheap hardware at the problem? For example, can you use a grid to solve a processing problem, or do you have to get a mainframe?

Mechanics

In order to use new hardware efficiently you should:

1. *Identify performance choke points.* Where are you having performance problems?
2. *Determine the possible hardware options.* Can you just upgrade a computer to fix the problem? If so, that may be the cheapest path. If you can rearchitect and add another machine of similar cost, that might be the best solution.

3. *Rule out architectural solutions.* Perhaps you can solve the problem purely with architecture. Keep in mind that this too has a price, so it may not be worth it. But sometimes you have made some miscalculations that send too much data over the network or to a particular machine, and you can fix those cheaply.
4. *Warm up the credit card.* When you know what to buy, and you have the money to buy it, go to the store and buy it. Have cash on hand for major hardware purchases and upgrades.

Example

I would imagine that anyone reading this book has thought about buying a bigger system at some point, perhaps that Cray T90 when it came out, or something similar. Therefore, an example is just overkill. There is, however, a funny counterexample. In the early nineties, when my machine had 8 MB of RAM (random access memory) in it and I thought that was great, I heard the following story:

A guy I worked with was supposed to build a sound recognition application for a small submarine that an unnamed navy wanted to build. The goal was to build a small, cheap submarine, perhaps around a million dollars or so. At the time, the best technology looked like Lisp, so they wrote the recognition software in that. When the demo day came, they fed in the first sound and out popped, "That is a whale." The program worked great. Then, they tried another sound, a few minutes passed, and out popped, "That is a blah blah submarine." Then, the kicker, they fed in a third sound, and an hour later, it said, "That is a blah submarine." The garbage collector had kicked in, and the whole program came to a crawl.

Now, the navy wasn't happy about this, so the sales guy jumped right in, saying, "For a couple million bucks we can put a gigabyte of RAM in." To which the navy replied, "We weren't planning to spend that much on the entire submarine."

In this example, the choke point is memory. There was a hardware option, but it was too costly. So the second choice was to find an architectural solution. In general, you always want to at least investigate the architectural solutions, Step 3, because they can be cheaper, although they won't always be.

Sometimes the cost of new hardware isn't worth the solution it provides. Of course, that's easy for me to say with my dual-processor machine with a gigabyte of RAM that only cost a couple hundred bucks.

CHAPTER 2

Persistence

In this chapter, we will explore some common persistence issues, along with refactorings to rectify these issues. The term *persistence* refers to the practice of storing and retrieving data. Such data could reside in a relational or object-oriented database, or perhaps even a flat file. In fact, the variety of such data source representations is staggering. Simply put, there is no single, universal format or medium for hosting raw data. There is also no universal method for representing this data in working memory. For example, an application could manipulate this data in memory-resident model objects or in data structures, such as C or C++ language data *structs* or COBOL copybooks.

For the purposes of our discussion, we can impose some simplifying assumptions. For example, our AntiPatterns and refactorings will assume that the underlying database is relational and thus accessible via the Java Database Connectivity (JDBC) API. Our in-memory data will reside in Java objects or components, under the auspices of persistence framework specifications, such as EJB and Java Data Objects (JDO).

We will use a sample financial services domain model as the basis of our AntiPattern discussion. In this model, illustrated in Figure 2.1, we will assume that we have customers who are associated with one or more addresses and accounts. Each account represents a particular product (for example, interest-bearing checking account, money market account) and can have one or more transaction entries, such as deposits and withdrawals.

These items will be represented as some combination of related Session and Entity Beans, and dependent objects. The AntiPatterns we discuss will highlight some specific design issues associated with the sample model, along with refactorings and solutions that address these issues.

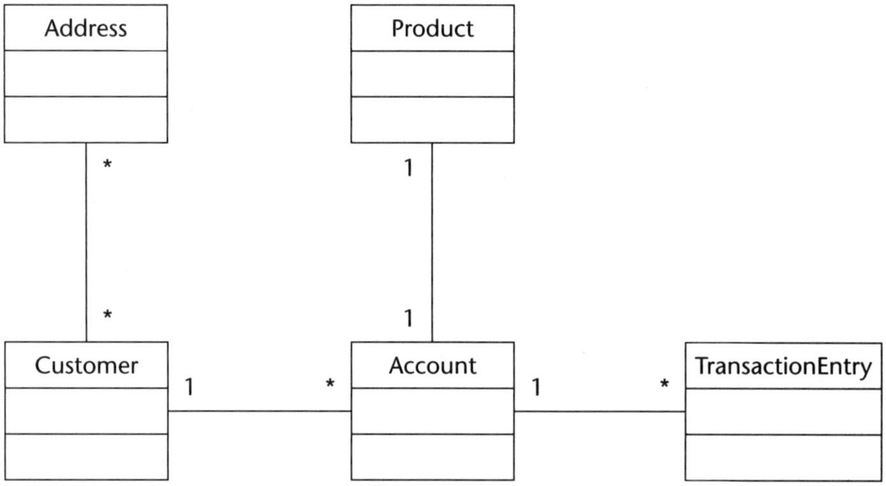

Figure. 2.1 Sample financial services domain model.

Dredge. Applications must frequently retrieve data from databases in order to drive query screens and reports. Applications that do not properly distinguish between *shallow* and *deep* information tend to load all of this information at once. This can lead to applications that outstrip available processing and memory resources and that cannot scale to meet user demands.

Crush. Shared access to data in a multiuser environment must be carefully coordinated to avoid data corruption. A *pessimistic* locking strategy can ensure such coordination—at the expense of performance—by allowing only one user to read and update a given data record at a time. An optimistic strategy can offer better performance by allowing multiple users to view a given data record simultaneously. However, great care must be taken to avoid data corruption and overwriting in a multiuser environment. The Crush AntiPattern illustrates the pitfalls of not taking the proper precautions in such an environment.

DataVision. Application component models should drive their underlying database schema—not the other way around. The DataVision AntiPattern shows the dysfunctional application model that can result from not heeding this advice.

Stifle. Most J2EE applications that deal with persistent data act as database clients, which converse with database servers over a network connection. These J2EE applications must make optimal use of network bandwidth in order to achieve the greatest levels of database scalability. The Stifle AntiPattern shows how such applications can be bottlenecked as a result of not optimizing the network pipeline for database communications.

AntiPattern

Dredge

Also Known As: Deep Query

Most Frequent Scale: Application

Refactorings: Light Query

Refactored Solution Type: Software

Root Causes: Inexperience

Unbalanced Forces: Complexity and education

Anecdotal Evidence: "We're running out of memory all over the place! We'll need to limit how much data our users can query at any given time . . . But what's a good limit?"

Background

A typical business application can consist of a wide variety of screens. Some screens resemble forms, allowing a user to view or possibly update a logical record of *deep information,* such as a given employee's personnel data. Some screens display several logical records of *shallow information,* such as a list of a company's employee identification numbers. The identification numbers represent individual employees. However, it is not necessary to load everything about each employee in order to build this screen. In fact, the only information required is the employee identification numbers, which is why such information is deemed shallow. An employee's complete data record can be loaded on demand (that is, when selected). The term, *lazy fetching,* refers to this strategy of loading data only when necessary. It enables systems to scale far better than would normally be possible if all of the data were always loaded upfront.

Unfortunately, many systems take a naïve approach to querying data. Instead of leveraging the efficiency characteristics of shallow queries, such systems use deep queries that often end up loading far more data than is necessary or even feasible. For example, a naïve application might display a list of employees by finding and instantiating every employee entity in the database. In a large company, with potentially hundreds of thousands of employees, such a deep query would likely exhaust all of the available application server memory and fail before returning any data.

In situations where large amounts of read-only data must be made available to users or other systems, it can be far more efficient to forgo the use of instantiating full-blown Entity Beans in favor of issuing a relatively lightweight query using JDBC. This concept is described in the *Light Query* refactoring.

General Form

This AntiPattern takes the form of session or DTOFactory façades that create large, deep graphs of Entity Bean instances in order to support the listing requirements of an application.

Symptoms and Consequences

Dredge typically takes a toll on processing and memory resources. Thus, the typical symptoms of Dredge are the depletion of those resources. These symptoms must be recognized and proactively addressed; otherwise, they could arise in a production environment where they might need to be addressed with rash purchases of additional memory and processing capacity. It may be virtually impossible to mitigate the effects of Dredge if end users have been materially affected by the AntiPattern. The symptoms and consequences of Dredge are described in the following:

- **Depleted resources and degraded performance.** The main symptoms of Dredge are a severe depletion of memory and resources, and degradation of performance on the application server whenever users start requesting lists of information. In these situations, an application suffering from Dredge will use deep information queries to create huge networks of Entity Bean instances, when a simple JDBC query of a subset of this information would have sufficed. As users open screens displaying lists of employees, customers, and accounts, the application server becomes increasingly bogged down in the process of locating and instantiating Entity Bean instances in order to support these screens. If some of these same entity instances are being updated by other users or processes, then the task of building the list screens could take an even longer time, depending on the transaction isolation levels being employed. For example, a deep query that attempts to load and instantiate an account entity that is being updated must wait for that update to complete if a serialized transaction isolation level is being used in conjunction with a database that enforces a pessimistic locking policy. In short, the symptoms of dredge are severely degraded performance as the number of concurrent users requesting lists—and the size and complexity of those lists—increases. Unfortunately, these symptoms rarely surface during unit testing or even system testing. During these phases, the amount of test data available is usually not sufficient to stress the system or indicate any problems. Therefore, list information screens will seem to be rendered with ease, despite the overhead of the deep queries providing the data. It is only during the transition phase, when the application is deployed with a full complement of business data and is being tested by a relatively large numbers of users, that the effects of Dredge become evident.
- **Increased hardware expenses.** One consequence of ignoring this AntiPattern is an increase in hardware expenses, because additional memory and processing resources must be purchased to combat the inefficiencies of the application and satisfy customers. Without such upgrades, an increase in the number of users could result in demand that outstrips the capabilities of the underlying hardware. Eventually, the application could become a victim of its own weight, becoming hopelessly bogged down and unresponsive to customer demands.
- **Loss of user confidence.** The most serious consequence is the loss of user confidence in the application and the entire development organization, as doubts of scalability and thoroughness of testing begin to emerge.

Typical Causes

The typical cause of Dredge is inexperienced architects, designers, and developers who have only a textbook understanding of J2EE application development. Such professionals do not understand that it is sometimes necessary—and entirely appropriate—to bypass the Entity Bean layer in order to access large volumes of database information. This typical cause is described below.

- **Inexperience.** Developers who have never built and fielded a J2EE application have no concept of what works and what does not. It may seem entirely appropriate to make liberal use of relatively heavyweight Entity Beans for every application query. After all, the entity layer is supposed to provide encapsulation of data and behavior and abstraction from the underlying database schema. Hence, using the entity layer would seem like a noble attempt to uphold the widely accepted benefits of its use. Using JDBC queries, on the other hand, would seem to counter these very same benefits, by tightly coupling the application to its underlying database schema. However, it takes real-world experience to know when the ideal is not ideal. Only an experienced architect, designer, or developer can understand that it is sometimes necessary to bypass the component framework or even denormalize database tables in order to achieve the kind of performance and scalability his or her customers require, as shown in Figure 2.2.

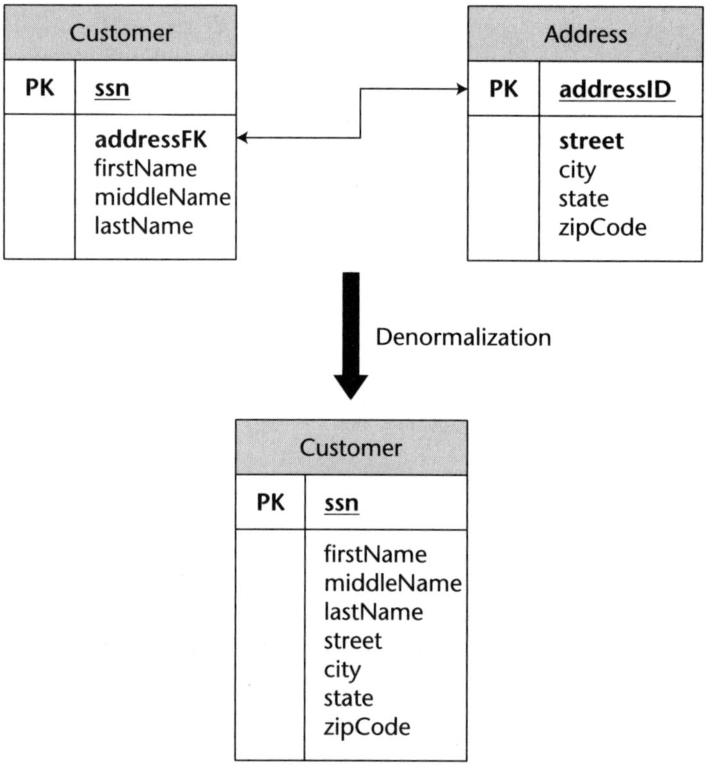

Figure. 2.2 Table denormalization for performance improvement.

Known Exceptions

The only acceptable time to make carte blanche use of deep queries is when the performance and scalability requirements of the application's stakeholders can still be satisfied despite their use. If this can be guaranteed, then it makes no sense to fix what is not broken. In this case, the simplicity of using a consistent mechanism for both persistence and data queries would outweigh the potential benefits of optimizing performance.

Refactorings

Light Query, found at the end of this chapter, is the refactoring that can be used to reduce the memory and processing requirements of database queries. Its conceptual underpinnings are based upon the Value List Handler and Value Object Assembler patterns, described in *Core J2EE Patterns: Best Practices and Design Strategies* (Alur, Crupi, and Malks 2001).

Use a Session or DTOFactory façade that uses JDBC scrollable result sets and cursor support to quickly access large amounts of read-only data within a reasonable memory footprint.

Variations

There are no variations of this AntiPattern.

Example

Suppose that a financial services application must present a tabular display of customer, account, and product information. A deep query could result in the instantiation of thousands of customer, account, and product entities—potentially exhausting all resources available to the application server environment.

Listing 2.1 is an example of a Session Façade method that might perform such a deep query.

```
...
public Collection getCustomerAccountInformation()
     throws CustomerProcessingException
{
Collection returnedInformation = new ArrayList();

// Get the default JNDI Initial context.
Context context = new InitialContext();

// Look up the Customer home.
Object obj = context.lookup("java:comp/env/CustomerHome");
```

Listing 2.1 CustomerFacadeBean.java. *(continued)*

```
// Downcast appropriately via RMI-IIOP conventions
CustomerHome custHome = (CustomerHome)PortableRemoteObject.narrow(obj,
     CustomerHome.class);
Collection customers = custHome.findAll();
Iterator custIter = customers.Iterator();
while(acctIter.hasNext()) {
     Customer aCustomer = (Customer) acctIter.next();
     Collection customerAccounts = aCustomer.getAccounts();
     Iterator custIter = customerAccounts.Iterator();
     while(custIter.hasNext()) {
       Account anAccount = (Account) acctIter.next();
       Product aProduct = anAccount.getProduct();
       ...
       // Get data from the Customer, Account, and Product beans.
       ...
       CustomerAccountDTO aCustAcctDTO = new CustomerAccountDTO();
       ...
       // Set data on a custom DTO that contains the
       // information required by the presentation tier.
       ...
       returnedInformation.add(aCustAcctDTO);
     }
}
```

Listing 2.1 *(continued)*

In this example, the Session façade acts as a DTOFactory, performing a deep query of every customer, account, and product in order to create custom DTO objects containing the information required by the presentation tier. This method is extremely expensive. For BMP and some CMP implementations, the initial fetch of N customers will result in N + 1 database fetches—one for the home findAll() invocation that retrieves all of the primary keys, and one for each of the *N* customer Entity Beans. In turn, the Product load could result in two database fetches (that is, one for the primary, one for the product itself), and a fetch of *M* Account entities could result in M + 1 database fetches (that is, one for the primary keys, one for each of the *M* accounts). In addition, there would be network and serialization overhead for each of the Entity Bean method invocations if remote interfaces were used. If this kind of solution is replicated wherever a list of information must be generated, the application will never be capable of scaling to any reasonable extent.

Related Solutions

There are a number of related solutions for this AntiPattern. Some follow the same general principle of using a façade that implements some relatively lightweight query mechanism for retrieving the desired information. Other solutions augment container functionality and efficiency, so that Entity Beans can still be used to provide the information.

The first is object/relational (O/R) mapping products. Some O/R mapping products, such as Oracle's Toplink, can augment the application server container with enhanced functional capabilities. For example, Toplink provides special mechanisms for implementing finders that can deal with large result sets. Toplink finders can be configured to leverage a proprietary feature, called *cursored streams*, and the cursor capabilities of the underlying database to shuttle result sets into memory in chunks. This allows such finders to partition extremely large result sets into smaller pieces that can be managed within a reasonable memory footprint. For example, a Toplink finder could locate all of the accounts associated with a large customer, using the implementation in Listing 2.2.

```
...
ReadAllQuery query = new ReadAllQuery();
ExpressionBuilder builder = new ExpressionBuilder();
query.setReferenceClass(AccountBean.class);
query.useCursoredStream();
query.addArgument("customerID");
query.setSelectionCriteria(bldr.get("customer").
like(bldr.getParameter("customerID")));
descriptor.getQueryManager().addQuery ("findByCustomerID");
...
```

Listing 2.2 Oracle Toplink finder.

Products such as Toplink are extremely powerful, but typically require developers to use proprietary APIs and mechanisms. As shown in the listing above, the Toplink query framework uses proprietary classes, such as *ReadAllQuery* and *ExpressionBuilder*. Extensive use of such classes could severely limit the portability of the applications that use them. The issue of vendor lock-in must be factored into the process of deciding whether to use a given product or technology.

Java Data Object (JDO) is another solution. An emerging specification for the storage, query, and retrieval of Java objects from a persistent store, JDO competes with EJB, offering a lightweight and compelling alternative to the overhead of Entity Beans. JDO offers the advantage of *transparent persistence*, where Java objects need no additional methods, attributes, or related visibility modifications in order to be persisted. Any changes to an object's state in memory will be persisted once the active transaction is committed.

JDO has tackled the issue of querying objects, and has more than one approach for accomplishing this task. Since JDO is relatively lightweight, its query capabilities could be used in a *Light Query* refactoring implementation. For example, a JDO query could query the database for all accounts belonging to a particular customer ID. These accounts would be implemented as Plain Old Java Objects (POJOs), instead of heavy-weight Entity Beans, as illustrated in Listing 2.3.

```
...
Query query =
persistenceManager.newQuery(
Account.class, "customer == \"" +
customerID + "\"");

Collection accounts = (Collection) query.execute();
Account anAccount = (Account) accounts.iterator().next();

// Extract account data from the instance.
String accountID = anAccount.getID();
...
query.close(accounts);
...
```

Listing 2.3 JDO query finder.

This example is by no means an exhaustive treatment of JDO. Several JDO books are available on the market, should you wish to study the subject further. JDO has gained considerable momentum in the software community. It will be an important tool in any Java developer's arsenal.

Crush

Also Known As: Overwrite, Stale Dominance

Most Frequent Scale: Application

Refactorings: Version

Refactored Solution Type: Software

Root Causes: Inexperience

Unbalanced Forces: Complexity and education

Anecdotal Evidence: "Our users are stepping all over each other's updates!"

Background

Applications are often challenged with the task of supporting transactional scenarios that would allow a user to read some data, modify the data, and then subsequently update the data in the underlying database. For example, a customer service representative at a local bank might need to bring up an account detail screen in order to make an important annotation. When the operator requests the screen, the data for the desired account is loaded from the database and presented in a form. The operator might take several minutes or even hours to do offline research before annotating the account data.

The time it took the operator to perform her research and save the form is called *user think-time*. This scenario is actually a long-running, logical transaction that involves user think-time. Because this think-time can be so long, it is not feasible to actually read, modify, and update the data in a single Atomic, Consistent, Isolated, and Durable (ACID) transaction. Instead, this set of steps must be implemented in separate transactions that are logically associated with the single, logical transaction of annotating an account. Thus, the reading of the data might happen in one ACID transaction, while the updating might happen in yet another. Because these steps cannot be covered within a single ACID transaction, they cannot be isolated from the actions of other users.

General Form

This AntiPattern is evidenced in applications that have long-running, transactional use cases with no discernable realization of these use cases in code. In other words, these transactional cases either have not—or cannot—be captured within a single container-managed Session Façade method or section of code bracketed by Java Transaction API (JTA) invocations. Instead, such use cases are implemented without ever considering how they can ever be executed in a transactional manner.

Symptoms and Consequences

Subtle data corruptions and overwriting are the symptoms of Crush. These symptoms can shake the faith of the most loyal user, as the stability and integrity of the application are brought into question. The symptoms and consequences of Crush are described below.

- **Intermittent data loss.** This is a particularly insidious symptom of this AntiPattern. An application support staff that is battling such issues is probably fighting a war with Crush.
- **Loss of user confidence.** Once enough users have been affected by the AntiPattern, they will quickly doubt the integrity of the application and the abilities of the development and testing organizations. Unfortunately, it is very difficult to detect the presence of this AntiPattern during unit or even system-level testing. It is only when the application is used by multiple concurrent users, that the probability of collisions increases enough to raise suspicion.

Typical Causes

The typical cause of Crush is inexperienced developers who have minimal practical understanding of implementing and deploying transactional information systems. This cause is described below.

- **Inexperience.** The typical cause of Crush is inexperience. Developers who have limited experience building transactional systems do not appreciate the variety and complexity of transactions and related issues. Transactions cannot always be neatly packaged into a Session Façade method or a snippet of code. Some transactions occur naturally in business—yet cannot be readily implemented in any one particular place. These are complex, yet common situations. In fact, the entire marketplace for commercial workflow engines exists to handle such situations—business transactions that can span extremely long periods and involve numerous people, events, and actions in the process.

Known Exceptions

There are no significant exceptions to this AntiPattern. If transactions must span user think-time, then there must be some way of dealing with the possibility of updating recent information with stale data. Unless this possibility is acceptable, there is no exception worth noting.

Refactorings

The best refactoring to apply to this AntiPattern is Version, detailed later in this chapter. This refactoring can be used to maintain version numbers and perform associated version checks within the Entity Beans and DTOs that support transactional scenarios involving user think-time. This effectively provides an optimistic locking strategy that can dramatically reduce the possibility of inadvertent data overwrites.

Variations

There are no variations of this AntiPattern.

Example

A Crush scenario between two operators is illustrated in Figure 2.3. After Operator A pulls up the account detail screen, she may take a long time to perform offline research before annotating the account and updating its data in the database. During that long span of user think-time, another operator (Operator B) could have performed the same logical operation on the very same account, taking only a few seconds to annotate and update the data. At this point, Operator A is working with a stale copy of the account data. Therefore, she is now operating under a false assumption regarding the state of the account. When she updates the account, she will overwrite Operator B's updates. In effect, Operator A is replacing the latest version of the account with stale data.

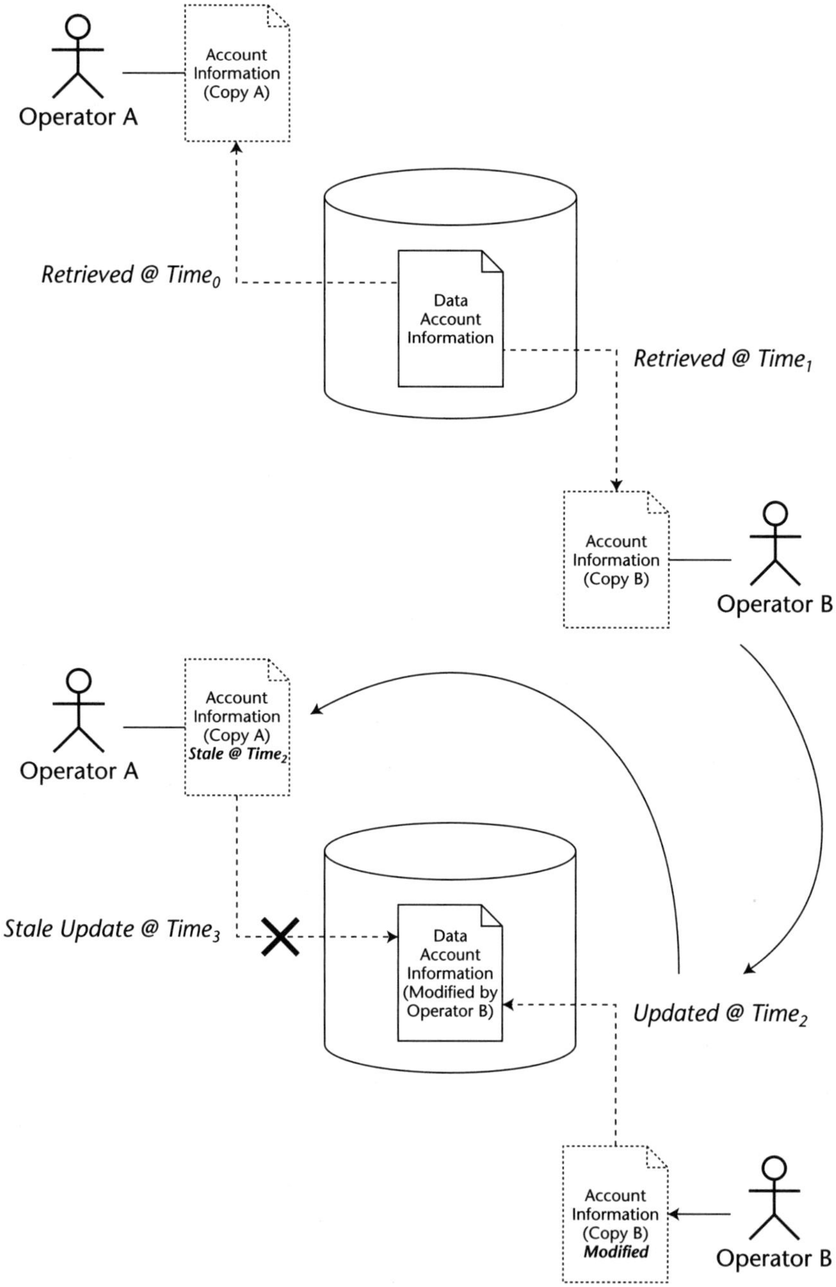

Figure. 2.3 Inadvertent overwrites between two operators.

This is the Crush AntiPattern in action, and it is disastrous. Unless Operator B happens to inspect the account in the near future, he will have no idea that his changes have been trampled by another user's updates. A system that suffers from Crush has no integrity because it cannot guarantee the validity of the data it presents or the durability of the changes it accepts. In situations like this, the application must allow multiple users to update account information, while allowing for think-time and preventing updates from being trampled by stale data.

In order to accomplish this, you must maintain version numbers in the Account Entity Bean and underlying database table, and in any DTOs that convey account information. This version information must be checked before any account can be updated. This is the essence of the Version refactoring, discussed later in this chapter.

Related Solutions

There are a number of different ways to address this AntiPattern. The main point of any solution is some ability to enforce an optimistic locking strategy. Users must be allowed to update the same data, but stale data overwrites must be detected and avoided. Some solutions can rely, almost exclusively, on any optimistic locking capabilities natively available within the underlying database. Other solutions can use other technologies, such as commercial O/R mapping products, like Oracle Toplink. Many of these products track and enforce object-level versioning semantics in order to support a robust optimistic locking strategy.

DataVision

Also Known As: Database Object

Most Frequent Scale: Architecture

Refactorings: Component View

Refactored Solution Type: Software

Root Causes: Inexperience

Unbalanced Forces: Maintainability and education

Anecdotal Evidence: "Our DBA group is developing the enterprise object model."

Background

A database schema should never be used to drive an application component model. Databases contain and maintain relationships between various pieces of data stored in tables. There is a formal, mathematical model for expressing and manipulating the data that resides within a relational database. Redundant data is maintained in foreign key columns in order to facilitate the process of joining data from separate tables. All of this is proven, sound technology, but it should not drive the design of your application components.

The reason is that relational database design and object-oriented design are distinctly different ways to view the world. Relational database design encompasses data, while object-oriented design encompasses both data (that is, state) and behavior. Thus, the application component model should be designed using object-oriented analysis and design methodologies—and this design should drive the underlying database schema. In effect, the database schema should primarily be designed to meet the data and behavioral demands of the component model. Additional database design modifications and tuning should only be performed if performance or scalability issues remain.

Application component models that have been developed from a database schema often end up suffering from an AntiPattern called *DataVision*. DataVision litters component models with poorly defined abstractions that are essentially blobs of data and functions with no crisp definition, boundary, or behavior. These abstractions masquerade as components, littering the application component model and increasing the complexity and the overall cost of maintenance.

General Form

This AntiPattern is usually evidenced by a large number of poorly defined session and Entity Beans. These components lack cohesion, often representing many things and yet nothing. They are usually contrived inventions that have no mapping to the business domain or any reasonable design construct.

Symptoms and Consequences

A dysfunctional application component model is often a symptom of DataVision. Such models often consist of mere blobs of data rather than cohesive objects with meaningful state and crisp behavior and boundaries. Because these constructs are byproducts of an underlying database schema and not the result of thoughtful domain and object-oriented analysis, they are usually difficult to understand and maintain. All of these factors raise the overall cost of application maintenance. The symptoms and consequences of DataVision are outlined next.

- **Abundance of pseudocomponents.** A symptom of DataVision is the abundance of pseudocomponents, or globs of data, within the application component model.
- **Dysfunctional component object model.** The consequence of this AntiPattern is an overly complicated and confusing component object model that is difficult to maintain.
- **Increased maintenance costs.** The longer-term consequences are increased maintenance costs and longer times being required to implement functional enhancements.

Typical Causes

Relational database modelers (such as DBAs) often embrace a data-centric perspective, and they tend to build models from that perspective. Object-oriented analysts typically build models based upon real-world abstractions. DataVision results when a data-centric perspective is used to create an object model. The resulting models typically consist of pseudo-objects that lack cohesion and clear state and behavioral characteristics. The typical causes of the DataVision AntiPattern are described in the following list.

- **Ongoing battles between DBAs and OO developers.** This AntiPattern lies at the center of the ongoing religious war between database and object-oriented architects, designers, and implementers. Some organizations give considerable power and authority to their database designers. In fact, it is common to hear of database organizations that have been charged with the responsibility of developing the enterprise object model. The models that result from these efforts are usually a disaster, bearing more resemblance to an entity-relationship (E-R) model than an object- or component-oriented model. Organizations that fail to respect the complexities of both the data and object-oriented worlds stand a very good chance of falling prey to this AntiPattern. Neither world should be responsible for dictating the designs of the other. Rather, both worlds must be designed by their respective practitioners, with the overall goal of complementing, reflecting, and supporting each other.

Known Exceptions

There really is no exception to this AntiPattern. Even when a legacy database is in place, there is no good reason to design a component object model from a data-driven perspective. Tools and technologies, such as CMP, JDO, and O/R mapping products can bridge the impedance mismatch between most database and component object models. Neither world has to benefit at the expense of the other.

Refactorings

Developers should be using the Component View refactoring, described in detail later in this chapter, to resolve this AntiPattern. This refactoring introduces a component-oriented perspective when developing an application's component object model. If possible, let this design drive the design of the underlying database schema. Use mapping technologies, such as CMP, JDO, and O/R mapping products to marry the two worlds. Apply database optimizations if performance or scalability issues remain.

Variations

There are no variations of this AntiPattern.

Example

Let us revisit the sample financial services domain model illustrated in Figure 2.1. Consider the many-to-many relationship between customers and addresses. A typical way to model this relationship in a relational database is to use separate tables for customers and addresses, while introducing a junction or join table to store the many-to-many mappings. A three-way join across all of these tables can be used to enumerate the many-to-many relationships between specific customers and addresses, as demonstrated in Figure 2.4.

Although the database schema illustrated in Figure 2.4 is entirely appropriate in the relational database world, it is not an optimal perspective for designing a component object model. Taking a data-driven approach to designing a component object model would create an entity component for each of the tables, as shown in Figure 2.5.

Although such a model could work, it would not be optimal or natural from an object-oriented perspective. For example, consider the *CustomerAddress* component. This component is completely contrived and has no mapping to the financial services domain. It is merely an artifact of the relational database schema, yet has no crisp state or behavior. Therefore, it should not be represented as a component.

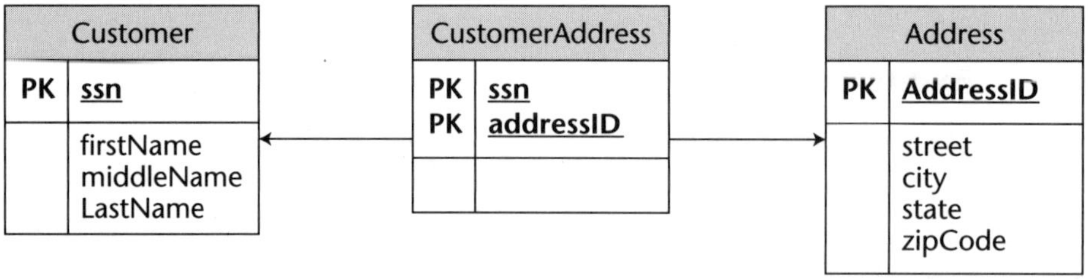

Figure. 2.4 Address-customer database schema.

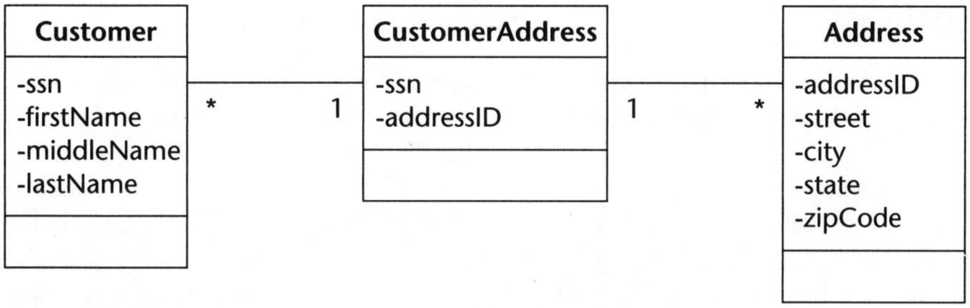

Figure. 2.5 Data-driven address-customer component model.

Related Solutions

There are no significant related solutions to this AntiPattern.

AntiPattern

Stifle

Also Known As: Choke Point

Most Frequent Scale: Architecture

Refactorings: Pack

Refactored Solution Type: Software

Root Causes: Inexperience

Unbalanced Forces: Education and resources

Anecdotal Evidence: "Java's just too slow to be used for any database-intensive work."

Background

There was a time when Java lacked sufficient power to be used for database-intensive applications. Now that JDBC 3.0 is available with functional advancements such as SavePoint processing and the ability to update database BLOB and CLOB columns, Java has shattered the old myths and silenced its naysayers. Even the JDBC 2.x release brought several key advancements, such as simplified connection pooling to reduce the overhead of establishing and relinquishing physical connections to the database and the ability to perform database updates in efficient batches. Unfortunately, many developers do not know about the advancements of JDBC 2.x and 3.0. Thus, they continue to miss the significant performance and functional enhancements that have been made available. Applications that do not leverage these enhancements suffer needlessly from the Stifle AntiPattern—a condition of poor performance caused by a general lack of knowledge of Java database technology and the full extent of what it has to offer.

General Form

This AntiPattern usually takes the form of code that fails to use the batch-processing capabilities of JDBC 2.x, and thus makes suboptimal use of the network pipelines connecting database clients and servers.

Symptoms and Consequences

The Stifle AntiPattern makes the database a bottleneck by making inefficient use of the network pipeline between J2EE database clients and database servers. Ultimately, this leads to poor performance and unhappy users. Following are the symptoms and consequences of Stifle:

- **Poor database performance.** The symptom of this AntiPattern is poor database performance, particularly in controlled, batch-processing scenarios where a large number of records must be inserted or modified in the database within a relatively short period. Another symptom of this AntiPattern is significant database server idle time. The combination of poor database performance and idle database resources suggests that the application is not making full use of the available network bandwidth between the application and the database servers. Therefore, the database server is starved for work, while the application is throttled by the overhead caused by spoon-feeding SQL commands to the database.
- **Unhappy users.** The consequence of not defeating this AntiPattern is needlessly slow database performance that can blow batch-processing windows and make business users and general application customers very unhappy.

Typical Causes

The typical cause of this AntiPattern is inexperienced developers who lack sufficient understanding of the JDBC mechanisms that can provide dramatic performance improvements. This cause is further elaborated below.

- **Inexperience.** The typical cause of this AntiPattern is inexperience. Developers who have learned JDBC 1.x and have grown used to its limitations may be reluctant to take the time to learn the capabilities of subsequent JDBC specification releases. However, with education and sufficient time for experimentation, developers can become aware of these capabilities and can use them to defeat the performance degradation associated with the Stifle AntiPattern.

Known Exceptions

There are no exceptions to this AntiPattern.

Refactorings

The Pack refactoring—found later in this chapter—can be used to avoid or alleviate the performance impacts of Stifle by using pooled JDBC database connections to minimize the overhead associated with managing such connections explicitly. In addition, JDBC 2.0–based batch updates are used to maximize the network pipeline between database clients and servers.

Variations

There are no variations of this AntiPattern.

Example

Let us suppose that the accounts stored in a financial application are frequently updated in a nightly batch. Specifically, a mainframe system that serves as the account of record for newly acquired, established, or closed accounts creates and sends a message containing these accounts to the financial application via MQSeries. Suppose that this financial application implements a message-driven bean (MBD) that can receive this message, extract its contents, and use this information to perform a potentially massive update of the underlying accounts database. It may be possible to circumvent the Entity Bean layer in favor of using lightweight JDBC SQL statements—assuming that the nature of the update is trivial (for example, toggling an open or closed indicator). The JDBC implementation could issue SQL INSERTs and UPDATEs on an individual account basis. However, if millions of accounts are being updated, this approach will not scale well and may run the risk of blowing the nightly batch-processing window. This means that the online portion of the application may have to remain closed until the updates are complete.

Consider Listing 2.4. The AccountBatchProcessingBean code shown in that listing uses the deprecated DriverManager approach to establish a connection to the database. This practice essentially grafts specific information about the driver into the application, thus complicating the code and hindering its portability. After this, the bean sends each SQL INSERT and UPDATE instruction separately to the database server. Although this gets the job done, it is extremely inefficient because it fails to make full use of the network bandwidth available between the application and database servers.

```
...
// Load the database driver and establish a connection...
Class.forName(databaseDriver);
Connection conn = DriverManager.getConnection(url,userID,password);
...
// Extract and loop through account data extracted from JMS Message
...
while(accountIter.hasNext())
{
...
Statement statement = conn.createStatement();
int rowsAffected = statement.executeUpdate(
"UPDATE ACCOUNT SET ...");
     ...
}
...
```

Listing 2.4 AccountBatchProcessingBean.java.

Related Solutions

There are no related solutions for this AntiPattern.

Refactorings

This section documents the refactorings referred to earlier in the AntiPatterns. These refactorings utilize a combination of persistence strategies and mechanisms to either prevent or neutralize a persistence AntiPattern. Some of the AntiPatterns in this chapter deal with the failure of developers to embrace the benefits of properly using certain J2EE standards, such as JDBC. The Light Query and Pack refactorings address these AntiPatterns. Other AntiPatterns deal with issues such as optimistic locking and poor object-oriented design. The Version and Component View refactorings deal with these issues, respectively.

Light Query. Applications can retrieve much larger volumes of shallow information more efficiently if lightweight JDBC queries are used in lieu of heavyweight entity beans.

Version. An application can support multiple, simultaneous logical transactions involving user think-time if the right versioning mechanisms and checks are put into place. Introduce versioning mechanisms into the entity and DTO layers, and check versions in the Session Façade layer.

Component View. Use proper object-oriented analysis and design to refactor pseudocomponents, which were originally conceived from an existing database schema or a data-centric mindset.

Pack. Use the batch-processing capabilities of JDBC 2.x (or greater) to optimize intensive database operations.

Light Query

Your application must present large lists of shallow information items to its users and allow those users to select an item in order to reveal its detailed, deep information.

Use lightweight JDBC queries and scrollable result sets to select potentially vast numbers of shallow list items. Use an additional JDBC query or Entity Bean fetch to retrieve the deep information for a selected shallow item.

```
Object obj = context.lookup("java:comp/env/CustomerHome");

CustomerHome custHome = (CustomerHome)PortableRemoteObject.
     narrow(obj, CustomerHome.class)
Collection customers = custHome.findAll();
Iterator custIter = customers.iterator();
while(custIter.hasNext()) {
   Customer aCustomer = (Customer)custIter.next();
   Collection accounts = aCustomer.getAccounts();
   Iterator accctIter = accounts.iterator();
   while(acctIter.hasNext()) {
     Account anAccount = (Account)acctIter.next();
     ...
   }
}
```

Listing 2.5 Deep query retrieval of account information.

```
DataSource ds = (DataSource)context.lookup("jdbc/FinancialDB");
Connection conn = ds.getConnection("user","password");
Statement stmt = conn.
   createStatement(ResultSet.TYPE_SCROLL_INSENSITIVE,
   ResultSet.CONCUR_READ_ONLY);
ResultSet resultSet = stmt.
   executeQuery("SELECT NAME, LNK_CUSTOMER, ... FROM ACCOUNT");
while (resultSet.next()) {
...
}
```

Listing 2.6 Refactored light query retrieval of account information.

Motivation

Applications often display lists of information to users. This information can be retrieved via deep queries that inflate and interrogate full-blown Entity Beans, in order to extract and return the data that is required to render the screen. This approach consumes a considerable amount of processing and memory resources, and can drastically hinder an application's ability to scale as the number of concurrent users and the amount of requested listing data increases. JDBC—a very popular Java 2 specification—can be used to access relational databases and tabular data sources (for example, spreadsheets) from within plain Java applications or bean-managed persistence (BMP) entities. Thus, the use of JDBC to combat the Dredge AntiPattern should require very little training in the development community. JDBC 2.x introduced a number of functional advancements, including scrollable result sets and enhanced cursor support, which are both critical to this refactoring.

A result set encapsulates the results of a SQL query and provides a cursor that can scroll from one logical record to another. In older versions of JDBC, this cursor could only scroll forward within a result set. However, starting with JDBC 2.0, cursors can scroll forward, scroll backward, and be set to an absolute record position within a result set. This kind of functionality mimics the typical operations of a user scrolling through a list of data. In fact, this very same functionality can be used not only to fetch list data, but also to allow users to navigate the data without bringing it all into memory at once.

Mechanics

The following is a list of steps, which must be followed in order to apply the Light Query refactoring. The first steps concentrate on locating instances of the Dredge AntiPattern—portions of the application that uses deep queries to produce potentially large lists of information. The next steps involve the use of a DTOFactory façade, which will use lightweight JDBC queries in order to generate the shallow lists. These façades could also be used to retrieve deep information for a selected shallow item.

1. Determine which types of lists an application must generate and provide to its clients. Take an inventory of the data composing these lists. It will be necessary to target the underlying data tables containing this information.
2. *Locate any logic currently responsible for generating these lists of information.* If the logic uses deep queries to generate these lists, then they become candidates for refactoring—particularly if the lists are very large. Also, take stock of which lists are already problematic from a performance or memory consumption perspective. If users are not able to view certain lists without severely degrading application performance, then such lists should be refactored first.

3. *Introduce or modify existing session or DTOFactory façades.* These components will be responsible for generating and returning shallow list information.
4. *Either introduce or use existing custom DTOs that will represent each logical row of list information.* The Session or DTOFactory façades mentioned above will ultimately create and return these DTOs to higher-level tiers. Each DTO should be a shallow data representation, containing only what is needed to display the list and the primary key for the corresponding record in the database. If the user selects an identifier, then a separate Façade method can use the primary key of the selected record to load the corresponding detailed data record.
5. *Use lightweight JDBC queries.* Implement session or DTOFactory Façade methods that use lightweight JDBC queries, and not heavyweight Entity Beans, to load the requested data.
6. *Deploy and test.*

Example

The first step in this refactoring is to identify the lists of information that an application is generating. The easiest way to do this is to locate such lists in the user interface. A typical business application has some query capability that produces a displayed list of results. Often the query is subtle—for example, the list of accounts that is displayed after a user enters a customer identifier.

The next step is to locate the logic that is currently responsible for generating these lists. Typically, this kind of code is located in a session bean or Plain Old Java Object (POJO) façade. If no such façade exists, it must be created. This façade must act as a DTOFactory, returning the desired list information in collections of custom DTO instances. Let us take the example of an application that must return a collection of customer and account information given a customer identifier.

For the purposes of our example, we will assume that there is no DTOFactory currently responsible for returning customer-account information, so we must create this factory class. We will create the *CustomerFacadeBean* Session Façade Bean, whose *getCustomerAccountInformation()* method will return collections of custom DTO instances.

```
public class CustomerFacadeBean implements SessionBean
{
...
public Collection getCustomerAccountInformation()
          throws CustomerProcessingException
{
```

```
        ...
    }
    ...
}
```

The next step is to define the custom DTO class that the *getCustomerAccountInformation(...)* method must create and return. We will create the *CustomerAccountDTO* class, which will act as the custom DTO for customer-account information.

```
import java.util.Collection;

 public class CustomerAccountDTO
 {
     private String customerFirstName;
     private String customerMiddleName;
     private String customerLastName;
     private Collection accountIDs;

     public String getCustomerFirstName
          { return customerFirstName; }
     public void setCustomerFirstName(String inValue)
          { customerFirstName = inValue; }
     public String getCustomerMiddleName
          { return customerMiddleName; }
     public void setCustomerMiddleName(String inValue)
          { customerMiddleName = inValue; }
     public String getCustomerLastName
          { return customerLastName; }
     public void setCustomerLastName(String inValue)
          { customerLastName = inValue; }
     public void addAccountID(String inValue)
          { accountIDs.add(inValue); }
     public String getAccountIDs
          { return accountIDs; }

}
```

The next step is to use a lightweight JDBC query within the *getCustomerAccountInformation ()* method. This query will retrieve the required information from the database in the most efficient manner. After a JDBC data source has been acquired, a database connection is established.

```
...
public Collection getCustomerAccountInformation()
          throws CustomerProcessingException
{
            Collection returnedInformation = new ArrayList();
            ...

     // Establish a result set that will not reflect changes to itself
     // while it is open (i.e., TYPE_SCROLL_INSENSITIVE vs.
     // TYPE_SCROLL_SENSITIVE) and cannot be used to update the
     // database (i.e., CONCUR_READ_ONLY vs CONCUR_UPDATABLE).

            Statement stmt =
               conn.createStatement(
                    ResultSet.TYPE_SCROLL_INSENSITIVE,
                    ResultSet.CONCUR_READ_ONLY);

     // Execute SQL query to retrieve shallow information, such as
     // the account name, customer ID (i.e. LNK_CUSTOMER a foreign
     // key reference to the Customer primary ID key)

            ResultSet resultSet =
               stmt.executeQuery(
                   "SELECT NAME, LNK_CUSTOMER, ... FROM ACCOUNT");
```

Finally, after executing the JDBC query, each row of returned information is transformed into a CustomerAccountDTO instance. A collection of these instances must be created and returned to the client.

```
            while (resultSet.next())
            {
              String accountName = resultSet.getString("NAME");
              String customerID = resultSet.getString("LNK_CUSTOMER");
              ...
              CustomerAccountDTO aCustAcctDTO =
                    new CustomerAccountDTO();

           aCustAcctDTO.setCustomerFirstName(...);
           aCustAcctDTO.setCustomerMiddleName(...);
           aCustAcctDTO.addAccountID(...);
              ...
              // Set data on a custom DTO that contains the
              // information required by the presentation tier.
              ...
              returnedInformation.add(aCustAcctDTO);
            }
            ...
     }
...
```

Your last step is to compile and test all of these changes to make sure the information list screens still functions properly. You should notice dramatic performance improvements in the screens and reports that deal with large amounts of data.

This shallow query implementation is far more efficient than its deep query functional equivalent, originally presented in the Dredge AntiPattern. Additional intelligence could be added to shuttle pages of shallow information to the client upon request, instead of returning all of them at once as implemented above. A stateful Session Bean façade could cache the shallow information, so that a user could page forward and backward through the information on subsequent invocations.

Version

Your application must allow multiple users to update the same data, with think-time, but must prevent updates from being trampled by stale data.

Use version numbers in the data components, underlying database, and any DTOs used to convey related information. Check version numbers for staleness before allowing any update to proceed.

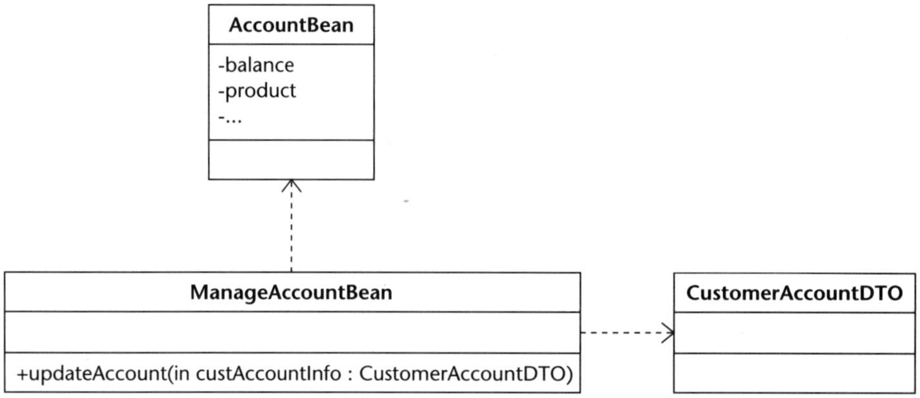

Figure 2.6 Before refactoring.

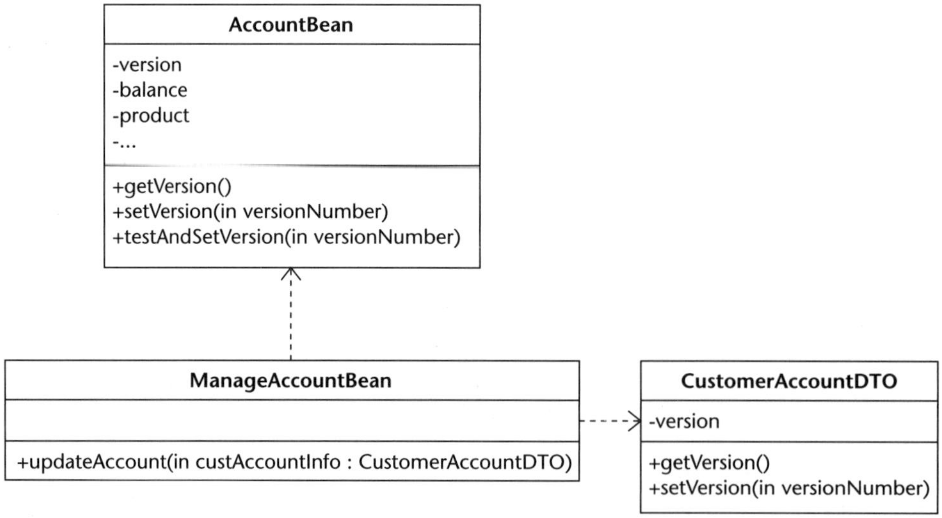

Figure 2.7 After refactoring.

Motivation

If logical business transactions involve user think-time, they cannot be wrapped within a single, ACID transaction. Instead, the logical transaction must be implemented in multiple ACID transaction segments, such as reading and subsequently updating the data. In this scenario, it is possible for different users to both read the same data. One user might take longer to modify the data and subsequently update the data in the database. The slowest user to update the information will overwrite the database with stale data. This severely compromises the integrity of the application, as it can no longer be trusted to present what is reality and preserve what has been modified.

Use version numbering to check for staleness before allowing an update to take place. This effectively implements an optimistic locking strategy within the application. It is acknowledged that the entire logical business transaction takes too long to isolate in its entirety. Therefore, an optimistic-locking approach at least guarantees that good data is not overwritten by bad data.

This refactoring is based on the Version Number persistence pattern described in Floyd Marinescu's *EJB Design Patterns: Advanced Patterns, Processes and Idioms* (Marinescu 2002).

Mechanics

The following is a list of steps, which must be followed in order to apply the Version refactoring. The first steps concentrate on locating instances of the Crush AntiPattern—portions of the application that use an optimistic locking strategy without the necessary versioning mechanisms in place. The next steps involve the introduction of versioning mechanisms and checks into the entity, DTO, and services layers.

1. *Determine the beans that must support an optimistic locking strategy within the application.* These beans must be enhanced to support the Version refactoring.

2. *Introduce versioning mechanisms into the entity layer.* Add a version number attribute to these Entity Beans, along with a version number column in their respective underlying tables. Implement a method in each optimistic Entity Bean that atomically checks version numbers and throws an exception if these numbers do not match.

3. *Introduce versioning mechanisms into the DTO layer.* Add a version number attribute to each DTO that conveys bean information, if applicable. Under EJB 2.x, this step is now largely irrelevant, because the need for domain DTOs has been eliminated by the efficiencies of local interfaces.

4. *Enforce version checking in the services layer.* Implement the procedure of invoking the version-checking method prior to updating an optimistically locked Entity Bean. This procedure should be coded in the Session Façade methods that perform the updates.

5. *Deploy and test.*

Example

Let us assume that we will use the AccountBean in Listing 2.7 as a basis for introducing a version-based, optimistic locking strategy in our financial services application. In this case, we must first introduce a version number attribute to the AccountBean and its underlying data, along with a new method for atomically testing the version number against a supplied value and either updating the version upon success or throwing a BadVersionNumberException instance upon a failed comparison.

```
public class AccountBean implements EntityBean
{
...
// Container-managed version number field

abstract public Long getVersion();
abstract public void setVersion(Version newVersion);
...

// New method to atomically test and update the version number
// if appropriate, otherwise throw an exception.

public void testAndSetVersion(Long inVersionNumber)
     throws BadVersionNumberException
{
     Long curVersion = getVersion();

     if (curVersion.equals(inVersionNumber))
{
     // Increment the version number.

     setVersion(inVersionNumber.longValue()+1);
}
else
{
     // Throw an exception, the version number
     // supplied is no longer valid (i.e., is stale).

          throw new BadVersionNumberException();
     }
}
...
}
```

Listing 2.7 AccountBean.java.

Next, although local interfaces deprecate the use of domain DTOs under 2.x, it is still entirely appropriate to use custom DTOs in order to convey information between the session and view-based application logic layers. Therefore, the custom DTO class must be modified to convey a version number, as shown in Listing 2.8.

```
public class CustomerAccountDTO
{
...
     private Long version;
     ...
     public Long getVersion() { return version; }
     public void setVersion(Long inVersion) { version = inVersion; }
     ...
}
```

Listing 2.8 CustomerAccountDTO.java.

Finally, we must enforce version checking in the services layer by adopting the policy of invoking the *testAndSetVersion(...)* method—shown in Listing 2.7—prior to updating the state of an AccountBean instance. If we perform this invocation within a transactional Session Façade method, then any update in progress will be rolled back if the version numbers fail to match. The following illustrates an introduction of this policy into the *updateAccount(CustomerAccountDTO)* method of the *ManageAccount* Session Façade Bean.

```
public void updateAccount(CustomerAccountDTO inAccountDTO)
{
...
Account anAccount;

try
{
     anAccount =
AccountHome.findByPrimaryKey(
     inAccountDTO.getAccountID());

     anAccount.testAndSetVersion(
     inAccountDTO.getVersion());

          // Update the account.

     anAccount.setBalance(inAccountDTO.getBalance());
          anAccount.setProduct(...);
          ...
}
     catch(Exception excp)
{
     // Ensure that the transaction is rolled back.

     context.SetRollbackOnly();
```

Listing 2.9 ManageAccountBean.java. *(continued)*

```
        throw new AccountProcessingException();
    }
    ...
}
```

Listing 2.9 *(continued)*

The *ManageAccount* Session façade's *updateAccount(CustomerAccountDTO)* method must successfully check the version number supplied in the DTO against the Entity Bean's version number before an update can proceed, as demonstrated in Listing 2.9.

Your last step is to compile and test all of these changes using simultaneous logical transactions involving user think-time. Now that this refactoring is in place, potential data corruptions and overwrites, caused by simultaneous access to shared data, will be flagged and avoided. If a user attempts to update data that has already been updated, he or she will receive a BadVersionNumberException. This is a clear indication that the user is attempting to update the shared data with a stale copy. The user can be directed to refetch a fresh version of the data record in order to start the updating process again.

Component View

Your application's component object model was designed from a relational database perspective. Hence, its objects are merely globs of data lacking crisp state, boundaries, and behavior.

Use solid object-oriented analysis and design principles to create an application object model. Let this model drive the design of the underlying database schema whenever possible. Tune the schema for performance, if necessary.

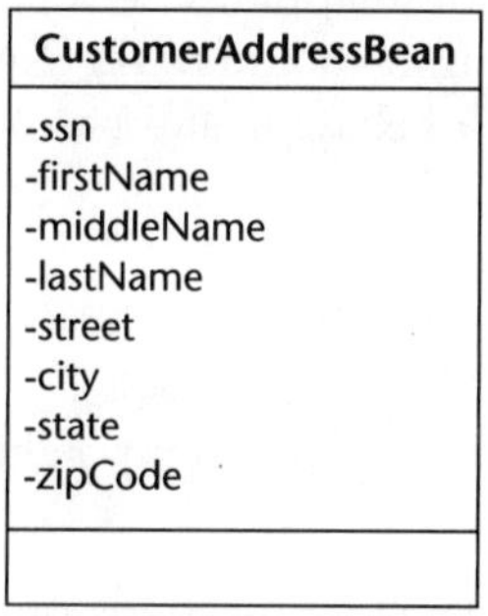

Figure 2.8 Before refactoring.

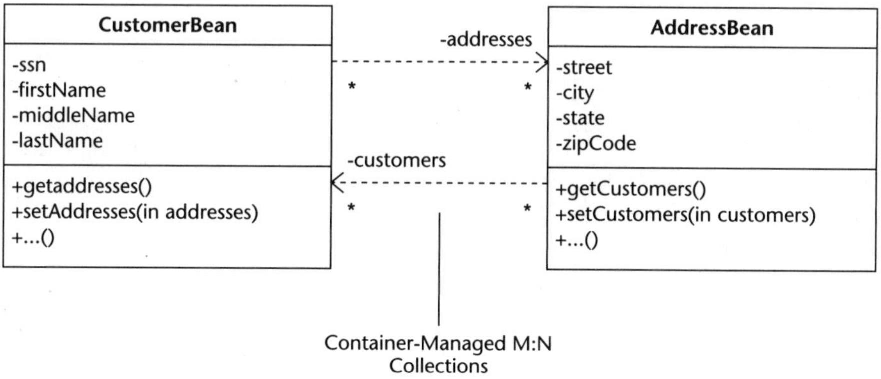

Figure 2.9 After refactoring.

Motivation

There is an ongoing battle between database architects and designers, and their object-oriented application architect and designer brethren. Some organizations feel one view should dominate them all. So it is not uncommon to see database organizations that are charged with the responsibility of designing the enterprise component model. This is a serious mistake. Such models often consider data without functionality—and that is only half of the component view of the world. Both aspects must be accommodated in any component model. In addition, a data-centric view often gives rise to components that are merely artifacts of relational database design.

For example, consider the *CustomerAddress* illustrated in Figure 2.5 of the *DataVision* AntiPattern. This component is really nothing of the sort. Rather, it is an artifact of the relational database model intended to codify the many-to-many mappings between customers and addresses. The table may certainly be needed, but it should never surface as a full-fledged component because it has no crisp state or behavior, and has no ties to the business domain.

Mechanics

The following is a list of steps that must be followed in order to apply the Component View refactoring.

1. *Identify pseudocomponents.* These globs of data have no crisp state, behavior, or ties to the business domain, and cannot be associated with any legitimate, object-oriented design construct.
2. *Think OO and components.* Use the collective power of objected-oriented analysis and design and J2EE component technology to eliminate pseudocomponents within the application component model.
3. *Deploy and test.*

Example

The first step of this refactoring is to identify pseudocomponents, which must be made more object-oriented. It is obvious that the CustomerAddress component is not a component but an artifact of a relational data-driven view of the world. EJB 2.x provides the tools necessary to drive this pseudocomponent out of the component object model and back into the database where it belongs.

The next step of this refactoring is to apply an object-oriented perspective in the redesign of the *CustomerAddress* pseudocomponent. This will yield a simpler model containing a direct many-to-many relationship between customers and addresses, as shown in Figure 2.10.

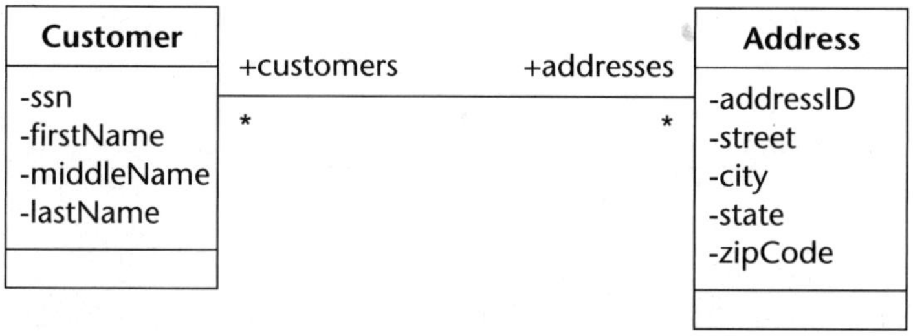

Figure 2.10 Component-oriented address-customer model.

However, there is no magic in this solution. The many-to-many mappings still need to be implemented, and an underlying junction table will still be needed in order to make these mappings durable. EJB 2.x and the collective powers of container-managed persistence (CMP) and container-managed relationships (CMR) enable us to specify these mappings transparently. The Customer and Address Beans will contain references to each other. However, the mechanics of the many-to-many mappings is swept out of the component object model and into the realm of deployment descriptors and database schemas. The first set of code is a snippet from Listing 2.9.

```
...
public class CustomerBean implements EntityBean
{
...
abstract public Set getAddresses();
abstract public void setAddresses(Set inAddresses);
...
}
```

This snippet, along with Listings 2.10 and 2.11, supports CMP many-to-many mappings between customers and addresses.

```
...
public class AddressBean implements EntityBean
{
...
abstract public Set getCustomers();
abstract public void setCustomers(Set inCustomers);
...
}
```

Listing 2.10 AddressBean.java.

```
...
<relationships>
<ejb-relation>
<ejb-relation-name>Customer-Address</ejb-relation-name>
<ejb-relationship-role>
<ejb-relationship-role-name>
Customers-Have-Addresses
</ejb-relationship-role-name>
<multiplicity>many</multiplicity>
<relationship-role-source>
<ejb-name>CustomerBean</ejb-name>
</relationship-role-source>
<cmr-field>
<cmr-field-name>addresses</cmr-field-name>
<cmr-field-type>java.util.Set</cmr-field-type>
</cmr-field>
</ejb-relationship-role>
<ejb-relationship-role>
<ejb-relationship-role-name>
Addresses-Have-Customers
</ejb-relationship-role-name>
<multiplicity>many</multiplicity>
<relationship-role-source>
<ejb-name>AddressBean</ejb-name>
</relationship-role-source>
<cmr-field>
<cmr-field-name>customers</cmr-field-name>
<cmr-field-type>java.util.Set</cmr-field-type>
</cmr-field>
</ejb-relationship-role>
</ejb-relation>
...
</ejb-jar>
```

Listing 2.11 Ejb-jar.xml deployment descriptor.

This solution allows the container to keep track of the mappings and ensure referential integrity without getting the application involved. This is a far cleaner approach than exposing such mechanical details in the component object model and application implementation code.

Pack

Your database-intensive Java applications suffer from poor performance, yet your database and network resources are largely idle.

Use data sources to encourage connection pooling and abstract driver details out of the application code. Use batched SQL instructions to take advantage of any network bandwidth available between the application and database servers.

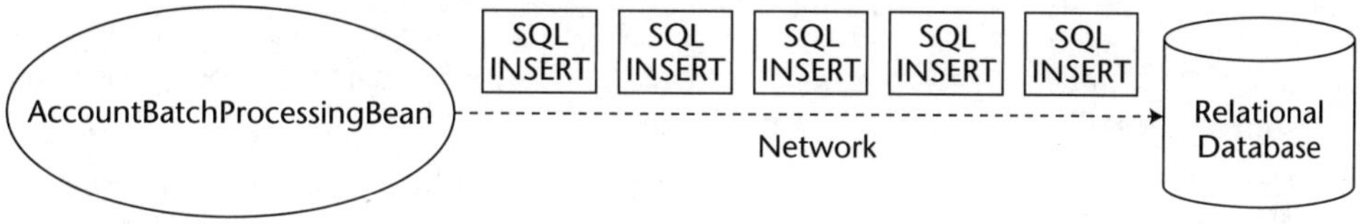

Figure 2.11 Before refactoring.

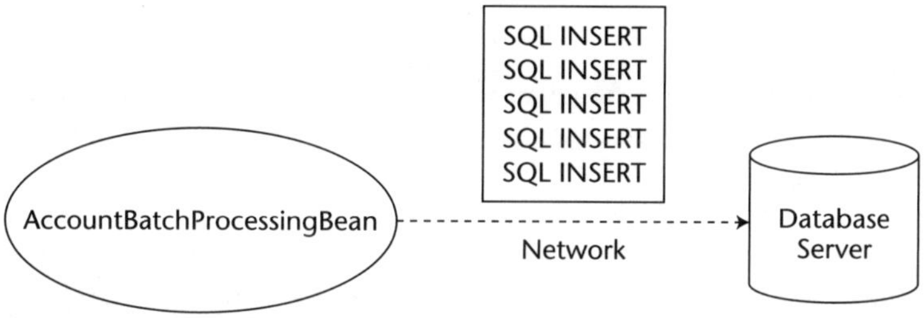

Figure 2.12 After refactoring.

Motivation

JDBC 2.x and 3.0 bring Java into the world of database-intensive computing. Many of the shortcomings of the earlier JDBC specifications have been rectified. Mechanisms are now available to make use of pooled database connections and take maximum advantage of available database and networking resources.

Mechanics

The following is a list of steps, which must be followed in order to apply the Pack refactoring.

1. *Switch to DataSources.* Replace DriverManager connection acquisition with data sources in order to encourage connection pooling and increased portability.
2. *Use batched SQL statements.* Instead of sending individual SQL statements over the network, use JDBC 2.x's batching capabilities to send multiple SQL instructions in one batch. This optimizes the network pipeline between the application and database servers, and improves database server utilization by reducing the amount of time the server sits idle while awaiting the next SQL instruction.
3. *Compile, deploy, and test.*

Example

Let us continue the example of the account batch-processing bean originally illustrated in Listing 2.4 of the *Stifle* AntiPattern. As discussed, this bean has performance problems and runs the risk of blowing its allowable batch window. The developer's gut reaction to this problem is to either move the entire process into the database as a stored procedure, or use a bulk-load facility instead of Java to update the table. There are times when performance requirements are so aggressive that such solutions represent the only reasonable courses of action. However, they should be avoided if possible.

Introducing stored procedures may boost performance, but their use severely hampers the portability of the application. Stored procedures also complicate application maintenance, because critical business logic is now implemented within the application and database servers. This means that typical application maintenance may require the efforts of both Java developers and DBAs, making maintenance complicated, expensive, and more difficult to plan. Using external bulk-data-loading utilities may be quick, but they are intrusive and can be difficult to synchronize with other aspects of the application. For example, the message-driven account batch-processing bean we have been studying might need to invoke some application-specific logic or process upon completion. Although this could conceivably be done with an external bulk data loader, it would be far more difficult and contrived, and would involve migrating some critical logic and controls out of the application and into the bulk-loader scripts. This approach actually compromises the encapsulation of the application, as critical steps that would have been performed internally are now migrated to an external agent. Unless the performance boost is necessary, this is a poor solution.

Very often, the real performance problem is either inside the database or between the application server and the database server. The first problem may be a database schema design or table segmentation and storage issue. A good DBA can tell if a database is thrashing because of a poor page allocation scheme. Such problems can be corrected, yielding substantial performance improvements without changing the application at all. The second problem can often be solved by simply batching the database update operations so that the network pipeline between the application and database servers is fully utilized. This step can improve performance by an order of magnitude, which is a considerable gain for such a modest change.

The code snippet below illustrates how simple it is to modify the batch-processing bean so that pooled connections and batched database commands are utilized. The first step in applying this refactoring is to establish a pooled database connection using a JDBC data source.

```
...
// Get the default JNDI Initial context.
Context context = new InitialContext();

// Establish a JDBC data source and connection.
DataSource ds = (DataSource)context.lookup("jdbc/FinancialDB");
Connection conn = ds.getConnection("user","password");
...
```

The next step is to introduce JDBC batch processing in order to optimize the network pipeline to the database server, as illustrated in Listing 2.12.

```
// Set autocommit off, so that the application is given a chance
// to handle any errors that occur during batch execution.
conn.setAutoCommit(false);

Statement statement = conn.createStatement();

// Build a batch of statements to be sent to the database
// in one shot.
...
for (int counter=1;counter<=BATCH_SIZE;counter++)
{
    ...
    statement.addBatch("UPDATE ACCOUNT SET ...");
    ...
}

int[] updateCounts = statement.executeBatch();
...
```

Listing 2.12 AccountBatchProcessingBean.java.

This refactoring can yield dramatic performance improvements without sacrificing the simplicity and portability of your application. This refactoring is an incremental improvement that is much simpler to implement and maintain, and is more portable than other possible solutions, such as using stored procedures or bulk data loaders.

CHAPTER

3

Service-Based Architecture

This chapter covers AntiPatterns associated with the implementation of a *service-based architecture* (SBA) within a multitier J2EE application. SBA is an architectural approach that centers on organizing the major business and technical system functions (that is, middle-tier functionality) into services—individual, self-contained process-oriented software components that are accessed exclusively through interfaces. Each service supports the processes (functions) related to a specific, coarse-grained business or technical abstraction or concern abstractions such as purchase order or application event. SBA advocates services that are generalized, enabling them to be used in multiple applications, supporting reuse of common, shared functionality. For instance, something like a product catalog service should be general enough to support an end-consumer shopping application *and* an internal inventory management application. Such a service supports the general processes associated with product catalogue information, and should be usable (and useful) in multiple contexts/applications that deal with product catalogue information. Thus, an SBA approach allows more rapid development by providing prebuilt, tested components that support the core underlying application business and technical logic. Application development is then reduced to using and coordinating the subset of services necessary for the application at hand, and implementing interfacing tiers (such as the user interface tier, integration tier, and more).

SBA is an architectural concept that is not specific to J2EE. SBA can and has been implemented with other platforms and technologies. CORBA is probably the most well-known and detailed definition of an SBA, defining a number of standard services that are important for distributed enterprise systems, including elements needed to support distributed access and interoperation by clients in a language and platform independent way. J2EE is fundamentally about supporting distributed enterprise systems, and a number of its core architectural aspects have been patterned after CORBA, such as JNDI, RMI, JRMP, EJB, and more. J2EE provides all of the necessary mechanisms to support the implementation of SBA.

The emergence of Web Services has also emphasized the general concepts of SBA. The term *service-oriented architecture* (SOA) has become prevalent in architectures that support Web Services, facilitating loosely coupled, distributed services that are vended as Web Service interfaces. Thus, service orientation within J2EE systems not only enhances reuse across related J2EE applications, but also facilitates the structure and principles needed to effectively vend business functionality as Web Services.

The J2EE specification defines a number of standard services that J2EE implementations must provide, including JTA, JNDI, and JMS. These serve as the base layer of technical capabilities that higher-level technical services and business services can be built on, to form a true SBA.

The following AntiPatterns can occur when developing service-based architecture:

Multiservice. A service that does too much, implementing multiple business or technical abstractions. This aggregates too much into a single service, reducing usability.

Tiny Service. A service that only implements part of an abstraction, with other sibling services implementing other processes within the abstraction. This requires several, coupled services to be used together, resulting in more development complexity and reduced usability.

Stovepipe Service. A service that is completely standalone, redundantly implementing common business or technical functionality required and implemented by other services, APIs, and more. This results in replicated and inconsistent functionality, increasing development effort and adversely affecting reliability and application correctness.

Client Completes Service. Business or technical logic that should be implemented within a service (such as validation of data, data access authorization checking, business rules, and more) is implemented in client components, and left out of the service. This results in incomplete/incorrect service functioning when the service is used by other clients.

Multiservice

Also Known As: The God Object, Big Ball of Mud

Most Frequent Scale: System

Refactorings: Interface Partitioning

Refactored Solution Type: Software

Root Causes: Ignorance, haste

Unbalanced Forces: Complexity and resources

Anecdotal Evidence: "Ouch! Some other developer just overwrote all my changes to the service!"

Background

The identification of business services is typically accomplished by analyzing requirements to identify core business entities and the key processes that operate on them. If use cases or user stories are used to capture requirements, these artifacts are oriented toward describing the distinct goals of the system, and serve to assist in this process. In a typical business system, there are usually a few core entities or documents (for example, orders, invoices, shipments, and so on), and a number of activities, processes, or workflows associated with them that the system is intended to support.

A common service AntiPattern is to map a broad set of processes and functions associated with several different entities or abstractions into a single service, resulting in a service which implements multiple abstractions, with poor cohesion between the set of methods.

General Form

Multiservice has a large number of public interface methods that cover a lot of different abstractions and processes. Essentially, multiple abstractions are being supported through a single service. For example, methods like createOrder, checkInventory, and makePayment in the same service support the distinct abstractions Order, Payment, and Inventory.

The following UML diagram (see Figure 3.1) depicts an example of this AntiPattern, in the form of a service interface. The important aspect that indicates the AntiPattern is that the different methods are operating on different core abstractions (order, payment, and inventory). Please note that this is a small, artificial example meant to illustrate and highlight the multiabstraction nature that characterizes a Multiservice, and a real Multiservice will typically have many methods associated with each of the different abstractions.

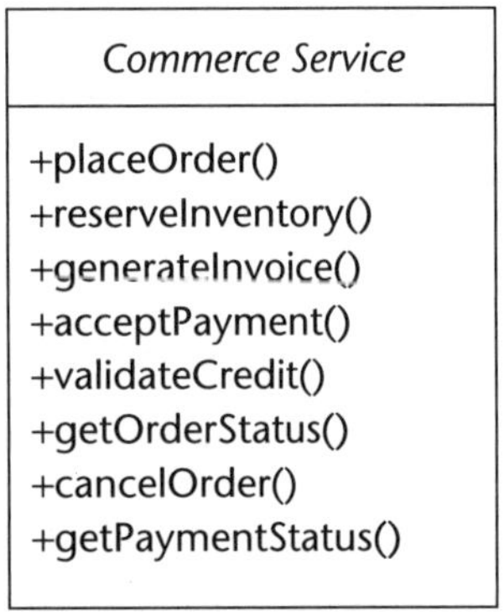

Figure 3.1 Multiservice.

Symptoms and Consequences

A Multiservice AntiPattern implements a number of abstractions and associated methods, which means that the service will be used in the implementation of many different applications. The result of this is greater coupling to a larger number of client implementation artifacts, and potentially multiple developers attempting concurrent development. A number of specific symptoms and consequences include:

- **A service has a large number of methods.** A service interface that defines a large number of methods (20–30) is likely covering too much ground, and implementing multiple abstractions.
- **Multiple core abstractions or data types are exchanged in a single service.** When there are methods within the same service that operate against different business or technical abstractions, like approve*Order*, track*Shipment*, and pay*Invoice*. This usually indicates that the service is not specifically handling one abstraction.
- **There are few (or possibly one) services within the system.** If services are handling too much, then naturally the individual services will be larger and there will only be a few, large services. The pathological case of this is having only one, God Object service that implements every core process.
- **The service implementation artifacts are being modified concurrently by multiple developers.** When a service implements a number of abstractions and associated methods, it effectively is implementing a broad range of system functionality and business processes. Typically, different developers implement different aspects and business processes within the system, but they will all need to be updating, implementing, and testing parts of the same service, and this will lead to contention and blocking across the development team.
- **Many client artifacts need to be rebuilt/redeployed when the service changes.** A Multiservice will support widely varying requirements in the system, and there will be many interface tier artifacts (such as servlets/JSPs or integration tier classes) that utilize the service, and are type-wise coupled to the service interface. Any changes to the service interface will require at least recompilation of coupled client code. In sizeable systems, this may also mean rebuilding of jar, war, or ear files, along with redeployment.
- **Unit testing of the service is time-consuming.** Unit testing of the Multiservice is problematic because the large number of methods and dependent entities and data types results in a very large number of tests. In order to pass the service, all tests must be completed, and there is a lower likelihood of this occurring when there are so many methods and tests to run. This results in greater, more complicated test development and execution time, and a higher percentage of time that the service fails to pass tests, holding up the release of the service for use by developers.
- **Deployment of the Multiservice may require special configuration, to support appropriate performance, pooling, and so on**. For services that are implemented using Session Beans, having one service that is used by many different

client components means that there will need to be many concurrent instances of the Session to support the clients. Typical session pool values may not be sufficient, requiring special setup, and tuning.

Typical Causes

The development of multiservices is typically related to insufficient requirements information, and/or inexperience in performing OO analysis, applying core OO principles, and so on. Some of the specific details include:

- **Nonexistent, thin, or poorly structured requirements**. The identification of distinct abstractions and processes is very dependent on the set of requirements that serve as the starting point. Requirements that are thin, muddy, or poorly structured make it difficult to recognize abstractions and processes.
- **Incorrect application of the Session Façade pattern.** The Session Façade pattern has been used in many EJB implementations to reduce the number of remote interactions between client and server, and to organize middle-tier behavior into layers of coarse-grained subsystems over finer-grained processes. This pattern has become so common that its use is often considered to be a given. However, inexperience or misunderstanding of the pattern can lead to creating a façade that is simply a mechanical aggregation of methods into a larger interface, without creating effective subsystem layers, and so on. The result can be a Session façade that is just a hodgepodge of methods, all assembled together, resulting in a large, muddy service.
- **Principles of high cohesion and low coupling not understood or applied adequately.** A good service abstraction will exhibit *low* coupling and *high* cohesion. Low coupling means that the service is type-wise coupled to a low number of other types, and interfaces. This indicates that the service is not trying to do too much, and allows the service to be reused more effectively. Cohesion refers to how related the methods themselves are. High cohesion means that the service methods are related because they operate against the same, underlying core abstraction. A Multiservice AntiPattern may result when these principles are not understood or applied.
- **Purely mechanical creation of service(s) to support the Web Services interface.** In some cases, the guiding principle behind the service delineation may in fact be the need to develop one or more Web Services, to vend new or existing functionality. A purely mechanical approach to defining the Web Service interface (and the interface of an underlying middle-tier service) may lump together all sorts of methods, without regard for any sort of business-related organization. For instance, there may be a number of distinct sessions that support different business abstractions such as OrderService or ShipmentService. But when it comes time to create a session to act as implementation for a Web Service, a Session façade is defined over all of these lower-level sessions, creating one, large, multiabstraction session or service.

Known Exceptions

The integration and usage of an external legacy system within a J2EE application (for example, using JCA connector) may be architected such that it is exposed as a service to the rest of the system, encapsulating any specifics about legacy integration, and enabling it to be used in a consistent manner. However, this may also lead to a service that presents the various processes and abstractions of the legacy system, resulting in something that looks like a Multiservice AntiPattern. These cases are somewhat of an exception, because the service interface is dependent on the unchangeable legacy system interface, and often there is a desire to isolate the legacy system functionality behind a single encapsulated component.

Refactorings

Refactoring of a Multiservice AntiPattern amounts to repartitioning the service's inappropriate interface methods to other services, to result in a single, well-defined abstraction. The Interface Partitioning refactoring found later in this chapter focuses on deciding what the core abstraction of the service should be, and moving the methods that don't fit that abstraction to some other service(s).

In many cases, there will be multiple existing services, so the target service may already exist. Conversely, a new service may need to be created, to support the abstraction and moved method(s). Deciding what methods should stay, which ones should be moved, and where they should be moved to focuses on identifying and deciding appropriate abstractions across the business and technical requirements. Thus, as multiple services are reexamined and modified through this process, the requirements may need to be reexamined, refined, and scrutinized to more clearly identify the core business and technical abstractions that should be supported through services.

Variations

In some cases, a service may implement a fat method that actually implements multiple processes against multiple abstractions. For instance, a service method that creates an order, creates an associated line item, and reserves inventory. In this case, the method itself must be repartitioned into separate methods, which then may need to be reassigned to appropriate services, such as Order Service or Inventory Service.

Many variations on the same basic method result in a lot of very similar looking methods, sometimes referred to as the *Swiss Army Knife* approach. When this is repeated for all the processes that the service supports, there could be many service interface methods to support just a few basic processes. Having all these variations can be confusing and prone to incorrect use. It is better to compact these into just a few, clear methods.

If someone is unsure about the requirements to be implemented, they may throw a lot of extra functionality, methods, and variations, just to cover themselves. This is defensive programming and will result in services that do a lot more than they need to, relative to the actual requirements. The real solution is to get more detailed requirements, validation from users, and business-level prioritization from stakeholders.

Example

Listing 3.1 illustrates the salient aspects of a Multiservice AntiPattern, in the form of a Java service interface. The core identifying aspect of a Multiservice AntiPattern is that it implements multiple core business and/or technical abstractions. This is manifested at the service interface as different public methods that involve different entities or abstractions. In this example, it can be seen that there are methods that operate on or involve different core business entities. For instance, the placeOrder() method creates a new instance of Order entity, while the reserveInventory() method attempts to reserve the specified quantity of Product entity. Overall, this Multiservice supports the entities Order, Product, Invoice, and Account. Note that each of these is a significant, core business abstraction, and typically will have many associated methods. So, while this example shows one method operating against each core entity, it is merely illustrative, and in reality, a typical multiservice will include many methods related to each entity, resulting in a service with many methods.

```
public interface MyService {

boolean placeOrder(HashMap orderData);

int reserveInventory(int productId, int quantity);

void generateInvoice(int orderId);

boolean acceptPayment(int invoiceId, float amount);

boolean validateCredit(int accountId, float amount);
}
```

Listing 3.1 Multiservice interface.

Related Solutions

When a fat method exists, you can refactor the multiple processes and/or scenarios that are supported by the method into distinct methods.

Tiny Service

Also Known As: Refactor Mercilessly

Most Frequent Scale: System

Refactorings: Interface Consolidation

Refactored Solution Type: Software

Root Causes: Ignorance

Unbalanced Forces: Complexity and resources

Anecdotal Evidence: "I read somewhere that each use case should map to a separate service."

Background

When a developer jumps on the idea of services, the process of mapping requirements to services may be done to excess, and principles of abstraction and cohesion not followed correctly. The process may be taken to extremes, where every individual responsibility and sequence of process is mapped into a separate service. The application of the Command pattern may also contribute to this, when developers decide that they should have individual components or services, each of which implements a command.

General Form

A tiny service is one that incompletely represents an abstraction, only implementing a subset of the necessary methods. The flipside of this is that there are usually multiple services that, taken together, completely implement the abstraction. Therefore, developers have to utilize multiple services to implement the complete set of requirements for the abstraction. In the extreme case, a tiny service will be limited to one method, resulting in many services that implement an overall set of requirements.

This AntiPattern is manifested as many small, specific services, with just a few methods, that implement just a subset of the overall processes for an abstraction or entity. This means that several services will implement processes against that one abstraction, meaning there will be several services that perform methods associated with Order, for example, and to effectively reuse that whole abstraction, all of those services must be used.

The following UML class diagram (see Figure 3.2) depicts this situation. Note that the different services are all related to the Order entity, and each implements just one, specific process for it. Note also that the names of the services themselves are specific to a process (such as Update or Approve) instead of being specific only to an abstraction. This suggests that the service is not supporting an abstraction per se, but just a specific process for that abstraction, and it is too fine-grained.

Symptoms and Consequences

The most significant issue with the Tiny Service AntiPattern is that multiple services are required to support one, core business abstraction, and without tying all the processes together into one service, developers need to know all the different services to use, and how they should be coordinated and sequenced to support one overall business process workflow. There are a number of specific symptoms and consequences as follows:

- **A service interface has few methods (possibly only one)**. When a service implements a small number of methods, this may indicate an incomplete service.
- **Multiple services support methods against the same core abstraction.** If there are methods in different services that perform different functions on the same abstraction (such as createOrder in one service and approveOrder in another), then this is a strong indicator that those services are incomplete and should be combined.

- **Implementation and maintenance of a particular area of application requirements requires changes to multiple services.** The implementation of business logic for a core business abstraction should be encapsulated within a single service.
- **Developers must know what multiple services are used for a specific business or technical area, and they must know how they operate together.** When process areas are spread across services, it is up to the client artifacts (and the developers creating those) to know which different services should be used together and how. This sort of knowledge is better encapsulated into coarse-grained methods within a single service.
- **Testing and validating a business abstraction requires testing of multiple services.** Ideally, a specific business process abstraction such as Order should have all of its processes implemented and contained within a specific service, such as an OrderManagement service. However, when those methods are spread around to multiple services, each of those must be tested and validated to validate that the overall business process area is complete and correct.
- **Performance may suffer with a large number of services.** If business processes require the use of multiple services to execute and complete, the overhead associated with locating and invoking many services can lead to degradation of performance, especially if the services utilize transactions and other container resources.

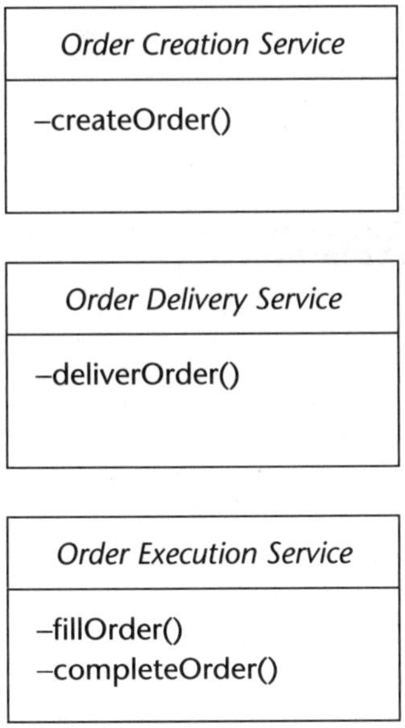

Figure 3.2: Tiny services.

Typical Causes

As in the case of the Multiservice AntiPattern, the most typical cause of tiny services is insufficient requirements and/or inexperience in the understanding and application of core OO principles such as abstraction, coupling, and cohesion. The following lists some specific causes:

- **Mapping of individual use cases into separate services.** Use cases are a common approach to documenting requirements, because they describe the business and technical processes in terms of goals and subgoals. These provide an appropriate basis for identifying services and methods. However, sometimes the mapping isn't done quite right, and each use case is mapped to a separate service. The correct approach is to map each use case to a public method, and combine all the associated use cases or methods that deal with one abstraction into the same service.
- **Use of the EJB Command pattern to define services.** The EJB Command pattern is typically applied in situations where verb-type components are desired within an architecture or design to support pluggable/interchangeable behaviors. Since a service could be thought of as a verb-type, large-grained, pluggable component, it may be tempting to apply the EJB Command pattern. However, this results in services that support one public operation, resulting in many related services to cover a single abstraction.

Known Exceptions

If a service is defined for the purpose of encapsulating access to a legacy system, ERP, or even an external Web Service, that access may be thin, meaning that only one or two key functions of those systems are accessed. This may lead to the service exhibiting a thin, seemingly incomplete interface. If the functionality accessed fits within a larger set of capabilities within the application, then there should be a more complete service, with the implementation accessing those external systems where applicable.

Refactorings

The significant issue with this AntiPattern is that related methods for a specific purpose or abstraction are scattered across separate services, making it difficult for developers to locate, understand, and use. The Interface Consolidation refactoring found later in this chapter is used to rectify this, by focusing on consolidating the separate but related services into single, more cohesive services. The basic approach involves examining the methods across a number of services, to determine what abstraction they are, in fact, operating against, and collecting these together into a single service. Often, the Tiny Service AntiPattern will manifest a number of services that have verb-like names such as OrderApprovalService, and the like. In these cases, the actual names of the services themselves will indicate what abstraction and what behavior is being implemented. In these situations, consolidation may be as easy as just gathering together all those very apparently related services into a single service.

Variations

One of the variations of this AntiPattern is the inappropriate application of the Command pattern to define services. The Command pattern is used to define single-method command-type objects that can be used interchangeably within an execution framework. Services, however, are intended to support a particular abstraction, so command-oriented services are really not appropriate. Command-type services can be consolidated into a single method on a service, with the different command implementations delegated to simple Java classes used by the service. The execution of the commands should be encapsulated within a service.

Example

Listing 3.2 depicts the interfaces of a number of tiny services. Each of these services supports a specific process related to the Order entity, and, taken together, support the processing for one abstraction—in this case, the Order entity. The OrderCreationService supports the specific process of creating Order instances (and providing Order Data Transfer Object instances) through its methods. The OrderUpdateService provides a method to update an existing instance of Order, and the OrderApprovalService provides one method to support approval process for Orders. Application client components that support Order processing must utilize each of these different services at different points within the client code, depending on whether an Order is being created or updated, and what state the object is in.

```
public interface OrderCreationService {
     OrderDTO createOrder(HashMap data);
     OrderDTO duplicateOrder(int orderId);
     OrderDTO duplicateOrder(OrderDTO order);
}

public interface OrderUpdateService {
     void updateOrder(OrderDTO orderData, int orderId);
}

public interface OrderApprovalService {
     boolean approveOrder(int orderId);
}
```

Listing 3.2 Tiny service interfaces.

Related Solutions

There are no significant related solutions for this AntiPattern.

AntiPattern

Stovepipe Service

Also Known As: Multilayer Service

Most Frequent Scale: System

Refactorings: Technical Services Layer

Refactored Solutions Type: Software

Root Causes: Avarice, ignorance, and haste

Unbalanced Forces: Complexity and resources

Anecdotal Evidence: "Hey, my service is completely self-contained."

Background

In addition to the core business process logic, business services within an SBA usually need to support a number of nonfunctional requirements such as persistence, security, workflow, auditing, and logging. Within a J2EE system, core technical requirements, such as persistence, are provided by the J2EE application server containers. However, other technical requirements, such as workflow execution, auditing, email notification, and so on, must be implemented on top of J2EE. In an SBA, the most natural approach is to create one or more technical services or components that implement these requirements, and develop a multilayered SBA, in which a layer of business services overlies and uses the set of shared technical services/components.

An AntiPattern that can crop up in these situations occurs when this separation of business and technical concerns is not done, and business services end up implementing a lot of nonfunctional, technical requirements. Because many of these requirements apply to many (or all) of the business services, the Stovepipe Service AntiPattern can arise, whereby different developers implement many of these deep services in parallel. Thus, each service ends up containing duplicated functionality, implemented in different ways by different developers. Although these services effectively support their public interfaces, the nonfunctional requirements operate inconsistently, and maintenance and evolution is a nightmare.

The diagram in Figure 3.3 depicts a couple of business services that contain some duplicated private methods (shown in bold). Notice that the duplicated methods are not really related to the service abstraction per se, but are implementing some fundamental infrastructure functions:

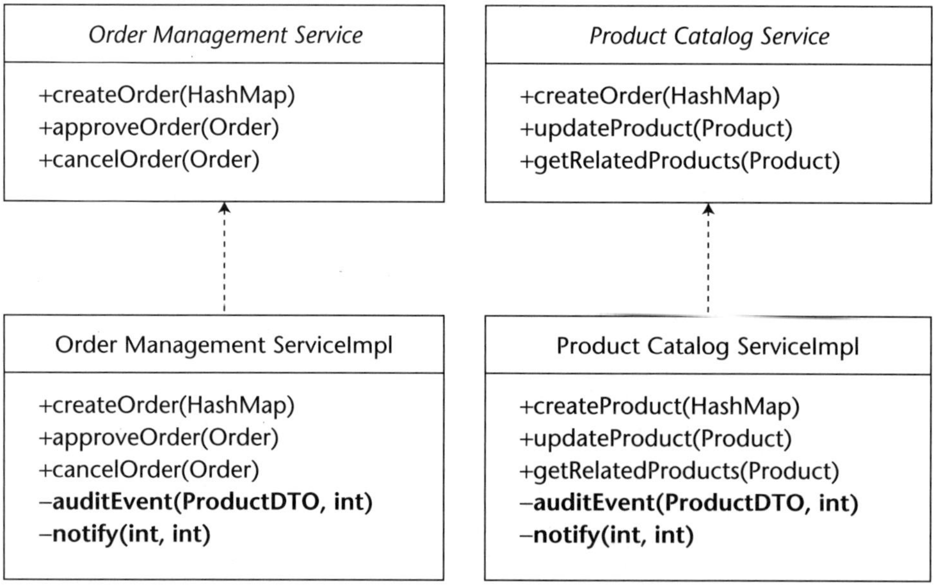

Figure 3.3 Stovepipe services.

General Form

A stovepipe service has a large number of private implementation methods that support common infrastructure functions. This internal implementation typically supports technical processes (such as logging, data validation, workflow, and notifications), but can also include common business processes such as data type conversion (currency conversion, for example). In most cases, the stovepipe service issue will occur across a number of services in an SBA, due to the overall development approach being taken or the degree and type of communication occurring (or not). The result leads to a number of stovepipe services that implement a lot of duplicated code, and inconsistent functionality.

The form that this takes will be a service that, from the interface, looks fine and appropriately represents the abstraction or concern it is intended for. However, the implementation classes and components behind the interface will contain a number of protected or private methods that do not seem to implement functionality for the abstraction, but instead perform infrastructure and utility functions such as application logging, auditing, and security checking. All of these kinds of functions are likely to be used across several services, but the stovepipe service will implement them internally.

Symptoms and Consequences

Services are intended to be the basis of encapsulated, shared implementation of core (middle-tier) requirements within a system. When services are implemented in a stovepipe fashion, the result will be considerably greater development time, inconsistent functioning, and poor extensibility. There are a number of systems and consequences that arise:

- **Service implementation is large, for example, with a lot of private methods.** When the private methods of a service implementation are numerous, this may be an indicator that it is covering too much ground and is a candidate for refactoring.
- **Infrastructure and utility functions are implemented inconsistently.** When underlying functionality is redundantly implemented, the implementation will likely vary, sometimes subtly, and this usually leads to differences in the operation between one service and another. For instance, logging may occur at different frequencies and dump the entries to different files.
- **Development time is considerably greater for stovepipe services.** When there are significant infrastructure requirements that are being implemented on top of the business functions, this will result in much greater development time.

Typical Causes

The most obvious reason for the occurrence of the Stovepipe Service AntiPattern is lack of communication and collaborative review during concurrent implementation of services. Also, if there is not specific effort or time taken to review and refactor the architecture and designs at key points in a project life cycle, then there will not be the process or mechanisms to recognize commonalities and factor them out. Specific details of these causes are provided below:

- **Inexperience in developing multilayered architectures.** In many cases, this AntiPattern is caused simply by inexperience in architecting multitier architecture. In two-tier architectures, the core business logic is tied into the presentation tier, or database tier, or some combination thereof. The conceptual move to a middle tier that only encapsulates the business and infrastructure logic (and is not specifically tier to presentation or DB) is itself a significant leap. Introducing multiple layers within the middle tier is something that requires experience in architecting *n*-tier systems, and practice separating process logic from client-tier implementation.
- **Insufficient communication, design/code reviews during service implementation.** If there is little communication and synchronization happening across developers and service development, then there will be little opportunity to recognize common implementation requirements and refactor them into other services. It is important to perform group design and code reviews during service implementation (not after, when everything is done). In other words, the development process should intrinsically include communication and sync-up between development team members throughout the course of development. Additionally, an iterative code/test/integrate approach, with short-term iterations, is useful and important to build in specific, frequent synchronization and validation milestones.
- **No after-the-fact implementation refactoring.** Even in cases where there are decent design practices, implementation of a service will inevitably realize additional requirements. This is especially true for technical requirements, that don't directly appear in requirements documents, but are nonetheless implicitly there, and are recognized and implemented during coding. These usually include requirements such as authorization, checking of operations or data (such as which roles can execute a particular interface method, and what properties of an entity can they see and modify), data validation (such as what the allowable ranges for values that the service can accommodate are), and logging (every time anyone touches or changes an entity, or executes a service method, a detailed log entry should be created). During requirement analysis, some of these very detailed issues may not be discussed (or there may be some general blanket statements for the whole system mentioning security, logging, and others). It is only when the actual implementation and testing occur that they are recognized, discussed, and implemented. Agile programming techniques and Extreme Programming advocate doing the simplest thing needed, but then there is still the need to do after-the-fact, incremental refactoring when these new requirements issues are introduced.

Known Exceptions

An acceptable exception to this AntiPattern is when an existing chunk of functionality already exists, and it is being wrapped in a service so that it can be integrated into an SBA to be used consistently and transparently as one of the services. The service implementation in this case may incorporate all sorts of its own functionality for common infrastructure requirements, such as logging, email notification, auditing, and security checking.

Another acceptable exception is the integration of third-party components as the implementation of a service. In this case, the imported implementation may carry along with it additional functionality that is coupled to its own security authentication store and mechanism, or a persistence layer, or the usage of XML for property data.

Refactorings

The basic refactoring of one or more stovepipe services is to factor out the similar common private methods into lower-layer technical services or utility classes. This Technical Services Layer approach (found later in this chapter) consists of conducting code reviews of the various service implementation artifacts, to identify private or protected methods that duplicate functionality across multiple services. Typically, infrastructure/technical requirements are the most likely to be refactorable, since they are typically shared by multiple business services. The result is a new set of underlying technical services that are shared by the business services. This also allows client components to directly use those technical functions when appropriate.

Variations

There are no significant variations to this AntiPattern.

Example

Listing 3.3 shows the implementation of a stovepipe service. The latter part of the class contains a number of private methods that implement generic technical requirements that are necessary for the complete and correct implementation of the public business methods. Since auditing and notification are likely common requirements across business services, this implies that there are other, duplicated implementations being used by the other services. The other services may also have internal implementations, exhibiting characteristics of a stovepipe service, or there may actually be Audit and Notification services that this service developer neglected to use.

```
public class ProductCatalogServiceImpl {

     public boolean updateProduct(ProductDTO product, int productId) {

          // Do product update stuff (left out for brevity)...

          // ** Perform the additional nonfunctional requirements:

          // Notify interested parties of product updates:
            notify(UPDATE, getLoggedInUser());

            // Audit the change, and who did it:
            auditEvent(product, getLoggedInUser());

            }

     // Other Product-related, public methods:
     public boolean createProduct(HashMap productData) { ... }


     // Here are the technical (nonproduct) private methods:
     private boolean auditEvent(ProductDTO product, int userId) {
            // Audit user actions
     }

     private void notify(int eventType, int userId) {
            // Email notification
     }
}
```

Listing 3.3 Stovepipe service.

Related Solutions

An alternate solution is to refactor the common technical functions into a generic abstract superclass that all services are derived from. This is a somewhat less desirable approach than creating layered technical services or classes, because it limits the use of the functionality to services only (whereas the main solution discussed above also allows other clients, the Web tier, and so on to directly use those services as well).

Client Completes Service

Also Known As: Incomplete Service

Most Frequent Scale: Architecture

Refactorings: Cross-Tier Refactoring

Refactored Solution Type: Software

Root Causes: Haste, apathy, and ignorance

Unbalanced Forces: Complexity and resources

Anecdotal Evidence: "Since our application is only going to be Web-based, all our input data validation is in Javascript."

Background

Services in general should be self-contained, encapsulated units of functionality that can stand on their own, and be usable by a variety of client types and application contexts. Occasionally, however, only the core business process workflow/sequencing is implemented within the service, and important supporting requirements are left to be implemented by clients, such as data validation, business rules, business event auditing, and so on. In order to complete the implementation of the business process, client artifacts that use the service must then implement these additional elements. This becomes problematic when multiple client components use the service, because each of them has to repeatedly implement the missing implementation that should reside within the service. This is particularly common in Web-based applications, where client-side data validation is done in Javascript to improve performance by reducing client/server interactions. While this may be an effective way to improve performance, if the validation is not also done in the service, then other clients of the service will be able to pass bad data or have to replicate data validation code.

In general, services need to implement all aspects of the processes they implement to ensure correct functioning when used by any kind of client. This may mean replicating some logic in clients (as in the Javascript/Web client case) and service implementations, but a service should always be complete and self-contained at any rate.

General Form

In this AntiPattern, the interface of the service represents a well defined abstraction, so from the external view, this appears to be a well-defined service. However, when the service is used, additional implementation is required by the client to use it properly. Nonfunctional requirements, such as data validation, security checking, event auditing, and so on, need to be implemented by the client using the service. In Web-based applications, this code usually shows up in JSP scriplet or custom tags, servlets, or business delegates (that wrap the usage of a service). Often, this code is added when the clients are being implemented and tested, as these important omissions are noted. If it is not recognized that these functions should be a fundamental aspect of the service itself, then it is too easy to think that it should be handled by client context and implemented there.

Symptoms and Consequences

The most significant symptom of this is the replication of similar, nonfunctional code in different client components and contexts. This will inevitably have an impact on system development time and correctness/completeness, because duplicated implementations are often not exactly the same, and there may be some client components that do not implement the needed functions. The specifics of the symptoms and consequences are as follows:

- **Client artifacts (JSPs, servlets, front controller, and so on) contain code to perform nonclient, server-side functions.** If nonfunctional requirement code begins to creep into client artifacts, this may be an indication that the service is not doing all that it should (it may also indicate that client developers don't know what the service actually does and are unnecessarily replicating code).
- **Some client interfaces (such as Business-to-Business (B2B)) may be able to pass bad data and perform unauthorized data access and manipulation.** In many cases today, the assumption with J2EE applications is that they will be accessed only through Web-based clients, and so it is okay to include client-side code to perform data validation and security checking. However, B2B integration often is included or added, essentially being another, different client. Without the appropriate implementation in the service itself, these clients can perform erroneous or unauthorized interactions.
- **In some cases, data validation and so on, functionality is implemented in multiple client components.** If multiple client components are utilizing the same process (for example, a Web page and integration component both support creating orders), then there may be duplicated implementations within each of these clients to cover the data validation and security checking.
- **Potentially different application behaviors when performing a function interactively vs. through a B2B component.** When duplicated implementations occur, they will not be coded in exactly the same way, and there may be differences in their actual effects. Testing different client accesses, using exactly the same input business data, may reveal these differences.
- **Unit tests for out-of-bounds conditions regarding data ranges and authorizations fail.** Due to differences in client implementations (or lack thereof), tests reveal that data is not being properly validated and rejected when it is out of bounds.
- **Unit test components need to implement a lot of code to properly test a service.** If some functional aspects of a service are left out (and implemented in Web clients), then other clients such as unit test components will also need to provide this implementation. In general, unit test clients should only need to do a minimum of setup and then invoke the service method, and all the actual functionality should be provided by the service itself.

Typical Causes

This AntiPattern is mainly the result of an insufficient understanding of the idea that services really need to be self-contained, standalone functional components. Shortcuts or alternate approaches are taken to improve performance, or reduce the amount of development time to create the services, but in the long run, this means that the service is really incomplete. The following defines some specific causes.

- **Web-centric approach to development.** In Web applications, there is often the thought that the Web client artifacts will be the only artifacts, and thus, it is not as critical to ensure that services themselves are standalone. However, later, other clients use the service too.
- **Poor communications between team members during development.** During development, developers working on presentation- or client-tier functionality introduce implementation to support requirements such as data validation, but this is not refactored into an underlying service because of poor communication. This may be due to team dynamics or the physical distribution of team members.
- **Schedule pressures don't allow major refactoring.** Projects are always under time pressure, but if there is no opportunity during development or after incremental releases to do reviews and refactoring, then the refactoring of common, underlying functionality may be identified but there may be no time to actually do it.

Known Exceptions

One exception to this AntiPattern is when it is clear from the outset that the system to be developed will only have one type of client interface (such as a Web interface), and its lifetime will be relatively short. However, this determination is tricky, because there have been many systems that were planned to be Web-only and short-term that have grown to be much more. Thus, unless these conditions are very well agreed upon, it is much better to assume the opposite and develop appropriate, self-contained services.

Refactorings

The chief refactoring required here is to move the infrastructure-related functionality from client into service. So, in Cross-Tier Refactoring, found later in this chapter, the client code that performs data validation, security checking, and so on is moved to or replicated in some form down to the service implementation. Note that it may be still acceptable to leave implementation in the client as well to support better performance, but the underlying services should be able to be used in a standalone way.

For example, if data validation is being performed in Javascript (or in JSP scriptlet, custom tags, or servlets), then some similar implementation needs to be part of the service implementation. As discussed in the Stovepipe Service AntiPattern, the ideal approach is to define another service that generically performs these actions for multiple services. For instance, if one of the processes is to validate that entity-based data elements are present and in the correct format, then metadata descriptions and rules about the entities can be used in conjunction with an Entity Validation service, so that any service that receives entity instance data can utilize that service to validate before moving on. Likewise, fine-grained security checking (that needs to ensure that a user/role can access, read, or edit some entity property) can be facilitated by a generic security service that utilizes security metadata about entities to perform its checking.

This allows any service, which is attempting to access or modify entity data, to utilize another service to provide authorization or deny it.

Variations

There are no significant variations of this AntiPattern.

Example

The diagram in Figure 3.4 depicts an example of this AntiPattern. This example shows a vertical slice through a typical multitier J2EE application that implements some functionality around Order creation and workflow. This slice includes a servlet Web-tier component that handles user interactions and responses, and interacts with an underlying business service that implements the actual order-related business logic. The servlet implements the typical methods to handle UI interactions (service, doGet, doPost). But there are also a couple of methods that implement non-UI functions more specifically related to the underlying service. The method validateOrderData() validates data values before passing them to the createOrder() service method, and the canApprove() method determines if the currently authenticated user is authorized to approve an order before invoking the approveOrder() service method. In both cases, these servlet methods are performing actions necessary to use an underlying service method.

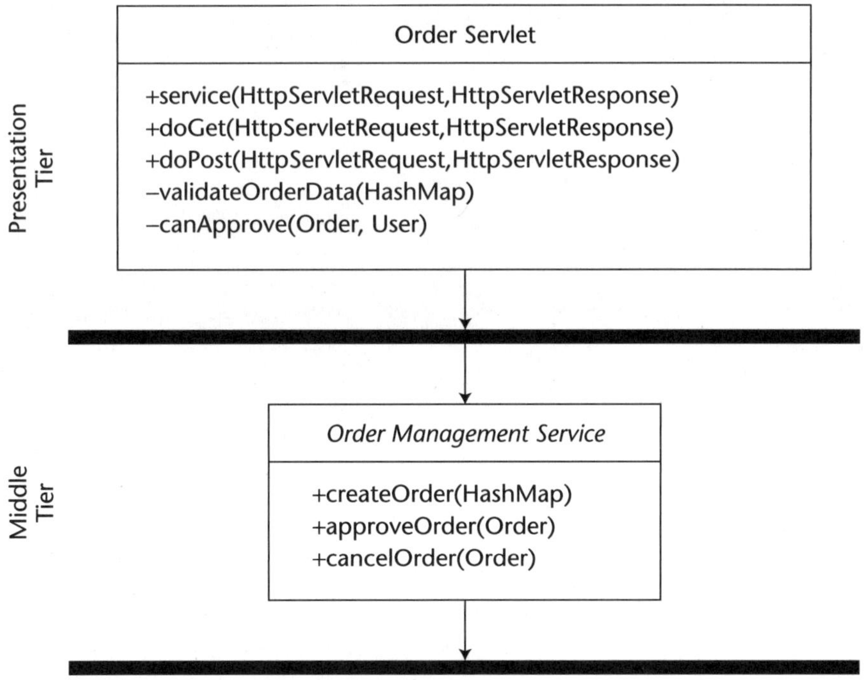

Figure 3.4 Service functionality in client tier.

This arrangement becomes an issue when another client (such as an integration client or another servlet) also needs to interact with the service. These other clients can invoke those same service methods with invalid data, and/or as an unauthorized user. Clearly, those two servlet methods are operational requirements of the service itself, and should be implemented there so that the service does everything it should, consistently for all clients.

Related Solutions

There are no related solutions for this AntiPattern.

Refactorings

The refactorings associated with SBA concentrate on improving the basic object-orientedness of the services, that is, making services exhibit better, more cohesive abstractions, as represented by their interfaces. Also, these refactorings support reduced coupling between services and client components that use the services, so that the services are more context-independent and reusable. Additionally, SBA is very centered on the idea of layered architecture, with independence and decoupling of the upper and lower layers. Some of the refactorings presented here are geared toward refactoring poorly layered, coupled tiers into more distinct and decoupled tiers.

Interface Partitioning. This refactoring partitions a large, multiabstraction service into multiple services that each represents a distinct abstraction. The service interface is the basis of this partitioning, because it represents the public view of the service that clients interact with.

Interface Consolidation. This refactoring consolidates a set of services that collectively implement a complete, single abstraction. Different service interfaces that operate against the same abstraction are consolidated (along with their implementations) into one service that represents a single cohesive abstraction.

Technical Services Layer. This refactoring is concerned with the layering of existing service implementations into multiple layers, for example, factoring out common technical and infrastructure methods of business services into the underlying technical and infrastructure services.

Cross-Tier Refactoring. This refactoring concentrates on moving an implementation across tiers to where it is more appropriate to be. The main example of this is moving business or technical process logic from the client tier down to the middle-tier services.

Interface Partitioning

A service interface has methods, which cover multiple abstractions and business process areas.

Partition the interface into separate services to yield better, more usable abstractions.

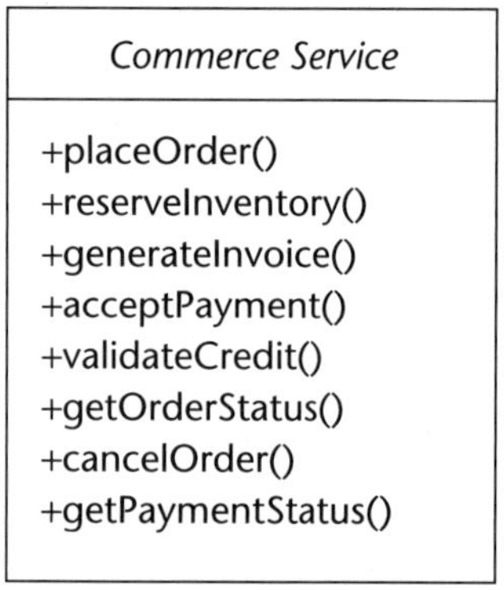

Figure 3.5 Before refactoring.

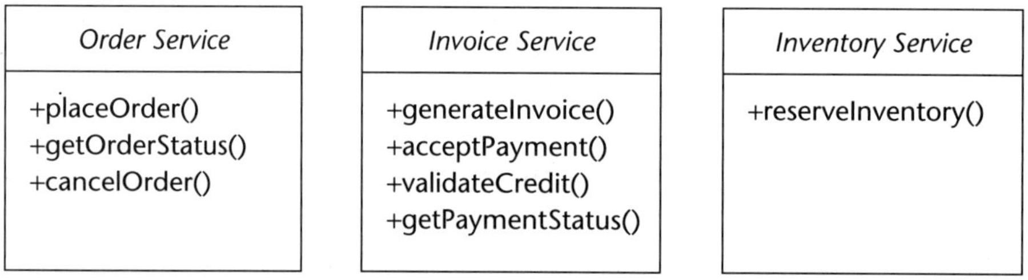

Figure 3.6 After refactoring.

Motivation

The architectural basis for services is centered on providing self-contained, encapsulated, cohesive units of functionality that support a specific abstraction and are loosely coupled to other services or components, allowing them to be used in a variety of applications. A significant aspect that affects a service's use and reuse is how correctly and completely the service supports its abstraction or concern. When a service does too much, as in the Multiservice AntiPattern, it supports multiple business entities or technical abstractions (such as Orders and Invoices), and the service is less usable because all of these abstractions are coupled within the service. Additionally, when a lot of varied application requirements are concentrated into one component, it is more likely that many developers will need to implement parts of the service, leading to contention and issues around coding, testing, and deployment. All of these factors end up leading to longer, more problematic development and reduced reuse potential.

In some cases, an interface represents several, related abstractions like a subtype hierarchy. For instance, when an account abstraction is recognized, an AccountManagementService is defined and over time a variety of distinctly different account types emerge. If all the common, variant, and unique processes associated with all the different account types are implemented through one service, this can be quite large, and does not explicitly expose the differences. It is better to refactor this service into a subtype hierarchy of services, or possibly hierarchy of service implementations, depending on the interface distinctions.

Mechanics

The basic mechanics of this refactoring involve examining the methods within a service interface, and determining which of those apply to the specific abstraction that the service is intended to support. In many cases, the name of a method will indicate its abstraction, for example, update *Order*, or approve *Invoice*. In other cases, it may not be so apparent, especially if the command pattern has been applied resulting in method names like doIt. In those cases, the method implementations themselves need to be examined to ascertain what core abstraction they are operating on.

1. *Identify the different abstraction(s) that the service is representing*. For each method in the service interface, identify the action and abstraction. The method name itself usually indicates the action, such as validateCredit or reserveInventory. Identifying the abstraction that the service method operates on is usually a matter of examining the method's name and/or arguments. Methods that create or generate instances will usually indicate the relevant abstraction by their name, such as generateInvoice. Methods that perform actions on existing instances will typically indicate the abstraction by one of the arguments to the method, in the form of an Entity reference, an instance of a Data Transfer Object (DTO), or possibly a primary key value. In these cases, the relevant abstraction is the Entity type, the Entity type that the DTO is representing, or the Entity type that is fetched using the supplied primary key. This process is repeated for all method signatures within the multiservice, to identify all the distinct abstractions operated on by the service.

2. *For each identified abstraction, create a new service interface and implementation class, and partition the related multiservice methods into the new service*. Each distinct abstraction identified in the previous step should end up being a separate service. The naming of this service should be indicative of the abstraction, such as OrderService or AccountService. For each service that is defined, the method signatures from the original multiservice interface that operate against that service's abstraction are partitioned to the new service. The implementation of the method is likewise moved over to the new service implementation class.

Example

The following provides a walkthrough of the Interface Partitioning process as applied to the Multiservice example presented in Listing 3.1.

The first step of the refactoring process examines each of the method interface signatures to determine the associated entity or abstraction.

We first examine the interface for creational methods, looking for hints within the method naming to indicate the abstraction. The placeOrder(HashMap) and generateInvoice(int orderId) methods indicate that they create instances of Order and Invoice, respectively, so the Order and Invoice abstractions are identified from these method signatures.

Next, we look for the methods that implement processes against existing instances of entities, examining the method arguments themselves to indicate the associated abstraction. The acceptPayment (int invoiceId, float amount) method accepts a payment amount against an Invoice (as indicated by the invoiceId argument), so this method identifies the abstraction Invoice. The validateCredit(int accountId, float amount) method validates the credit worthiness of an Account (indicated by the accountId argument). Thus, this method identifies the abstraction Account. The reserveInventory(int productId, int quantity) method reserves the quantity of product (as indicated by the productId argument), indicating that the abstraction in this case is Product.

By examining these method interfaces and implementations, we have determined that the abstractions supported by this service are Order, Invoice, Account, and Product.

The next step in this process involves defining new services to implement each distinct abstraction. From the process described above, we define the following new service interfaces:

```
public interface OrderService { }
public interface InvoiceService { }
public interface AccountService { }
public interface ProductService { }
```

Finally, once these service interfaces are defined, we then partition the methods from the existing multiservice into the appropriate separate services. The earlier step, which involved identifying the abstraction for each method, has already indicated this mapping, so the next step is simply placing those method signatures within the new service interfaces, as shown below in Listing 3.4:

```
public interface OrderService {
boolean placeOrder(HashMap orderData);
}

public interface ProductService {
int reserveInventory(int productId, int quantity);
}

public interface InvoiceService {
void generateInvoice(int orderId);
boolean acceptPayment(int invoiceId, float amount);
}

public interface AccountService {
boolean validateCredit(int accountId, float amount,);
}
```

Listing 3.4 Multiservice partitioned into multiple, distinct services.

Interface Consolidation

An abstraction and related processes are scattered across a number of services.

Consolidate separate interface methods that support the same abstraction, to form a more cohesive, self-contained, and usable abstraction.

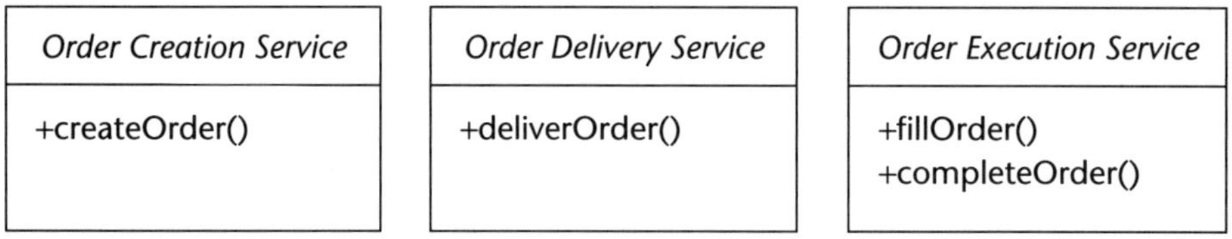

Figure 3.7 Before refactoring.

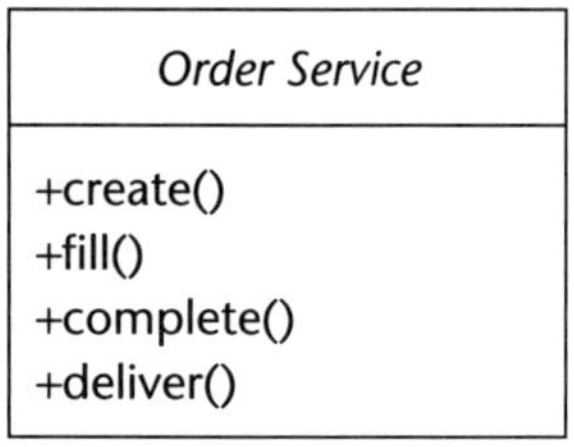

Figure 3.8 After refactoring.

Motivation

A key benefit that is intended to accrue from the use of service-based architecture is the ability to locate, understand, and use and reuse core business and technical functionality within a number of different end-user requirements and even separate applications. A well-defined business service implements all the relevant processes associated with a specific business abstraction or entity; therefore, it is inherently coupled to the attributes and properties of that entity. When the operations for a specific abstraction or entity are scattered over multiple services (as in the Tiny Service AntiPattern), each of those services is coupled to that one entity. This is a problem when changes or extensions to the entity occur, because all of those services potentially need to change. Developers need to know what *set* of services are potentially affected and how they should change. This translates to greater development time, and a greater burden on developers to know what collective set of services are related to a specific entity.

The motivation of Interface Consolidation is to join together into one unit the parts of separate services that actually support a single abstraction.

Mechanics

The basic approach in this refactoring is to locate the methods across a set of services that support one specific abstraction or entity, and aggregate them together into a single service. The mechanics of the actual process are based on first examining the service and method names, because these often indicate related items. For instance, if there is an approveOrder method on one service, and updateOrder on another, then the naming of these indicate that they are both related to the Order entity. The names of the services themselves may be named in a similar manner, for example, OrderApprovalService and OrderUpdateService.

Another important technique is to look for all the services and methods that use or depend on a specific entity or abstraction. For instance, all the services that interact with either the Order entity EJB or OrderDTO Data Transfer Object may actually be supporting the Order abstraction. These kinds of determinations can be made by looking at the service method arguments, to identify types or indirect references to types represented as entity primary keys.

1. *Identify the different abstraction(s) across all of the services.* Each service interface needs to be examined, to identify the distinct abstractions that are actually present. For each method in each service interface, identify an action and abstraction. The techniques described above in the Interface Partitioning refactoring can be applied in the same way here. Tiny services tend to be very specific in nature, so it is likely that the name of the service itself indicates the action and abstraction. For instance, a service named OrderApprovalService indicates that the action is approval, and the abstraction is Order.

2. *For each identified abstraction, define a new service interface and implementation class, and consolidate each of the related tiny service interface methods into the new service.* Each distinct abstraction that was identified in the previous step is used to create a new service interface and implementation class. Then, each of the tiny services' methods are moved over to the new services, based on the associated abstraction that was identified in the previous step. The result of this should be a set of services, one for each distinct abstraction, and each one containing the complete set of methods that operates against that abstraction.
3. *Update the service method implementations.* After the consolidation of the services, existing method implementations may need to be updated to correctly locate and use the correct (new) service.

Example

The following provides a walkthrough of Interface Consolidation refactoring, applied to the tiny services example presented previously in Listing 3.2. The first step involves examining each of the existing services to determine the set of abstractions. In the tiny services example presented earlier, the names of the services (OrderCreationService, OrderUpdateService, and OrderApprovalService) provide clear indication that they all relate to the Order entity. So, in this case, there is just one abstraction—Order—that is identified in this step.

The next step is to create a new service interface and implementation components to support the abstraction identified. In this case, the one abstraction identified is Order, so an OrderService is defined:

```
public interface OrderService { }
```

The final step is to consolidate the separate services and associated methods into the one new service interface, as shown below in Listing 3.5:

```
public interface OrderService {
     OrderDTO create(HashMap data);
     OrderDTO duplicate(int orderId);
     OrderDTO duplicate(OrderDTO order);
     void update(OrderDTO orderData, int orderId);
     boolean approve(int orderId);
     boolean cancel(int orderId);
}
```

Listing 3.5 Tiny services consolidated into a single service.

Technical Services Layer

A number of services contain duplicated implementations of common technical functions.

Factor out the duplicated technical functions within the service implementations into an underlying layer of shared technical services.

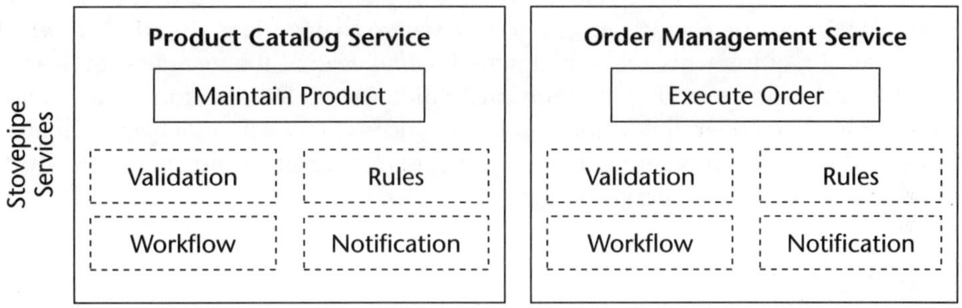

Figure 3.9 Before refactoring.

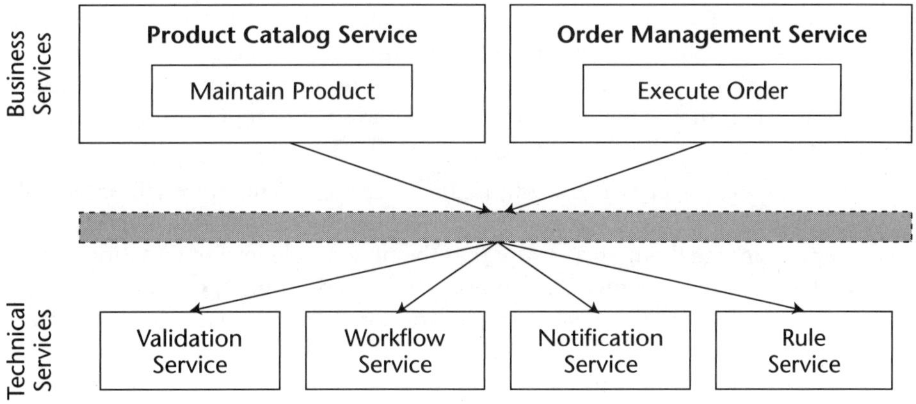

Figure 3.10 After refactoring.

Motivation

A core concept behind SBA is that services in general should be self-contained and loosely coupled components, allowing the services to be used in multiple applications and contexts. However, within most business services, there are a number of technical or nonfunctional requirements that need to be supported, such as application logging, data validation, instance-based security checking, and transactional event auditing. In a well-layered SBA, these general technical functions would generally be implemented as a set of technical services underlying the business services, motivated by the same rationale as the business services (such as single implementation, reusable by multiple clients). The Stovepipe Service AntiPattern discussed above is a situation in which these technical requirements are implemented *within* each of the business services by different developers, resulting in multiple, different implementations. The consequences are a greater overall development effort, inconsistent behavior across different services, and a significantly longer time to perform maintenance and enhancements to meet technical, nonfunctional requirements.

Mechanics

The basic approach to implementation Refactoring is to identify the duplicated common functionality across a set of services, and factor this out into another (usually technical) service or component. In many cases, these functions will be technical and infrastructure types of functions that are not specifically associated with the abstraction that the service supports.

1. *Review implementation classes of services to identify common or similar private or protected methods.* This can be a bit tricky when services have been implemented by different developers, because method naming can be done quite differently. A large part of successful implementation repartitioning is centered on being able to identify common behavior in the face of widely different naming and style conventions.
2. *Factor out the common code into new, technical service(s).* This step will potentially require some analysis of the multiple implementations that are currently present, to merge them and ensure that the new, single implementation accommodates all the requirements and variations of individual (possibly slightly different) ones. Essentially, this is a step of mining the existing implementations to understand the actual requirements and process steps, and merging them together so that the new implementation can accommodate all the current client usages.
3. *Refactor business services to remove any duplicated versions of these functions, and replace them with references to the new technical services.* The refactored stovepipe service, or any other services that redundantly implement these technical functions, are refactored to remove their own implementation and use the new technical services.

Example

The following provides a walkthrough of Technical Services Layer refactoring, applied to the Stovepipe Service AntiPattern example presented previously in Listing 3.3.

The first step involves reviewing the implementation class(es) of existing services to identify common utility or technical functions that are occurring repeatedly across the services. In the stovepipe service example presented earlier, the auditEvent() and notify() methods are features that are not specific to the Product service abstraction, but are common to multiple business services. So, these are identified as methods that should be factored out of this business service.

The next step involves factoring out those common utility or technical functions into new, technical services. Because the notification and audit functions are distinct functions that operate against different abstractions (Notification and Audit Event), this indicates that separate technical services—AuditService and NotificationService—are justified, and created as shown below:

```
// New technical service:
public interface AuditService {
void auditEvent(DTO dto, int userId);
}

// New technical service:
public interface NotificationService {
void notify(int eventType, int userId);
}
```

The final step involves refactoring the existing stovepipe service to remove its local implementation of those functions and utilize the new technical services instead. This is shown below in Listing 3.6:

```
public class ProductCatalogServiceImpl {
public boolean updateProduct(ProductDTO product, int productId) {

          // Do product update stuff (left out for brevity)...

          // ** Perform the additional nonfunctional requirements:

          // Notify interested parties of product updates:
          NotificationService notif = getNotificationService();

          notif.notify(UPDATE, getLoggedInUser());

          // Audit the change, and who did it:
          AuditService audit = getAuditService();
```

Listing 3.6 Stovepipe service refactored into business service plus technical services. *(continued)*

```
audit.auditEvent(product, getLoggedInUser());
}

public boolean createProduct(HashMap productData) { ... };
}
```

Listing 3.6 *(continued)*

Cross-Tier Refactoring

Nonfunctional requirements such as data validation are implemented in client code and not in the underlying service, resulting in an incomplete service when it is used by some other client.

Move the client-based functionality into the service so that it is truly complete and self-contained.

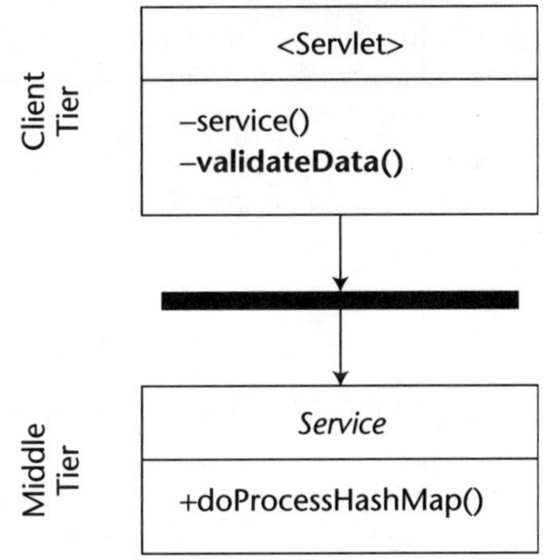

Figure 3.11 Before refactoring.

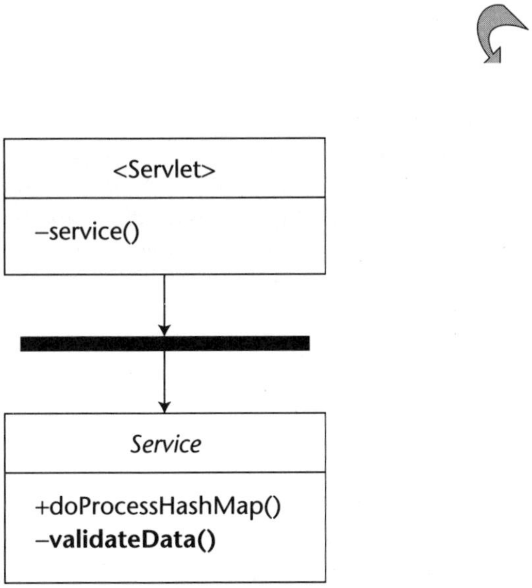

Figure 3.12 After refactoring

Motivation

As mentioned several times already in this chapter, a well-defined service should be relatively self-contained and usable by multiple clients, including Web-tier clients, integration clients, and even unit-test clients. However, as discussed in the Client Completes Service AntiPattern, important functionality can end up in client components and not in the services. This is especially common when SBA-based applications implement one client approach to start with. In these cases, it is easier to bleed service functionality up into client components, because the overall system functionality is still complete. It is later, when additional clients are developed (such as integration clients), that the omissions in the service become apparent. The consequence is that additional clients need to reimplement some of the missing functionality, or refactor it down into the services as described in this refactoring. At any rate, implementing middle-tier functionality within client components can result in longer development and significant refactoring with new application requirements.

Cross-Tier Refactoring moves the middle-tier functionality down into the appropriate services, and refactors the clients to use those services.

Mechanics

The basic approach to this refactoring is to move or duplicate client-based implementation down into middle-tier services. The actual mechanics depends somewhat on the client artifacts. For instance, data validation in Javascript requires some new, Java-based implementation within the services, so the code cannot be directly moved. For other Java-based client artifacts (JSP scriptlet, custom tag code, or servlet code) there is more opportunity.

1. *Identify service-related functions that are currently implemented in client components.* Within client components, look for functions that aren't specifically related to presentation concerns and that must be executed before invoking a service method.

2. *Refactor these methods down to an appropriate service.* In some cases, these should reside on a specific business service. But often, these kinds of functions are general mechanisms such as data validation that should be used with many business services. In these latter cases, the functions should be relocated to existing or new technical services.

Example

The following provides a walkthrough of this refactoring, as applied to the Client Completes Service AntiPattern example presented in Figure 3.4.

The first step involves identifying service-related functions implemented within client components. In reality, this usually occurs when some other client attempts to use the service, and either fails (because something like data validation isn't done), or test cases reveal that unauthorized clients can still execute the service methods. But ideally, this is done during design or code review steps before these other situations arise.

As indicated in bold in Figure 3.13 below, two private methods are identified as methods of this type. The validateOrderData() method validates data before calling any of the OrderService methods, and the canApprove() method performs authorization checks as a precursor to calling the Order Service method approveOrder(). Neither of these methods has anything to do with Web browser interactions or presentation, and both are used in preparation for calling service methods.

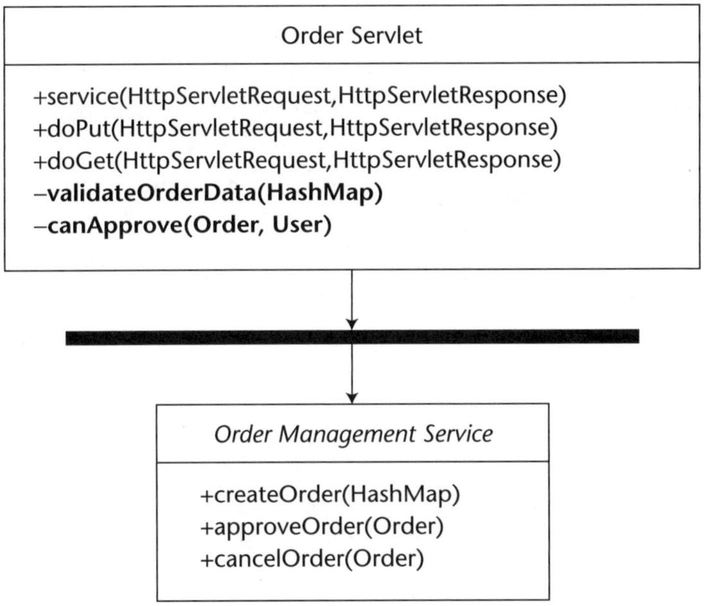

Figure 3.13 Service-related functions identified in client tier.

Once the service-related methods are discovered or identified, they are refactored into the appropriate underlying service. In this case, there is a close relationship between the OrderServlet and the OrderService, so these two methods are reallocated onto the OrderService, as shown in Figure 3.14.

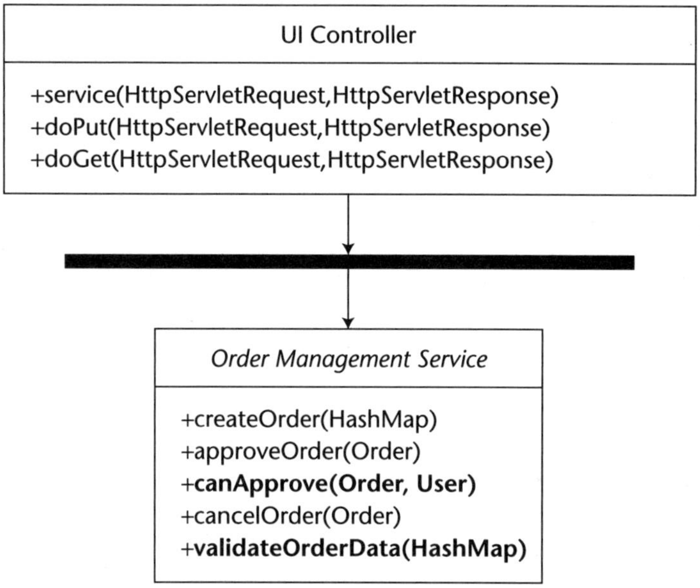

Figure 3.14 Client to service refactoring.

CHAPTER 4

JSP Use and Misuse

This chapter is about the use and misuse of JSP technology. An organizing principal used to build the user interface of J2EE applications is called Model-View-Controller (MVC). The Model is made up of the entities (not necessarily EJBs, but the abstractions) that make up the application. Examples of model objects include things like Customer, Account, or ElectronicBill. These classes are the nouns in the vocabulary of the problem, the things that are acted upon or do the acting in the application. The View is the way that the Model is displayed in a user interface. View examples include things like CustomerInfoScreen or ScheduleRecurringPaymentScreen, among others. View objects will have a display component and will provide display of and allow updates to the model information. Controllers provide the glue that translates user actions in the View into method calls on the Model.

This technique for grouping objects can be very powerful if done correctly and will allow different user interfaces to drive the Controller and Model. For example, imagine scheduling a bill payment in the online bill payment service that can be done from a browser. If we apply MVC to building this application, we will have a model that encapsulates all the business data and rules; none of the essence of the application will be in the UI code. Updating the application to add a UI for cell phones would simply require new code for that device. None of the underlying model code would have to change to accommodate the new view. If we do not apply MVC and instead embed Model or Controller code into our View, we will be hard pressed to provide a cell phone UI. The typical J2EE UI is delivered to the user in the form of HTML rendered in a browser. JSPs are the typical way to write the UI for J2EE applications.

Acting in the View role, JSPs play an important role in any J2EE application. However, the typical misuse of JSPs involves confusing this role as View, and building Controller or even Model code right into the JSP. While this approach works for very small applications, it is unwieldy in large enterprise applications. What ends up being built is impossible to maintain as the complexity of the code in the JSP grows. Many of the AntiPatterns documented in this chapter arise because of failing to maintain this separation of concerns.

In the J2EE community, the MVC pattern is often referred to as Model 2. Early JSP specifications releases (pre-1.0) referred to two models for programming with JSPs. Model 1 used JavaBeans as a combined Controller and Model. Model 2 suggested Servlets as controllers, with JavaBeans as the model and JSPs as the view. The article at http://developer.java.sun.com/developer/onlineTraining/JSPIntro/contents.html has an interesting explanation and history of the Model 2 term. As you are reading other literature on the subject of JSPs, you can mentally translate the Model 2 term to MVC adapted to the J2EE technologies of JSPs, JavaBeans, and Servlets.

The AntiPatterns covered in this chapter are briefly summarized here.

Ignoring Reality. This AntiPattern is about the tendency of developers to ignore the reality that errors do happen. All too often users are served Java stack traces which causes them to lose confidence in the application and, if not dealt with, can eventually lead to the project being canceled.

Too Much Code. This AntiPattern is about how much Java code ends up in a JSP when developers are either not aware of or do not apply the principals of logical separation of tasks among the layers of J2EE. The main consequence of this AntiPattern is a very brittle and hard-to-maintain user interface.

Embedded Navigational Information. This AntiPattern is about the common practice of embedding links from one page to the next into JSPs. The Web site that results from applying this AntiPattern is hard to change and to maintain.

Copy and Paste JSP. The Copy and Paste JSP AntiPattern is about copying and pasting JSP code. Seems that this AntiPattern should go away some day, but for some reason developers that would never copy and paste Java code have gotten into the habit of copying and pasting JSP code from page to page. When this AntiPattern is applied, the typical result is a hard-to-maintain system that has user-confusing subtle differences from page to page.

Too Much Data in Session. This AntiPattern covers the tendency of developers to use the session as a giant flat data space to hang everything they might need for their application. The result is often seemingly random crashes and exceptions because data is put into the session with conflicting keys with different types.

Ad Lib TagLibs. The Ad Lib TagLib AntiPattern is about the way that TagLibs are used to do what they are not intended to do. Often TagLibs become the dumping ground for code when developers first realize that all the code in their JSPs (i.e., when they realize the symptoms of the Too Much Code AntiPattern) is causing major maintenance problems. The result is more or less the same; the application is much harder to maintain than it should be.

AntiPattern

Ignoring Reality

Also Known As: No Errors Happen Here

Most Frequent Scale: Application

Refactorings: Apply Error Page

Refactored Solution Type: Software

Root Causes: Haste, apathy, and ignorance

Unbalanced Forces: Functionality and resources

Anecdotal Evidence: "Error page? What's an error page?" "That is such a waste of time, no exceptions come out of the JSPs; they are too simple."

Background

This AntiPattern is about the tendency of new developers to ignore the reality that errors do happen and users hate to seem them. For whatever reason, developers either think that exceptions will never be thrown or that even if they are thrown users will not mind seeing a stack trace from time to time. In reality errors do happen in server-side code and users quickly lose confidence in an application that shows some strange-looking error message. When you fail to recognize that errors happen, you inevitably end up harming user confidence. For example, when users see a stack trace in their browser they become very skeptical of the quality of the application. Once a development team has lost the users' confidence, it is very hard to regain.

All too often programmers pick up a new technology and start building software based on it. The examples that come with the new technology's download bundle are often seen as the best practices for the new technology when, in fact, the examples were thrown together at the last minute by the development team. The thinking goes that if an example was good enough for the definer of the technology then surely it's good enough for the application. The typical JSP example says nothing about handling errors or managing exceptions, so the typical new JSP developer will tend to Ignore Reality and not plan for errors happening.

Another reason that we ignore the reality of errors happening is that we get pushed into a corner by deadlines and just throw what we know to do out the window, and do what we can to meet the deadline. This is never a comfortable situation and many things that we wish we had not done end up in our code. The stack traces end up in the JSPs because the Web container has the rendering of each JSP in a try-catch block. The browser's request is filtered to the Web container, which in turn renders the JSP. If, during rendering, the JSP encounters an error and an exception is thrown, the container will first look for an error page; if none is found, most containers will just print the stack trace to the output that is returned to the browser. If an error page is specified in the JSP, then the container renders the error page instead.

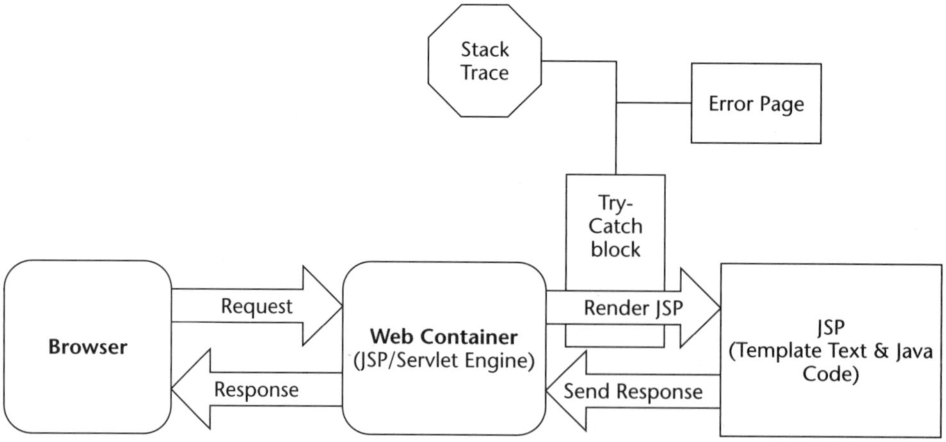

Figure 4.1 Rendering a JSP.

General Form

This AntiPattern takes the form of a JSP without an error page directive. It is very easy to spot and can almost be found automatically. All that need be done is scan each JSP for an error page directive; if none is found, then there is some work to be done.

Symptoms and Consequences

The symptoms of being stuck in this AntiPattern are obvious, especially to users who do not know or care about stack traces or anything else related to Java. Users quickly lose confidence in a system that presents them with an unintelligible error message.

- **Stack Traces in Web Browsers.** This is the most common symptom of Ignoring Reality. The typical user does not know anything about Java and does not want to know about it. They have a job to do, and the software we are writing is supposed to help them do that job. When a user sees a stack trace, the typical response is to get scared that the application is going to corrupt the data.
- **Loss of User Confidence.** The most common consequence is the loss of user confidence. Once user confidence is gone, it is very hard to regain.

Typical Causes

Typically, inexperienced developers who just plain don't know how to handle errors in a JSP cause this AntiPattern. Management can sometimes cause this AntiPattern as well by driving the schedule over quality.

- **Lack of understanding of error processing.** Sharp newbies not given time to experiment or adequate training to appreciate the issues will often be subject to this AntiPattern. Also, a lazy attitude towards maintainability and modularity can contribute to this AntiPattern.
- **Schedule-driven corner cutting.** Failure to accurately assess the time needed for application development leads to a feeling that there is no time to do the right thing, just time to do what it takes to meet the deadline. One major contributor to corner cutting is scope creep. Users, or even developers, dream up new things for the application to do and the time necessary to build in the required features often passes while the new features are implemented.
- **Flat denial.** Finally, developers, from time to time, just deny that exceptions will come from their code and refuse to plan as if they will.

Known Exceptions

The only known acceptable exception to Ignoring Reality occurs when the JSP is used in some form of integration testing. Typically, a developer testing back-end processes with a JSP wants to see a stack trace if something goes wrong. Most of the times, though, there are better means of testing available than JSPs. If you are tempted to test your back-end code with JSPs, look into Cactus. It is a JUnit derivative built specifically to test back-end J2EE code.

Refactorings

Ignore Reality is basically about not programming defensively and expecting everything that could go wrong to go wrong. The Introduce Error Page refactoring will go a long way towards helping you keep users' confidence despite something going astray on the server.

To work your way out of Ignoring Reality use the Introduce Error Page refactoring. The process is basically to put error page directives into your JSPs so that the users do not end up with a stack trace in their browser. This refactoring will cause your JSPs to be more realistic in handling errors.

Variations

This is a simple AntiPattern and does not have any significant variations.

Example

This is a simple example JSP that is Ignoring Reality. The timer bean can throw an exception from time to time (due to failure to contact the time server, for example), and this JSP ignores that. If an exception is thrown from the getNow() method, the server will return the stack trace from the exception.

```
<%@ page isELEnabled="true" %>
<html>
  <head>
    <title>Welcome To This Page</title>
  </head>
  <jsp:useBean id="timer" class="com.util.Timer"/>
  <body>
    <table>
      <tr>
        <%-- timer is a bean that returns a formated date --%>
        <td>Welcome it's ${timer.now}.</td>
      </tr>
    </table>
  </body>
</html>
```

Related Solutions

Another way to fix this AntiPattern is to implement the Front Controller pattern from *Core J2EE Patterns* by Alur, Crupi, and Malks (Alur, Crupi, and Malks 2001), and not allow exceptions to be thrown from the request processing method at all. The Front Controller will catch any *throwable* exceptions from the processing and implement its own forwarding to an application-wide error page. This strategy is less desirable because the front controller will reimplement something that the controller provides.

AntiPattern

Too Much Code

Also Known As: Bloated Do-Everything JSP

Most Frequent Scale: Application

Refactoring: Beanify, Introduce Delegate Controller, Introduce Traffic Cop

Refactoring Type: Software

Root Causes: Ignorance, apathy, and sometimes haste

Unbalanced Forces: Functionality and schedule

Anecdotal Evidence: "Hey man, it works; what's the problem?"

Background

A lot of Java code ends up in a JSP when the fundamental purpose of JSPs is forgotten or thrown out. In building JSPs, the focus should be on writing the user interface and not the application proper. JSPs are so flexible and easy to deploy and work with that the temptation is great to push validation, SQL, or whatever into the JSP. Before you know it, the whole application state is creeping into the HttpSession, and the JSP is stuck in the Too Much Code AntiPattern.

As mentioned in the introduction to this chapter, the main purpose of JSPs is to provide the view in the MVC triad. This AntiPattern comes into play mostly when developers fail to maintain that separation of concerns between the Model, View, and Controller. The reason that this is such an issue is the mixed development model of HTML and Java that ends up in the JSPs caught in this AntiPattern. When you build HTML applications, this requires following certain processes and using a paradigm and skill set that are very different from the processes, paradigms, and skill sets that are used for Java development. Systems built without the separation of concerns recommended by the MVC pattern are harder to maintain because of the differences inherent in developing HTML and Java applications. One application that a colleague was called in to rescue had a JSP that had so much Java code embedded in it that the Java runtime could not load the resulting Java class that was generated from the JSP. The length of the generated servlet method that builds the response exceeded the 64K limit on method size. Needless to say, this one page was a big part of the application. Imagine how hard that page was to maintain.

General Form

This AntiPattern takes the form of large JSP files with lots of Java code in scriptlets.

Symptoms and Consequences

Applications caught in this AntiPattern are usually hard to maintain. The JSPs are also hard to understand, which leads to numerous problems in changing the JSPs to fix bugs or update functionality.

- **Bugs in scriptlet code.** If the code in a JSP is complex enough to have to look through it to find a bug, then the JSP is almost certainly caught in the Too Much Code AntiPattern.
- **Difficulty maintaining a JSP.** If your JSPs are stuck in the Too Much Code AntiPattern, there will be maintenance problems in fixing bugs in the JSP as well as extending it to meet future requirements.
- **Compiler errors while deploying a JSP.** The Too Much Code AntiPattern is also implicated if the Java code in your JSP is complex enough to have a compiler error. Any code in a JSP should be minimal single-line scriptlets that are very unlikely to have compiler errors.

- **Steep learning curve for new team members.** A major consequence to leaving your JSPs in the Too Much Code AntiPattern is the learning curve faced by new developers joining the team. The code in a JSP is difficult to read and even more difficult to debug.
- **Impossible to reuse functionality.** If your JSPs are trapped in the Too Much Code AntiPattern, the code will be very hard to reuse in other contexts because it's embedded in the JSP and cannot be invoked from anywhere else.

Typical Causes

Either not knowing or not understanding the MVC design pattern most typically causes this AntiPattern.

- **Lack of undersanding of the role of JSPs.** The instance of the Too Much Code AntiPattern is often a result of a bright developer getting just deep enough into the JSP specification to be dangerous. Given the great flexibility inherent in JSP development, it is very easy to continue in a lack of understanding of the role of JSPs. The huge JSP that could not be loaded because the method was too long, as mentioned in the background given above, was a result of this instance of the AntiPattern. Basically, a large portion of the business process the application was written to manage was implemented in the JSP. The developers were very good at writing JSPs, but they failed to see the bigger picture of how to build J2EE applications.
- **Stuck in the past.** Another major driver behind the Too Much Code AntiPattern is being stuck in the past. It is rare that a developer has no experience other than J2EE and JSP. Often there has been extensive work done in other systems like Visual Basic, Oracle Forms, or Powerbuilder. These systems are essentially two tiers in nature, and all the code must live in the UI because that is the only place it can be captured. Habits developed in this environment die slowly and poor JSPs are a result.
- **Schedule-driven corner cutting.** Developers pushed by schedule can find themselves trapped in this AntiPattern. When the schedule is not viable and not changeable, inexperienced developers often find themselves doing whatever it takes to meet the deadline. JSPs that are impossible to maintain often result.

Known Exceptions

There are no known exceptions to the Too Much Code AntiPattern. Any time that a large amount of code is in a JSP, the maintainability, readability, and understandability of that JSP will suffer.

Refactorings

To navigate your way out of the Too Much Code AntiPattern, there is a set of related refactorings to consider. They are, in no particular order, Beanify to help get model code into the right place, Introduce Delegate Controller to help get controller code into the right place, and Introduce Traffic Cop to get the page flow code into the correct place. All three of these refactorings can be found later in this chapter.

If the rogue code in the JSP relates to keeping track of information for the model of the application, then Beanify is an appropriate refactoring to fix the page. Often, code found in JSPs pushes and pulls data in the HttpSession. The Beanify refactoring provides the mechanisms to move the data out of the session and put it into a JavaBean that is kept in the session (yes, the data is still in the session, but now behavior is attached to that data in the form of a JavaBean). Once the code and its data are refactored into a JavaBean, the code will no longer be in the JSP.

If the JSP has a lot of code that is managing business processes or doing validation across different business objects, then Introduce Delegate Controller is a good choice to refactor the JSP. Introduce Delegate Controller provides the mechanism to remove the controller code from the JSP and place it into a separate class.

Sometimes JSPs end up with navigational code in them (code that specifies which page to navigate to next). Use Introduce Traffic Cop to remove that code and consolidate the navigational information in the Traffic Cop controller. Once this is done the JSP will be free of the navigational code and thus have far less code.

These three refactorings can often be used in concert to get the Java code out of the JSP and into a class where it belongs. The three refactorings combine to allow JavaBeans to capture the data and behavior, and controllers can be used to manage the flow of the application. The refactorings section below, which documents these refactorings, discusses strategies to use them together.

Variations

This AntiPattern varies a lot in scope and quantity of code in the JSP. The more code that is in your JSP, the more likely you will need to apply more than one refactoring. No matter how much code is in the JSP the symptoms are more or less the same. Reuse is almost impossible and maintenance is difficult. On one extreme there is the JSP that results in Java classes that are too big to be loaded, with model and controller code embedded throughout; on the other end are a few lines of business logic code inhibiting reuse. Most occurrences of this AntiPattern are on the light end and will not require vast amounts of refactoring.

Example

This is an example JSP that renders a login page for a Web application. As you can see in the listing for Login.jsp, there is a lot of code in scriptlets in this JSP. There are several aspects of the MVC pattern that are being broken here. The JSP is directly accessing the database with JDBC calls and then placing the data into the session. That code is part of the model and controller abstractions. As the amount of data contained in the session grows, the maintenance of the application will become almost impossible. No one doing maintenance on the application will be able to tell how the data got into the session or if it should be edited or not. With JSPs in the Too Much Code AntiPattern, we are almost back to the bad old days with C programming when all the data for the application resided in a shared memory space and any function that imported the correct header could access and modify the global data. We have rightly rejected that kind of programming, but like a ghoul that just won't die, the lazy practices of putting data in a global shared space keep coming back.

Another aspect of the AntiPattern that this JSP displays is the coding of application flow into the JSP. Notice that if there is an error, this JSP redirects the response to itself again; if the user is valid, then this page redirects the response to the HomePage.jsp. Coding in this style is very hard to maintain; for example, if the name of HomePage.jsp ever needed to change, this JSP would need maintenance. No big deal for an application with six pages, but that kind of maintenance point is a very big deal for an application with 600 pages.

Here is the code for Login.jsp, Listing 4.1.

```
... <%
 // Looking up values in the session
 String wrongLogin  = (String)session.getAttribute("message");
 Long ownerId = (Long)session.getAttribute("ownerId");

Boolean validUser = (Boolean)session.getAttribute("validUser");
 // Get info from the request and look that info up in the database
 String userName = request.getParameter("uname");
 String passwd = request.getParameter("passwd");
 if(userName != null) {
  ...
  // What happens if the schema changes? We have to update our UI code!
  String query = "select OWNERID from SITE_USER where UNAME = '" +
           userName + "' AND PASSWD = '" + passwd + "'";
  try {
    ...
    // Execute the query, i.e., look to see if the user exists
    rset = stmt.executeQuery(query);
    // Get the ownerID.
    if(rset.next()) {
      ownerId = new Long(rset.getLong("OWNERID"));
      validUser = new Boolean(true);
    } else {
      validUser = new Boolean(false);
    }
    ...
  } catch(SQLException sql) {
    // Clean up if there are errors
    ...
  }
```

Listing 4.1 Login.jsp. *(continued)*

```
    // Keep track of the user.
    session.setAttribute("validUser", validUser);
    if(validUser.booleanValue() == true) {
      // Keep the owner's ID around in the session.
      session.setAttribute("ownerId", ownerId);
      // Remove the wrongLogin message since we did log in.
      session.removeAttribute("message");
      // If it's a valid user then redirect to HomePage
      response.sendRedirect("HomePage.jsp");
    } else {
      session.removeAttribute("ownerId");
      session.setAttribute("message",
                 "User Name or Password incorrect, please reenter");
      response.sendRedirect("Login.jsp");
      return;
    }
  }
%>
<html>
...
 <body>
...
   <form name="loginForm" action="Login.jsp" method="post">
     <table>
       <tr>
         <td>User Name:</td>
         <td><input type="text" name="uname"/></td>
       </tr>
       <tr>
         <td>Password:</td>
         <td><input type="password" name="passwd"/></td>
       </tr>
       <tr>
         <td align="center" colspan="2">
           <input type="submit" name="Submit" value="Done"/>
         </td>
       </tr>
     </table>
   </form>
 </body>
</html>
```

Listing 4.1 *(continued)*

This page has way too much code in it. Less than half of the page is HTML; the remainder is Java.

Related Solutions

Doing away with JSPs completely is one of the solutions that has been pursued. Several open-source Web-based MVC implementations are available and do not use JSPs at all. Velocity from the Jakarta project is a great example. There is no chance to pollute the view with model or controller code because there is nowhere to hang the code.

The AntiPattern Embedded Navigational Information is often tied to this one. JSPs with lots of code often end up with navigational information embedded in them.

Embedded Navigational Information

Also Known As: Broken Links Waiting to Happen

Most Frequent Scale: Application, Microarchitecture

Refactorings: Introduce Traffic Cop

Refactoring Type: Software

Root Causes: Ignorance, haste, and apathy

Unbalanced Forces: Complexity and education, functionality and Schedule

Anecdotal Evidence: "Why do I have to update every stinking JSP every time I add or rename a page?"

Background

A JSP that contains the names of files that can be navigated to is brittle with respect to change. That resistance to change is what makes the Embedded Navigational Information AntiPattern so painful to be stuck in. Whenever a change is made to a filename, every single JSP that references it must also be updated. On small projects, this might not be very much overhead, but on big projects, it can be a killer.

General Form

This AntiPattern usually shows up as highly coupled JSPs that are hard to rearrange. A typical place to find the navigational information is in buttons and other action elements. If the filenames are hard-coded into the links actions for the forms, buttons, and so on, the application will be very hard to rearrange.

Symptoms and Consequences

The symptoms of this AntiPattern are obvious when you hit them but they can be hard to find and can sometimes remain hidden, lurking to affect your users, which will result in a loss of user confidence.

- **Page Not Found errors.** Typically, developers will notice these errors after renaming a JSP. Since the filenames are embedded in the JSP, any name change of a file will cause an error if every instance of that filename is not updated. Particularly frustrating is the way that the error can lie undetected for a long time before being found. When the error finally does surface, it is hard to identify the root cause because the page was renamed some time ago, and it is not obvious what to tie the error to.
- **Loss of user confidence.** As described in the Ignoring Reality AntiPattern, users do not understand (nor should they have to) the intricate details of how J2EE applications work. When they see a Page Not Found error, they quickly lose confidence in the application. No matter how hard we work to look for every instance of a JSP name in every JSP file in the system, it is almost inevitable that something will be missed.
- **Difficult to modify application flow.** Another consequence of this AntiPattern is the difficulty in changing the flow of the application. As the users' needs change over time, the flow of the application will have to change. For example, new pages might need to be inserted in a process. These changes are harder to implement if the page names are directly embedded in the JSPs.

Typical Causes

This AntiPattern is usually caused by a lack of experience or knowledge. A new developer typically has not been hit with the consequences and will thus not be wary of putting navigational information into her JSPs.

- **Lack of knowledge.** The typical new developer has not developed an architecturally focused approach to building applications. As a result, there is typically no thought about the division of responsibility or loose coupling. In trying to build things the easy way, developers end up losing user confidence because their code is trapped in the Embedded Navigational Information AntiPattern.

Known Exceptions

For real applications, there are no real exceptions to the Embedded Navigational Information AntiPattern. This AntiPattern always makes it harder to change the application flow and leads to a loss of user confidence when the changes are not introduced flawlessly.

Refactored Solutions

The best way to get out of the Embedded Navigational Information AntiPattern is to introduce a controller that will contain the flow directing code that was in the JSP. Use the Introduce Traffic Cop refactoring to remove the code and consolidate the navigational information in the Traffic Cop controller. See the Introduce Traffic Cop refactoring later in this chapter for more information.

Variations

Inexperienced developers will sometimes embed a Traffic Cop controller into their JSPs. When the controller is embedded in the JSP, though, there is no way to reuse the controller code. The inevitable result is copying and pasting that code from JSP to JSP.

Example

This example is from a banking application that allows users to schedule and review online bill payments. The following JSP allows the users to view currently scheduled payments. From this page, users can navigate to four different screens. Figure 4.2 is a graphical representation of the navigational options.

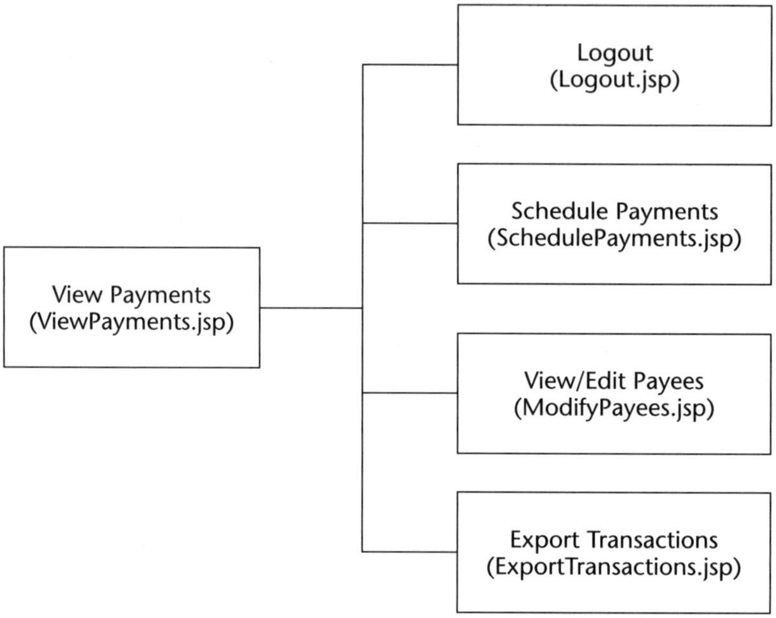

Figure 4.2 Options from the view payments screen.

In the snippet below, each of the four filenames is hard-coded into the JSP.

```
. . .
<table>
  <tr>
    <td><a href="Logout.jsp">Logout</a></td>
  </tr>
  <tr>
    <td><a href="SchedulePayments.jsp">Schedule Payments</a></td>
  </tr>
  <tr>
    <td><a href="ModifyPayees.jsp">View/Edit Payees</a></td>
  </tr>
  <tr>
    <td><a href="ExportTransactions.jsp">Export Transactions</a></td>
  </tr>
</table>
. . .
```

If any of these JSP files are renamed or moved to another directory, this JSP will have to be updated. That makes this ViewPayments.jsp brittle and resistant to changes.

Related Solutions

The Struts framework from the Jakarta project (jakarta.apache.org) takes the Traffic Cop approach to solving this AntiPattern. The ActionServlet has an XML configuration file that specifies the JSP filenames, and the JSPs refer only to the Actions that are invoked to make transitions to new pages. Be aware that moving your application to Struts will cause a major reworking of the user interface. It is recommended that you first refactor your JSPs to get rid of all the code in them before you attempt to move your UI to Struts.

AntiPattern

Copy and Paste JSP

Also Known As: Spaghetti Code

Most Frequent Scale: Idiom

Refactorings: Introduce Template

Refactoring Type: Software

Root Causes: Haste and apathy

Unbalanced Forces: Schedule and complexity

Anecdotal Evidence: "Why does this menu look so different from the other menu?"

Background

The Copy and Paste JSP AntiPattern describes the tendency of developers to copy and paste HTML and scriptlet code from JSP to JSP because they want to achieve consistency in their user interfaces. The problem is, of course, that in copying and pasting any code you end up with duplicate maintenance points; inevitably, one copy is updated and the others are not. The resultant JSP code is always harder to maintain than it should be. Applications built with this AntiPattern typically become very hard for the users to understand and use because of the subtle inconsistencies that creep in over time. In one application in particular that I worked on, there was so much JSP code duplicated that the development team gave up on trying to achieve consistency.

General Form

A very typical form for this AntiPattern to take is applications that have a menu on one side and a header and/or footer with the content in the bottom right pane. All too often, the header and menu is copied from page to page. Figure 4.3 has a diagram that illustrates this problem.

When put together in a diagram like this it seems silly that someone would copy and paste the menu, header, or footer, but it happens repeatedly.

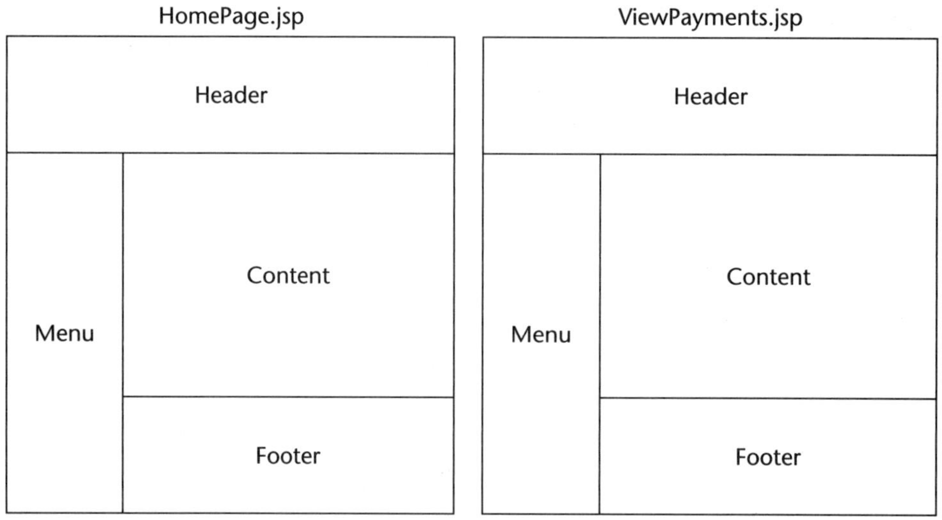

Figure 4.3 Copied and pasted header, footer, and menu.

Symptoms and Consequences

Any time that code is copied and pasted between two source files the copies will diverge. Over time, it will become hard to recognize that the two snippets were once one. This divergence will lead to major maintenance headaches because it is insufficient to fix the bug in only one place.

- **Subtle inconsistencies.** A typical symptom of being caught in the Copy and Paste JSP AntiPattern is having subtle inconsistencies in the user interface of the application. Over time, the copies of the UI elements are changed subtly and differently in the various copies. These kinds of inconsistencies are very irritating to users; they make the application much harder to use than it should be because each interaction is slightly different in meaning from the other interactions.
- **Maintenance nightmares.** As a consequence of being stuck in this AntiPattern is that maintenance of the application will be much harder than it otherwise would be. Each change or enhancement requested by the users will result in having to check each JSP for a copy of what is changing.

Typical Causes

Most of the time developers in a hurry cause this AntiPattern. As the scheduled deadline approaches, developers get nervous and do things they know are bad for the code base just to hit the dates. In some cases, this AntiPattern is caused by code that was intended only to demonstrate that an application could be built ending up becoming the application. Demos are notorious for being slapped together with a lot of copying and pasting of code.

- **Schedule-driven corner cutting.** Developers pushed by schedule can find themselves trapped in this AntiPattern. When the schedule is not viable and not changeable, inexperienced developers often find themselves doing whatever it takes to meet the deadline. JSPs that are impossible to maintain often result. For some reason, developers seem to think that doing the wrong thing (that is, copying and pasting) will reduce the time needed to build the application. The exact opposite is almost always true.
- **Demo creep.** Another typical cause of this AntiPattern is the all-too-frequent occurrence of the demo application becoming the real application. It is almost always better to throw away the demo code and start over than it is to try to change the demo code into actual code.

Known Exceptions

Sometimes it is acceptable to copy whole interrelated sets of JSPs across applications rather than attempt to properly parameterize the JSPs so they work in both contexts.

You only want to do that, however, if the two applications will be perceived by the user as different applications. There are no exceptions to this AntiPattern within the same application.

Refactorings

The best way to get out of the Copy and Paste JSP AntiPattern is to create templates of the parts of your JSPs that you are tempted to copy. Templates work great for consolidating and reusing the different pieces of the presentation layer of an application. The Introduce Template refactoring has more detail and examples to solidify how to refactor out of this AntiPattern.

Variations

The typical variations in this AntiPattern come in the form or degree of pervasiveness. The more code that has been copied between JSPs, the more important it is to refactor the JSPs.

Example

This example is the code for the JSPs described by Figure 4.3. The JSP has three sections: a menu on the left side, a header on the top, and the content on the bottom right. This is the initial page that the user will see after logging in. The problem with this JSP is that each of the sections is inside this page. The rest of the pages in this application are supposed to have the same format. If the application is to be consistent, the code must be copied into the rest of the pages. Listing 4.2 shows the code for HomePage.jsp.

```
<%@ page isELEnabled="true" %>
<html>
  <head>
    <title>iBank BillPay Online</title>
    <link rel="stylesheet" href="css/ibank.css" type="text/css" />
  </head>
  <jsp:useBean id="userCtx" class="ibank.UserContext"
               scope="session"/>
  <body>
    <table border="0" cellspacing="0" cellpadding="0" summary="">
      <tr>
        <td style="align:center;width:121px;height:20px;">
          <img src="img/logo.gif" alt="iBank" border="0">
        </td>
        <td style="text-align:center;width:165px;height:20;">
          <a class="BorderButton" href="${userCtx.nextNav}">
            ${userCtx.loginTitle}
          </a>
```

Listing 4.2 HomePage.jsp.

```
        </td>
      </tr>
    </table>
    <table>
      <tr>
        <td>
          <table>
            <tr>
              <td><a href="SchedulePayments.jsp">
                     Schedule Payments</a></td>
            </tr>
            <tr>
              <td><a href="ViewPayments.jsp">
                           View/Edit Payments</a></td>
            </tr>
            <tr>
              <td><a href="EditPayees.jsp">View/Edit Payees</a></td>
            </tr>
            <tr>
              <td><a href="ExportTransactions.jsp">
                           Export Transactions</a></td>
            </tr>
          </table>
        </td>
        <td>
          <%-- Content Section --%>
          <table>
            <tr>
              <td> Current Balance: </td>
              <td> ${userCtx.currentBalance}</td>
            </tr>
            <tr>
              <td> Current Pending: </td>
              <td> ${userCtx.currentPending} </td>
            </tr>
          </table>
        </td>
      </tr>
    </table>
  </body>
</html>
```

Listing 4.2 *(continued)*

The rest of the JSPs in this example application will have more or less the same HTML except for the content section. The menu and header sections are copied to each "normal" JSP in this application. This copied-and-pasted code might work fine for the first iteration, but over time, things change and the copies will inevitably diverge. As an example, imagine that a requirement is introduced that the menu must be location sensitive. For about half the pages, the menu must be different from the rest of the pages. Now, each of these location-sensitive pages must be updated. The updates will be hard to achieve accurately because of the number of places in the code that must be updated.

Related Solutions

JSPs that are infected with this AntiPattern are often infected with the AntiPattern Too Much Code in the JSP as well. Having both AntiPatterns is a double whammy; not only is there too much code in the JSP but that code has been copied into multiple JSPs. So solving this AntiPattern will often lead to solving the other, and vice versa.

If you are doing new development, a good pattern to apply to keep out of this AntiPattern is the Composite View Pattern documented by Alur, Crupi, and Malks in *Core J2EE Patterns* (Alur, Crupi, and Malks 2001), which is a great Web adaptation of the Composite pattern from John Vlissides and colleagues in *Design Patterns* (Gamma, Helm, Johnson, and Vlissides 1996).

AntiPattern

Too Much Data in Session

Also Known As: Global Data Space

Most Frequent Scale: Idiom, Microarchitecture

Refactorings: Beanify, Introduce Delegate Controller, Introduce Traffic Cop

Refactoring Type: Software

Root Causes: Ignorance, haste, or apathy

Unbalanced Forces: Complexity

Anecdotal Evidence: "What was that key again?"

Background

This AntiPattern harkens back to the day when we had global data spaces available from C programs. All that we needed to do was import the proper header, and we could write to any variable in the shared space any time we wanted to. The session provides a place for developers to put data under a name. What makes it hard to deal with is the global nature of the data; any part of the application can write anything into the space. Various JSPs can stomp on each other's data by writing some other data into the session under the same key. The worst case is when alternate JSPs write different kinds of data into the session with the same key. For example, if one JSP places a String under the key *myKey* and another JSP places an Integer into the session under the same key, most likely a *ClassCastException* will occur the next time either of the pages is displayed.

Code trapped in this AntiPattern violates the fundamental principal of encapsulation inherent in object-oriented programming. The whole idea of OO is to encapsulate the data of your application with the behavior. Applications stuck in this AntiPattern have their data in the session and the behavior in the JSP.

General Form

The general form of this AntiPattern involves a lot of code in the JSP manipulating data in the session. The typical JSP caught in the Too Much Data in Session AntiPattern uses the session as a place to put data between invocations or to pass state from JSP to JSP. Most of the manipulation of the data belongs in either a model or controller class. Instances of the AntiPattern are violating the basic division of responsibility defined by the MVC pattern. JSPs caught in this AntiPattern are typically caught in the Too Much Code in the JSP AntiPattern.

Symptoms and Consequences

You will typically discover that you are trapped in this AntiPattern when you start to have trouble with the data you have placed in the session. The consequences end up being severe if this AntiPattern is not dealt with.

- **Problems keeping track of keys.** Applications trapped in this AntiPattern usually have problems keeping track of the keys that are used in the application. Various means to keep track of the keys have been observed. If you are putting both your keys and the type of object placed with that key into the session into a spreadsheet, you are probably stuck in this AntiPattern.
- **Bugs galore.** Systems trapped in this AntiPattern typically also get a lot of bad behavior like ClassCastExceptions being thrown from code in the JSP. Because there is so much code in the JSP to manage the data, there are bugs in the JSP. Anyone who has ever been stung by this AntiPattern knows how hard it is to find and fix bugs in the code in a JSP.
- **Performance problems.** Typically an application trapped in this AntiPattern ends up with performance problems, especially in clustered environments

where the entire session state must be copied into each session in the cluster. The vast amount of data causes bottlenecks in updates as the other sessions are updated. Even in environments that are not clustered there will be major performance hits if the session ever has to be pacified by the server.

- **Maintenance Headaches.** Applications caught in the AntiPattern will also have a hard time changing over time. The link between the functionality in the JSP and the data in the session become lost over time. As a result, developers end up having to use trial and error to introduce changes. A change is introduced and the page is invoked from a browser; if nothing bad happens right away, then we hope for the best. But since any JSP in the application could be affected by a change to the data in the session, the whole application should really be tested after each change. No one wants to perform a full integration test after every small change to a JSP.

Typical Causes

Developers that are new to J2EE usually cause this AntiPattern. However, once in a while a developer can get lazy and fall into this AntiPattern.

- **Lack of knowledge.** Developers that either do not know the basics of OOP or forget the basics for some reason when they start building Web applications typically cause this AntiPattern. The inexperienced developer will not see the classes that could easily be created from all the related data that is being put into the session. Just because we have a giant flat dataspace (the session) does not mean that we should use it.
- **Lazy programmer.** Another major cause of this AntiPattern is developers just becoming lazy in building good software. It is often a lot quicker and easier in the short run to just put one more key into the session. In the long run, though, this approach leads to very hard-to-maintain systems.

Known Exceptions

There are no known exceptions to this AntiPattern. It is always a bad idea to put individual data values into the session.

Refactorings

Use Beanify (found later in this chapter) to get the data that is in the session organized into classes. Remember to use principals of object-oriented design (one of the major reasons for this AntiPattern is developers forgetting these principals and building a giant flat dataspace in the session). The JavaBeans will typically be either model objects related to the business process the application is supporting or controller classes related to the way the user interface interacts with the underlying model.

Use this refactoring to get rid of the data used for application flow that is being kept in the session. Often data needed to manage the "process flow" of the application is kept in the session, which makes that data (and thus the application flow) subject to all the consequences of being stuck in the AntiPattern. Namely, any JSP in the application can override the way the application flows by writing different or, worse yet, wrong data into the session. Using the Introduce Delegate Controller refactoring (found later in this chapter) introduces a controller class that keeps track of the data needed to manage the application flow. In addition to removing data from the session, a lot of code can be removed from the JSPs.

This refactoring can be used to remove any navigational type data that might be stored in the session. Inexperienced or lazy developers will often put flags or other small pieces of data into the session to let subsequent pages know how to construct links. This practice can lead to hard-to-understand and -maintain user interfaces. Introduce Traffic Cop (found later in this chapter) will help unwind this mess and make things a lot more straightforward and easier to maintain.

Variations

The way this AntiPattern manifests will vary with the reasons that the data is kept in the session in the first place. There are three basic types of data kept in the session: application data to populate forms, application state data to manage processes, and data related to navigating through the pages of the application.

Application data kept in the session is usually something like a customer's name and address. This data is kept under keys like userName or address and is likely to run into conflicts with other JSPs that need to keep data with similar use. As described earlier, the data ends up being switched by both JSPs back and forth. When the data is retrieved and cast in the different contexts, there is a potential class cast exception if the data is of different types.

Application state data that is kept in the session is usually something like a flag indicating if the current user is logged in or not. The code in the JSPs usually looks like this: each user-sensitive JSP has a check for this flag, and if it's found the JSP is available; otherwise, it's not and the user is redirected to a login page. Application flow logic like this is best implemented in a controller instead of a JSP.

Finally, the session can end up being a place where navigational data is stored. For example, when a form is being filled in, some choices that the user makes can lead to different pages. As these choices are made, flags or other small indicators are placed into the session. JSPs retrieve these indicators and use them to render the HTML for the page differently. This kind of processing really belongs in a Traffic Cop or Delegate controller. When changes are made to the way this processing happens, the code in each of the JSPs that are written this way will have to be updated.

Example

Listing 4.3 shows a JSP caught in the Too Much Data in Session AntiPattern. Notice that there are several keys used here (message, ownerId, and so on) to keep track of all the data that has been placed into the session. There is also a lot of code used to manipulate the data in the session.

```
<%@ page import="java.util.*" %>
  <%
  String wrongLogin  = (String)session.getAttribute("message");
  Long ownerId = (Long)session.getAttribute("ownerId");
  Boolean validUser = (Boolean)session.getAttribute("validUser");
  // Make sure the user is OK.
  String userName = request.getParameter("uname");
  String passwd = request.getParameter("passwd");
  try {
    ownerId = DBAccess.getOwner(userName, passwd);
  } catch(Throwable t) {
    validUser = new Boolean(false);
    ownerId = null;
  }
  if(userName != null) {
    // Also set the user state to true or false.
    session.setAttribute("validUser", validUser);
    if(validUser.booleanValue() == true) {
      // Keep the owner's ID around in the session.
      session.setAttribute("ownerId", ownerId);
      // Remove the wrongLogin message since we did log in.
      session.removeAttribute("message");
      // If it's a valid user then redirect to HomePage
      response.sendRedirect("HomePage.jsp");
    } else {
      session.removeAttribute("ownerId");
      session.setAttribute("message",
              "User Name or Password incorrect, please reenter");
      response.sendRedirect("Login.jsp");
      return;
    }
  }
  %>
<html>
  <head>
    <title>iBank Login Page</title>
    <link rel="stylesheet" href="css/ibank.css" type="text/css" />
  </head>
  <body>
    <table border="0" cellspacing="0" cellpadding="0" summary="">
      <tr>
        <td style="align:center;width:121px;height:20px;">
          <img src="img/logo.gif" alt="iBank" border="0">
        </td>
      </tr>
```

Listing 4.3 Login.jsp. *(continued)*

```
        <tr>
          <td>
      <% if(null == wrongLogin) { %>
         Please Type Your User Name and Password Below.
          <% } else { %>
         <span style="color=#ff0000"><%=wrongLogin%></span>
          <% } %>
          </td>
        </tr>
      </table>
      <form name="loginForm" action="Login.jsp" method="post">
        <table>
          <tr>
            <td>User Name:</td>
            <td><input type="text" name="uname"/></td>
          </tr>
          <tr>
         <td>Password:</td>
            <td><input type="password" name="passwd"/></td>
          </tr>
          <tr>
         <td align="center" colspan="2">
              <input type="submit" name="Submit" value="Done"/>
         </td>
          </tr>
        </table>
      </form>
    </body>
  </html>
```

Listing 4.3 *(continued)*

The data for a User class is being kept in the session here. Inexperienced developers often miss the lack of encapsulation because they have not trained themselves to think that way yet. In this JSP, the user name and login status are kept in the session under keys. What happens if the application needs more data kept around about the user, for example, a banner welcoming the user with his or her full name? Just about every JSP would have to start managing a new keyed value in the session, say, usersFullName. To further complicate matters, what happens if another JSP, say, the registration page, happens to already be using that key? Unless the changes to add the banner are made in a very disciplined way, the registration page will almost certainly suffer from bugs because one of its keys has been manipulated elsewhere.

Notice also that this example is also conditionally rendering links to the next page as well as deciding where to forward to next based on data that is stored in the session. The big problems come up again in maintenance or enhancements. If one of the keys used by this page is added to the session by another page, this page will suffer and likely stop working.

Related Solutions

Struts (a project from Apache's Jakarta) is a great example of a way to keep data out of the session and in application objects. The Struts framework is an implementation of the MVC design pattern built using patterns that keep the JSP code out of this AntiPattern. For example, the ActionForm objects are *beanified* versions of sets of keys that would otherwise end up on the session. If you are in a position to be able to rewrite your UI, Struts is a great option that you should look at. If you are stuck in this AntiPattern and can't rewrite your UI, the best way out is to apply the refactorings recommended earlier.

Ad Lib TagLibs

Also Known As: Quirky Kitchen Sink

Most Frequent Scale: Architecture, Development

Refactoring: Beanify; Introduce Delegate Controller

Refactoring Type: Software

Root Causes: Ignorance, sloth

Unbalanced Forces: Functionality and resources

Anecdotal Evidence: "Hey, look, I can update the database while I'm generating some HTML."

Background

TagLibs are generally poorly understood and poorly implemented. Many of the examples that are available are not written with the MVC pattern in mind, instead the TagLibs try to be model and controller in addition to view. Like many of the other AntiPatterns in this chapter, Ad Lib TagLibs is borne from a misunderstanding of the role of TagLibs in the architectural landscape of J2EE. The TagLibs are part of the view for the application and are merely a convenience to help reuse HTML generating code. Developers that are starting to realize the problems inherent in having a lot of Java code in their JSPs often turn to TagLibs and repeat the same architectural mistakes that were made in the JSP; they just move the model or controller code into the TagLib from the JSP. While it is easier to find bugs when they occur in a TagLib than it is when the code is directly in the JSP, it is not easy to reuse model code that is embedded in a TagLib.

General Form

Ad Lib TagLibs usually takes the form of a big or very big class implementing each tag. The class does HTML generation and lots of business logic and often interacts with other TagLibs. If your tags interact with the HttpServletSession very often, perform involved calculations, or update the database, you are probably suffering from the Ad Lib TagLibs AntiPattern.

Symptoms and Consequences

You will notice that you are in this AntiPattern when your Tags become hard to use either because of bugs or because of the way they are hard-wired to work in only one situation.

- **Problems finding and fixing bugs.** While finding bugs in a TagLib class is often easier than finding the same bug in code embedded in a JSP, it is still harder to find the bug when it's in a TagLib, especially when the TagLib is implementing some business logic.
- **Inability to use new UI technologies.** If business logic or application flow logic is embedded in the TagLib, it will be difficult to put a new kind of user interface on the application because the business problem the application is supposed to solve is coded in part of the UI.
- **Difficulty in reuse.** When a TagLib is doing some HTML generation, some database access, and some application flow management, it will be very hard to put that tag into any JSP other than the one it was originally written for. The logic to access the database and manage the application flow is presumably specific to the particular JSP and will not be reusable in other JSPs.
- **Large number of attributes on the TagLib.** Another indicator that you are stuck in the Ad Lib TagLib AntiPattern is the number of attributes allowed on your tag. Typically what happens to cause the attribute count to grow is that

attempts are made to reuse the TagLib. With each new reuse attempt, something must be parameterized in order to generalize the TagLib to work in the situation. Sometimes that is a legitimate way to make the TagLib more reusable. More often than not, though, the TagLib will have big chunks of code that is only executed if one of the attributes is set. If your TagLibs have conditional code as described here, you are probably stuck in this AntiPattern.

- **Adding functionality introduces bugs.** With very large and complex TagLibs (as with most large and complex classes) adding functionality becomes very difficult to do without introducing bugs. If you are seeing bugs crop up with even minimal changes to your TagLibs, you are probably stuck in this pitfall.

Typical Causes

Inexperienced developers most commonly cause this AntiPattern, either through a lack of understanding or being stuck in habits formed around another technology.

- **Well-meaning lack of knowledge.** Typically, TagLibs end up stuck in this AntiPattern because developers know that they need to get the java code out of their JSPs. Mistakenly, they move the code wholesale from the JSP into a TagLib. Lack of understanding of MVC and the place of TagLibs in that pattern is one of the root causes of this AntiPattern.
- **Stuck in the past.** Developers new to J2EE from two-tier development systems often try to build a two-tier system with JSPs. When the Ad Lib TagLibs AntiPattern is caused by being stuck in the past, the JSPs are seen not only as the view but also as everything else—database access, business logic, application flow, and so on. All these other kinds of code end up in the TagLibs.

Known Exceptions

There are no known exceptions to Ad Lib TagLibs. But it is difficult sometimes to draw the line regarding what "business logic" is. Some developers think that all validation is business logic; others claim that making sure that a number field contains only numbers is a UI validation. So, as this debate rages, some of the data validation for your application might end up in a TagLib and be perfectly fine. In deciding if your TagLib code has crossed the line into this AntiPattern, ask yourself if the validation being performed involves more than one attribute. If so, that almost certainly belongs in the model classes. If the validation is simply involved in the conversion of the data from a String to an Integer, then that code can reside in either the view classes (that is, the TagLib) or in the model class. The important thing to avoid is putting obvious business logic into your TagLib code; for example, do not put balance calculations for an online store into a TagLib.

Refactorings

Refactoring Ad Lib TagLibs (found later in this chapter) occurs at two levels. First, we have to refactor the TagLibs themselves to get the business logic out of the tag and into either a model or controller class. Once that is done, we also have to refactor the JSP to use the tag according to its new design and make sure that the JSP will work properly with the changes.

Often tags caught in the Ad Lib TagLib AntiPattern will have model code and data kept either as part of the tag or in the session. To get out of the AntiPattern, the tag needs to be refactored to put this data and code together into a bean. In addition, the JSP that uses the Tag is likely placing some of the data into the session or into an attribute of the Tag. Appling the Beanify refactoring (found later in this chapter) to both the TagLib and all the JSPs that use it will help get your application out of this AntiPattern.

If the Tags in your application are used to manage the flow, then the Introduce Delegate Controller refactoring (found later in this chapter) will help you to properly move the controller code out of your tags and into a controller where it belongs.

Variations

This AntiPattern varies with the kind of code kept in the TagLib. If the code is related to the model or business logic, then the TagLib will tend to have a lot of database-oriented code. If, on the other hand, the TagLib has a lot of application-flow-type logic in it, then there will be code that conditionally creates links or conditionally forwards to other pages in the application. Depending on the kind of code that is in the TagLib, the consequences to understandability and maintainability can be mild or severe.

Example

Here is an example of a tag that is stuck in the Ad Lib TagLib AntiPattern. The tag processes payments for displaying in a table. This class renders a table containing the pending payments for the online bill payment customer. Rendering a table is a great task for a tag; running calculations and manipulating data is what has gone wrong with this tag. The first sign of problems is in the setPageContext method of the tag.

```
public void setPageContext(PageContext pageContext) {
  super.setPageContext(pageContext);
  UserContext uc = (UserContext)pageContext.getSession().
                    getAttribute(UserContext.USERCTX_KEY);
  Long ownerId = uc.getUserId();
  getData(ownerId);
}
```

Notice that data is being extracted from the session here. Extracting data from the session in a tag is not good practice. It becomes very hard to debug a tag or discover why its not working if part of the tag's information comes from the session and another part of the data comes to it via the attributes in the JSP. If the tag needs some data from the environment, it should be made explicit in the form of an attribute. When the tag is stuck in this AntiPattern, the bean must be explicitly referenced with a jsp:useBean tag. Here is the code for the JSP:

```
<td>
  <jsp:useBean id="userCtx" class="ibank.Web.UserContext"
               scope="session"/>
  <ibank:payments/>
</td>
```

The tag is easy to invoke but will be hard to maintain over time because the link between the jsp:useBean tag and the ibank:payments tag is not explicit. Someone later during a maintenance cycle could easily mistakenly remove the jsp:useBean tag and cause the ibank:payments tag to stop working.

Another issue it is necessary to address in this example code is writing template text from within a tag. It is much simpler to keep pure template text in your JSP. Here is the code for the addHeader method:

```
private void addHeader(StringBuffer buf) {
    buf.append("<tr>");
    buf.append("<th align=\"left\" width=\"275\">");
    buf.append("Payee Name</th>");
    buf.append("<th align=\"left\" width=\"128\">");
    buf.append("Date To Send</th>");
    buf.append("<th align=\"left\" width=\"128\">");
    buf.append("Amount</th></tr>");
}
```

This code is hard to maintain and even harder to get right. Because the HTML is coded in a Java class, it must be recompiled before you can look at the result and make sure that it looks good. If the width of 275 is not right for Payee Name, then you will have to recompile and redeploy it to change it to 280, and so on until you get the width right.

This Tag also has database access code. Remember that the tag is part of the view and should not be involved with accessing databases or performing business logic tasks. As a result of getting the data itself, this tag cannot be reused anywhere else. For example, in the online bill payment application, you want to be able to view the historical payments. Because this tag gets the pending payments from the database, it cannot be used to display the historical payments. One way to approach a solution is to add another parameter to the tag that tells it which kind of payment to retrieve and display. While that approach seems good on the surface, it will lead you further into this AntiPattern. Making the tag understand even more of the business logic of the application prevents that business logic from being reused elsewhere without copying and pasting. Adding that kind of code to the tag also further departs from the MVC approach.

The user's historical payments are passed into the tag instead of the pending payments. Reuse is one of the primary drives to get and keep controller code out of your tags.

Related Solutions

Ad Lib TagLibs comes at its root from the same issues that most of the AntiPatterns in this chapter stem from, not properly applying MVC concepts to building the code. So, the same types of solutions present themselves here in a slightly different form. The JSTL template library has many good examples of writing good TagLibs that are not mired in this AntiPattern. The URI-related i18n (internationalization) and formatting tags are very good. Struts is another source for some good tags.

Refactorings

This section documents the Refactorings referred to earlier in the AntiPatterns. The typical refactoring will help your code to migrate from where it is in whatever AntiPattern it is trapped in towards a better design. Most of the AntiPatterns in this chapter deal with developers not understanding MVC, and most of the refactorings focus on helping the code to become a better reflection of MVC.

Beanify. Data encapsulated with its functionality is one of the fundamental tenants of object-oriented programming. Beanify provides the mechanics for you to get unorganized data out of your session and organize it into a bean. Having your data encapsulated in a bean will improve the reliability and maintainability of your application.

Introduce Traffic Cop. An application that has all the navigational information hard-coded into the servlets and JSPs will be much harder to change than it should be. The Introduce Traffic Cop refactoring will help you to move all that navigational information out of the individual servlets and JSPs and place it into a central servlet.

Introduce Delegate Controller. When a single controller is responsible for all the application logic, the controller will be very hard to change or update. For any reasonably sized application, the class will become almost impossible to follow because it is so big. The Introduce Delegate Controller refactoring will help you to pull small interrelated pieces of functionality out of the overly big controller and into smaller controller classes. The big controller can then delegate that functionality to the smaller controller.

Introduce Template. JSP code is very hard to maintain when it is copied and pasted into several different JSPs. As with any other programming technology, copying and pasting leads to hard-to-change code. The Introduce Template refactoring provides practical help in getting the common parts of your JSP ready to be reused in a template.

Remove Session Access. Tags that depend on data in the session are hard to learn and use because they will fail to work if the data is not in the session. This is especially frustrating to developers trying to use the tag for the first time because it is not apparent that the data must be placed into the session. The Remove Session Access refactoring provides the mechanics that will help you to get the session access requirement out of your tags.

Remove Template Text. Servlets that have a lot of HTML encoded in them in the form of strings are hard to understand and maintain, which leads to difficult maintenance and a higher bug rate. The Remove Template Text refactoring will help you to get the HTML out of your servlets and into JSPs, where it can more easily be manipulated with tools that understand the syntax of HTML.

Introduce Error Page. Developers have a tendency to ignore the fact that the typical user does not know anything about Java and does not want to know. When a server-side exception is raised and is sent back to the user as a stack trace, the users will quickly lose confidence in the application. This refactoring will guide you through introducing error pages into your JSPs so that users will get simple error pages and not stack traces when server-side exceptions are thrown.

Beanify

You have code in your JSP that refers to data stored in the session.

Encapsulate the data into a JavaBean and use jsp:useBean to access the data.

```
<%
Boolean validUser = (Boolean)session.
                        getAttribute("validUser");
String buttonTitle = "Login";
String url = "Login.jsp";
if(null != validUser && validUser.booleanValue()) {
  buttonTitle = "Logout";
  url = "Logout.jsp";
}
%>
```

Listing 4.4 Before refactoring.

```
<jsp:useBean id="userCtx" class="ibank.web.UserContext"/>
...
<a class="BorderButton" href="${userCtx.nextNav}">
  ${userCtx.loginTitle}
</a>
```

Listing 4.5 After refactoring.

Motivation

Web designers typically create and maintain JSPs. Java developers build and maintain the business logic. The knowledge base of a Web designer does not typically include Java and the particulars of scriptlets, declarations, and expressions. Likewise, Java developers don't usually make the best Web designers. In order for this division of labor to be as efficient as possible, there needs to be as much division in the two aspects of the application as there is in the division of labor in creating it.

Even if our Web designers have an understanding of Java, the business logic should not be embedded in the JSPs. As has been discussed, embedding code in the JSP diminishes maintainability and clouds the division of labor. The JSP is intended to provide the user interface and should get data from a model and not have to have any business logic embedded in it.

Mechanics

Here are the steps to perform this refactoring:

- **Create a JavaBean to hold the data for the JSP. If you already have a bean you can reuse it.** Follow good OO practices when defining your beans. The data and functionality should be a logical package.
- **Add an attribute to the bean for each unique key used in a session.setAttribute( ) or session.getAttribute( ) call.** Start by looking through the JSPs for any calls to either of these methods. More than one bean class might be needed depending on how much data is stored in the session. Just make sure to keep in mind OO concepts when creating your beans.
- **Add a jsp:useBean action to the JSP.** Keep in mind that this will create the bean if it does not already exist and will use an existing instance if it is already there. Most of the time a controller creates the bean and places it in the session for the JSPs to use.
- **Remove all calls to session.getAttribute( ) and replace with expression language statements.** The expression language allows you to access the attributes of your beans without using any scriptlet code.
- **Remove all calls to session.setAttribute( ).** Depending on how far you are going with the refactoring, you should either be putting the data manipulation code into the delegate controller (if you are applying the Introduce Delegate Controller refactoring as well), or, if you do not have a delegate controller, replacing the setAttribute calls with jsp:setProperty tags.
- **Deploy and test.**

Example

In the following JSP, we see a lot of code. This kind of code is typical of JSPs stuck in the Too Much Code or Too Much Data in Session AntiPatterns. You could also see code like this in JSPs using TagLibs stuck in the Ad Lib TagLib AntiPattern. The idea of this refactoring is to encapsulate the data being manipulated in the session into a JavaBean. The following scriptlet is an example of what you might find in your JSPs.

```
<%
  String message  = (String)session.getAttribute("message");
  Boolean validUser = (Boolean)session.getAttribute("validUser");
...
  if(validUser.booleanValue() == true) {
    session.setAttribute("message",
                         "Wrong login please retype");
...
%>
...
<tr>
  <td>
    <% if(null == message) { %>
    Please Type Your User Name and Password below.
    <% } else { %>
```

```
      <span style="color=#ff0000"><%=message%></span>
      <% } %>
    </td>
  </tr>
```

The first step to making this JSP better is to create a JavaBean to hold the data that you will remove from the session. The next step is to add the properties that you remove from the session to the new bean. The two properties in this example are extracted and placed into a JavaBean like this.

```
public class UserContext {
    private boolean validUser = false;
    private String message = null;

    public UserContext() {
    }

    public void setValidUser(boolean flag) { validUser = flag; }
    public boolean isValidUser() { return validUser; }

    public void setMessage(String msg) { message = msg; }
    public String getMessage() { return message; }
}
```

Next, use the jsp:useBean action to create an instance of the new bean and rework the rest of the page to remove any use of getAttribute or setAttribute, and instead use the bean that you created. Here is the code for the JSP after these steps are applied:

```
<jsp:useBean id="userCtx" class="ibank.Web.UserContext"
             scope="session"/>
...
<tr>
  <td>
    <c:choose>
      <c:when test="${userCtx.validUser}>
    <span style="color=#000000>
      </c:when>
      <c:otherwise>
    <span style="color=#ff0000>
      </c:otherwise>
    </c:choose>
      ${userCtx.message}
    </span>
  </td>
</tr>
```

The *choose* tag from the JSTL was used to pick the color. Whenever possible, it is preferable to use the JSTL over scriptlet code so that you better isolate the Web developers from having to understand Java. The JSTL was specifically designed to look a lot like JavaScript, which Web developers are already familiar with.

Finally, you must deploy and test the new code. Because this example is small, there was not a significant reduction in the size and complexity of the page. In a larger, more complex page however, the amount of simplification can be significant.

Introduce Traffic Cop

You have several hrefs that explicitly name a JSP in your application. Furthermore, the links are conditional or in some other way dependent on application logic.

Move the forwards and the condition checks out of the JSP and into a controller.

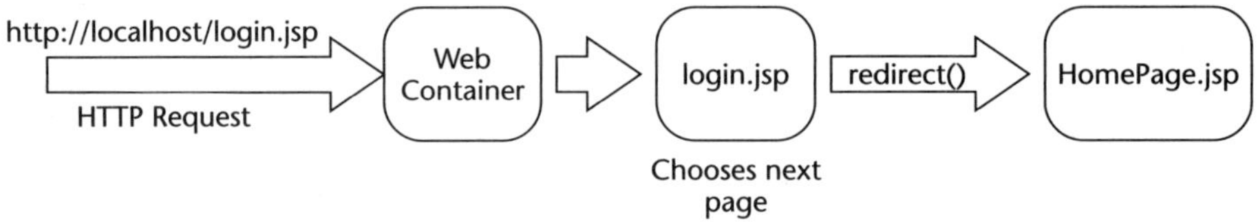

Figure 4.4 Before refactoring.

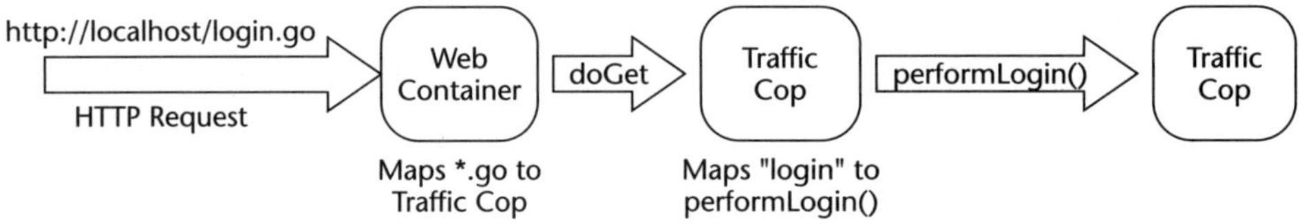

Figure 4.5 After refactoring.

Motivation

Putting navigational information in JSPs makes a Web site harder to maintain. One reason is that the "site map" is embedded into the various JSPs and will be very hard to change unless each JSP is reviewed. This architecture makes the site hard to change because the way that users move through the site is spread out over all the JSPs instead of being maintained in one spot.

When the site map is maintained in one central spot, the application becomes easier to maintain and change. Organizational changes, such as moving JSPs into subdirectories, becomes as simple as updating the central repository that the Traffic Cop uses. This has the added benefit of the site layout being easy to see.

Mechanics

Here are the steps to perform this refactoring.

1. *Build a page transition diagram that depicts the links between your pages.* While this step is not strictly required, it is very helpful when you are trying to make sure that all page transitions are happening properly. As an alternative, you can use HTTPUnit or Cactus (testing tools based on JUnit) to build tests asserting the current navigational structure of the application and run them periodically as the pages are refactored.
2. *Create a Servlet that will act as your Traffic Cop and will front the requests made to the application.* The Traffic Cop will have all the navigational information for your application and will use that information to correctly redirect each request made.
3. *Initialize this Traffic Cop with the navigational information captured earlier in your diagram.* Using a HashMap is an easy and quick means to do this. The keys are just strings, and the values are the names of the JSP pages.
4. *Name each of the arcs or lines between the pages.* Action-oriented names work best, such as *login* or *showPendingPayments*. These are the names of the processes your application will be performing for the user.
5. *Replace any direct references to other JSPs with the names of the arcs.* Look for jsp:include, jsp:forward, and/or href attributes. Do no more than can be easily verified in each iteration through this process. You want to be able to easily verify that what you have done still works when you are done so, do the refactoring in manageable chunks.

6. *Move any conditional checks from the JSP into your Traffic Cop.* You can use the Delegate Control refactoring to keep the Traffic Cop from becoming unwieldy. If your Traffic Cop has too many lines of code, it will be very hard to maintain and understand.
7. *Update your Web.xml file to register your Traffic Cop.* Register your new Traffic Cop Servlet to intercept all requests that conform to a certain pattern so that your Web resources (JSPs, other servlets, and so on) can ensure that their requests will be routed though your Traffic Cop. It is convenient to use a pattern that ends in an action-oriented word like *.go or *.do.
8. *Deploy and test.*
9. *Repeat until the whole site map is implemented in your Traffic Cop.* This step is, of course, optional; this refactoring can be done all at once or piecemeal, as makes sense. Make sure that you test thoroughly, though, because it will be hard to find a bug related to this refactoring three months later (unit tests are the key to refactoring).

Example

Let's start with ViewPayments.jsp and look at how the links from this page are implemented. Notice that several of the links are hard-coded. Applying the Introduce Traffic Cop refactoring will make this page much more resilient to change.

```
<table border="0" cellspacing="0" cellpadding="0" summary="">
  <tr>
    <td style="align:center;width:121px;height:20px;">
      <img src="img/logo.gif" alt="iBank" border="0">
    </td>
    <td style="text-align:center;width:165px;height:20;">
    <%
      Boolean validUser = (Boolean)session.getAttribute("validUser");
      if(null != validUser && validUser.booleanValue()) {
    %>
      <a class="BorderButton" href="Logout.jsp">Logout</a>
    <% } else { %>
      <a class="BorderButton" href="Login.jsp">Login</a>
    <% } %>
    </td>
  </tr>
</table>
```

Notice that the validation check for the user and the pages to navigate to are directly embedded in this page. This makes the pages hard to maintain and resistant to change. Building a site navigation tree is the first step in refactoring this page. Figure 4.6 shows the map for this page. This is a subset of the whole site; it's fine to start with a subset of the pages in the application or to even refactor one page at a time.

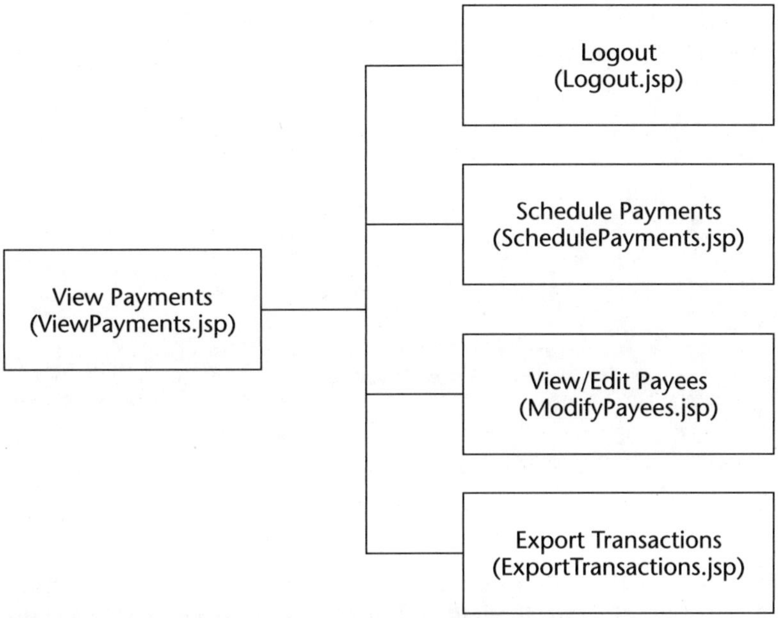

Figure 4.6 ViewPayments.jsp navigation map.

Test cases are also needed to ensure that this refactoring is implemented properly. Here is the code for a Cactus test:

```
class ViewPaymentsCactusTest extends ServletTestCase {
    . . .
    // Uses the Cactus integration with HttpUnit to do some
    // assertions about the titles of returned pages.
    public void
        endViewPaymentsNav(com.metaware.httpunit.WebResponse response)
        throws Exception {
        WebLinks links[] = response.getLinks();
        for(int i = 0;i < links.length;i++) {
            WebResponse response = links[i].click();
            String expectedTitle =
                (String)expectedTitles.get(link.getText());
            String title = response.getTitle();
            assertEquals(expectedTitle, title);
        }
    }

    public void setUp() throws Exception {
        expectedTitles("Logout", "Logout of The Application");
        expectedTitles("Login", "Login to The Application");
        expectedTitles("Schedule Payments", "Schedule Payments");
    }
    . . .
}
```

Notice that the Cactus test class navigates away from this page via the links found. As the links are traversed, an assertion is made that the page returned has the correct title. These tests will ensure that the application will continue to function as it did previously as the refactoring proceeds. Now that a test is in place and can be run against the refactored JSP, the page can finally be refactored.

```
<table border="0" cellspacing="0" cellpadding="0" summary="">
  <tr>
    <td style="align:center;width:121px;height:20px;">
      <img src="img/logo.gif" alt="iBank" border="0">
    </td>
    <td style="text-align:center;width:165px;height:20;">
      <a class="BorderButton" href="trafficCop?toDo=logout">
        Logout
      </a>
    </td>
  </tr>
</table>
```

The href now refers to something called trafficCop and is passing a single parameter toDo and setting its value to logout. To make this link work, we have to put the navigation into the Traffic Cop class. Here is the code that will cause the navigation to happen properly:

```
public void init() throws ServletException {
    uriMap.put("logout", "Logout.jsp");
}

public void doGet(HttpServletRequest request,
                  HttpServletResponse response)
    throws ServletException, IOException {
    String toDo = (String)request.getAttribute("toDo");
    String newURI = (String)uriMap.get(toDo);
    Boolean validUser =
        (Boolean)request.getSession().getAttribute("validUser");
    RequestDispatcher reqDisp = null;
    if(null != validUser && validUser.booleanValue()) {
        reqDisp = request.getRequestDispatcher(newURI);
    } else {
        reqDisp = request.getRequestDispatcher("index.jsp");
    }
    reqDisp.forward(request , response);
}
```

This code initializes the uriMap with the abstract name logout that you expect to get in your doGet method. This step is encoding the site map into the Traffic Cop. In doGet, you retrieve the attribute and look up the URI you should go to. You moved the code that was in the JSP into the Traffic Cop so if the user is valid, then you link to logout. If the user is not valid, you forward to your mapped URI; if the user is invalid, you send him or her back to the welcome page. All this code is specific to the logout value for the toDo attribute. In real systems, there will be several different values that will come in for this key. The doGet method could have an if/if else/else block to manage this or you could apply the Introduce Delegate Controller refactoring while applying this refactoring.

Now, to make this all work you have to update the Web.xml file to get trafficCop requests sent to your Traffic Cop servlet. To accomplish this, the following elements need to be added to the Web.xml file for the Web application.

```
<servlet>
  <servlet-name>TrafficCop</servlet-name>
  <servlet-class>TrafficCop</servlet-class>
</servlet>
...
<servlet-mapping>
  <servlet-name>TrafficCop</servlet-name>
  <url-pattern>trafficCop</url-pattern>
</servlet-mapping>
```

The final step is to deploy and test the application. Once you are satisfied that your application works as it should, you can proceed to the rest of your JSPs (one at a time) and refactor them to take advantage of your new Traffic Cop. Make sure to consider the Introduce Delegate Controller refactoring before you finish because it is very helpful to apply both refactorings at the same time, especially if the application has several JSPs.

Introduce Delegate Controller

Your code to manage application flow is one big if/else if/else block and is impossible to maintain.

Create specialized controllers that can be delegated to.

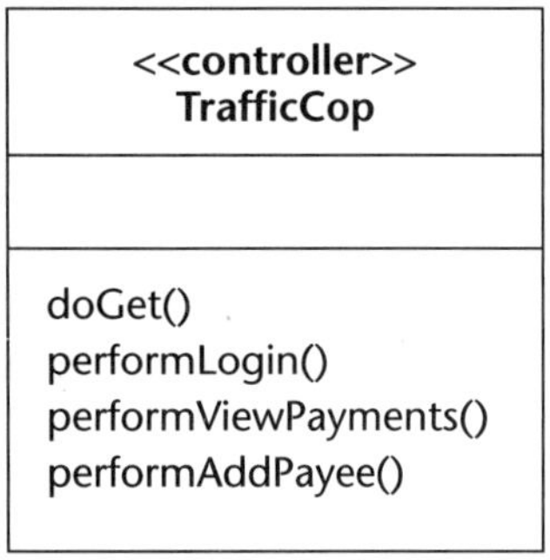

Figure 4.7 Before refactoring.

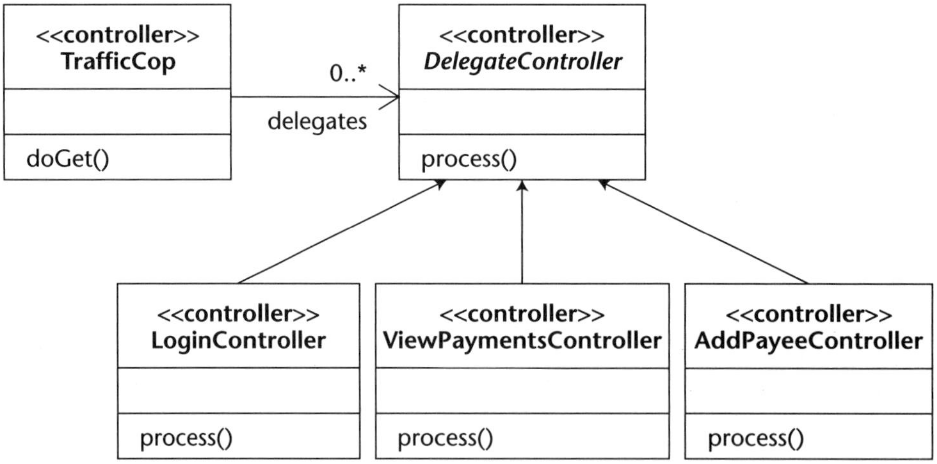

Figure 4.8 After refactoring.

Motivation

It is never a good idea to have a "kitchen sink" type class where everything in the world is thrown into one method. In big systems, unless there is a delegating mechanism, the Traffic Cop will become a kitchen sink. Even if the system is not that big there can be an unmanageable amount of code in the doGet and doPost methods on the Traffic Cop.

This refactoring will help to normalize the code into an easier-to-maintain set of classes that together accomplish the same thing but in a much more manageable way. Look at Figure 4.9 for an architectural diagram of what the outcome of this refactoring will look like.

Each request that comes into the Traffic Cop is delegated to one of the delegate controllers which handles all the state changes on the model objects as well as finding the JSP to forward to. Prior to applying this refactoring, all the functionality contained in the delegate controllers must be implemented in the Traffic Cop, which makes that class unwieldy at best and impossible to maintain at worst.

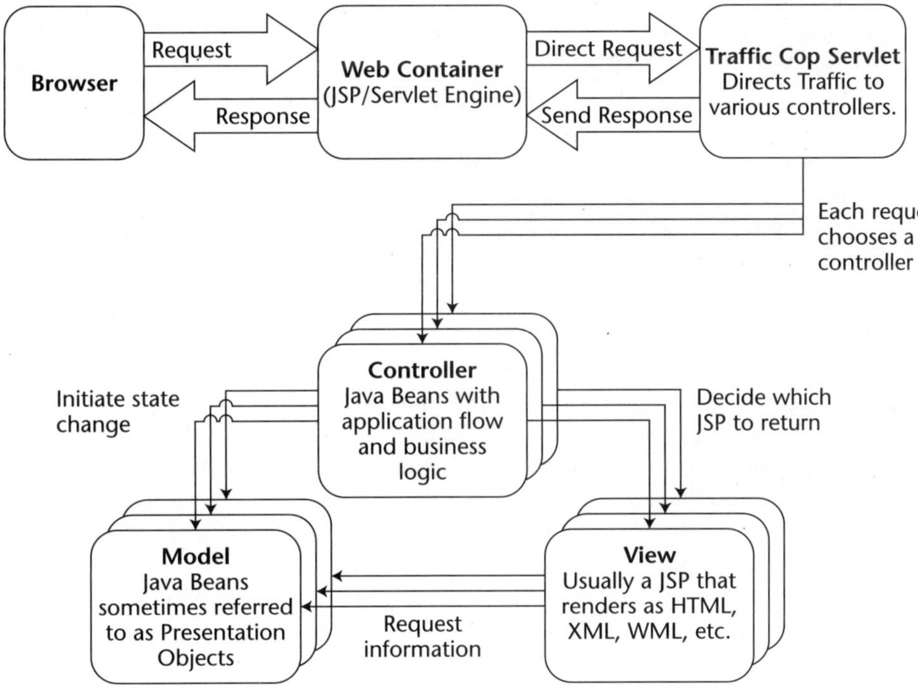

Figure 4.9 Controller delegation.

Mechanics

Here are the steps to perform this refactoring:

1. *Define an interface with a single method that will perform the delegated behavior.* Choose a method name such as *process* or something similar to capture the active nature of this method. The method needs at least the request and response objects as arguments. It is also good to include some indicator of why this delegate was chosen. This argument depends on the strategy chosen to key the delegates. See the example for further discussion of this topic.
2. *Build a delegate controller that implements the interface for each conditional statement in the main method of the Traffic Cop.* This is not intended to say that each if statement needs a new controller, but rather to say that each group of functionality that is chosen is based on the state of the system. The example has more detail about how to do this step.
3. *Copy the code from the conditional branch into the body of the newly defined method.* Clean up the code so that it uses only the parameters passed into the process method. This step can require a bit of refactoring of the Traffic Cop; resist adding additional instance variables to the delegate or additional parameters to the process method, though.
4. *Add a Map instance variable to the Traffic Cop to hold the group of delegate controllers.* The controllers are keyed on the subject of the conditional statements. The subject for the conditional is often a string that comes in on the request as part of the URL. These strings are usually the names of the arcs between pages that were discussed in the Introduce Traffic Cop refactoring. See the example for more detail.
5. *Create an instance of the newly defined controller in the init method and add it to the map.* Each controller will be instantiated and placed into the map while the Traffic Cop is being initialized. At some point, you might consider putting this information into a configuration file and making the initialization code for the Traffic Cop generic to just loop over a list of class names, instantiating an instance of the class and placing it into the map under a key that is also kept in the configuration file.
6. *Replace the code in the Traffic Cop in the body of the conditional with a call to the delegate controller.* Use the map and the key defined in the init method to find the controller. The code in the conditional was copied into the delegate controller; all we are doing in this step is replacing the copied code with a call to the controller.
7. *Deploy and test.*
8. *Repeat for each delegate controller needed.*

Example

This example will show the steps to take in a typical Traffic Cop implementation that is way too complex and bloated to move its code to several delegate controllers. Here is the code that will be refactored with the conditionals and code in place:

```
public class MyTrafficCop {
...
public void doGet(HttpServletRequest request,
                  HttpServletResponse response)
        throws ServletException, IOException {
        String toDo = (String)request.getAttribute("toDo");
        String newURI = (String)uriMap.get(toDo);
        Boolean validUser = (Boolean)request.getSession().
            getAttribute("validUser");
        String userName = (String)request.getSession().
            getAttribute("userName");
        if(toDo.equals("logout")) {
            RequestDispatcher reqDisp = null;
            if(null != validUser && validUser.booleanValue()) {
                reqDisp = request.getRequestDispatcher(newURI);
            } else {
                reqDisp = request.getRequestDispatcher("index.jsp");
            }
        } else if(toDo.equals("viewPayments")) {
            List payments = getPayments(userName);
            request.getSession().addAttribute("payments", payments);
        }
        reqDisp.forward(request, response);
    }
...
}
```

This is a limited example of what would be required in an entire application but it serves to illustrate this refactoring. The rest of the code can be found in the code available on the companion Web site for this book.

The first step in this refactoring is to build an interface that each of the delegate controllers will implement. The following code for the interface defines one method of accomplishing this process that takes the expected parameters as well as a string. The *name* parameter is passed by the Traffic Cop servlet to the delegate controller so that the delegate can know why it was chosen if it needs to.

```
public interface ForwardController {
    /**
     * This method processes the request and returns a string that
     * tells the controller the name of the place to go next.
     */
    public String process(HttpServletRequest request,
                          HttpServletResponse response,
                          String name) throws ServletException;
}
```

Next, you must create a controller that implements the ForwardController interface for each of the conditional statements in the doGet method. The first controller in this example is the ViewPaymentsController delegate. The code from the Traffic Cop related to viewing the payments needs to be copied into the process method on the ViewPaymentsController. Remember that you need to move all the code in the Traffic Cop to the delegate. If entire methods are copied, they will often need to have their signatures changed so the new method will have access to the session.

```
public String process(HttpServletRequest request,
                      HttpServletResponse response,
                      String name) throws ServletException {
    HttpSession session = request.getSession();
    String retVal = "view.payments";
    String name = (String)session.
        getAttribute(Constants.USER_NAME_KEY);
    // Perform a query and get the data.
    getPayments(name, session);
    return retVal;
}
```

Next, you have to refactor the Traffic Cop code so that it takes advantage of the new controller. Here is the new code for the doGet method:

```
public void doGet(HttpServletRequest request,
                 HttpServletResponse response)
    throws ServletException, IOException {
    // Process the request.
    String requestURI = request.getRequestURI();
    // Find the name of this request.
    int lastDot = requestURI.lastIndexOf(".go");
    int lastSlash = requestURI.lastIndexOf('/');
    String name = requestURI.substring(lastSlash + 1, lastDot);
    ForwardController fc = (ForwardController)controllerMap.get(name);
    if(null == fc) {
        throw new ServletException("Poor configuration, there is no " +
                                   "controller avalible to process the " +
                                    name + ".go request");
    }
    //Find the URI to forward to.
    String responseKey = fc.process(request, response, name);
    String newURI = (String)uriMap.get(responseKey);
    if(null == newURI) {
        throw new ServletException("Poor configuration, there is no " +
                                     "uri to forward the " +
                                     responseKey + " response from the " +
                                     " controller.");
    }
    RequestDispatcher reqDisp = request.getRequestDispatcher(newURI);
    reqDisp.forward(request, response);
}
```

Finally, you need to deploy and test the application. When you are satisfied that the newly placed delegate controller is functioning properly move on to the next conditional from your old Traffic Cop implementation. If you are familiar with Struts, you might notice that this is very similar, at least in concept, to the Action servlet that comes with Struts. If you are in a position to be able to switch your application over to Struts, then by all means do so; you will not have to maintain this code if you do. But if you are not able to make the switch, this refactoring will clean up your JSPs and your Traffic Cop as well.

Introduce Template

You have copied and pasted pieces of JSP code into many different JSPs.

Introduce reusable pieces of JSP and include them instead of copying and pasting the code.

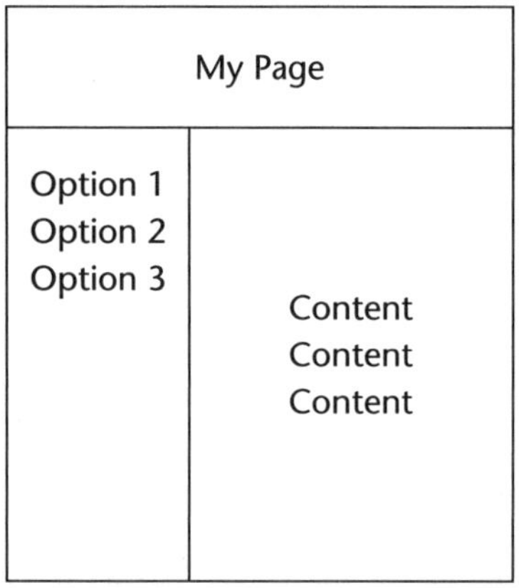

Figure 4.10 Before refactoring.

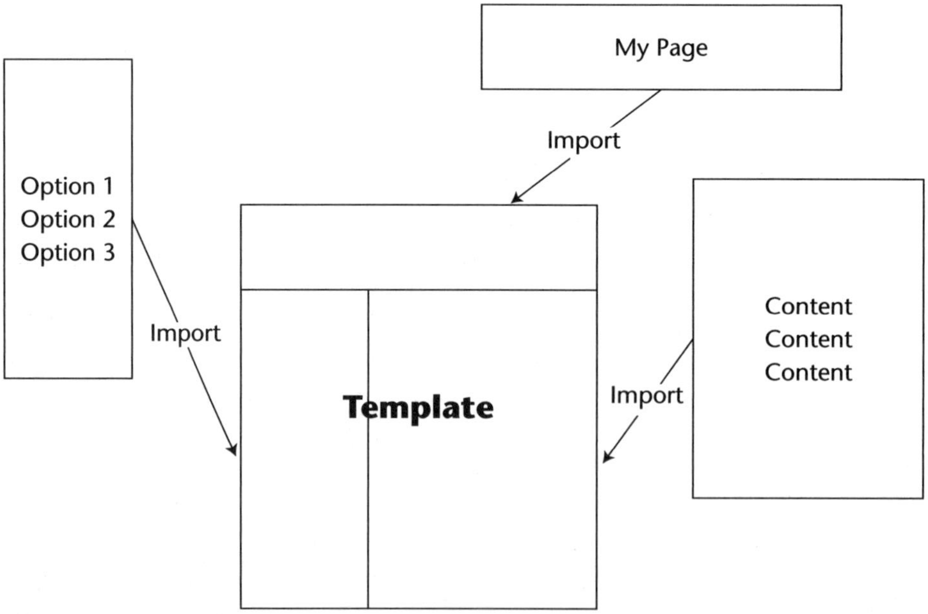

Figure 4.11 After refactoring.

Motivation

Applications should strive for conformity across the different pages that compose that application. Often, in an attempt to achieve that conformity, pieces of HTML/JSP are copied and pasted between pages. When the application changes, each place that the JSP code has been copied must be updated. This process often leads to confusing and hard-to-use UIs that perform and look the same across most, but not all, of the breadth of an application. Use this refactoring to capture the reusable pieces of the UI.

It is a good idea to have applied the Beanify, Introduce Delegate Controller, and/or Introduce Traffic Cop refactorings to remove as much Java as possible from the JSPs before starting this refactoring. It is important to remove as much Java code as you can from your JSPs because it is much more difficult to build templates from JSPs that include scriptlets.

Mechanics

Here are the steps to perform this refactoring:

1. *Identify the sections of your user interface that you want to be common*. Typical common sections are headers, footers, and menus along the right and/or left side of the pages.
2. *Identify pages that currently implement these pieces of the UI*. It's best to have a repeatable unit test for the pages that you start with so that the refactoring can proceed confidently.
3. *Move the common pieces into their own files*. Make sure that you use the current pages code as a starting point.
4. *Identify the simplest page that can use the templates and start there*. It is a good idea to perform this refactoring one page at a time to help avoid missing any subtitles on a particular page.
5. *Remove the code that implements the common piece from the JSP*.
6. *Include the template in the JSP. Use jsp:include or the JSTL import tag*.
7. *Deploy and test. It is a good idea to deploy and test for each JSP you refactor in this way*. In some simple cases, you can replace each of the common pieces of the UI in a single JSP before moving on.
8. *Repeat for each common element and each JSP that will use the templates*. It is a good idea to deploy and test the application, at least for every page if not for each template placement.

Example

In this example, you will add templates to the user interface for iBank, a fictitious online bank that allows its customers to pay their bills online. The UI for iBank has two sections that should be common: the banner across the top and the menu that is on the left side. For this example, you will refactor two JSPs: the ViewPayments.jsp and

HomePage.jsp. Here is the code for the menu that was copied into both JSPs. There is other code that is copied into both JSPs, but for brevity it is not all shown.

```
<table>
  <tr>
    <td>
      <a href="NotImplemented.jsp">Schedule Payments</a></td>
  </tr>
  <tr>
    <td><a href="ViewPayments.jsp">View/Edit Payments</a></td>
  </tr>
  <tr>
    <td><a href="NotImplemented.jsp">View/Edit Payees</a></td>
  </tr>
  <tr>
    <td>
      <a href="NotImplemented.jsp">Export Transactions</a>
    </td>
  </tr>
</table>
```

The first step is to identify the common elements, which you have already done. The next step is to identify the pages that currently implement these pieces. You have also done that, and the two pages you will start with are ViewPayments.jsp and HomePage.jsp. The next step is to make a template for the common pieces that you will use. You will start with the menu and move it to a file called Menu.jsp. You will then replace the menu code in one of the JSPs (start with HomePage.jsp because it is a simple page) with one line of code, like this:

```
<jsp:include page="Menu.jsp"/>
```

The next step is to deploy and test the application. After you are sure the refactoring has been successful, move on to the next piece of the UI that you want to be common. Next, you move the content from the HomePage.jsp into a new file called HomePageContent.jsp. Here is the code for the HomePageContent.jsp:

```
<table border="0" cellspacing="0" cellpadding="0" summary="">
  <tr>
    <td style="align:center;width:121px;height:20px;">
      <img src="img/logo.gif" alt="iBank" border="0">
    </td>
    <td style="text-align:center;width:165px;height:20;">
      <%
      Boolean validUser = (Boolean)session.
                                   getAttribute("validUser");
      if(null != validUser && validUser.booleanValue()) {
      %>
      <a class="BorderButton" href="Logout.jsp">Logout</a>
      <% } else { %>
```

```
        <a class="BorderButton" href="Login.jsp">Login</a>
        <% } %>
      </td>
    </tr>
  </table>
```

Then, place a fresh import into the HomePage.jsp file, like this:

```
<jsp:include page="HomePageContent.jsp"/>
```

Creating the HomePageContent.jsp file and setting up the jsp:include was very straightforward in this example. Most of the time it will be more complex to move the code out of the original JSP and into something that can be included, especially if there are scriptlets in the code. Typically, what happens is that the code in the scriptlet will refer to or make use of variables that are declared elsewhere in the page, which will create a dependency between what should be moved and the rest of the JSP. The best way to work around this issue is to vigorously apply the other refactorings in this chapter to remove as much code as you can from your JSPs before you try to put them into the template.

Remove Session Access

You have code in your tag that uses the session to access data.

Change the tag so that the required data is passed in as a parameter.

```
public void setPageContext(PageContext pageContext) {
  super.setPageContext(pageContext);
  MyStuff stuff = (MyStuff)pageContext.getSession().
                    getAttribute("MyStuff");
  doStuff(stuff);
}
```

Listing 4.6 Before refactoring.

```
public MyStuff getStuff() {
  return stuff;
}
public void setStuff(MyStuff stuff) {
  this.stuff = stuff;
}
public void setPageContext(PageContext pageContext) {
  super.setPageContext(pageContext);
}
```

Listing 4.7 After refactoring.

Motivation

Accessing data stored in the session from your TagLib causes maintenance headaches and often leads to unintended consequences when the data in the session changes. The more the session is used by the tag, the more brittle the coupling becomes until any change you make in any JSP (or controller that manipulates the session) causes problems in the tags.

Having the tag use data directly from the session also inhibits reuse of the tag. If the tag accesses the data directly from the session instead of having it passed in via an attribute, the tag will only be useful with the set of data in the session.

Mechanics

Here are the steps to perform this refactoring:

1. *Identify the data that is being accessed through the session.* Look for calls to getAttribute or setAttribute in your servlets for the data that you are keeping in the session.
2. *Add an attribute to your tag for each piece of data.* Each of the attributes in the session can become a get/set pair and an instance variable on your tag. Refactor the remainder of your code to use the instance variables you have created. Keep in mind that the tag might not need the exact data that it is getting from the session. Look for what your tag is actually using in rendering the HTML and seek to provide that data as a property. Update your tld file to reflect the new attributes you have defined on your tag.
3. *Update your JSP to pass in the required data.* Remember to use the expression language instead of java expressions.
4. *Deploy and test.*

Example

Let's take a closer look at PaymentsTag to illustrate this refactoring. The tag is currently getting the user context from the session and then using that JavaBean to get at the data it needs to render the HTML. Here is the initial content of the setPageContext method.

```
public void setPageContext(PageContext pageContext) {
  super.setPageContext(pageContext);
  UserContext uc = (UserContext)pageContext.getSession().
                     getAttribute(UserContext.USERCTX_KEY);
  Long ownerId = uc.getUserId();
  getData(ownerId);
}
```

The first step is to identify the data that is being used from the session and turn that into a property on the tag. The tag is currently getting the UserContext from the session. The next step is to add an attribute to your TagLib to get the data passed into the tag instead of having to retrieve it from the session.

One approach to applying this refactoring would be just simply pass the UserContext instance as an argument into the tag. While that approach would work, if we dig a little deeper, you can see that the Tag is not really interested in the UserContext at all but instead is interested in the ownerId value. And taking it a step further, you can see that the only reason that the tag needs the ownerId is to get the list of Payment objects from the getData method. And with this you finally arrive at what the Tag actually needs, the list of Payment objects. So, instead of using brute force when applying the steps, spend some time thinking through what your tag really needs to render the HTML.

To fix this tag, a straightforward moving of ownerId to a property is not what is needed. Instead, you want to have the payments collection passed to this tag. As a side benefit of doing this properly, you can get rid of the query that is being executed by this tag. Remember that tags are part of the view and should try not to have model- or controller-oriented code. With this change, the getData method can be removed from this tag. So with all that in mind, we arrive at the following code.

```
public void setPageContext(PageContext pageContext) {
  super.setPageContext(pageContext);
}
public void setPayments(List payments) {
  this.payments = payments;
}
public List getPayments() {
  return payments;
}
```

The next step is to update the tld file to reflect the new attribute that has been defined on the tag. Here is the relevant piece of the updated tld file for reference:

```
<tag>
  <name>payments</name>
  <tag-class>ibank.web.PaymentsTag</tag-class>
  <body-content>JSP</body-content>
  <description>
    Displays the owners payments in a table
  </description>
  <attribute>
    <name>paymentLists</name>
    <required>true</required>
    <rtexprvalue>false</rtexprvalue>
  </attribute>
</tag>
```

The next step is to update the JSP to use the new tag appropriately. Here is the invocation of the tag:

```
<iBank:payments paymentList="${userCtx.pendingPayments}">
```

Finally, the JSP and Tag are deployed and tested. When you are sure that your tag functions properly for the current JSP, move on to the next until you have successfully updated each JSP to use the new tag.

Remove Template Text

You have code that merely writes out large amounts of template text.

Move the template text back into the JSP and have the tag build only the HTML that involves calculations or other programming tasks.

```
private void addHeader(StringBuffer buf) {
  buf.append("<tr>");
  buf.append("<th align=\"left\" width=\"275\">");
  buf.append("Payee Name</th>");
  buf.append("<th align=\"left\" width=\"128\">");
  buf.append("Date To Send</th>");
  buf.append("<th align=\"left\" width=\"128\">");
  buf.append("Amount</th></tr>");
}
```

Listing 4.8 Before refactoring.

```
<tr>
  <th align="left" width="275">Payee Name</th>
  <th align="left" width="128">Date To Send</th>
  <th align="left" width="128">Amount</th>
<tr>
```

Listing 4.9 After refactoring.

Motivation

It is hard to maintain template text in a tag so it is best to leave it out of the tag and in the JSP. For example, in the code at the beginning of this refactoring, if someone decided that using a bold font was better than using the <th> element, this code would have to change and subsequently be recompiled and redeployed before it could be tested. There is also the hassle of making sure we get the syntax right before we deploy the application. For example, what if instead of switching to bold, the class of the element was to be specified as font-family:Arial,sans-serif; font-weight:bolder; font-color:#663300;? Our code would have to change to look like the following:

```
private void addHeader(StringBuffer buf) {
  buf.append("<tr>");
  buf.append("<th align=\"left\" width=\"275\">");
  buf.append("Payee Name</th>");
  buf.append("<th align=\"left\" width=\"128\" ");
  buf.append("class=\"font-family:Arial, sans-serif;");
  buf.append("font-weight:bolder; font-color:#663300;\">");
  buf.append("Date To Send</th>");
  buf.append("<th align=\"left\" width=\"128\">");
  buf.append("Amount</th></tr>");
}
```

Notice that the specification of the class for the second heading cell is broken up into many lines. While this makes the line much easier to read in Java, it is harder to make sure that the specification has good syntax for the browser. Many subtle mistakes have been caused by template text in a tag having hard-to-see syntax errors embedded in the strings. It is best to keep this kind of text in the JSP where it is more straightforward to deal with.

Mechanics

Here are the steps to perform this refactoring.

1. *Identify the template text that can be moved.* Some template text should not be moved. For example, the template text that is repeated with each iteration should be kept in the tag if your tag iterates over a collection.
2. *Put the template text into all the JSPs that invoke this tag.* If there are many, you should consider using the Introduce Template refactoring discussed earlier in this chapter.
3. *Remove the code from the tag that was generating the template text.*
4. *Deploy and test.*

Example

Let's go back to the PaymentsTag.java and ViewPayments.jsp to see how to accomplish this refactoring. The first step is to identify the template text that can be moved from the tag. Here is some sample code in the PaymentsTag.java file that is writing template text out to the response:

```
private void addHeader(StringBuffer buf) {
    buf.append("<tr>");
    buf.append("<th align=\"left\" width=\"275\">");
    buf.append("Payee Name</th>");
    buf.append("<th align=\"left\" width=\"128\">");
    buf.append("Date To Send</th>");
    buf.append("<th align=\"left\" width=\"128\">");
    buf.append("Amount</th></tr>");
    }
```

This method has no function other than to write out the header for the table. It is much better to remove this kind of code from the tag and place it in the JSP instead. The next step is to put the template text back into the JSP. The JSP originally looked like this:

```
<td>
  <ibank:payments payments="${userContext.pendingPayments}"/>
</td>
```

And it is changed to look like this:

```
<td>
  <table>
    <tr>
     <th align="left" width="275">Payee Name</th>
     <th align="left" width="128">Date To Send</th>
     <th align="left" width="128">Amount</th>
    <tr>
    <ibank:payments payments="${userCtx.pendingPayments}"/>
  </table>
</td>
```

The JSP has become longer, but now you can use a WYSIWYG (What You See Is What You Get) JSP/HTML editor to perform maintenance on this part of your JSP instead of having to update anything in the tag. HTML is more natural in JSP than it is encoded into strings in Java code anyway.

Next, you have to tackle the Java code for PaymentsTag. Start with the setPageContext method. The only thing this method was doing was getting a handle on the ownerId, and since you have eliminated your need for this data, that method can be completely deleted. This would be a good time to perform a compile and test cycle.

Next, you need to look at the doEndTag and see how it changes. The initial code looked like this:

```
public int doEndTag() throws JspException {
  StringBuffer buf = new StringBuffer("<table>");
  addHeader(buf);
  addPayments(buf);
  addFooter(buf);
  buf.append("</table>");
  try {
    pageContext.getOut().print(buf.toString());
  } catch(IOException ioe) {
    throw new JspException(ioe.getMessage());
  }
  return EVAL_PAGE;
}
```

You can now safely remove all the code that was generating template text. In particular, you can remove the addHeader and addFooter methods as well as the open and closing table elements. Notice that the new version of the JSP has all this code in it.

The new code is much simpler. The only responsibility left for the tag is to render the table rows for each payment. Here is the new code for the doEndTag method:

```
public int doEndTag() throws JspException {
  StringBuffer buf = new StringBuffer();
  addPayments(buf);
  try {
    pageContext.getOut().print(buf.toString());
  } catch(IOException ioe) {
    throw new JspException(ioe.getMessage());
  }
  return EVAL_PAGE;
}
```

Introduce Error Page

You have JSPs that return a stack trace to your user.

Create an error page and add an error page directive to each JSP.

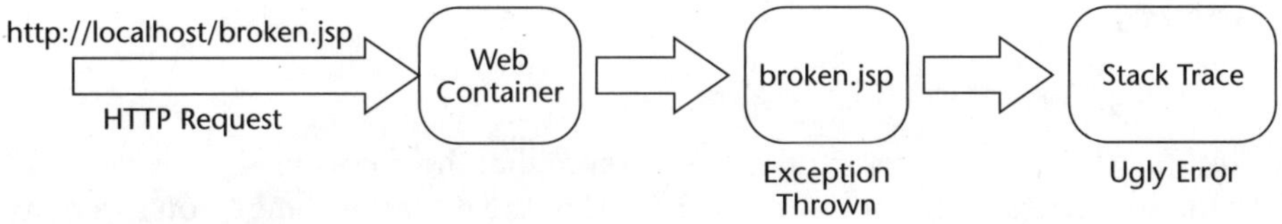

Figure 4.12 Before refactoring.

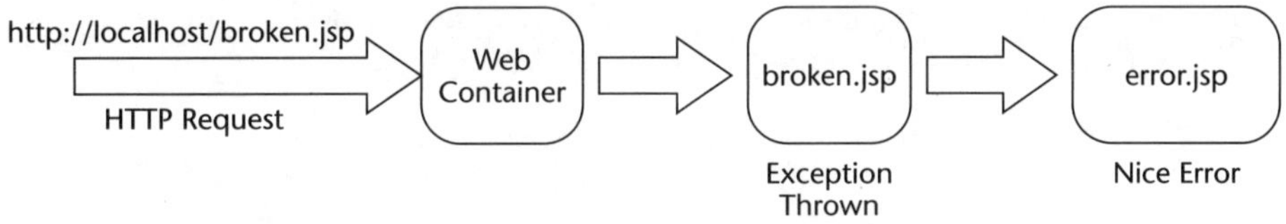

Figure 4.13 After refactoring.

Motivation

Users quickly lose confidence in an application that responds to any request with a stack trace. For some reason, developers often feel that users are willing to live with an absolutely unintelligible (to them anyway) message. While some users are more tolerant of bad behavior from an application, no user should be forced to put up with it.

Mechanics

Here are the steps to perform this refactoring:

1. *Create a JSP to act as your error page.* Make sure that the message is nonconfrontational in nature. For example, instead of the message being "You forgot to enter the data," have your message say, "Some data was missing from the form."
2. *Look into each JSP in your application to make sure that it has an error* ***page*** *directive.* The error page directive is easy to look for with a simple search tool such as grep or with the Windows Explorer search utility. Any JSPs that do not have the directive need to be edited.
3. *For each JSP that does not have an error page directive, add one.* Make sure the directive points to your newly created error page JSP.
4. *Deploy and test.*

Example

Here is an example of a JSP (part of the HomePage.jsp for the iBank application that you saw earlier) that could throw an exception and return the stack trace to the user. Because this JSP has no error page directive, it needs to be refactored.

```
<%@ page isELEnabled="true" %>
<html>
  <head>
    <title>iBank BillPay Online</title>
    <link rel="stylesheet" href="css/ibank.css" type="text/css" />
  </head>
  <jsp:useBean id="userCtx" class="ibank.UserContext"
               scope="session"/>
  <body>
    <table border="0" cellspacing="0" cellpadding="0" summary="">
      <tr>
        <td style="align:center;width:121px;height:20px;">
          <img src="img/logo.gif" alt="iBank" border="0">
        </td>
```

```
        <td style="text-align:center;width:165px;height:20;">
          <a class="BorderButton" href="${userCtx.nextNav}">
            ${userCtx.loginTitle}
          </a>
        </td>
      </tr>
    </table>
  </body>
</html>
```

The first step in this refactoring is to build an error page. In this example, you will build a very simple error page. For your application, you will probably want to do a more extensive error page that provides more useful information to your user. Here is the code for this example's error page:

```
<%@ page isErrorPage="true" %>
<html>
  <body>
    An unexpected condition has occurred. Please back up
    and try your request again.
  </body>
</html>
```

The next step is to examine each of your JSPs looking for an error page directive, and if one is not found, add one. Here is the line to add to your JSP to have it reference the error page you created.

```
<%@ page errorPage="error.jsp" %>
```

As an alternative to putting an error page directive in each of your JSPs, you can set a default error page in the deployment descriptor for your Web application (web.xml). The XML to associate the error.jsp error page with any java.lang.Throwable that is thrown and not caught elsewhere is listed here.

```
<web-app>
 ...
  <error-page>
    <exception-type>java.lang.Throwable</exception-type>
    <location>error.jsp</location>
  </error-page>
...
</web-app>
```

Finally, the application should be deployed and tested. When you are satisfied that the changes were successful, proceed to the rest of the JSPs in your application.

CHAPTER

5

Servlets

This chapter covers some of the repeated ways that servlets are misused. Servlets are part of the presentation tier of J2EE. Their official function is to provide a response to a request. That means that servlets provide a standard API for servers to be extended by third parties so that requests made of that server can be met in customized ways. In most real-world applications of servlets, the server that is extended is an HTTP server and the servlet customizes the way HTML is returned.

There are two major areas of HTTP server customization that servlets are involved in: managing traffic and building the response that is returned to the requestor. Servlets are very effective at directing and managing traffic. In the MVC (Model, View, Controller) paradigm, the servlet is a controller. On the Web, a controller directs application flow from page to page and transfers data to and from Web pages and data objects. Figure 5.1 shows a typical layout of servlets, JSPs, and model objects.

Not applying this paradigm leads to many of the misuses of servlets. Servlets can be used as views and even models (although that would be convoluted at best) but they are not well suited for that functionality. Their main purpose is to control the page flow of the application and to direct the delegation of the response's rendering. Here is the list of servlet AntiPatterns covered in this chapter.

Including Common Functionality in Every Servlet. This is a slight variation of the copy-and-paste AntiPattern that is so common in other systems and that is discussed in Chapter 7, "Session EJBs". The consequences are a brittle Web site that is hard to change and maintain. Even if the code is in a utility class and not copied into each servlet, the Web site is still hard to maintain because the flow of the application is hard-coded into the servlet.

Template Text in Servlet. This refers to the tendency of some developers to put hard-coded strings of HTML into their servlets. When applications are stuck in this AntiPattern, you will have a hard time fixing bugs in the HTML that is generated because the HTML is embedded in Java code instead of being in an HTML file.

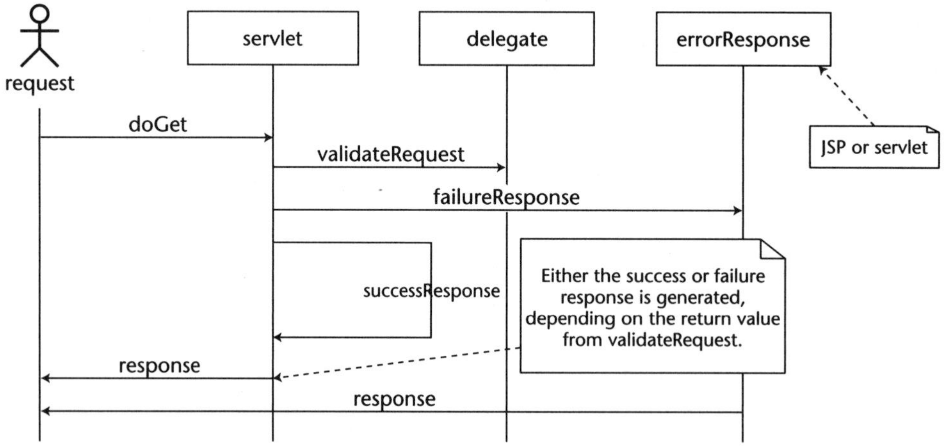

Figure 5.1 Servlets in MVC for the Web.

Using Strings for Content Generation. In many cases, a servlet will have HTML embedded in it, and the content cannot be removed. When strings are used to generate the content, the servlet and the HTML that it generates are much harder to maintain than they could be.

Not Pooling Connections. Connections are expensive in time and resources to open and keep open. Applications stuck in this AntiPattern will suffer from performance problems in all aspects that relate to accessing the database.

Accessing Entities Directly. A servlet should not remotely access an EJB entity via a fine-grained API. The overhead of marshaling and unmarshaling the data involved in the remote call will cause the application to slow to a crawl.

NOTE **Servlet and HttpServlet**

In this chapter the term *servlet* is used interchangeably for either a servlet or an HttpServlet. If it makes a semantic difference in the text, HttpServlet will be used for clarity.

AntiPattern

Including Common Functionality in Every Servlet

Also Known As: Spaghetti Code

Most Frequent Scale: Application

Refactorings: Introduce Filters

Refactored solution type: Software

Root Causes: Ignorance

Unbalanced Forces: Complexity and schedule

Anecdotal Evidence: "This same bit of code is in every servlet. There must be a better way!" "We can't change the authentication protocol. We would have to update everything!"

Background

In many Web applications, there is a need to apply pre- and postprocessing of requests and responses. Preprocessing includes functionality such as making sure that the user is authenticated or logging the request for analysis. Postprocessing examples include things like applying XSL transformations to the response. Often this code is put into a servlet's doGet or doPost method. It is also common to find this code in a utility class that is called by the servlet.

This was a great approach to achieve pre- and postprocessing under older versions of the servlet specification. However, in the 2.3 version of the specification, filters were introduced. With the introduction of filters, some of the old patterns have become AntiPatterns because the old approach caused added complexity and maintenance overhead to the code. Filters and the deployment descriptor support for them allow the process (when and in what order the pre- and postprocessing is applied) to be captured once instead of being embedded in each servlet. In addition, the code for doing the pre- or postprocessing is captured once in the filter implementation instead of being essentially copied and pasted to several places.

General Form

Typically, this AntiPattern takes the form of a servlet's performing one or more tasks to validate the request before generating the response or to modify the response in some way before it is delivered. In the worst case, the code is embedded directly in the doGet or doPost method. If the strategy for performing the validation or modification changes, each servlet must also be changed. The process of applying the change across each servlet is tedious and error prone.

Another common way to validate or modify the request and response is to delegate to another class to check the validity or perform the modification. Figure 5.2 depicts a sequence diagram illustrating the typical sequence for a validation.

The delegate tests the request and determines if it is valid (one common check would be to make sure the user is authenticated). If the request is valid, control is returned to the servlet, which is free to render the response. If the request is invalid (in whatever way the delegate determines), then control is passed to the errorResponse object that renders the response.

The modification of the response before it is rendered to the client is depicted in the sequence diagram in Figure 5.3.

The delegate updates the response before it is sent to the client. XSL transformation on the output before it is sent to the client is a typical scenario in which this approach is used.

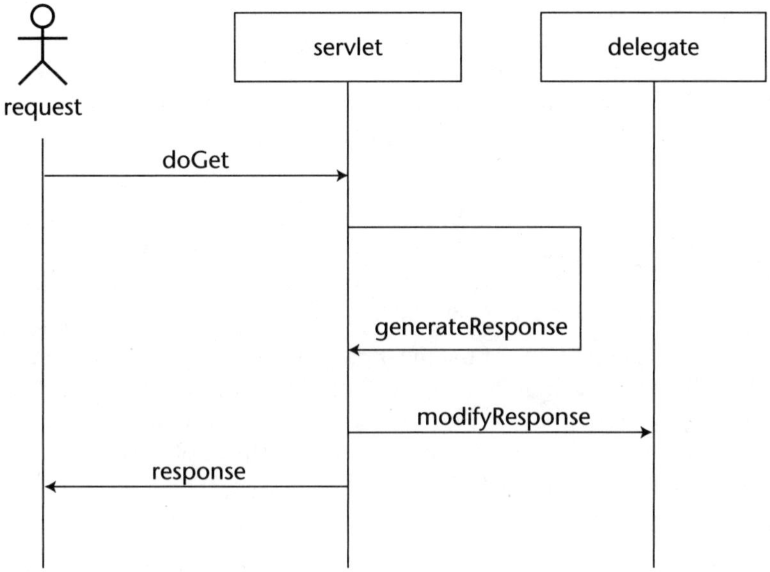

Figure 5.2 Delegated validation before generation.

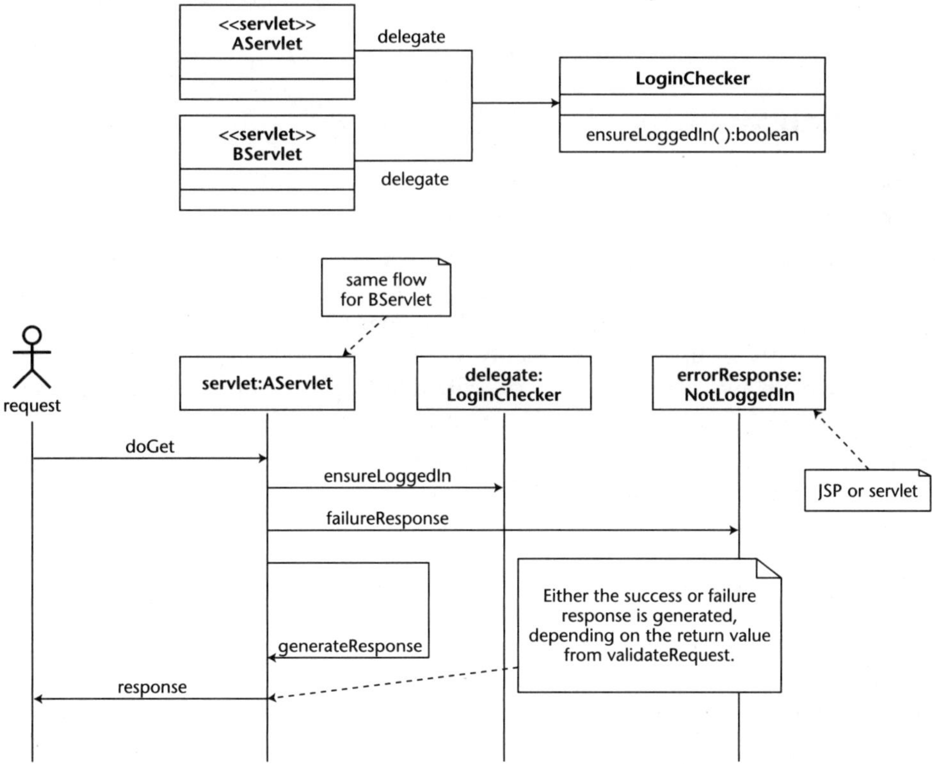

Figure 5.3 Delegated modification of response after generation.

Symptoms and Consequences

Most applications caught in this AntiPattern are much harder to change than they should be. Fixing bugs becomes a detective activity, not just looking for the cause of the bug but also looking for all the places that it exists. Over time, the user experience also becomes inconsistent.

- **Difficult to change.** Applications caught in this AntiPattern tend to be resistant to change since the flow of the application is embedded in the servlets. If another validation or transformation is needed, then each servlet that has the original transformation will have to be updated.
- **Inconsistent user experience.** One of the most painful consequences for users is the way that applications caught in this AntiPattern become inconsistent over time. Typically, what happens is that some of the servlets are updated but one is missed. Users are left confused as to why most of the application behaves in one way but one page behaves differently.
- **Maintenance headaches.** Having code stuck in this AntiPattern leads to lots of maintenance headaches. One of the biggest issues is having the processing steps embedded in each of the servlets. Another potentially painful consequence related to maintenance is that the code that performs the transformation or validation must be copied from servlet to servlet instead of being put into a utility class.

Typical Causes

This AntiPattern is usually caused by habits formed when building applications that conformed to the older version of the servlet specification.

- **Unsupported processing.** The lack of support in the servlet specification for the pre- and postprocessing of requests and responses prior to the 2.3 release is probably the most typical cause. Because so many Web applications had requirements to support functionality of this nature, Patterns and idioms developed to shoehorn pre- and postprocessing into existing implementations of the specification. The result was code that follows this AntiPattern.
- **Habits.** Another typical cause is developers not staying current and continuing to build applications with old approaches.

Known Exceptions

Many Web applications exist that follow this AntiPattern. The cost of doing a massive reworking of all of them makes this impractical. Better to approach the biggest problems first. As these applications evolve, it is a good idea to refactor the pre- and postprocessing to follow the latest version of the specification. Over the long haul, code that is updated to the latest release of the specification will be easier to maintain (in most cases) and will be easier to port to newer versions of application servers as they are released.

Known Exceptions

There is no exception to this AntiPattern for new development. If you are building new servlets, they should leave pre- and postprocessing to filters.

Refactorings

Including the Common Functionality in Every Servlet AntiPattern is best refactored by introducing filters to the code. Filters provide a way to do pre- and postprocessing and to have the order of that functionality be configured in the deployment descriptor. If the common code in your servlet is generating template text, consider the Use JSPs refactoring. The Introduce Filters and Use JSPs refactorings can be found later in this chapter.

Apply the Introduce Filters refactoring to your servlets that are stuck in this AntiPattern. It is also important to review your JSPs for pre- and postprocessing as well. A common idiom in the past was to create a custom tag that checked whether the user was authenticated. It is much better to use a filter for this requirement.

Apply the Use JSPs refactoring to your servlets that have template text repeated in several places. After applying this refactoring, you might need to consider applying the Introduce Template refactoring described in Chapter 4 to templatize the JSPs.

Variations

The most common instance of this AntiPattern occurs when it is used to preprocess the request to ensure that it is valid or to postprocess the response to transform it into a format acceptable to the requesting client. Another common variation is to use it to ensure that a user is authenticated. Another common variation is the repeated generation of template text that is included in many servlets.

In addition to the way that this AntiPattern affects servlets, it can also occur in JSPs. This AntiPattern is another major contributor to the Too Much Code in the JSP AntiPattern documented in Chapter 7. Authentication is a prime example of this kind of repeated code. Often a custom tag is written that makes sure that the user is authenticated, and if not, redirects the user to a login page, which is bad, or relies on code placed directly into the JSP, which is worse.

Example

In this example, we will look at validating a user. The code in Listing 5.1 is stuck in this AntiPattern because the validation is coded in the servlet. The example is very simple. If the user is valid (that is, has logged in successfully), then the servlet generates some HTML; otherwise, the user is directed to the Login page. Here is the code for the ValidateUser servlet.

```
public class ValidateUser extends HttpServlet {

    /**
     *  Simply forwards to the doGet method so that this servlet
     *  can respond to post
     */
    protected void doPost(HttpServletRequest req,
                          HttpServletResponse resp)
        throws ServletException, IOException {
        doGet(req, resp);
    }

    /**
     *  Checks to see if the user is valid and then forwards
     *  to the Login servlet if not
     */
    protected void doGet(HttpServletRequest req,
                          HttpServletResponse resp)
        throws ServletException, IOException {
        HttpSession session = req.getSession();
        boolean validUser = validateUser(session);
        if(validUser) {
            // If the user is valid generate the HTML.
            PrintWriter pw = resp.getWriter();
            resp.setContentType("text/html; charset=ISO-8859-4");
            . . .
            pw.flush();
        } else {
            // Otherwise forward to the login servlet
            ServletContext ctx = session.getServletContext();
            RequestDispatcher login = ctx.getRequestDis
                patcher("/Login");
            login.forward(req, resp);
        }
    }

    /**
     *  Makes sure the user is valid
     */
    private boolean validateUser(HttpSession session) {
        Object token = session.getAttribute(Login.USER_VALID_KEY);
        boolean flag = false;
        if(null != token) {
            flag = true;
        }
        return flag;
    }
}
```

Listing 5.1 ValidateUser servlet.

All the servlets in this application that rely on a valid user being logged in will have to have the validate-and-forward code repeated. When this code is copied to many different servlets, the flow of the application is captured in many different places. If that flow ever needs to be changed, then each of the servlets will have to change.

The validation logic could be placed in a shared utility class as a static method but the if/else block would have to remain. The if/else block is, in essence, directing the flow of the application. It is best if the flow of the application is kept separate from the code that generates the pages for the application.

Related Solutions

The Introduce Traffic Cop or Introduce Delegate Controller refactorings from Chapter 4, "JSP Use and Misuse," can sometimes provide help in getting repeated code out of your servlets. The application of a Traffic Cop can have the same positive effect on your servlets as it does on the JSPs, namely the embedded navigational information is abstracted out of the servlets and placed into a central location.

AntiPattern

Template Text in Servlet

Also Known As: Needless Complexity

Most Frequent Scale: Application

Refactorings: Use JSPs

Refactored Solution Type: Software

Root Causes: Ignorance

Unbalanced Forces: Education

Anecdotal Evidence: "This servlet is huge! What is this supposed to do, anyway?"

Background

Servlets began as a way to generate dynamic content for the Web and have more or less migrated to being a means to provide controller logic for Web applications. Since JSPs were introduced, the servlet is no longer the best technology to use to generate HTML, especially when a large percentage of the text is static. However, many applications exist that do use servlets to generate the static as well as the dynamic content. Developers who have not stayed current with the J2EE specification are still writing servlets that do nothing more than push static HTML text into the output they return. This leads to code stuck in this AntiPattern.

General Form

The typical form of this AntiPattern is a large servlet class that has mostly static HTML text being written into the response stream. In the most extreme cases, there is nothing but HTML in the servlet. In these extreme cases, the servlet might as well be a static HTML page because there is no processing happening in the servlet.

Symptoms and Consequences

The symptoms of this AntiPattern are a little harder to spot. If you are experiencing maintenance headaches with your servlets, you should take a look at the ratio of business logic to HTML when writing code. If the ratio is very low, you are probably stuck in this AntiPattern.

- **Low business logic to HTML writing ratio.** A typical symptom to look for that will help you to find this AntiPattern in your application is a low ratio of business logic code to the code that is simply putting static HTML into the response. If there is little business logic code and lots of static HTML writing, the code is likely caught in this AntiPattern.
- **Maintenance headaches.** The typical consequence of being stuck in the AntiPattern and not doing anything about it is increased maintenance costs. New features or extensions will be hard to introduce as well because it will be hard to tell where to put the logic in the midst of all the HTML generation code.

Typical Causes

This AntiPattern is usually the result of developers not being very experienced with servlet development.

- **Pursuit of simplicity.** Often developers looking at the short run think that just putting the static HTML into their servlet will be easier or simpler because everything for the response is in one place. In the very short run, this assumption is probably correct. In the long run though, it is a major issue for maintenance and enhancement.

- **Old habits.** Developers who have been building J2EE applications for some time have developed the habit (and the processes to support it) of putting the HTML into a servlet. These habits often resist changing to the point of driving new servlets into this AntiPattern.

Known Exceptions

Older applications had no choice but to do all HTML generation from their servlets. Almost all servlet implementations today support JSPs along with servlets so there is no reason or excuse to build a new implementation of this AntiPattern, and there are no known exceptions.

Refactorings

JSPs were designed to contain static HTML. The Use JSPs refactoring (found later in this chapter) will help you rework your servlets that are stuck in this AntiPattern, so they take advantage of JSPs.

Look for ways to isolate to JSPs the HTML that is being built in your servlets. The static HTML text can be captured in a way that is much easier to maintain and understand by keeping it in a JSP instead of writing it to the response in a servlet.

Variations

This AntiPattern varies with the way that the static content is generated. There is sometimes a group of methods that creates the various sections of the page via the output stream being passed around. In servlets generated in this way, the output stream is passed to the content-generation methods, and they write out their respective static HTML. Other variations include creating entire frameworks from scratch to manage building HTML content.

Example

This example demonstrates the AntiPattern in the form of a fictitious ski report from various ski hills around Summit County, Colorado. The servlet in Listing 5.2 displays a table of the snow conditions at the various resorts. This servlet is full of static HTML text being written to the response.

```
public class SkiReport extends HttpServlet {
    /**
     *  Build the table of ski hill reports.
     */
    protected void doGet(HttpServletRequest req,
                         HttpServletResponse resp)
        throws ServletException, IOException {
        resp.setContentType("text/html; charset=ISO-8859-4");
```

Listing 5.2 SkiReport servlet. *(continued)*

```
        PrintWriter pw = resp.getWriter();
        HttpSession session = req.getSession();
        // Build the headers and top-level stuff.
        pw.print("<!DOCTYPE HTML PUBLIC \"");
        pw.print("-//W3C//DTD HTML 4.0 Transitional//EN\"");
        pw.print("\"http://www.w3.org/TR/REC-html40/loose.dtd\">");
        pw.print("<html>\n<head>\n");
        pw.print("<title>Template Ski Reports</title>");
        pw.print("</head>");
        // Start the body.
        pw.print("<body>");
        pw.print("<b>Template Text Ski Report</b>");
        pw.print("<table border=\"1\">");
        // Header row
        pw.print("<tr>");
        pw.print(headerCell("Mountain"));
        pw.print(headerCell("Base"));
        pw.print(headerCell("Peak"));
        pw.print("</tr>");
        List reports = getReports();
        Iterator itr = reports.iterator();
        while(itr.hasNext()) {
            Report report = (Report)itr.next();
            pw.print("<tr>");
            pw.print(bodyCell(report.getMountain()));
            pw.print(bodyCell(report.getBase()));
            pw.print(bodyCell(report.getPeak()));
            pw.print("</tr>");
        }
        pw.print("</table>");
        pw.print("</body>");
        pw.flush();
    }

    private String headerCell(String value) {
        // The string concatenation approach
        return "<th>" + value + "</th>";
    }

    private String bodyCell(String value) {
        // The string concatenation approach
        return "<td>" + value + "</td>";
    }

    /**
     *  Get the list of reports. In a real-world application you'd
     *  go get the information from a Web Service offered by the
     *  ski hills.
     */
```

Listing 5.2 *(continued)*

```
    public List getReports() {
        List reports = new ArrayList();
        reports.add(new Report("Breckenridge", "4\" 3'", "9\" 2'"));
        reports.add(new Report("Copper Mountain", "3\" 9'", "8\" 1'"));
        reports.add(new Report("Vail", "7\" 9'", "12\" 2'"));
        reports.add(new Report("Keystone", "5\" 3'", "10\" 2'"));
        return reports;
    }
}
```

Listing 5.2 *(continued)*

Notice the ratio here between static HTML writing and business logic is large. Almost all the code in this servlet is focused on generating HTML. Virtually this whole servlet could be in a JSP. The getReports method is the only business code. If there are problems in the way the HTML looks, the servlet will have to be modified, recompiled, and redeployed.

Related Solutions

If it is not possible to refactor your servlet using the Use JSPs refactoring in this chapter, take a look at the Use JDom refactoring in this chapter. For cases where the content must be kept in the servlet, using JDom will make the code easier to understand and maintain. In refactoring your way out of this AntiPattern, be careful not to get trapped in the Too Much Code in the JSP AntiPattern in Chapter 4. As you move the static HTML out of your servlet, it will be tempting to move some of the Java code into scriptlets. Resist this temptation because you will end up in that AntiPattern, and then you will have the set of consequences that are inherent in that AntiPattern.

AntiPattern

Using Strings for Content Generation

Also Known As: Impossible-to-Follow Code

Most Frequent Scale: Application, System

Refactorings: Use JDom

Recfactored Solutions Type: Software

Root Causes: Ignorance

Unbalanced Forces: Training and deadlines

Anecdotal Evidence: "I really don't want to have to change that code; I have looked at it. That one method must be two miles long."

Background

HTML generation has traditionally been coded with string concatenation, meaning that, one piece at a time, strings that make up the page are added together via the + operator. Not only is this very slow, but it is also virtually impossible to debug the HTML that is generated by this technique. The resultant code is stuck in the Using Strings for Content Generation AntiPattern.

General Form

Typically this AntiPattern takes the form of a huge doGet or doPost method that concatenates strings and writes the out to the response stream. This form of the AntiPattern leads to the hardest to maintain code and thus is the most important to refactor.

Another common form is a servlet with many private methods that are passed a StringBuffer to append to. In this form of the AntiPattern, the doGet or doPost method becomes the driver for calling several different content-generation functions. While this form is better and easier to maintain than the Huge Method AntiPattern, it will still be hard to fix the HTML that is generated from this instance of the Using Strings for Content Generation AntiPattern.

Symptoms and Consequences

You will notice that you are stuck in this AntiPattern when you have a hard time fixing bugs or your performance is very bad. If you choose to ignore the AntiPattern, the maintenance will become more and more difficult.

- **Problems finding and fixing bugs.** Servlets stuck in this AntiPattern will have hard-to-find bugs. Bugs in both the HTML that is generated and the business logic that the servlet is supposed to perform will be hard to find because both kinds of code tend to be intermixed. Also, if you fix a bug in the HTML generation code, it is likely to cause a different bug in the business logic code.
- **Performance.** Performance problems often arise in servlets caught in this AntiPattern due to all the string concatenation. Removing all string concatenation in favor of StringBuffer append operations is the typical first pass at improving performance. However, that approach still leaves the servlet stuck in this AntiPattern facing the more serious consequences of HTML errors and maintenance headaches.
- **HTML errors.** One of the more serious consequences of being stuck in this AntiPattern is poorly formed HTML such as mismatched begin and end elements. The really frustrating part is that most HTML browsers are very forgiving of missing closing elements. The browser just guesses where you wanted the closing element. While that is convenient for someone writing HTML by hand, it leads to lots of formatting bugs in generated HTML because the browser inevitably guesses wrong. The result often looks very strange on the user's browser.

- **Maintenance headaches.** Maintenance problems are another major consequence of being stuck in this AntiPattern. Servlets caught in this AntiPattern tend to have very long methods (more than one page of code), which are hard to follow. The confusing code is difficult to change correctly.

Typical Causes

Inexperience on the part of developers causes this AntiPattern.

- **Lack of knowledge.** The usual cause of this AntiPattern is that the developer just does not know a better way. Most examples of code for servlet writing contain string concatenation code, and people very typically just follow the examples they are given. Developers usually copy and paste the example and modify it slightly to meet their specific requirements. It is not altogether foolish to copy and paste an example. However, unless the example was written in light of the big-picture architectural needs of a the specific project, it is likely that the sample code will have a naive approach to solving the problem at hand.

Known Exceptions

Very small utility servlets that render one or two lines of HTML will not usually manifest this AntiPattern. There is just not enough code that it will become hard to follow. Be careful, though, when you are evaluating whether or not your servlets are stuck in this AntiPattern; just because you think that 50 lines of HTML is not very much does not mean that others will agree. Try to refactor any servlet that has more than a handful of lines in it that use static strings.

Refactorings

Refactoring the Using Strings for Content Generation AntiPattern can be done in two different ways. The choice should be made based on the difficulty of pulling the HTML generation out of the servlet. If the static HTML and dynamic content are closely intertwined so that removing the static HTML will be virtually impossible without major rewriting, then look at the Use JDom refactoring (found later in this chapter) as a help in refactoring. You might also consider using some other refactoring to clean up the servlet to tease apart the HTML generation from the business logic. Fowler's Extract Method, found in Martin Fowler's *Refactoring: Improving the Design of Existing Code* (Fowler 2000) is probably the best place to start. Otherwise, you should look at the Use JSPs refactoring (found later in this chapter) and try to remove the static HTML altogether.

If you must keep the HTML generation embedded in your servlets, use the Use JDom refactoring to simplify the code and make it easier to maintain. Using JDom will make your code much cleaner and easier to maintain than leaving it with HTML and Java intermixed.

If it's possible to remove all HTML from your servlets, do so with the Use JSPs refactoring. Applying this refactoring is a lot like getting rid of Java code from a JSP, as documented in several of the refactorings in the previous chapter. You should always be looking for ways to preserve the separation of concerns in your code. JSPs are the view/HTML technology for J2EE, and servlets are the controller technology.

Variations

This AntiPattern will vary in scope, that is, the amount of static HTML in the servlet, as well as the means used to get the static HTML into the response. There are three ways that the response will be generated. First, the static strings can be written directly onto the OutputStream or PrintWriter. This approach is usually the first approach that a new developer takes; it is also one of the hardest to maintain. The next means to get the static HTML into the response is to concatenate all the strings together with a + operator, then write the resultant string to the response. This approach is usually the poorest performing but it will be easier to maintain than writing directly onto the response stream. Finally, you can create a StringBuffer and append the strings to that. This approach will perform better than string concatenation with +, but will still result in hard-to -debug and -maintain code.

Example

This example is a reimplementation of the Snow Report example from the Template Text in Servlet AntiPattern example. The servlet in Listing 5.3 generates and returns the snow conditions at several Summit County ski resorts in an HTML table. This version of the servlet demonstrates all the variations of this AntiPattern. Some HTML is written directly to the response stream, some is concatenated with the + operator, and some is appended to a StringBuffer. The typical servlet is probably going to stick with one of these approaches. This example has all three simply to illustrate the variations.

```
public class SkiReport extends HttpServlet {
    /**
     * Build the table of ski hill reports.
     */
    protected void doGet(HttpServletRequest req,
                         HttpServletResponse resp)
        throws ServletException, IOException {
        resp.setContentType("text/html; charset=ISO-8859-4");
        PrintWriter pw = resp.getWriter();
        HttpSession session = req.getSession();
        // Uses the direct print approach
        putHeader(pw);
        pw.print("<body>");
        pw.print("<b>SkiReport</b>");
        // Uses the string buffer approach
```

Listing 5.3 SkiReport servlet.

```
        putReport(pw);
        pw.print("</body>");
        pw.flush();
    }

    private void putReport(PrintWriter pw) throws IOException {
        StringBuffer buf = new StringBuffer(128);
        buf.append("<table border=\"1\">");
        // Header row
        buf.append("<tr>");
        buf.append(headerCell("Mountain"));
        buf.append(headerCell("Base"));
        buf.append(headerCell("Peak"));
        buf.append("</tr>");
        List reports = getReports();
        Iterator itr = reports.iterator();
        while(itr.hasNext()) {
            Report report = (Report)itr.next();
            buf.append("<tr>");
            buf.append(bodyCell(report.getMountain()));
            buf.append(bodyCell(report.getBase()));
            buf.append(bodyCell(report.getPeak()));
            buf.append("</tr>");
        }
        buf.append("</table>");
        pw.print(buf.toString());
    }

    private String headerCell(String value) {
        // The string concatenation approach
        return "<th>" + value + "</th>";
    }

    private String bodyCell(String value) {
        // The string concatenation approach
        return "<td>" + value + "</td>";
    }

    /**
     *  Put the header onto the output stream.
     */
    private void putHeader(PrintWriter pw) throws IOException {
        pw.print("<!DOCTYPE HTML PUBLIC \"");
        pw.print("-//W3C//DTD HTML 4.0 Transitional//EN\"");
        pw.print("\"http://www.w3.org/TR/REC-html40/loose.dtd\">");
        pw.print("<html>\n<head>\n");
        pw.print("<title>SkiReports</title>");
        pw.print("</head>");
    }
```

Listing 5.3 *(continued)*

```
    /**
     *  Get the list of reports. In a real-world application you'd
     *  go get the information from a Web Service offered by the
     *  ski hills.
     */
    public List getReports() {
        List reports = new ArrayList();
        reports.add(new Report("Breckenridge", "4\" 3'", "9\" 2'"));
        reports.add(new Report("Copper Mountain", "3\" 9'", "8\" 1'"));
        reports.add(new Report("Vail", "7\" 9'", "12\" 2'"));
        reports.add(new Report("Keystone", "5\" 3'", "10\" 2'"));
        return reports;
    }
}
```

Listing 5.3 *(continued)*

Notice how hard it is to see what the HTML will eventually look like by viewing the Java code in this example. In a small example like this, if the ending head tag or the ending table tag were left out, the report would probably be rendered just fine in most browsers, but just think of what would happen if this were generating a large amount of HTML. It becomes much more likely that the tables would render improperly as more HTML was generated. To see what the page will look like after it's rendered requires running the servlet and getting the HTML so it can be viewed in a browser. Blurring the lines between view and controller like this makes the servlet harder to understand, debug, and maintain.

Related Solutions

See the Template Text in Servlet AntiPattern earlier in this chapter for another approach to getting out of this AntiPattern. Simple HTML can more easily be captured in a JSP. There are many tools that will help to ensure the correctness of the HTML in a JSP, but as mentioned, it is difficult to ensure the correctness of the HTML when it's embedded in Java code.

Not Pooling Connections

Also Known As: Thrashing Connections

Most Frequent Scale: Application, Framework

Refactorings: Pack (Chapter 2, "Persistence")

Refactored Solution Type: Software

Root Causes: Ignorance and sloth

Unbalanced Forces: Education and schedule

Anecdotal Evidence: "What is going on? The SLQ has been tuned to death and the application is still too slow!"

Background

Establishing a connection to a database (or most external resources for that matter) is an expensive operation. It can take 10 times as long to establish the connection as it does to process a simple query. So, we should try to limit the number of connections that we create and do as much with the connection as we can before we release it.

A naïve approach to getting data into a servlet is connecting to a database with the JDBC DriverManager class. In fact, most JDBC examples are written in just this way. Unfortunately, many developers copy and paste what they see in examples and slightly modify it for their use. The result is that the servlets that take this approach are establishing a fresh new connection to the database with each invocation. Many performance problems attributed to servlets can be traced to this naïve approach to connecting to the database.

General Form

The most typical instance of this pitfall involves a servlet directly opening a connection to the database, interacting for some time, then closing the connection. In small systems, this is no big deal; in big systems, though, connections being constantly opened and closed will cause the application to perform poorly.

Symptoms and Consequences

You will notice that you are stuck in this AntiPattern when the performance of your application becomes hard to live with.

- **Poor performance.** The most obvious symptom and consequence of this AntiPattern is poor performance. Establishing a connection to the database is costly in terms of resources and time. The fewer times a connection must be opened the better. If your code is caught in this AntiPattern, the performance will be poor with large numbers of concurrent users or when the number of transactions is high.
- **Poor scalability.** An enterprise application typically needs scalability in the number of users and the transactions per second. If each transaction and user needs his or her own connection, the application will fail to scale up as it should.
- **Maintenance headaches.** There is additional maintenance in having the code to establish database connections in each servlet that accesses the database. If the connection information changes, then each servlet will have to be updated.

Typical Causes

Developers who are new to J2EE typically cause this AntiPattern.

- **Lack of experience.** New developers often do not recognize the impact of opening connections on performance. The typical new developer does not realize the scalability requirements or the importance of pooling connections to achieve them.
- **Configuration resistance.** Some developers are resistant to learning new configurations. In order for a servlet to connect with a pool, that pool must be configured (usually in the deployment descriptor). Many developers do not want to take the time to learn the configuration for JDBC pools.

Known Exceptions

Small applications intended to serve only a few concurrent users or process a few transactions a second can function with this AntiPattern because they do not have the scalability requirements of a typical Web application. Before you use this exception to justify keeping that JDBC connection code in your servlet, remember that applications usually live well beyond their expected lifespan, and become much bigger than they were ever expected to be. So refactor this AntiPattern if you can.

Refactorings

This AntiPattern is fixed by using connection pools instead of the DriverManager interface, as in the Pack refactoring found in Chapter 2. Chapter 2 deals with issues related to accessing and using databases and covers the need to use connection pools in depth.

This refactoring is straightforward and will produce a lot of performance gain in situations where connections are being opened and closed frequently. Adding batched SQL statements will also provide another gain in performance if your servlets are sending a lot of SQL to the server.

Variations

The basic scalability problems faced in this AntiPattern can apply to JSPs as well if the JSPs use database connections directly. Because JSPs are turned into servlets after compilation, they should be approached with the same care, to achieve performance gains.

Example

In this sample servlet, a table is built that contains all the customers in our database. The connection is established, used, and relinquished on each invocation of the servlet. The putReport method builds the static HTML and then gets the dynamic content with the getCustomers method. The getCustomers method is connecting to the database with the DriverManager API and will perform very slowly with many users. In a real-world application, the servlet would implement some sort of scrolling technique as well, because there would be no way to display a million customers. For this example though, let's assume that the database has only a few records, as found in Listing 5.4.

```
public class CustomerReport extends HttpServlet {

    /**
     *  Build a table of the customers in the database.
     */
    protected void doGet(HttpServletRequest req,
                         HttpServletResponse resp)
        throws ServletException, IOException {
. . .
        putReport(pw);
. . .
    }

    /**
     *  This method writes out the report on the customers.
     */
    private void putReport(PrintWriter pw) throws IOException {
        StringBuffer buf = new StringBuffer(128);
        buf.append("<table border=\"1\">");
        // Header row
        buf.append("<tr>");
        buf.append(headerCell("First Name"));
. . .
        buf.append(headerCell("Zip Code"));
        buf.append("</tr>");
        List customers = getCustomers();
        Iterator itr = customers.iterator();
        while(itr.hasNext()) {
            Customer customer = (Customer)itr.next();
            buf.append("<tr>");
            buf.append(bodyCell(customer.getFirstName()));
. . .
            buf.append(bodyCell(customer.getZipCode()));
            buf.append("</tr>");
        }
        buf.append("</table>");
        pw.print(buf.toString());
```

Listing 5.4 Customer report servlet.

```
    }
. . .
    /**
     *  Fetch a list of customers from the database and build a bunch of
     *  simple JavaBeans to hold the data.
     */
    public List getCustomers() {
        List customers = new ArrayList();
        try {
            // Make sure that the driver is loaded.
            Class.forName("org.gjt.mm.mysql.Driver");
            String url = "jdbc:mysql://localhost:3306/book";
            // This line is the culprit.
            // Each display of the servlet will cause
            // a new connection to be created and opened
            Connection conn = DriverManager.getConnection(url, "book",
                                                          "book");
            Statement stmt = conn.createStatement();
            String query = "SELECT fName, lName, street, city, " +
                "state, zipCode FROM Customer ORDER BY lName";
            ResultSet rset = stmt.executeQuery(query);
            while (rset.next()) {
                String fName = rset.getString("fName");
                String lName = rset.getString("lName");
                String street = rset.getString("street");
                String city = rset.getString("city");
                String state = rset.getString("state");
                String zipCode = rset.getString("zipCode");
                customers.add(new Customer(fName, lName, street,
                                           city, state, zipCode));
            }
            conn.close();
            stmt.close();
            rset.close();
        } catch(ClassNotFoundException e) {
            e.printStackTrace();
        } catch(SQLException sqle) {
            sqle.printStackTrace();
        }
        return customers;
    }
}
```

Listing 5.4 *(continued)*

Notice also that the database connection information is coded directly in this servlet. Over time, the connection information will probably change, and this servlet will have to change as a result. It is far better to have the connection information in one place in the configuration file.

Related Solutions

The Accessing Entities Directly AntiPattern will have similar issues with scalability, although for very different reasons. If the servlet is refactored to use an EJB back end instead of using JDBC directly, the database connection issue is pushed down to the EJB layer. In fact, if container-managed persistence is used, then the container will automatically pool the connections to the database (for most J2EE implementations). In addition, the Stifle AntiPattern in Chapter 2 is closely related to this AntiPattern.

AntiPattern

Accessing Entities Directly

Also Known As: Molasses

Most Frequent Scale: Application

Refactorings: Façade (Chapter 6, "Entity Beans")

Refactored Solution Type: Software

Root Causes: Ignorance

Unbalanced Forces: Education

Anecdotal Evidence: "This application is so slow!"

Background

This AntiPattern documents the performance problems encountered when servlets use the entity layer directly. Entities are positioned in the J2EE space as the way to get to the database and often developers turn to them to avoid coding their own JDBC calls. Because they are EJBs, entities are effective at getting data back and forth from the database within the proper transactional context; however, they are ineffective as a distribution technology because of the multitude of instances and the fine-grained nature of their APIs. We'd never want to populate an HTML table by calling simple getter methods on a remote interface. Establishing the connection, marshaling, and unmarshaling the data is too much overhead to get a string from the entity layer into the presentation layer.

In older versions of the EJB specification, the only interface available for entities was remote. Many patterns were developed to work around the performance issues related to the remoteness of entities. The basic tenet of these patterns was to bundle the data into one package and send it over the remote connection via one method invocation. Most of these patterns were basically the same and eventually became collectively known as the Data Transfer Objects Pattern. Many J2EE applications use this pattern to get data to and from entities. With the advent of EJB 2.0, however, there is another, better, option. Entities can have a local interface. The container does not create marshal and unmarshal code for local interfaces, so the overhead of invoking a local method is much lower.

In many cases, it is not appropriate for servlets to take advantage of local interfaces, however. When a large-scale J2EE application is rolled out into a production environment, the Web tier is often run on a different machine from the EJB tier. In topologies like that, it is not possible for the servlet to get to the local interface of an entity.

General Form

The simplest form of this AntiPattern is a servlet looking up the home interface for the entity via JNDI, invoking a finder that returns an instance of the entity, and invoking the fine-grained API. A particularly bad performance problem is iterating over a collection of entities. Figure 5.4. is a sequence diagram showing a simplified view of building an HTML table from a collection of Customer entities.

For every entity found (the finder is not shown in the diagram), two remote method invocations will be done. This will lead to performance problems, even with relatively small sets of entities.

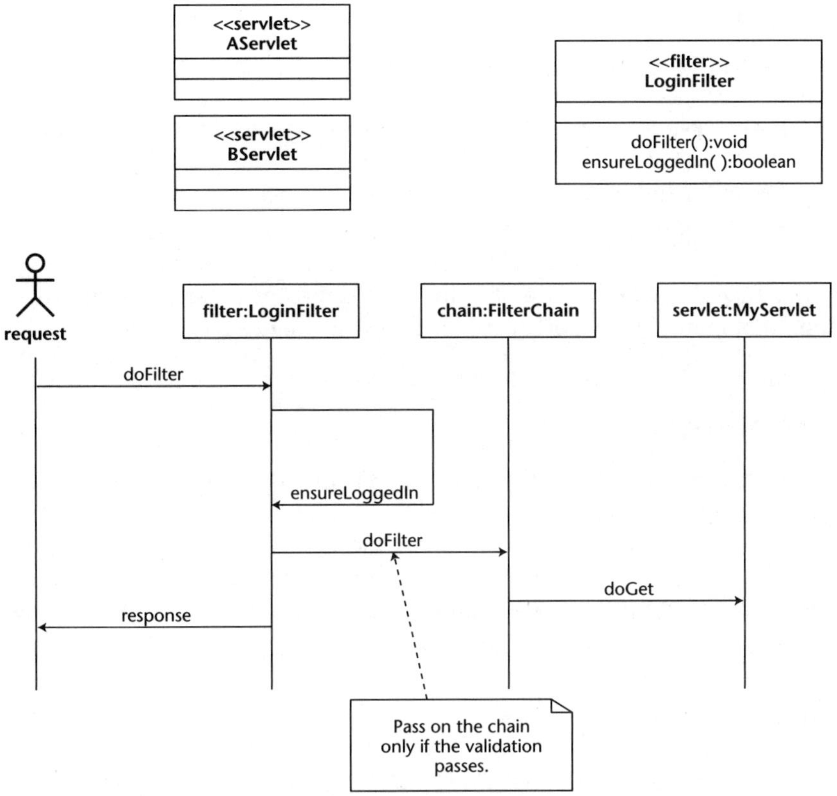

Figure 5.4 Populating a table with entity data.

Symptoms and Consequences

In a typical development environment, this AntiPattern is sometimes hard to spot, but once it gets into an environment that is more representative of the real world, the performance problems will become painfully apparent.

- **Performance problems.** This AntiPattern will become apparent when performance problems become apparent in development. Typical performance problems include a several-second delay in displaying a page. The major problem in finding this AntiPattern is that the performance problems are not usually apparent. Small data sets, which usually lead to small pages, don't turn into multiple-second delays in rendering a page. When the application goes into an environment more representative of the real world, the performance problems will start to manifest themselves.
- **Loss of user confidence.** The most major consequence of any code stuck in an AntiPattern is a loss of confidence in the development team by the users the application is supposed to serve.

Typical Causes

New developers usually cause this AntiPattern.

- **Lack of experience.** This AntiPattern is almost always caused by lack of experience. Developers new to J2EE are not always aware of the ramifications of distributed computing and tend to not think about these issues.
- **Unrealistic expectations.** Sometimes the AntiPattern can be caused by an expectation that the application will never have to scale up anyway so it's not a big deal to take the simple route. This instance is mostly a management problem, though, of failing to properly capture the performance requirements.

Known Exceptions

There is no known exception to this AntiPattern. The severity of the consequences, however, will be mild on small-scale applications. The cost of the refactoring should be considered for truly small applications. If you know the short- and long-term scalability requirements and they are met with the current implementation, then there is no need to refactor. If you are doing any new development, make sure not to get trapped in this AntiPattern.

Refactorings

This AntiPattern is best addressed by placing an EJB session over the entities that the servlet needs access to. The session can aggregate the data needed into a JavaBean and return it in one remote call.

The Façade refactoring in Chapter 6 provides guidance on how to migrate your code from accessing entities directly to using a façade that covers the entities. In Chapter 6, you will find an in-depth discussion on the Façade Pattern and how you can refactor your code to perform much better by retrofitting this pattern onto your existing code. Rather than repeat the whole discussion here, you are referred to Chapter 6.

Variations

This AntiPattern varies only in the kind of entities being accessed. Some servlets stuck in this AntiPattern access remote entities; others access local entities. Servlets that access remote entities will suffer from performance problems. Servlets that access local entities will not be flexible in the way they can be deployed.

Example

The servlet found in Figure 5.5 finds several instances of the Invoice entity EJB and iterates through them, building a table of the results of the fetch. Anytime that you are accessing an entity from a servlet, you should examine it carefully. You are almost always putting your code into this AntiPattern.

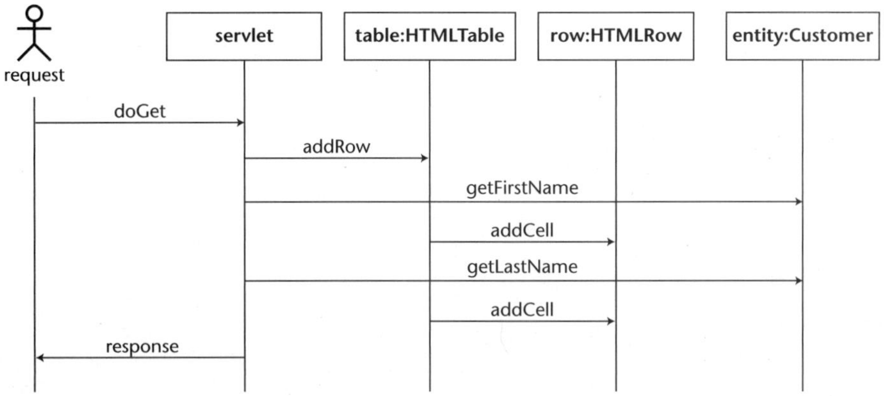

Figure 5.5 Invoice report servlet.

Each request sent to the Invoice is a remote method call. This configuration will perform very poorly. The overhead of creating a remote connection for each call will cause the application to crawl.

This sequence diagram skips some obvious steps; namely, there is no reference to looking up the home interface. In a real application, though, you should use the Service Locator Pattern found in Alur, Crupi, and Malks' *Core J2EE Patterns* (Alur, Crupi, and Malks 2001).

Related Solutions

Applications that are built with servlets directly accessing entities might have addressed the performance issues by aggregating entities into megaentities. If your application is doing that, take a look at the Coarse Behavior AntiPattern and the Local Motion and Strong Bond refactorings in Chapter 6 for insight into how to make your implementation better.

Refactorings

This section documents the refactorings referred to earlier in the AntiPatterns. The typical refactoring will help your code to migrate from where it is in whatever AntiPattern it is trapped in towards a better design. The AntiPatterns in this chapter address several different issues. The refactorings captured here cover the unique issues related to refactorings. The two persistence-related AntiPatterns, Not Pooling Connections and Accessing Entities Directly, have their refactorings in Chapter 2 and Chapter 4, respectively.

Introduce Filters. Filters provide the perfect place to put functionality that is common across several servlets. Instead of coding the way the application is supposed to use that common functionality into the servlets themselves, externalize that information into your deployment descriptor and put the functionality into a filter. This refactoring takes you through the steps to introduce filters into your application and remove the common functionality from your servlets.

Use JDom. HTML in your servlet in the form of hard-coded strings causes many maintenance headaches. JDom is a much better way to generate HTML from a servlet. This refactoring takes you step by step through removing the strings from your servlet and replacing them with JDom-generated XHTML.

Use JSPs. Instead of having HTML in your servlets, use JSPs to capture the plain HTML and include the JSP from within your servlet. Having the plain HTML for your application embedded in your servlet will cause maintenance headaches; HTML code embedded in Java code is very hard to debug. This refactoring takes you step by step through the process of removing the HTML from your servlet and replacing it with a JSP import.

Introduce Filters

You have embedded code in many servlets that applies the same pre- or postprocessing to the requests that are serviced.

Place the common functionality into a filter and control the applicability and order of the pre- or postprocessing with the deployment descriptor.

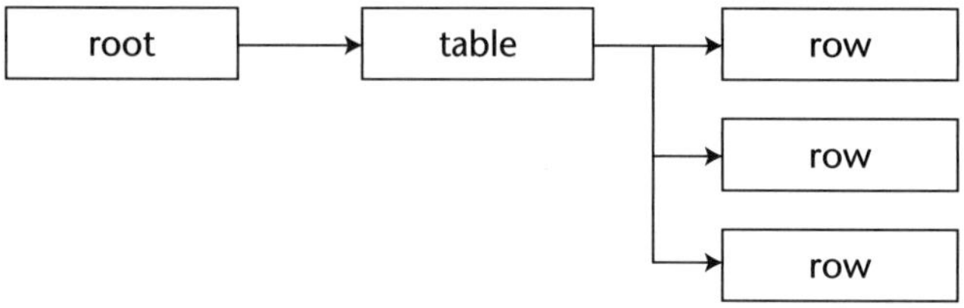

Figure 5.6 Before refactoring.

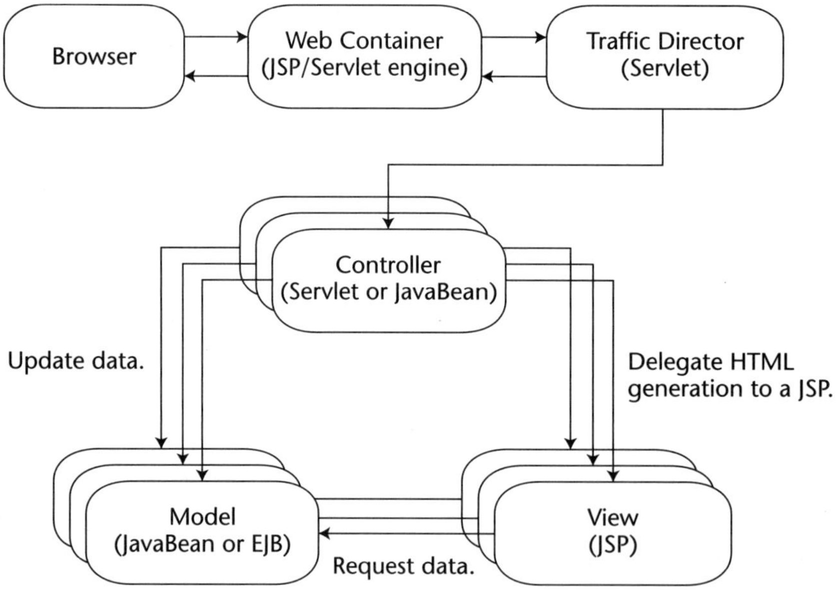

Figure 5.7 After refactoring.

Motivation

The main reason to apply this refactoring is to consolidate and simplify code to make it easier to understand and maintain. This refactoring is especially effective at getting rid of the Including Common Functionality in Every Servlet AntiPattern. Pre- or post-processing on a request or response that is implemented in servlets is harder to maintain than the same functionality implemented with filters. Because the container implements most of the processing-oriented code through its interpretation of the deployment descriptor, a lot of code that would otherwise be in a servlet is now implemented by the container. Another reason that filters make the same functionality easier to maintain is the encapsulation of the pre- and postprocessing responsibility behind the filter interface. With this refactoring in place, the servlets will not have to know the APIs for several different utility classes to accomplish the pre- and post-processing. In fact, the servlets will no longer need to be aware that any pre- and postprocessing is taking place.

Mechanics

Here are the steps to perform this refactoring:

1. *Identify any pre- or postprocessing code that is common across your servlets*. Typical places to find repeated code are the beginning and end of doGet or doPost methods. Don't forget to consider your JSPs as well. They can have a lot of repeated code that could be deleted with the application of a filter.
2. *For every common block of code or pre- or postprocessing utility class that was found, create a filter implementation class*. Break the filters across functional boundaries, that is, build encapsulated filters that accomplish one pre- or postprocessing task.
3. *Build the deployment descriptor*. Make sure to follow the code in the servlet to ensure that the filters are applied in the correct order.
4. *Remove the pre- or postprocessing code from one of the servlets*. Comment out the code to start with, just in case you need to refer to the code while debugging the filter. After all tests have been passed, the commented-out code can be deleted.
5. *Deploy and test*.
6. *Repeat for each servlet and each filter*. This step will be much easier if you have a good set of repeatable unit tests.

Example

In this example, we will refactor a servlet that has preprocessing code embedded in the doGet method. The first step is to identify the preprocessing code. The servlet in Listing 5.5 logs all the parameters that are passed to it in the doGet method. The application that this servlet is part of has a requirement that all form parameters must be logged. In order to implement this requirement, every servlet must implement this functionality. Here is the code for the BuzzyServlet. The form parameters are logged in the logParameters method.

```
public class BuzzyServlet extends HttpServlet {
     // In a real app you should keep strings like the
     // name of this logger in a static final public
     // variable and import that class.
     private static Logger logger =
          Logger.getLogger("ServletParameterLogger");

     /**
      * Constructor for BuzzyServlet.
      */
     public BuzzyServlet() {
          super();
     }

     public void doGet(HttpServletRequest request,
                          HttpServletResponse response)
          throws ServletException, IOException {
         logParameters(request);
          // Do the buzzy business process.
     }
     private void logParameters(HttpServletRequest request) {
         Enumeration enum = request.getParameterNames();
          StringBuffer buf = new StringBuffer(128);
          while (enum.hasMoreElements()) {
               String name = (String) enum.nextElement();
               String values[] = request.getParameterValues(name);
               buf.append("parameter = ");
               buf.append(name);
               buf.append(" values = {");
               for (int i = 0; i < values.length; i++) {
                    buf.append(values[i]);
               }
               buf.append("}\n");
          }
          logger.fine(buf.toString());
     }
}
```

Listing 5.5 BusyServlet.

This servlet has the logging hard-coded into it. There is little flexibility for changing the way this servlet logs other than just turning off the logger. If the need arises to change the way that the parameters are logged, then this servlet will have to be changed. In addition, since every servlet in the application is supposed to be implementing the same kind of logging, they will all have to be updated as well. This refactoring will help us to remove this integration between the Buzzy business process and the logging and, in turn, remove all the logging from all the other business processes in this application.

We have accomplished the first step in this refactoring by identifying the common logging code. The next step is to create a new filter class for each piece of common code. Because we only have one common piece of functionality, we only need one filter class. Our new filter class can be found in Listing 5.6.

```
public class LoggingFilter implements Filter {
     // In a real app you should keep strings like the
     // name of this logger in a static final public
     // variable and import that class.
     private static Logger logger = Logger.
                              getLogger("ServletParameterLogger");

     public void doFilter(
          ServletRequest request,
          ServletResponse response,
          FilterChain chain) {
          Enumeration enum = request.getParameterNames();
          StringBuffer buf = new StringBuffer(128);
          while (enum.hasMoreElements()) {
               String name = (String) enum.nextElement();
               String values[] = request.getParameterValues(name);
               buf.append("parameter = ");
               buf.append(name);
               buf.append(" values = {");
               for (int i = 0; i < values.length; i++) {
                    buf.append(values[i]);
               }
               buf.append("}\n");
          }
          logger.fine(buf.toString());
     }

     public void destroy() {
     }

     public void init(FilterConfig config) {
     }
}
```

Listing 5.6 LoggingFilter.

The next step is to build the deployment descriptor. The filter must be applied to all servlets in our simplistic application, so we give it a URL specification of '*'. The next step is to comment out the old code from the servlet and then deploy and test the application. When we are satisfied that the application is working properly, we can go back and delete the commented-out code from the servlet. Finally, if there were more servlets or JSPs that had other pre- or postprocessing, we would apply this process again until our application was free of repeated pre- and postprocessing code.

Use JDom

Your servlets perform poorly and are almost impossible to maintain.

Use JDom to build an object representation of the HTML document.

```
protected void doGet(
    HttpServletRequest req,
    HttpServletResponse resp)
    throws ServletException, IOException {
    resp.setContentType("text/html; charset=ISO-8859-4");
    PrintWriter pw = resp.getWriter();
    HttpSession session = req.getSession();
    resp.setHeader("title", "Stock Report");
    String content = "<body><b>Stock Report</b>";
    content += "<table><tr>";
    content += headerCell("Symbol");
    content += headerCell("Value");
    content += "</tr>";
    content += "<tr>";
...
}
```

Listing 5.7 Before JDom refactoring.

```
protected void doGet(HttpServletRequest req,
                     HttpServletResponse resp)
                     throws ServletException, IOException {
    resp.setContentType("text/html; charset=ISO-8859-4");
    PrintWriter pw = resp.getWriter();
    HttpSession session = req.getSession();
    resp.setHeader("title", "Stock Report");
    Element body = new Element("body");
    Element title = new Element("b");
    title.addContent("Stock Report");
    body.addContent(title);
    Element table = new Element("table");
    Element row = rowCell(table);
...
}
```

Listing 5.8 After JDom refactoring.

Motivation

String concatenation is very hard to maintain as a means of writing HTML. The structure of the HTML is hard to see, so things like closing tags are often missed. While most browsers will work even with missing tags, the sloppiness of the HTML that is generated makes it hard to debug and maintain. It is much easier to debug and maintain a highly structured document like XHTML that is produced from JDom.

If you have the ability to remove all static text from your servlet, you should look at the Use JSP refactoring in this chapter. The better the roles of the different technologies are preserved, the more maintainable your software will be. Servlets are better suited for controller-like code, as documented in the introduction to this chapter, than to generating static HTML.

Mechanics

Here are the steps to perform this refactoring:

1. *Save a copy of the generated HTML.* This copy will be used to validate the output from the updated code. If you have a good set of unit tests, you can skip this step.
2. *Make sure you understand the structure of the HTML.* A diagram can be used to capture this structure if need be. See the example for a simple diagram of a document's structure.
3. *For each element in the document, create a new JDom Element.*
4. *Put the structure of the document together by adding child elements to parent elements as required.*
5. *Remove the string concatenation code from your servlet.* Comment out the code to start; it will help you debug the new code.
6. *Deploy and test.* If you don't have good unit tests, you can open the copy of the HTML you made in the first step, in a browser window, and invoke the servlet from a second browser window and visually compare the two.

Example

In this example, we will see a page that displays stock quotes in a table. The first step in this refactoring is to save a copy of the HTML for use later in validating that the changes you have made do not result in a different page being delivered to the client. The next step is to make sure that you understand the structure of the document. An effective tool to use is a diagram of the elements in the document. Here is a diagram depicting the DOM structure of the example document.

An actual stock quote page would, of course, be much more complex than what is depicted here. Remember that the point of diagramming the DOM for your page is not to fully explode out what will be needed for the resultant document but to give yourself a guide for how to implement the complex or dynamic pieces of the document. So, keep the diagram as simple as possible.

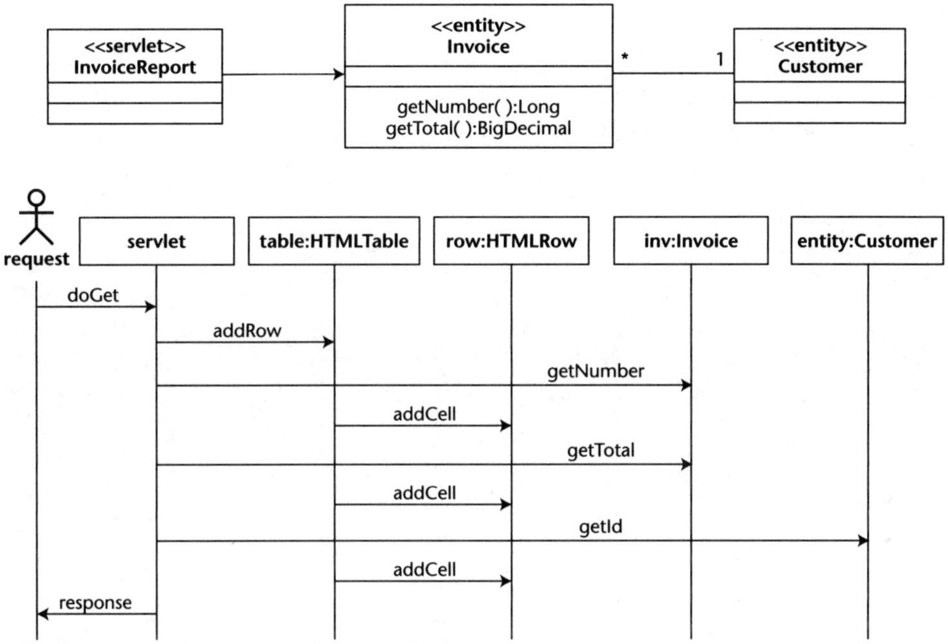

Figure 5.8 HTML structure of the document.

Listing 5.9 shows some of the code from the example, which builds the response via string concatenation.

```
public class StockTable extends HttpServlet {
    /**
     *  Build the table of stock price reports.
     */
    protected void doGet(
        HttpServletRequest req,
        HttpServletResponse resp)
        throws ServletException, IOException {
        resp.setContentType("text/html; charset=ISO-8859-4");
        PrintWriter pw = resp.getWriter();
        HttpSession session = req.getSession();
        resp.setHeader("title", "Stock Report");
        String content = "<body><b>Stock Report</b>";
        content += "<table><tr>";
        content += headerCell("Symbol");
        content += headerCell("Value");
        content += "</tr>";
        content += "<tr>";
        content += bodyCell("APPL");
        content += bodyCell("14.75");
```

Listing 5.9 StockReport servlet. *(continued)*

```
        content += "</tr>";
        content += "<tr>";
        content += bodyCell("JDSU");
        content += bodyCell("2.75");
        content += "</tr>";
        content += "</table>";
        content += "</body>";
        pw.print(content);
        pw.flush();
    }

    private String headerCell(String value) {
        // The string concatenation approach
        return "<th>" + value + "</th>";
    }

    private String bodyCell(String value) {
        // The string concatenation approach
        return "<td>" + value + "</td>";
    }
}
```

Listing 5.9 *(continued)*

Notice that the output (the result sent back to the client browser) is going to be one continuous line with no newlines, spaces, or other things that make the HTML much easier to read and debug. Some might argue that newlines could be placed into the concatenation along with tabs and so on. That is one path to take; however, as the structure of the document grows, the complexity of managing the indent level and other factors in formatting code become hard to keep track of.

The next step in this refactoring is to replace each element that we are creating with an equivalent JDom element and then construct the tree with the JDom elements. Listing 5.10 is the refactored code for the StockReport servlet. The string concatenation has been completely deleted and replaced with JDom calls.

```
public class StockTableRefactored extends HttpServlet {
    /**
     *  Build the table of stock price reports.
     */
    protected void doGet(HttpServletRequest req,
                         HttpServletResponse resp)
                         throws ServletException, IOException {
        resp.setContentType("text/html; charset=ISO-8859-4");
        PrintWriter pw = resp.getWriter();
        HttpSession session = req.getSession();
        resp.setHeader("title", "Stock Report");
```

Listing 5.10 Refactored StockReport servlet.

```
        Element body = new Element("body");
        Element title = new Element("b");
        title.addContent("Stock Report");
        body.addContent(title);
        Element table = new Element("table");
        Element row = rowCell(table);
        headerCell("Symbol", row);
        headerCell("Value", row);
        row = rowCell(table);
        bodyCell("APPL", row);
        bodyCell("14.67", row);
        row = rowCell(table);
        bodyCell("JDSU", row);
        bodyCell("2.56", row);
        body.addContent(table);
        Element html = new Element("html");
        html.addContent(body);
        XMLOutputter out = new XMLOutputter();
        out.output(html, pw);
        pw.flush();
    }

    private Element headerCell(String value, Element row) {
        Element th = new Element("th");
        row.addContent(th);
        return th.addContent(value);
    }

    private Element bodyCell(String value, Element row) {
        Element td = new Element("td");
        row.addContent(td);
        return td.addContent(value);
    }

    private Element rowCell(Element table) {
        Element tr = new Element("tr");
        table.addContent(tr);
        return tr;
    }
}
```

Listing 5.10 *(continued)*

Even in this simplified example, you can see an improvement in the structure of the code. In a larger example that had more complex HTML, the difference would be amazing, especially if there were any attempt to make the resultant HTML readable. When JDom prints out the XHTML, it will be clean, human-readable, and properly formatted, so it will be much easier to debug the generated HTML than the flat string concatenation code.

Use JSPs

Your servlet is full of HTML code and is hard to follow and maintain as a result.

Copy the template text to a JSP and use the forward mechanism to get the template text into the result.

```
protected void doGet(HttpServletRequest req,
                         HttpServletResponse resp)
        throws ServletException, IOException {
        resp.setContentType("text/html; charset=ISO-8859-4");
        PrintWriter pw = resp.getWriter();
        HttpSession session = req.getSession();
        // Build the headers and top-level stuff.
        pw.print("<!DOCTYPE HTML PUBLIC \"");
        pw.print("-//W3C//DTD HTML 4.0 Transitional//EN\"");
        pw.print("\"http://www.w3.org/TR/REC-html40/loose.dtd\">");
        pw.print("<html>\n<head>\n");
        pw.print("<title>Template Ski Reports</title>");
        pw.print("</head>");
        // Start the body.
        pw.print("<body>");
        pw.print("<b>Template Text Ski Report</b>");
        pw.print("<table border=\"1\">");
...
}
```

Listing 5.11 Before JSP refactoring.

```
protected void doGet(
    HttpServletRequest req,
    HttpServletResponse resp)
    throws ServletException, IOException {
    List reports = getReports();
    HttpSession session = req.getSession();
    session.setAttribute("ski.reports", reports);
    session
        .getServletContext()
        .getRequestDispatcher("iBank/SkiReport.jsp")
        .forward(req, resp);
}
```

Listing 5.12 After JSP refactoring.

Motivation

HTML in Java is hard to maintain and debug. The Java compiler looks at HTML as just another string and does not know or care that there is supposed to be structure to those strings. Also, the only way for us to see the actual HTML that will come out of the servlet is to run it through the container. This is a difficult and lengthy process to test if our HTML is correct. If the HTML is captured in a JSP, though, there are many tools that exist to validate and view the HTML that will result from the JSP. This refactoring is very useful in resolving the Template Text in Servlet AntiPattern.

Mechanics

Here are the steps to perform this refactoring:

1. *Save a copy of the HTML that is output from your servlet.* You will use this to compare the refactored output with the old output. If you have a good set of tests, you can skip this step.
2. *Create a new JSP and copy all the obvious static HTML that you can from the servlet.* Take note of where the static HTML wraps some dynamic content. Knowing that will become important as you seek to blend the servlet and the JSPs.
3. *Add a jsp:useBean action to the new JSP so the page will have access to an instance of the newly created bean.* The servlet will be creating the instance and putting it into the session as a request scope variable. Remember to use a naming convention that will provide a unique name across the request; the 2.4 version of the servlet spec recommends that you use the same names you use for packages.
4. *Define a JavaBean to hold the data needed by the page.* The list of attributes can be updated as you go along, so don't worry about getting it perfect the first time. Consider the Beanify refactoring from Chapter 4 for more details on creating a JavaBean for your servlet.
5. *Change the servlet to remove the static HTML and place the bean into the session under the name you used in the jsp:useBean tag earlier.* You should also comment out the static generation code and forward to the JSP to get the static content at this step.
6. *Deploy and test.*

Example

This example will begin with the SkiReport servlet that was presented earlier as Listing 5.2 in the Template Text in Servlet AntiPattern. This servlet is almost entirely HTML generation.

The only real business code in this entire servlet is the creation of the list of report objects. Fortunately, this servlet is already using a JavaBean to hold the data so we can reuse that and we do not have to introduce one to complete this refactoring.

The first step in this refactoring is to save a copy of the HTML output so that you can compare it with the outcome of your refactoring. Again, if you have unit tests you can skip this step. The next step in this refactoring is to create a new JSP to hold the static text. Listing 5.13 is the JSP for the ski report with all the obviously static text copied into it.

```
<%@ page isELEnabled="true" %>
<%@ taglib uri="/WEB-INF/tld/c.tld" prefix="c" %>
<head>
<title>SkiReports</title>
</head>
<body>
  <b>SkiReport</b>
  <!-- This will create a new empty list if the
            servlet did not set the value. -->
  <jsp:useBean id="ski_reports" class="java.util.ArrayList"
                          scope="session"/>
  <table border="1">
    <tr>
      <th>Mountain</th>
      <th>Base</th>
      <th>Peak</th>
    </tr>
    <c:forEach var="report" items="${ski_reports}">
      <tr>
        <td>${report.mountain}</td>
        <td>${report.base}</td>
        <td>${report.peak}</td>
      </tr>
    </c:forEach>
  </table>
</body>
```

Listing 5.13 The SkiReport JSP.

The next step is to define a JavaBean that will serve to hold the data for the servlet to pass to the JSP via a bean in the session. Listing 5.14 is the bean that we will be using in the JSP to populate the table.

```
public class Report {
    private String mountain;
    private String base;
    private String peak;
    public Report(String mnt, String base, String peak) {
        mountain = mnt;
        this.base = base;
        this.peak = peak;
    }
```

Listing 5.14 The Report JavaBean.

```
    public String getMountain() {
        return mountain;
    }

    public String getBase() {
        return base;
    }

    public String getPeak() {
        return peak;
    }
}
```

Listing 5.14 *(continued)*

The next step is to change the servlet. We need to delete the static HTML, place the bean into the session, and forward to the new JSP. Listing 5.15 shows the new code for the servlet.

```
public class SkiReport extends HttpServlet {
    /**
     *  Build the table of ski hill reports.
     */
    protected void doGet(
        HttpServletRequest req,
        HttpServletResponse resp)
        throws ServletException, IOException {
        List reports = getReports();
        HttpSession session = req.getSession();
        session.setAttribute("ski_reports", reports);
        session
            .getServletContext()
            .getRequestDispatcher("/chap08/SkiReport.jsp")
            .forward(req, resp);
    }
    /**
     *  Get the list of reports. In a real-world application you'd
     *  go get the information from a Web Service offered by the
     *  ski hills.
     */
    public List getReports() {
        List reports = new ArrayList();
        reports.add(new Report("Breckenridge", "4\" 3'", "9\" 2'"));
        reports.add(new Report("Copper Mountain", "3\" 9'", "8\" 1'"));
        reports.add(new Report("Vail", "7\" 9'", "12\" 2'"));
```

Listing 5.15 The refactored SkiReport. *(continued)*

```
        reports.add(new Report("Keystone", "5\" 3'", "10\" 2'"));
        return reports;
    }
}
```

Listing 5.15 *(continued)*

Now, the only code that is kept in the servlet is the code that manages the data. The HTML is rightly kept in the JSP, where it can be managed by the appropriate tools. No longer will you have to update the servlet, recompile it, and redeploy your whole Web application just to find out that you have the width of a column set to 55 percent and it is too wide. Because the HTML is in a JSP, you can use one of the great WYSIWYG JSP editors to manage the width of the columns.

CHAPTER 6

Entity Beans

This chapter covers some common problems associated with using Entity Beans, along with cogent refactorings to resolve these problems. Arguably, the most controversial facet of J2EE, Entity Beans have been both embraced and maligned by the many application architects, designers, and developers who have encountered them. Those who favor Entity Beans often cite their inherent support for container-managed persistence, transaction, and security as key benefits of their use. Those who dislike entities are quick to mention their network and transactional overhead and raise doubt about their ability to scale under pressure. Both sides have valid points.

As the EJB specification has evolved, however, many of the traditional scalability concerns involving Entity Beans have become moot. EJB 2.x has ushered in several advancements in Entity Bean technology, such as local interfaces, container-managed relationships, and a portable query language called EJB QL. Thus, many of the J2EE patterns that applied to EJB 1.x have become irrelevant under EJB 2.x or—even worse—have become AntiPatterns themselves. This chapter will describe some of these AntiPatterns, along with additional ones that occur frequently during the course of applying this important technology.

We will use a sample financial services domain model as the basis of our AntiPattern discussion. In this model, we will assume that we have customers who are associated with one or more addresses and accounts. Each account represents a particular product (such as an interest-bearing checking or money market account) and can have one or more transaction entries, such as deposits and withdrawals.

These items will be represented as some combination of related Entity Beans and dependent objects. The AntiPatterns we discuss will highlight some specific design issues associated with the sample entity model, along with refactorings and solutions that address these issues.

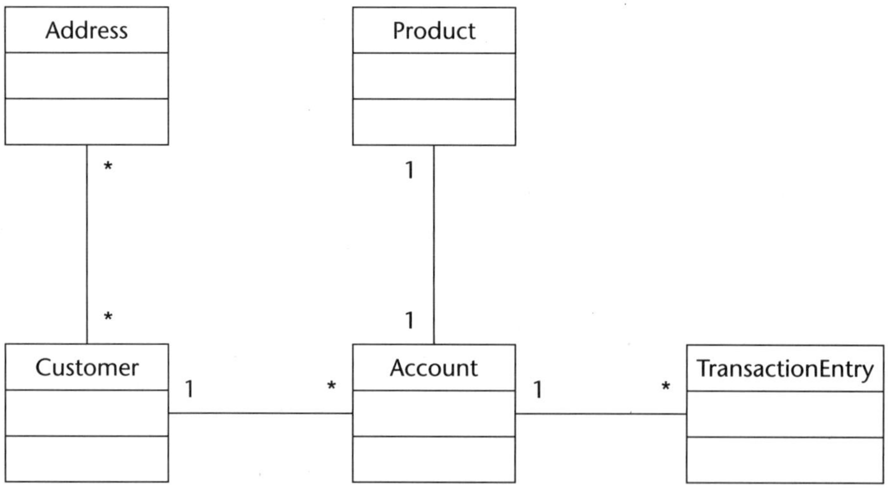

Figure 6.1 Sample financial services domain model.

Fragile Links. Hard-coded JNDI lookups on Entity Beans can cause a system to become brittle and more resistant to change. Use EJB references to add a layer of abstraction that will insulate your applications from deployment time changes.

DTO Explosion. A common mistake is to make the entity layer responsible for accepting and returning view-oriented DTO instances. This reduces the reusability of the entity layer, because it is wedded to a particular application's user interface or reporting requirements. Decouple the entity layer from higher-order tiers by moving all custom DTO operations to an independent DTO Factory.

Surface Tension. Sometimes the sheer number of explicit custom DTO classes, and the complexity of their interrelationships and interfaces, can make an application very difficult to maintain. Collapse particularly unwieldy DTO graphs into a single generic DTO, in order to reduce complexity and improve maintainability.

Coarse Behavior. Developers introduce unwarranted complexity by building coarse-grained entities under EJB 2.x (or greater) environments. Use fine-grained Entity Beans and container-managed relationships (CMR) to replace deprecated, coarse-grained composite entities.

Liability. Distributed applications often suffer severe performance degradation due to expensive, fine-grained invocations across the network. Introduce a façade component, which will present a simplified remote interface to clients and perform fine-grained invocations within a single process.

Mirage. Projects often shun the benefits of moving to CMP because of fear. Introduce CMP incrementally, using bean extensions and deployment descriptor settings, to avoid having to do a wholesale conversion.

Fragile Links

Also Known As: Hard-Coded References

Most Frequent Scale: Application, Microarchitecture

Refactorings: Alias

Refactored Solution Type: Software

Root Causes: Haste, apathy, and ignorance

Unbalanced Forces: Maintainability and time

Anecdotal Evidence: "Nobody's ever going to change this stuff at deployment time!"

Background

Hard-coded JNDI lookups on Entity Beans can cause a system to become brittle and more resistant to change. At deployment time, a JNDI tree—such as the one illustrated in Figure 6.2—could morph into something the original developer did not expect. In this situation, hard-coded references to that tree could fail. The EJB specification supports component reusability by allowing such references to be aliased and specified at deployment time. Because hard-coded links are essentially frozen within compiled .CLASS files, they cannot be dynamically introspected and altered using the convenient deployment tools provided by most commercially available, J2EE application server environments. Hence, the pervasive use of hard-coded links not only increases the possibility of widespread breakages throughout the application, but also hampers the reusability of the application components that use them.

General Form

This AntiPattern takes the form of explicit references to dependent EJBs within the JNDI tree. Specifically, references to beans under the *java:comp/env/ejb* JNDI location are an indication that hard-coded bean locations are probably being grafted into the application, based upon the often false assumption that locations will never change upon deployment.

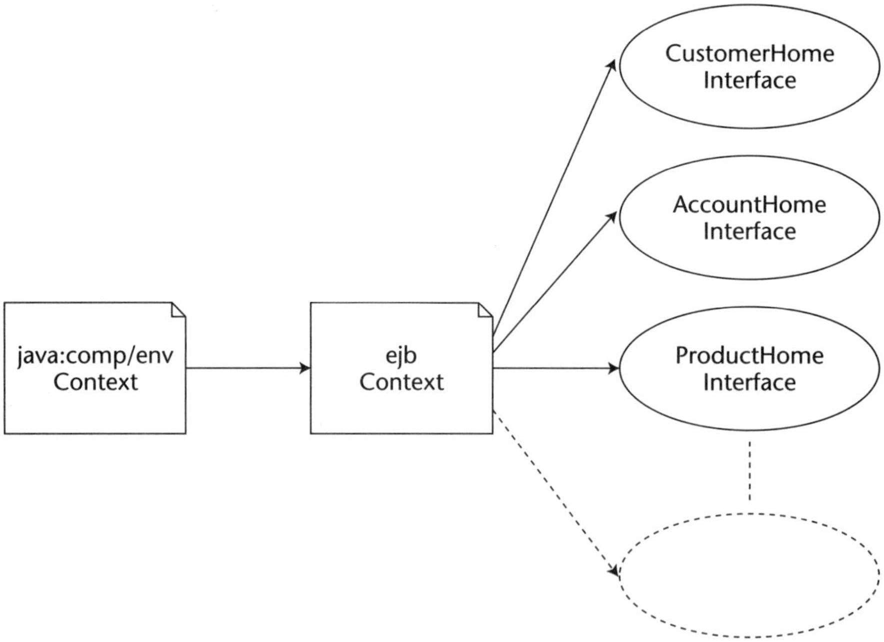

Figure 6.2 Standard EJB-JNDI tree.

Symptoms and Consequences

Hard-coded JNDI references to beans and services can be problematic in a dynamic deployment environment. Stack traces and JNDI lookup errors are often a symptom of broken JNDI references. The consequences of using these links are inflexible, unreliable applications. These symptoms and consequences are detailed below.

- **Stack traces throughout the application.** The main symptoms of Fragile Links are stack traces that appear throughout the application as it attempts to locate beans and services that are no longer located where the original developer intended. Some of these exceptional conditions may be severe enough to halt the application rather abruptly. However, a more insidious situation can occur if the failure to locate dependent beans is somehow masked via exception handling. For example, implementing *try-catch* blocks around bean lookups that simply swallow exceptions without performing any value-added handling (for example, throwing a descriptive exception to a responsible, higher-level application component), could cause the application to stumble on null bean references at some later point in time, under seemingly unrelated circumstances. Presumably, such stumbling would result in *NullPointerException* stack traces that a developer could use to investigate the problem. However, it can be extremely difficult to correlate these traces to the failed JNDI lookups that caused them. Unfortunately, these symptoms rarely surface during unit testing or even system testing. The developers who initially coded the links are unlikely to test the consequences of relocating beans and services upon deployment. Such scenarios usually extend beyond the field of vision of the typical developer. System testing groups are unlikely to fare any better, because their activities usually (and rightfully) focus on the verification of test cases that are based upon business use cases and not alternative deployment scenarios.
- **Reduced reusability.** A consequence of ignoring this AntiPattern is that the reusability of the application can be hampered by the inflexibility of hard-coded links. The application may need to be deployed in an environment that levies specific requirements on the topology of JNDI trees either because of standards or because of a need to avoid naming collisions with other application components. An application suffering from this AntiPattern would not be suitable in such environments, thus limiting its overall reusability.
- **Widespread breakage.** Another consequence of ignoring this AntiPattern is widespread breakage throughout the application, which could lead to a lack of user confidence in the application and its sponsors and developers.

Typical Causes

The typical causes of the Fragile Links Anti-Pattern are a misunderstanding of the EJB specification and the true meaning of reuse, as detailed below.

- **Misunderstanding the EJB specifications.** A typical cause of the Fragile Links AntiPattern is a lack of understanding of improved mechanisms defined within the EJB specification. This development problem can be resolved with sufficient training and education. Developers who are not knowledgeable about new advancements in the EJB specification will not use these features or will use them improperly.
- **Misunderstanding reuse.** Another cause of the Fragile Links AntiPattern results from taking a myopic view of software reusability. Most developers embrace the notion of reuse at the code and design levels but stumble in grasping the true power of reusable components and make the mistake of thinking that things should remain static upon deployment. The latter two points are an oxymoron. Components cannot be truly reusable if their implementation effectively pins them to a specific environment.

Known Exceptions

The only acceptable exception to not hard-coding links occurs when it is certain that there will be no chance of deploying the application in an environment that will differ from what has already been hard-coded in its implementation. For example, an application may be deployed in a military environment with a dedicated hardware suite and a strict deployment protocol that prohibits changes at deployment time.

Refactorings

The Alias refactoring (found in this chapter) introduces EJB References as aliases for dependant EJBs and services. EJB References introduce aliases, which can be referenced instead of addressing specific portions of the JNDI tree. This will decouple the implementation code from the actual locations of EJBs and services, allowing those components' locations to be specified when the application is deployed.

Variations

There are no variations to this AntiPattern.

Example

This is an example of a hard-coded reference to the Account bean's home, which is assumed to reside within the *ejb* context.

```
// Get the default JNDI Initial context.
Context context = new InitialContext();

// Look up the Account home.
Object obj = context.lookup("java:comp/env/ejb/AccountHome");

// Downcast appropriately via RMI-IIOP conventions.
AccountHome acctHome = (AccountHome)
javax.rmi.PortableRemoteObject.narrow(
obj, AccountHome.class);
...
```

Because the AccountHome is addressed explicitly, and is assumed to reside within the default EJB JNDI context, this code will not support the flexibility to relocate the AccountHome interface at deployment time. If the AccountHome interface is relocated, the code will break and possibly cause the application to fail.

Related Solutions

There is no related solution for this AntiPattern.

DTO Explosion

Also Known As: Tangled Up in Views

Most Frequent Scale: Application

Refactorings: Local Motion, Exodus, Flat View

Refactored Solution Type: Software

Root Causes: Inexperience

Unbalanced Forces: Complexity and education

Anecdotal Evidence: "Of course! Using entities is expensive. They should always accept and return Data Transfer Objects (DTOs) in order to cut down on networking overhead."

Background

The use of DTOs in the public interface and creation methods of Entity Beans and homes is a deprecated, EJB 1.x pattern. Domain DTOs are transfer object versions of domain entities. The following listing is an example of a read-only, domain DTO that is based upon the Account Entity Bean presented earlier. The DTO in Listing 6.1 could provide read/write capabilities with the addition of mutator (that is, setter) methods.

```
...
public class AccountDTO
{
    private String id;
    private BigDecimal balance;
    private ProductDTO product;
    private Collection transactionEntries;
...

    public Collection getTransactionEntries()
        { return this.transactionEntries; }

    public ProductDTO getProduct(){ return this.product; }
    public BigDecimal getBalance(){ return this.balance; }
    public String getId(){ return this.id; }
    ...
    }
...
}
```

Listing 6.1 AccountDTO.java.

Under EJB 1.x, this pattern aims to reduce the network and serialization overhead of fine-grained Entity Bean invocations by wrapping several pieces of entity data into serializable objects, which could be conveyed en masse using a single entity method (that is, getDTO, setDTO) invocation. Unfortunately, this practice often has a negative impact on the overall maintainability of systems, because a distinct DTO class must be created and maintained for each Entity Bean class in the system. Keeping the Entity Beans and their associated DTOs synchronized becomes a significant challenge as the underlying Entity Bean model evolves. Changes to an Entity Bean's attributes require similar changes to the corresponding DTO class. In addition, since domain DTOs often reside in the higher-level application tier, their use often makes the lower-level domain tier dependent on the higher-level application logic tier, which is an undesirable outcome. *Custom DTOs*, which provide use-case-based views of the domain layer, levy additional dependencies on the domain tier if used directly with entities. In this situation, custom DTOs and Entity Bean methods must be maintained for each new or modified view required by the presentation layer. The demands of a specific presentation layer are essentially grafted onto the domain layer, thus influencing its design and ultimately reducing its reusability.

General Form

This AntiPattern takes on two forms. The first form is the presence of a large, often unwieldy, number of DTO classes, which implies that a huge effort is required to maintain their synchronization with respective Entity Bean classes. The second form is the presence of Entity Beans that have been scarred by the imprints of view-based DTOs. These unfortunate Entity Beans have dramatically reduced prospects for reusability because they have been coupled to a specific application's view requirements.

Symptoms and Consequences

When the number of DTO classes in an application becomes unwieldy, they can be very difficult to keep synchronized with the entity layer. An excessive amount of effort expended in this task is often a symptom of the DTO Explosion AntiPattern, as described in the following list:

- **DTO/entity synchronization.** A typical symptom of this AntiPattern is that a project must allocate a significant and increasing amount of labor and time to synchronizing its DTO and Entity Bean classes. When a project finds itself crushed under the weight of having to change multiple components across multiple architectural layers because of relatively modest Entity Bean modifications, then it has clearly become a victim of this AntiPattern. Another symptom of this pattern is that application designers and implementers start writing off the possibility of reusing fundamental business components in response to new management initiatives. A deeper look often reveals that the business components cannot be reused because they have been polluted with a myriad of custom-DTOs in order to accommodate the relentless pace of changes in view, presentation, and reporting requirements.
- **Waste.** The consequences of this AntiPattern are increased maintenance costs, wasted resources, and disposable components.

Typical Causes

The typical causes of this AntiPattern are a lack of understanding of the latest EJB mechanisms, and a misunderstanding of the nuances of intertier coupling. Combine these causes with constant schedule pressure, and you have a recipe for this AntiPattern, as described below:

- **Stuck in the past.** This results from the general tendency of individuals to gravitate toward what they already know. Since there is a considerable learning curve associated with J2EE and its component specifications, one might feel the need to leverage what has already been learned rather than explore new options. In a more static environment, such as CICS development under the z/OS mainframe environment, this practice is not only acceptable but also prudent. Too many people have invested too many years making mistakes and ultimately learning the best combination of features and practices in that environment. There is no reasonable justification for someone deviating from dependable patterns of usage.

However, in a J2EE/EJB environment, this assumption is patently incorrect. The specifications are still quite fluid. New features are being introduced with each revision of the J2EE and component specifications, in order to improve robustness and address issues. For example, someone who harbors an EJB 1.x mindset in an EJB 2.x environment is missing incredible advancements, such as local interfaces and container-managed relationships (CMR). These people are more likely to waste time and resources writing unnecessary code to address issues that are automatically solved if the proper EJB 2.x mechanisms are used.

- **Failure to understand the impact of intertier coupling.** Inexperienced designers and developers often underestimate the negative impact of excessive coupling, especially between architecture tiers. It might not even occur to the typical developer that coupling an application's domain tier to its higher-level view tiers is bad. However, with appropriate training and experience, most developers will realize and avoid the negative effects of excessive coupling on component reusability.
- **Schedule-driven corner cutting.** Developers subjected to intense schedule pressures can lapse into this AntiPattern. In this situation, developers will often make hasty decisions that will eventually compromise the reusability of their designs for the sake of schedule and to address relentless requirement changes. For example, it is much simpler to add new DTOs and related dependencies to the entity layer in order to meet rapidly changing view-related requirements, than it is to carefully consider the best place to maintain and access these DTOs.

Known Exceptions

There are no exceptions to this AntiPattern.

Refactorings

You can use two refactorings to deal with this AntiPattern: Local Motion and Exodus, both found in this chapter.

Forgo the use of DTOs in favor of fine-grained entity access using local interfaces. (See the *Surface Tension* AntiPattern, found in this chapter, to address situations when it is preferable to maintain a pervasive DTO-based architecture.) Because of advancements in the EJB specification, such as Local References, DTOs are no longer a necessity for invoking Entity Beans efficiently.

In situations where DTOs are still in use (such as EJB 1.x environments and under the conditions described in the *Flat View* model), you can use Exodus to move the creation and manipulation of DTOs out of Entity Beans and into a special category of classes called *DTO Factories.* These factory classes or components assume the responsibility for handling DTOs, thus decoupling the domain layer from the view-related demands of higher-order tiers.

For entities that have a large number of methods, it may be easier to not only use DTOs, but also to use generic ones that are based on collection classes, such as java.util.HashMap. This is an example of the Flat View refactoring found later in this chapter. (See the *Surface Tension* AntiPattern for additional information about this refactoring.) This refactoring can also be used to simplify the task of conveying DTO hierarchies.

Variations

This AntiPattern can vary considerably in scope and severity, but the symptoms are more or less the same. However, the DTO/Entity synchronization issue is probably a more common symptom than the Entity/DTO intertier dependency issue, because many developers have probably approximated the concept of a DTO Factory during their application of what is arguably the most popular J2EE pattern, the Session façade, as described in Alur, Crupi, and Malks' *Core J2EE Patterns* (Alur, Crupi, and Malks 2001).

Example

Suppose that we need our sample entity model to support a Web screen that displays the primary address and a list of idle accounts for a given customer, where an idle account is one for which no activity has posted for the past 90 calendar days. Our system could shadow each domain entity with a domain DTO, which could be used to set or get entity attribute values in bulk, instead of issuing attribute-level method invocations. DTO set and get methods could be added to each Entity Bean and dependent object, as shown in Figure 6.3.

One approach to building custom DTOs is to hold Entity Beans responsible for gathering or disseminating view-based information. Thus, a given Entity Bean must rummage through a nest of associated entities in order to collect and aggregate domain-level DTOs into higher-level, view-based custom DTOs. The first issue with this approach is that it greatly increases the amount of coupling between the designated entity and its affiliated beans and DTOs.

This phenomenon is shown in Figure 6.3, where the Customer entity must not only be coupled to the Address and Account beans, but also to the AddressDTO, AccountDTO, and TransactionEntryDTO objects in order to satisfy the requirement of displaying idle customer account information on the user interface. If an additional screen must be added to display a list of accounts and respective product types for a given customer, then a new method must be added to the Customer bean, along with additional implementation code and a dependency on ProductDTO. Each time an additional customer-related view is required, we must modify the customer entity and rebuild the domain layer.

The second issue is that these custom DTOs typically reside within the application layer, where they are referenced by servlets and JSP <usebean> tags. Thus, they should never be referenced by a lower-level layer, such as the domain layer.

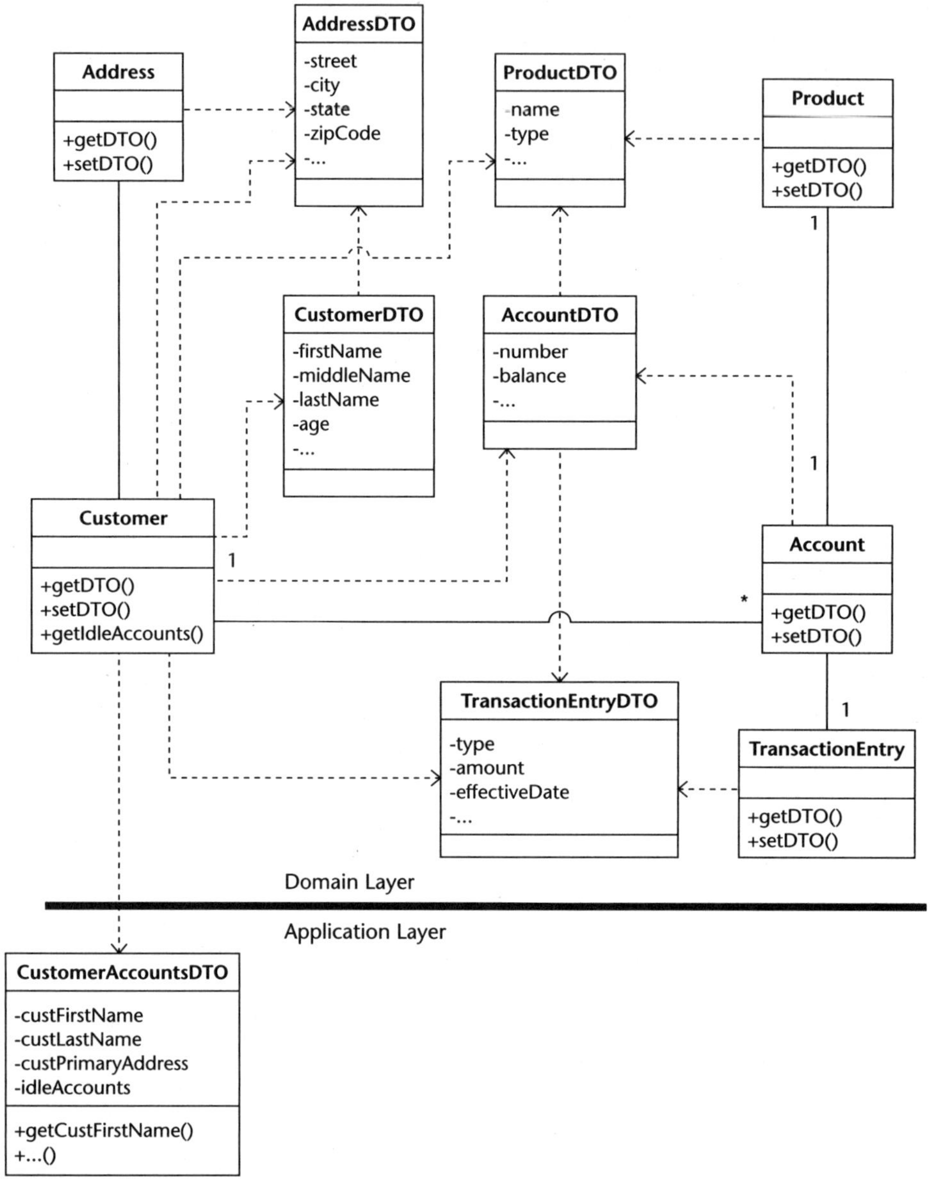

Figure 6.3 DTO dependencies and related methods.

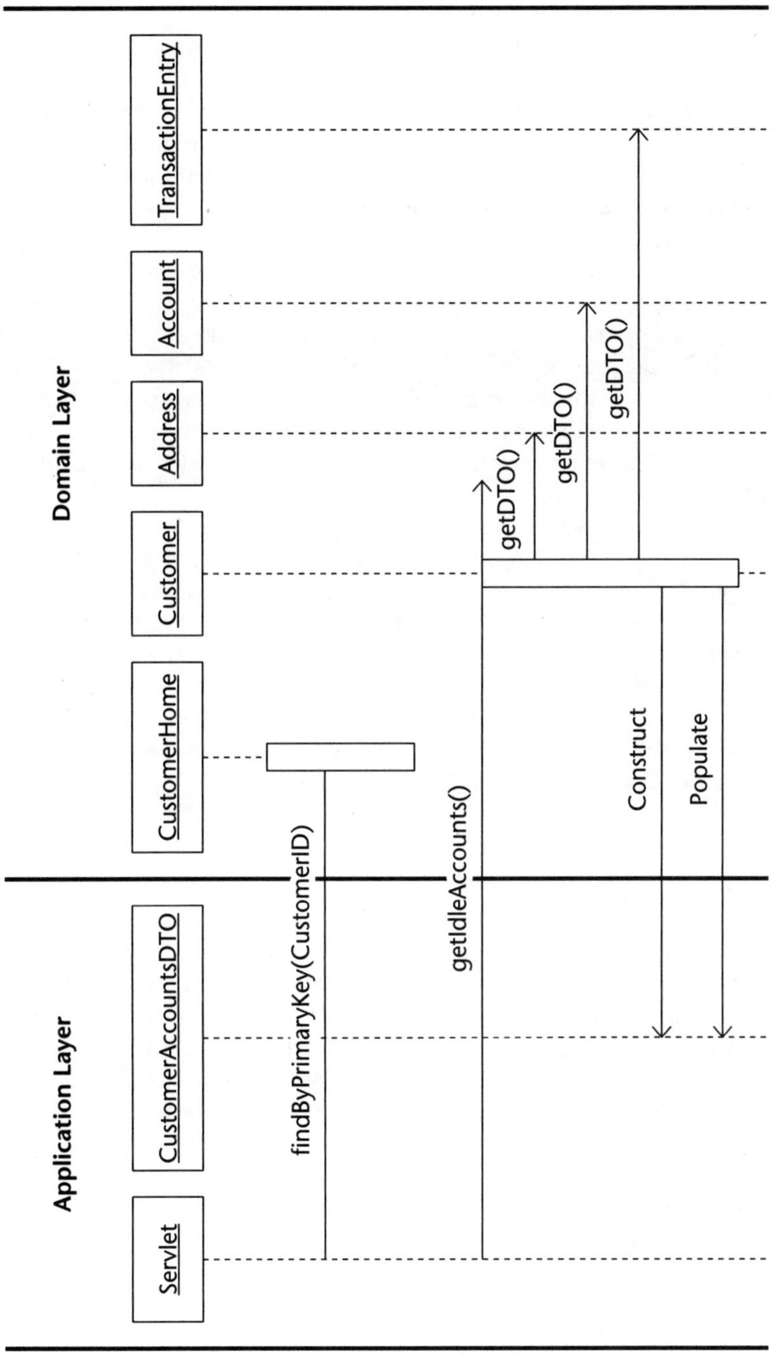

Figure 6.4 Retrieve idle customer accounts sequence diagram.

Since entities are responsible for creating and returning custom DTOs, they become inherently dependent on these DTOs and the application layer, as shown in Figure 6.4. This gives rise to two significant problems. First, a cyclic dependency is introduced. The application logic layer defines the custom DTO types, but expects custom DTO instances to be created and returned by the domain layer. The domain layer depends on the application-layer custom DTO type definitions in order to handle and create their instances. This cyclic dependency is not only architecturally bad, but also can lead to serious build-related issues.

The second problem is the decreased reusability of the domain layer, because of its dependency on a specific application-logic layer. The specific screens and view-related requirements of our sample application may be entirely different from those of another application. However, the Customer entity should be reusable across a wide range of application's, including those with differing user interfaces and those without any (that is, batch applications). Unfortunately, this example essentially grafts a particular applications user interface requirements onto the Customer entity, which significantly reduces its reusability.

Another problem with this approach is that it contributes to the proliferation of DTO types, which can become a maintenance nightmare. As new view-related requirements are levied, new custom DTO classes must be introduced, and new dependencies on domain DTOs must be leveraged. It becomes more difficult to keep the Entity Bean and domain DTO classes synchronized as the number of classes increases. The whole DTO concept was meant to combat the network overhead associated with invoking Entity Beans and conveying information between clients and servers. However, if the application is running under an EJB 2.x environment, then any DTOs that are not explicitly conveyed across the network can be eliminated by using the Local Motion refactoring.

Related Solutions

Some combination of identified refactorings and related solutions can be applied to this AntiPattern, depending on a number of factors. Such factors might include the specification level of EJB that is available and the overall complexity of the application and the average surface area (that is, size and complexity) of its Entity Beans. For example, it is unlikely that DTOs can be eliminated in an EJB 1.x environment—particularly for mission-critical systems that need to scale well. The network and serialization baggage of 1.x Entity Beans precludes the widespread elimination of DTOs. Therefore, the Local Motion refactoring mentioned in this profile would probably not be applicable to such environments. However, it might still be entirely appropriate to explore the Exodus refactoring by introducing DTO factories into the services layer that can build complex, view-oriented DTOs from the more basic domain DTOs being exchanged between the services and domain layers. This would still reduce overall coupling, while accommodating the performance advantages of exchanging domain DTOs between Entity Beans and Session Bean facades.

The Surface Tension AntiPattern, along with its Flat View refactoring, are related to this AntiPattern because they address the issue of unwieldy DTOs, from the perspective of both minimizing the total number of distinct DTO classes within a system and reducing overall exposure to very large entity interfaces.

Surface Tension

Also Known As: Boundless Interface

Most Frequent Scale: Application

Refactorings: Flat View

Refactored Solution Type: Software

Root Causes: Ignorance and haste

Unbalanced Forces: Maintainability and resources

Anecdotal Evidence: "Whenever we change entity attributes, we check the entire code base so that we can fix everything that ends up breaking."

Background

Some of the Entity Beans within an application could have a large number of attributes and associated methods. For example, our Product entity could contain tons of attributes to describe the various facets of a particular financial product. In addition, some of the application screens could require very complex DTO hierarchies and graphs to be created and transmitted in order to properly convey the relevant information. The larger and more complex these DTO networks and component interfaces are, the more difficult they become to navigate and maintain. At some point, some client—perhaps a session or message-driven bean, servlet or JSP—may need to invoke a potentially unwieldy number of Entity Bean attribute methods. Additionally, during the course of maintenance, it may be necessary to add, modify, or delete entity attributes and associated methods. This will most likely require a number of related changes to the surrounding client code invoking those methods. The greater the number of explicitly coded, entity attribute method invocations, the tighter the level of coupling between the Entity Beans providing these methods and the code that invokes them. All of this makes the system brittle and more difficult to maintain.

General Form

This AntiPattern is usually evidenced by large numbers of explicit get and set method invocations against the larger domain objects within the system. This phenomenon is evidenced by a large number of explicit get and set calls against Entity Beans (via local interfaces) and DTOs that have been shuttled across the network.

Symptoms and Consequences

The symptom of the Surface Tension AntiPattern is increased maintenance, while the consequence is lengthened change cycles, as described below.

- **Increased maintenance.** Coding and invoking get and set methods is both tedious and prone to error, and adds little in the way of actual business logic. However, in the end, the data must still be moved. Therefore, some method or mechanism for accomplishing this must be practiced. When developers start spending an inordinate amount of time massaging the parts of the system that deal most directly with moving data in and out of entities and DTOs, then it is likely that this AntiPattern has taken hold. When projects become unable to support routine screen field changes or modification of data items within the domain layer without being crushed by changes in the entity/DTO interface code, then it is evident that this AntiPattern has used the weapon of tight coupling to rob the system of its agility.
- **Lengthened change cycles.** The consequence of this AntiPattern is the inability to support routine maintenance and requirement changes in a timely fashion. The business users and customers of the system are the ones most likely to be directly affected. They may become frustrated with the inability of the information technology organization to meet the changing requirements of the business. Over time, this erosion of confidence can have drastic repercussions, including reduced funding for future technology projects and outsourcing.

Typical Causes

This AntiPattern is usually caused by architects and designers who lack a full understanding of the nature of coupling and its impact on the flexibility and maintainability of systems.

- **Misunderstanding coupling.** The early warning signs of large Entity Bean and DTO interfaces are apparent during design, but often go unnoticed throughout implementation. Only after the system is sent to the field and must respond to the changing needs of the business do the architects, designers, developers, and management realize the error of their ways.

Known Exceptions

There are no exceptions to this AntiPattern.

Refactorings

For entities that have a large number of entity attributes and associated methods, it may be easier to not only use DTOs, but to use generic ones that are based on collection classes, such as java.util.HashMap. This is an example of the Flat View refactoring (found later in this chapter). This enables a collection of data to be transported without creating a custom DTO class to represent that data. This refactoring can also be used to simplify the task of conveying DTO hierarchies.

Variations

The type of coupling associated with this AntiPattern can occur in several places. Systems that are based on the EJB 1.x standard tend to suffer more because DTOs are used more extensively. In these systems, the coupling problem can involve domain DTOs that are exchanged between the service and domain layers, along with custom DTOs that are vended from the service layer to the application logic layer. EJB 2.x-based systems that make judicious use of local interfaces will tend not to suffer from this AntiPattern between the service and domain layers. However, they can still become victims of it between the service and application logic layers, where custom DTOs are conveyed between clients and servers in order to reduce network overhead.

Example

Suppose that we have an application that needs to show detailed information about the contents of its entire domain object graph on one or more screens. Since this graph resides on the server, it should be converted into serializable DTOs, which are then shipped to the client where they can be cached for the rendering of one or more screens. Assuming that our application is based on EJB 2.x, and we have successfully applied the Local Motion refactoring, the sequence of invocations involved in constructing and conveying this graph of serializeable objects may resemble what appears in Figures 6.5 and 6.6.

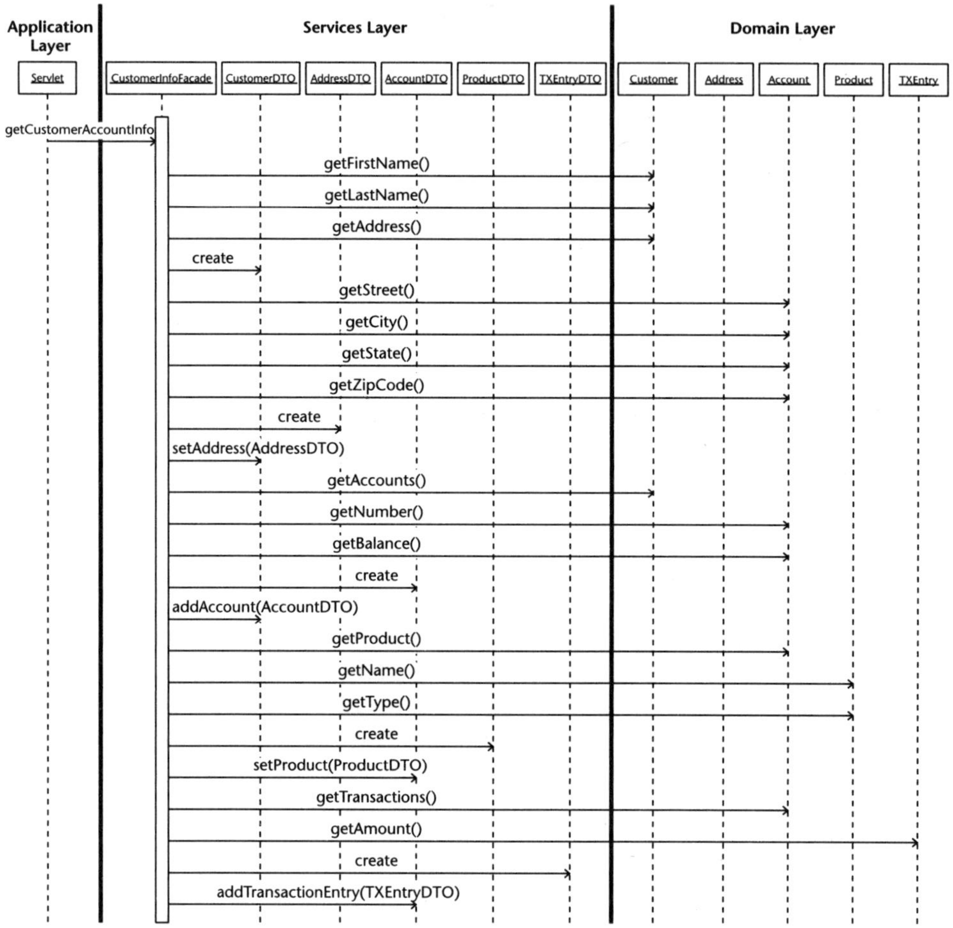

Figure 6.5 Sequence diagram—DTO graph construction.

Although local interface operations are efficient, it may take a huge number of them to create the desired DTO graph. Also, remember that not only are these invocations required in creating the graph within the service and domain layers, but similar invocations will also be required in navigating and reading the graph once it gets to the application-logic layer. What happens when new business requirements are levied, and additional customer, address, account, or transaction information must be shown on the screens? What happens when this specific scenario is extrapolated to payroll, marketing, and manufacturing screens, which require entirely different graphs of information from Entity Beans we have not yet even discussed?

Obviously, this seemingly straightforward, brute-force approach can fall apart once an application becomes sufficiently large and complex. This is where the more generic and dynamic approach outlined in the Flat View refactoring can prove extremely helpful.

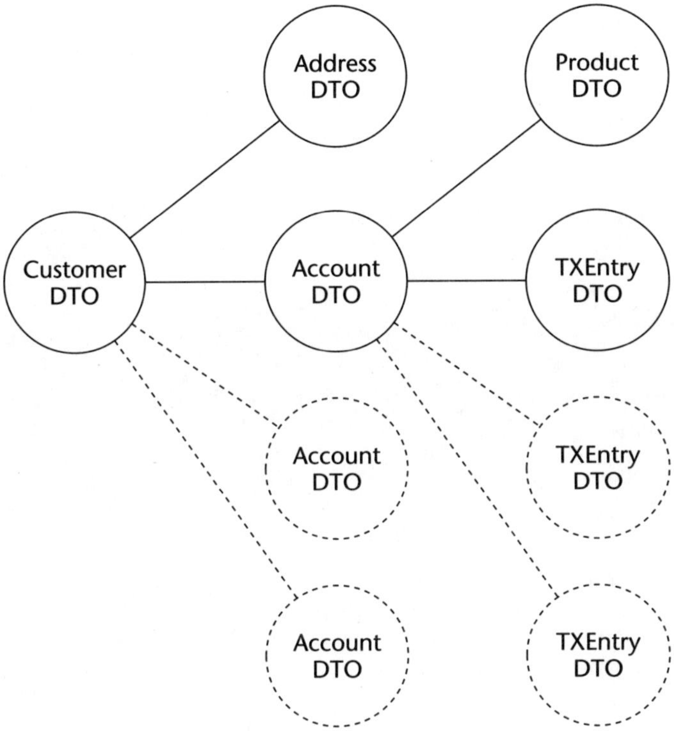

Figure 6.6 DTO graph visualization.

Related Solutions

The DTO hierarchies could be conveyed as XML and be vended to clients. This becomes particularly compelling if the client is actually some system engaging in a business-to-business (B2B) conversation with the application that is vending the XML. Expressing the DTO hierarchies in XML could produce a solution that has far less coupling than a solution leveraging explicit method invocations.

Coarse Behavior

Also Known As: Composite Entity

Most Frequent Scale: Architecture

Refactorings: Local Motion, Strong Bond

Refactored Solution Type: Software

Root Causes: Ignorance

Unbalanced Forces: Education and resources

Anecdotal Evidence: "EJBs are real resource hogs. We need to use composites."

Background

Coarse-grained or composite entities have been traditionally used to combat the networking overhead associated with Entity Beans. Because Entity Bean interfaces extend java.rmi.Remote, their use incurs a considerable amount of serialization and internal overhead. Even when clients and servers are co-located, there is no guarantee that a particular application server environment will be smart enough to optimize all calls using standard Java object references. Instead, such invocations always run the risk of having to pass through the considerable machinery of stubs, skeletons, and additional classes originally intended to support the invocation of methods and the movement of parameters and return structures over the network.

The composite entity concept, as shown in Figure 6.7, is straightforward. In order to reduce the overhead of interacting with Entity Beans, reduce their number by representing some of these beans as plain old Java objects (POJOs), whose lifetimes depend on a coarse-grained control object. This control object could be a composite Entity Bean or a coarse-grained POJO controlled by an Entity Bean.

This practice not only reduces the number of Entity Beans and bean interactions in an application, but also reduces the number of interbean relationships. Under EJB 1.x, this is important because such relationships are not only expensive but also tenuous

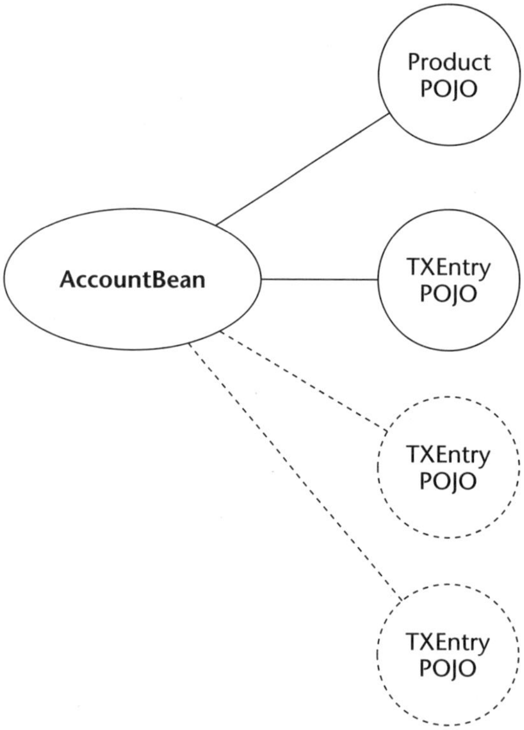

Figure 6.7 Conceptual composite entity.

because they rely on references to objects that might be remote and could become unavailable without notice. Under EJB 1.x, composite entities typically load and save their dependents explicitly, using bean-managed persistence (BMP) code that either resides within the bean itself or within a separate, but related, data-access object (DAO) that is solely responsible for persisting the object graph.

EJB 2.0 introduces a number of advancements, including local interfaces and container-managed relationships (CMR), which make the practice of creating composite entities not only unnecessary but also undesirable. With local interfaces, Entity Beans are no longer confined to the role of mere aggregations of persistent, dependent objects. Rather, Entity Beans can be as fine-grained as the domain model objects they represent. In addition, EJB 2.x's CMR supports robust relationship semantics between entities, including automatic lazy-fetching and cascade deletions—capabilities that would normally have been hand-coded in the composite Entity Bean or its DAO. These capabilities effectively deprecate the notion of composite entities.

Composite entities have become an AntiPattern because they work against the advantages of EJB 2.x. Because a composite's dependent objects are typically POJOs, they cannot be created or managed by the container. Instead, they must be tied to the life of the composite via BMP code. This hurts the cause of EJB 2.x, which now provides this functionality with CMP. Because composite BMP code is no longer necessary, and significantly increases overall complexity, it must no longer be pursued. In fact, composites should now be disaggregated into distinct entities that fall under the management of CMP and CMR.

General Form

This AntiPattern usually takes the form of large Entity Beans, whose state contains attributes that could have been associated with another Entity Bean, or contains actual instances of POJOs that could have been represented as Entity Beans. These coarse-grained beans typically use a considerable amount of BMP to load and store other objects.

Symptoms and Consequences

The symptoms and consequences of Composite Entity are increased complexity, reduced maintainability, and increased development time, as described below.

- **Increased complexity.** A symptom of this AntiPattern is a relatively small number of persistent domain objects represented as large and overly complicated Entity Beans. These Entity Beans are usually littered with complex BMP code that manipulates and manages the persistence of the POJOs. Such BMP code often includes complex, hand-coded logic to implement features such as lazy-fetching and cascaded deletions.
- **Reduced maintainability.** Inability to introduce new dependent domain objects without significantly reworking the BMP code within affected composites.

- **Increased development time.** Significant time and energy are spent designing and then allocating domain objects to be aggregated within composites. In addition, a lot of time and energy is spent coding memory management strategies (that is, lazy loading), in order to avoid the danger of loading portions of the composite object graph that will not be needed.

Typical Causes

The typical cause of this AntiPattern is being stuck in the past. Developers who have learned EJB 1.x and have grown used to its limitations are usually quite skeptical of the promises of EJB 2.x.

- **Stuck in the past.** The efficiency of container-managed operations is often doubted because of the considerable limitations of earlier implementations. However, those who have embraced the notion of composites have shown an ability to understand the benefits of pattern development. Therefore, they are capable of understanding the limitations and potential damage of AntiPatterns, given the proper training. Both education and sufficient time for experimentation are needed before developers will abandon this AntiPattern.

Known Exceptions

The one exception to this AntiPattern is the relatively rare situation in which portions of the underlying database cannot be mapped to the application domain model. This can happen with data stores that were designed to support legacy systems with different internal business models than the newer application being supported. In these cases, it may make sense to make localized use of a composite in order to manage this orphan data via BMP.

Refactorings

It may be best to forgo the use of DTOs in favor of fine-grained entity access using local interfaces. This is described in the Local Motion refactoring, found later in this chapter. (See the Surface Tension AntiPattern to address situations in which it is preferable to maintain a pervasive DTO-based architecture.)

Also, it may be helpful to disaggregate composite entities and dependent objects into finer-grained Entity Beans. Use CMP for basic persistence and CMR for robust relationships between the new entities.

Variations

This AntiPattern shares some common ground with the Mirage AntiPattern, described later in this chapter. Both assume the presence of BMP Entity Beans that should be refactored to take advantage of the advanced CMP and CMR capabilities of EJB 2.x. In fact, it may be necessary to consider some of the Mirage refactorings when preparing to defeat the Coarse Behavior AntiPattern.

Example

Let us suppose that AccountBean, in our sample financial application, is a composite entity consisting of dependent Product and TransactionEntry POJOs. This would imply that the persistence of Product and TransactionEntry instances is managed within the ejbLoad, ejbStore, and ejbRemove methods of the Account bean or that it is handled by a DAO. Our example does not include DAOs, so we can assume the former. An example of a bean-managed composite entity is shown in the AccountBean.java listing that follows.

The Account composite entity has a 1:1 relationship with Product and a 1:m relationship with its TransactionEntry instances. For EJB 1.x BMP entities, these relationships, along with the internal attributes of the Account (that is, number and balance) are maintained as attributes within the bean implementation class.

```
...

public class AccountBean implements EntityBean
{
     ...
private String number; // The primary key
private BigDecimal balance;

// Product and TransactionEntry relationships...
private Product product;
private ArrayList transactionEntries;
...

public Product getProduct() { return product; }
public void setProduct(Product inProduct){ product = InProduct; }

public Collection getTransactionEntries()
     { return transactionEntries; }
public void setTransactionEntries(Collection InTXEntries)
     { transactionEntries = (ArrayList) InTXEntries; }
...
```

Relationships, whether bean or container managed, must be reflected in the underlying database in order to be durable. For example, the 1:1 relationship between Account and Product can be represented by adding to the Account table a foreign key (FK) that references the primary key (PK) of its subordinate in the Product table. The Account PK is its number, while the Product PK is a synthetic object identifier (OID). This mapping is shown in Figure 6.8.

The 1:m relationship between Account and TransactionEntry can be represented by adding to the TransactionEntry table, a foreign key that references the primary key of its owner in the Account table. TransactionEntry instances are uniquely identified by an OID PK. This mapping is shown in Figure 6.9.

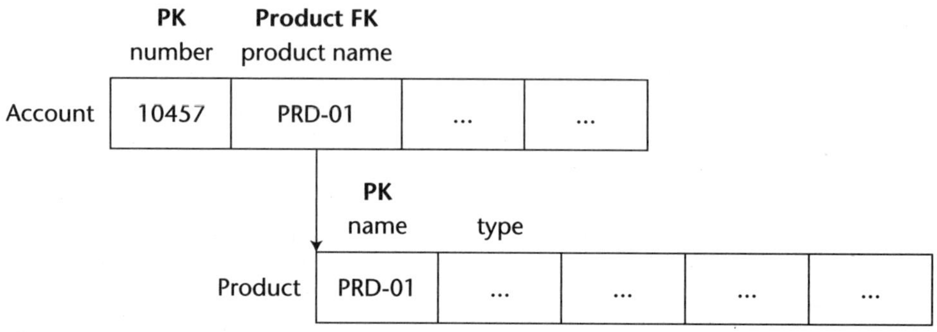

Figure 6.8 Account-product 1:1 cardinality database schema.

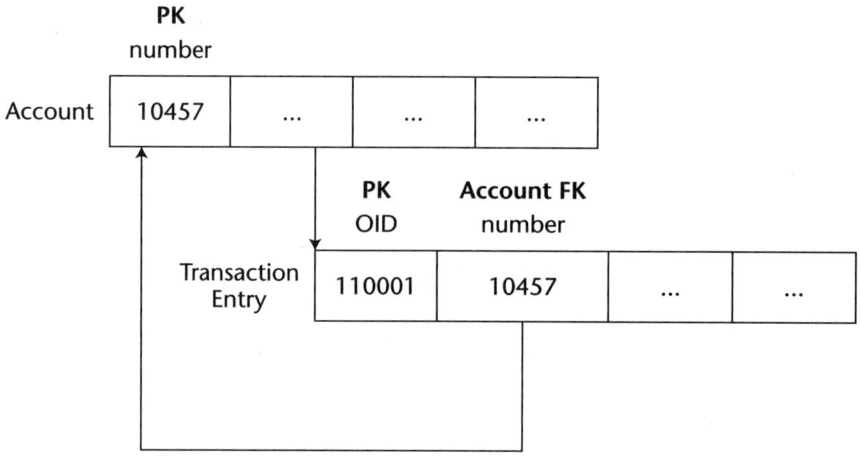

Figure 6.9 Account-TransactionEntry 1:m cardinality database schema.

Most of the persistence management of the Product and TransactionEntry dependent objects happens in the Account entity's *ejbCreate(), ejbLoad(), ejbStore(),* and *ejbRemove()* methods. For example, the ejbCreate() method must insert the Account into the database, along with its associated Product and TransactionEntry instances if they have already been assigned on the bean.

```
...
    public void ejbCreate()
    {
        // 1: If product has been assigned, then SELECT a product
        //    OID value from a database SEQUENCE or OID table.
        //
        // 2: SQL INSERT the Account, setting the Product FK
        //    to the OID that was fetched In Step 1.
        //
        // 3: If transactionEntry Instances have been assigned,
        //    then SELECT OID values for each Instance, using a
```

```
//    database SEQUENCE or OID table.
//
// 4: SQL INSERT each TransactionEntry into the underlying
//    table using the OIDs that were fetched In Step 3 as
//    PK values.  For each record, set the Account FK to
//    the PK of the currently executing Account bean.
}
```

For ejbLoad(), it is necessary to not only load the Account bean from its underlying table, but also use the fetched Product FK to load the Product instance from its underlying table. For the 1:m relationship with TransactionEntry, ejbLoad() can fetch all records from the TransactionEntry table where the Account FK equals the PK of the Account bean.

```
    ...
    public void ejbLoad()
    {
        // 1: SQL SELECT the Account, fetching the Product FK
        //    in addition to the account data.
        //
        // 2: SQL SELECT the Product using the Product FK as a
        //    PK In the Product table.
        //
        // 3: Populate the Account bean's attributes with the
        //    fetched data, including the Product instance.
        ...
        product = new Product();
        product.setName(...);
        product.setType(...);
        ...
        // 4: SQL SELECT TransactionEntry where the Account FK
        //    equals this bean's PK.
...
    }
```

The ejbStore() method must not only persist the state of the Account bean, Product, and TransactionEntry dependent objects—but it must also persist the relationships as FK column values. Therefore, when persisting the Product object, ejbStore() must update the object's state in the Product table. ejbStore() must also update each TransactionEntry instance in its underlying tables, which includes setting each record's Account FK to the PK of the currently executing Account bean.

```
    ...
            public void ejbStore()
    {
         // 1: SQL UPDATE the Product with the contents of the
         //    product attribute.
         //
```

```
            // 2: SQL UPDATE each TransactionEntry using its Instance
            //    state within the transactionEntries attribute.
            //    For each TransactionEntry record, set Its Account FK
            //    to the PK of the currently executing Account bean.
            // 3: SQL UPDATE the Account, updating the Product FK with
            //    the persisted Product's PK.
...
      }
      ...
```

Finally, the ejbRemove() method must remove the state of the Account bean from the underlying database. Since Products can exist without accounts, ejbRemove() will not delete the associated Product from the database. However, because each Account is composed of its TransactionEntry instances, it will be necessary for ejbRemove() to delete all of the transaction entries associated with the account.

```
      ...
      public void ejbRemove()
      {
            // 1: SQL DELETE TransactionEntry where the Account FK
            //    equals the PK of the currently executing Account
            //    bean.
            //
            // 2: SQL DELETE the Account.
...
      }
```

All of this explicitly coded logic is required in order to support the bean-managed Account composite and its dependent Product and TransactionEntry instances. This kind of code is often complex and prone to error.

Related Solutions

The Best of Both Worlds and Strong Bond refactorings (found later in this chapter) are related in their aim to replace BMP and bean-managed relationships with CMP and CMR. This is essential for replacing composites and dependents with fine-grained entities and relationships.

Liability

Also Known As: Overly Dependent

Most Frequent Scale: Architecture

Refactorings: Façade

Refactored Solution Type: Software

Root Causes: Ignorance and haste

Unbalanced Forces: Education, resources, and time

Anecdotal Evidence: "Transactions are complicated and must be managed explicitly."

Background

In the Surface Tension AntiPattern example (found earlier in this chapter), we considered the scenario of creating a graph of serializeable DTOs on the server, and then returning the graph over the network to the client in order to support the rendering of screens. In that example, as shown in Figure 6.5, a DTO Factory object was responsible for retrieving data from the graph of server-side entities, building the graph of DTO objects, and then returning this graph to the client. In order for this to work, the DTO Factory must implement a remote interface so that it is accessible over the network. A DTO Factory that is a Session Bean will not only support this requirement, but can provide additional benefits, such as the ability to be governed by declarative security and transaction management. In turn, these benefits provide even more benefits, as transactions are now localized on the server instead of being distributed across the client and server platforms. This is consistent with the generally accepted principle of avoiding distributed, long-running transactions that can adversely affect overall system performance with excessive resource locks and reduced concurrency. The declarative transaction management benefit is consistent with the goal of deferring as much functionality as possible to the underlying J2EE container.

The DTO Factory, as described here, is a session façade—or a simplifying component that encapsulates some underlying level of complexity. In this case, the complexity is the actual work of navigating the domain layer in order to construct and return a DTO graph. A client that uses the façade will not have to use the Java Transaction API (JTA) to explicitly manage a distributed transaction. Rather, a container-managed transaction can be wrapped around the invoked session façade method, thus pinning its scope to the server and relieving the client of any responsibility. The benefits of the façade extend to the server as well. For example, security management can be simplified by being applied at the coarse-grained façade level instead of the much finer-grained Entity Bean level. In addition, underlying Entity Beans can simply support (via the *tx_supports* transaction declarative) the transaction that the container provided for the invoked façade method, so that any Entity Bean operations that occur within the scope of this method will fall under the scope of its transaction.

All of these benefits are well understood. The Session Façade pattern—as described in Alur, Crupi, and Malks' *Core J2EE Patterns* (Alur, Crupi, and Malks 2001) —is one of the most popular J2EE patterns being used today. Unfortunately, there are still many applications that do not use facades. These applications end up suffering from increased complexity and reduced scalability and maintainability. Clients become liable for explicitly managing their transactions, while administrators become liable for defining security at the fine-grained Entity Bean level. In short, these applications suffer from the Liability AntiPattern.

General Form

The Liability AntiPattern usually takes the form of an abundance of explicit JTA calls, where clients have assumed the responsibility of explicitly managing distributed transactions. Within these transactions, there are direct manipulations of one or more entity-beans.

Symptoms and Consequences

The symptoms of Liability span everything from weighty distributed transactions to network saturation. In short, the numerous symptoms of this AntiPatterna are obvious:

- **Complicated transaction management.** Complicated, distributed transactions that originate from the client
- **Expensive client interactions.** Direct and remote client interactions with Entity Beans
- **Performance problems.** Severe performance bottlenecks, caused by the excessive network and serialization overhead of interacting with fine-grained Entity Beans over the network
- **Complexity.** Dramatically increased complexity throughout the system
- **Network saturation.** Caused by an excessive number of remote invocations and object serializations
- **Inter-tier coupling.** High levels of coupling between clients and business domain layer
- **Duplicated code.** Large amounts of repetitive code as common business processes are duplicated throughout the client, instead of being implemented in one place (as in a session façade method)

Typical Causes

Liability usually results from a couple of misunderstandings that are described below.

- **Misunderstanding the effects of coupling.** Developers, who do not understand the negative impact of coupling clients to the domain layer, are likely to fall into this AntiPattern.
- **Misunderstanding performance implications.** Developers who do not understand the performance consequences of long running distributed transactions will fall prey to this AntiPattern as well.

Known Exceptions

There are no known exceptions to this AntiPattern.

Refactorings

The primary refactoring to use on this AntiPattern is Façade, found later in this chapter. Use a Session façade to hide the complexity that is involved in performing a business process.

Variations

Strictly speaking, façades do not have to be remotable objects. If an application is small, and its Web and business layers will always be co-located, then it is unnecessary to introduce Session Beans. Instead, the façade can be a POJO that provides the benefits of encapsulation without the overhead and complexity of an EJB.

Example

Suppose that our earlier example of creating reading server entities in order to create and return DTO hierarchies to the client is reversed. Instead of displaying information, we may have screens that update data across a graph of related entities. Perhaps our screens allow us to change customer attributes and add new customer accounts. In this scenario, it is crucial that all of the data be committed to the entity graph under the principles of ACID (that is, atomic, consistent, isolated, and durable) transactions. Specifically, the entity updates should be all or nothing. If an error occurs at any time during the process of updating the entity graph, then the entire save process must be rolled back and abandoned.

However, a system that suffers from the Liability AntiPattern may not even perform the save under transactional control. Rather, this system may simply attempt to update the Entity Bean graph directly from the client, outside of transaction control.

Related Solutions

There are no related solutions to this AntiPattern.

Mirage

Also Known As: Great Expectations

Most Frequent Scale: Architecture

Refactorings: Best of Both Worlds

Refactored Solution Type: Software

Root Causes: Ignorance and haste

Unbalanced Forces: Education and time

Anecdotal Evidence: "We code all of the bean persistence by hand. It's always faster that way."

Background

Some situations require the use of bean-managed persistence (BMP). For example, some applications must work with nonrelational data stores or sources that cannot be abstracted as a javax.sql.DataSource. However, these cases are becoming increasingly rare, as J2EE application servers continue to improve their support for various types of data stores. One notable example is IBM's Websphere Application Server, Version 5.0, which uses Java Connector Architecture (JCA)-based DataSources to encapsulate non-relational data stores. Such data stores could include object-oriented database management systems (OODBMSs) or hierarchical database systems, such as IBM's mainframe-based Information Management System (IMS).

Additional examples of situations that might require BMP include the need to split beans across tables. Some J2EE application servers—notably BEA's Weblogic Server 7.0—have raised the functionality bar by providing custom container-managed persistence (CMP) extensions in order to support the mapping of an Entity Bean across multiple tables. In addition, there are a number of object-to-relational (O/R) mapping products, such as Oracle's Toplink, that can augment a CMP implementation with incredibly powerful features, such as the ability to split beans across tables or even use native stored procedures for database access. Finally, the EJB specification is continually evolving. Many of these issues are actively discussed in the J2EE standardization committees. As such, they stand a good chance of being addressed in later versions of the EJB specification.

Unless you are now dealing extensively with non-relational databases, require bean data to be split across tables, or are working with an application server that has poor CMP support, it is no longer necessary or desirable to use BMP. Applications that make extensive and unnecessary use of BMP are more difficult to develop and maintain. Valuable time is spent writing persistence code that could be better spent focusing on business logic and other functionality that cannot be readily purchased. Developers often feel they can create a more scalable solution using BMP and are hesitant to let go of this task, citing their skills in writing optimized SQL and the supposed risk of delegating such critical tasks to the container. However, such optimizations are often merely a mirage. Good CMP implementations can use a combination of efficient SQL and caching strategies to outpace most BMP efforts, while simplifying implementation and enhancing the portability of the application. When one considers the additional benefits of container-managed relationships (CMR) and built-in referential integrity, cascaded delete, and lazy-fetch support, the whole value proposition of CMP becomes even more compelling. It is this value proposition, along with the pace of advancements in the EJB specification, which leads us to conclude that using BMP, where not necessary, is an AntiPattern.

General Form

The Mirage assumes the form of Entity Beans that are overly complicated with hand-coded persistence and relationship management code. Mirage can also assume the form of large numbers of DAO classes, which end up assuming the responsibility for managing the actual persistence of the Entity Beans.

Symptoms and Consequences

When projects spend an inordinate amount of time massaging and fine-tuning JDBC calls instead of focusing on analysis, design, and the fulfillment of business requirements, it is obvious that Mirage has taken hold, as described below.

- **Time wasted coding JDBC.** Countless projects waste good intellectual capital, essentially creating object-to-relational mapping products from scratch. Unless a company is in the business of creating such products, these efforts represent a colossal waste of resources. The focus of any application development project should be the full satisfaction of its stakeholders. As such, it is far more productive to spend time analyzing and fulfilling their requirements than building unnecessary infrastructure code.

Typical Causes

The Mirage AntiPattern results from inexperience, skepticism and fear, as described below.

- **Inexperience.** Architects, designers, and developers who are not cognizant of the advancements in the EJB specification will not realize the benefits of exploiting its full capabilities. Those who have been burned in the past by the promises of older products will remain skeptical of the promises of EJB 2.x. Finally, those who are afraid to relinquish control of explicit database access will be both fearful and resent the idea of replacing their fine-tuned persistence code with container-generated JDBC.

Known Exceptions

There are some exceptions to this AntiPattern, although the list will continue to shorten as the EJB 2.x specification evolves, and its commercial implementations improve. The first exception is if you have a requirement to make significant use of non-relational data stores, such as OODBMs and hierarchical database systems. The second exception is if the application server being used offers poor CMP support or performance.

Refactorings

It may not be possible to make a wholesale from BMP to CMP in an application. Simply put, there may be some things that BMP must remain in place to handle. For example, an application may have an Entity Bean that spans multiple tables, or whose persistent state is kept in a hierarchical or object-oriented database. Thus, it may be necessary to keep BMP in some portions of the application. The Best of Both Worlds refactoring (found later in this chapter) will enable you to introduce CMP incrementally, while allowing BMP to serve in those situations for which it is still required.

Variations

There are no significant variations on this AntiPattern.

Example

Suppose that our financial services example has been using BMP entities all along. Now, suppose that we wish to incrementally introduce CMP into the example. After considering the bean-managed composite Account entity, described in the Coarse Behavior AntiPattern, we may decide to convert only the Account bean and its dependent objects into fine-grained CMP beans using CMR. In the AccountBean pseudocode extract below, there is a considerable amount of coded logic required to establish and maintain the 1:1 relationship with a product and a 1:m relationship with transaction entries. When applied across large applications, BMP code can account for more of the overall code base than the actual business logic. This means that developers, whose collective talents would be better spent on the business problem at hand, are often consumed with the menial, error-prone, and largely unnecessary task of persisting bean graphs.

```
public class AccountBean implements EntityBean
{
     // Account PK
     private String identifier;

     // 1:1 Product bean reference
     private Product product;

     // 1:M TransactionEntry bean references.
     private Collection transactionEntries;

public Product getProduct()
     { return product; }

public void setProduct(Product product)
     { this.product = product; }

public Collection getTransactionEntries()
     { return transactionEntries; }

public void setProduct(Collection transactionEntries)
     { this. transactionEntries = transactionEntries; }

public void ejbLoad()
{
     // 1: SQL Select the Account bean.
     //
     // 2: JNDI lookup of ProductHome
     //
     // 3: Call ProductHome.findByAccount, passing
     //    this account's identifier (i.e., PK)
     //
```

```
        // 4: JNDI lookup of TransactionEntryHome.
        //
        // 5: Call TransactionEntryHome.findByAccount,
        //    given the account PK.
    }

    public void ejbStore()
    {
        // 1: SQL UPDATE this Account, which stores
        //    the Product's foreign key.
    }
    }
```

Related Solutions

There are no related solutions to this AntiPattern.

Refactorings

This section documents the refactorings referred to earlier in the AntiPatterns. These refactorings utilize a combination of strategies and mechanisms to either prevent or neutralize an Entity Bean AntiPattern.

Local Motion. Most applications to not invoke their Entity Beans remotely. Instead, they are invoked by collocated Session Façade beans, which, in turn, are invoked remotely by application clients. In this scenario, the Entity Bean invocations can be far more efficient if those beans support a local interface. Session façades can use the local interface instead of the slower, more heavyweight remote interface.

Alias. Application code that references the actual JNDI locations of EJBs and services could break if those components are relocated at deployment time. Use EJB references to add a layer of abstraction that insulates the application from such deployment-time changes.

Exodus. Entity beans are often stuck with the responsibility for creating and returning custom DTOs to support screens and reports. This limits the reusability and maintainability of the entity layer, because the entity layer becomes dependent on higher-order, view-oriented DTOs that may be specific to a particular application. Add a DTO Factory component to the services layer. This component will be responsible for creating and manipulating custom DTO instances. This decouples the entity from the custom DTOs, which ultimately improves reusability.

Flat View. Entity Beans and DTOs that have a large number of getters and setters tend to increase coupling with client components. In addition, exceptionally large numbers of DTO classes can be difficult to maintain. Use a flat generic DTO to reduce the number of explicit DTO classes and DTO getters and setters within an application.

Strong Bond. Bean-managed interbean and bean-to-dependent-object relationships are no longer necessary under EJB 2.x (or greater). Use container-managed relationships (CMR) to implement these relationships without writing a single line of code.

Best of Both Worlds. Moving from BMP to CMP can be done incrementally. Simply introduce CMP implementations and modify existing BMP implementations to extend their CMP counterparts. Now, the choice of implementation can be specified at deployment time.

Façade. Java can do database-intensive operations. Simply use the batch-processing capabilities of JDBC 2.x (or greater) to optimize the network pipeline between database clients and servers.

Local Motion

Expensive remote interfaces are used throughout the system, even where not required.

Use EJB 2.x local interfaces for Entity and Session Beans that will not be accessed or tested remotely.

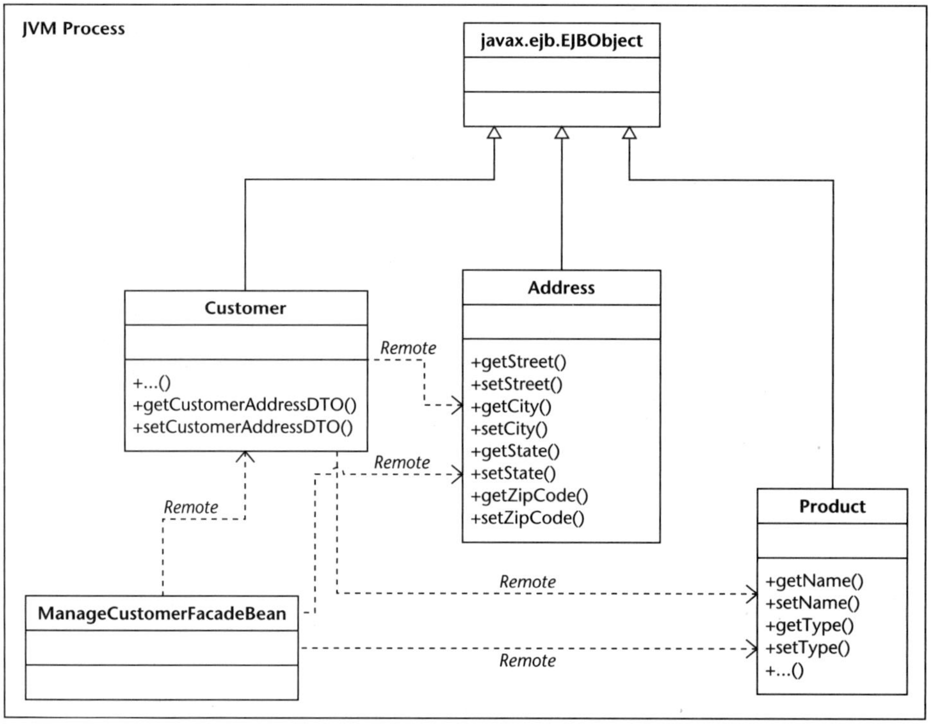

Figure 6.10 Before refactoring.

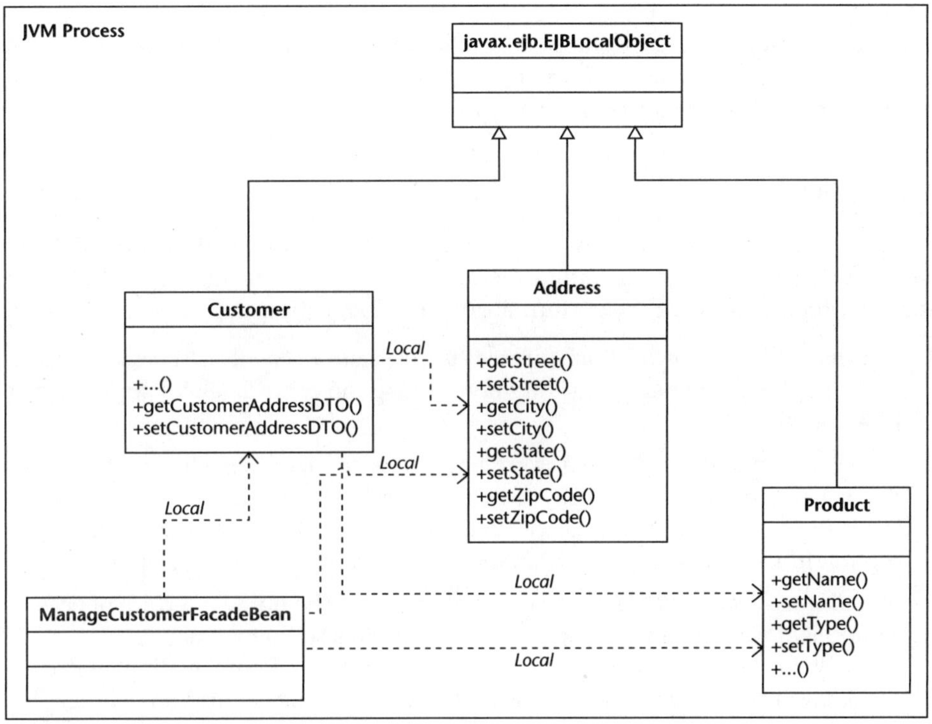

Figure 6.11 After refactoring.

Motivation

Most developers are familiar with the EJB 1.x specification and its reliance on EJB interfaces that extend java.rmi.Remote. Thus, they may continue to make blanket use of remote interfaces, even when working in an EJB 2.x environment. With proper education, developers can understand the choices that EJB 2.x offers, and the considerable benefits associated with using local interfaces where appropriate.

The term "local interfaces" actually refers to a set of interfaces called javax.ejb.EJBLocalObject and javax.ejb.EJBLocalHome. These interfaces allow their implementers to respectively perform the roles of EJB objects and EJB homes without incurring the overhead of their remotable javax.ejb.EJBObject and javax.ejb.EJBHome counterparts. Unless a Session or Entity Bean will be accessed remotely, there is no need for it to support a remote interface.

Using local interfaces not only improves the performance of an application, but can also simplify its overall design. For example, EJB 1.x applications typically used domain data transfer objects (DTOs) to convey Entity Bean attributes en masse. This practice was followed in order to reduce the overhead associated with making fine-grained invocations against Entity Bean interfaces. Although DTOs were helpful, they were also problematic because they often exploded in number and had to be synchronized with their entity counterparts. Under EJB 2.x, an Entity Bean that is fronted by a Session façade can support a local interface so that fine-grained access is as efficient as invoking a method on a plain old Java object (POJO). For the most part, this makes the use of domain DTOs between session and Entity Beans unnecessary.

Mechanics

The following is a list of steps which must be followed in order to apply the Local Motion refactoring. These steps outline a strategy for using local interfaces wherever possible in order to improve the performance of EJB invocations.

1. *Determine which components are invoked over the network and which ones are not.* The ones that are never accessed remotely are good candidates for supporting a local interface.
2. *Use local interfaces where appropriate.* Change the interface of each component that is never invoked over the network so that it extends javax.ejb.EJBLocalObject instead of javax.ejb.EJBObject. Remove all references to java.rmi.RemoteException from the interface. Local interfaces cannot throw these exceptions.
3. *Introduce local home interfaces as appropriate.* Change the home interface of each component that is never invoked over the network so that it extends javax.ejb.EJBLocalHome instead of javax.ejb.EJBHome. Remove all references to the java.rmi.RemoteException from the home interface. Local home interfaces cannot throw these exceptions.
4. *Modify deployment descriptors.* Change any ejb-jar.xml descriptor stanzas that reference the bean so that the new local object and home interfaces are used instead of the previous remote interfaces.
5. *Deploy and test.*

Example

The very first step in applying this refactoring is to identify the EJB components that are accessed remotely and the ones that are not. If your application only exposes Session Bean façades to remote clients, while invoking collocated Entity Beans within the façade implementation, then the Session Beans must support remote interfaces. However, the Entity Beans can support local interfaces, which the Session façades can use to improve the performance of Entity Bean invocations.

For example, suppose that we have an Account Entity Bean that supports only a remote interface, but is never accessed remotely. This means that collocated Session Bean façade interactions with the Account entity will incur the unnecessary overhead of the remote interface.

```
...

import java.rmi.RemoteException;
import javax.ejb.EJBObject;
```

```
public interface Account extends EJBObject
{
...
     public BigDecimal deposit(BigDecimal amount)
throws RemoteException;
     public BigDecimal withdraw(BigDecimal amount)
throws RemoteException;
...
}
```

The primary problem is that the Account bean interface extends javax.ejb.EJBObject, which is an interface that ultimately extends java.rmi.Remote. Because this Entity bean should never be accessed remotely, it should not incur the baggage of providing a remote interface.

Therefore, the next step in this refactoring is to change the Account interface so that it supports a local interface. We accomplish this by modifying the Account interface so that it extends javax.ejb.EJBLocalObject, which provides the necessary EJB interface definitions without extending java.rmi.Remote and incurring the associated invocation overhead.

```
...
import javax.ejb.EJBLocalObject;

public interface Account extends EJBLocalObject
{
...
     public BigDecimal deposit(BigDecimal amount);
     public BigDecimal withdraw(BigDecimal amount);
...
}
```

The next step is to modify the Account's home interface, so that it no longer extends javax.ejb.EJBHome, but instead extends its local equivalent—the javax.ejb.EJBLocalHome interface.

```
...
import javax.ejb.EJBLocalHome;
...

public interface AccountHome extends EJBLocalHome
{
...
public Account create(String Id, BigDecimal balance)
             throws CreateException;

public Account findByPrimaryKey(String Id)
    throws FinderException;
...
}
```

The next step in this refactoring is to modify the Account bean's deployment descriptor in order to enforce the local interface. To do this, edit the ejb-jar.xml file containing the deployment descriptor for the bean.

```
<ejb-jar>
  <enterprise-beans>
    <entity>
      <ejb-name>Account</ejb-name>
...
 <home>AccountHome</home>
      <remote>Account</remote>
...
```

Replace the <home> and <remote> element tags with <local-home> and <local> tags, respectively.

```
     ...
 <local-home>AccountHome</local-home>
      <local>Account</local>
...
```

The list step of this refactoring is to compile, deploy, and test the changes. Now that this refactoring is in place, co-located invocations between Session façades and co-located Entity Beans should perform much better.

Finally, this refactoring has operated under the assumption of switching a bean from remote to local interfaces. However, it is possible for a bean to support both types of interfaces simultaneously. To accomplish this, simply be additive in applying this refactoring. For example, instead of modifying the AccountHome.java and Account .java files, add two new ones—AccountLocalHome.java and AccountLocal.java—that contain the local interface definitions. Likewise, instead of replacing the remote tags within the Account's deployment descriptor, simply add the local tags. This way, clients can choose either to continue using the Account bean via its remote interface, or to use the new local interface. This approach can be used to incrementally introduce local interfaces to an application.

Alias

Code makes explicit references to the actual JNDI locations of EJBs and services.

Use EJB References to introduce a level of abstraction between the code and desired EJBs and services so that the actual location of these dependents can be specified at deployment time.

```
// Get the default JNDI Initial context.
Context context = new InitialContext();
// Look up the Account home.
Object obj = context.lookup("java:comp/env/ejb/AccountHome");
```

Listing. 6.2 Before refactoring.

```
// Get the default JNDI Initial context.
Context context = new InitialContext();
// Look up the Account home.
Object obj = context.lookup("java:comp/env/FinancialServices/Accounts");
```

Listing. 6.3 After refactoring.

Motivation

Hard-coding references to EJBs will introduce brittleness to an application. If the application must be deployed in an environment which, for one reason or another, will not accommodate the JNDI trees that have been hard-coded into the implementation, then the application will fail to deploy within that environment. This consequence effectively limits the reusability of the application and its components.

For example, consider the code example that was introduced in the Fragile Links AntiPattern described earlier. This code assumes the specific location of the AccountHome interface during its lookup.

```
// Get the default JNDI Initial context.
Context context = new InitialContext();

// Look up the Account home.
Object obj = context.lookup("java:comp/env/ejb/AccountHome");
```

```
// Downcast appropriately via RMI-IIOP conventions...
AccountHome acctHome = (AccountHome)
javax.rmi.PortableRemoteObject.narrow(
obj, AccountHome.class);
...
```

The EJB specification recommends, but does not require, placing beans that are referenced from other beans under the *java:comp/env/ejb* context. Therefore, it is possible that beans can reside elsewhere within the JNDI tree. EJB references can be introduced to accommodate this possibility.

Using EJB references in lieu of hard-coded references introduces a protective layer of abstraction, which will enhance the reusability of application components by making them capable of adapting to environments with different deployment characteristics.

Mechanics

The following is a list of steps that must be followed in order to apply the Alias refactoring. These steps outline a strategy for using EJB references to increase deployment flexibility.

1. *Determine and list the EJBs and services upon which a given application component depends.* A simple way to accomplish this step would be to scan the source code for the application component, looking for the JNDI lookup. Inspect each lookup, distilling a list of those involving dependent EJBs and services.
2. *Replace explicit, hard-coded links to dependent EJBs and services with aliases or EJB References.*
3. *Modify deployment descriptors.* Each component that uses an EJB Reference must contain a deployment descriptor definition that provides additional information about the reference. For example, the JNDI location of the referenced component must be specified, along with the .jar file in which the component resides.

Example

The first step in this refactoring is to identify the services and EJBs referenced within the application. A simple way to accomplish this is to scan the source code for JNDI lookups. Some of these lookups may be candidates for refactoring. For example, the following line of code assumes that the AccountHome will reside under the default *ejb* JNDI context. However, if AccountHome is relocated to another JNDI context at deployment time, this code will break.

```
// Look up the Account home.
Object obj = context.lookup("java:comp/env/ejb/AccountHome");
```

Therefore, the next step in this refactoring is to replace this hard-coded link with an EJB Reference, as follows.

```
// Look up the Account home.
Object obj = context.lookup("java:comp/env/FinancialServices/Accounts");
```

This seemingly trivial change eliminates the assumption that the AccountHome will always be located where the EJB specification recommends. Using the EJB reference, or alias, called *Accounts* will decouple the application code from the actual location of the AccountHome interface. This concept allows application components to be mapped to custom JNDI trees upon deployment. An example of such a JNDI tree is shown in Figure 6.12.

The final step is to modify the deployment descriptor, in order to tie the *Accounts* alias to the actual location of the AccountHome interface in the deployment descriptor of the calling component.

```
...
<entity>
...
     <ejb-name>Customer</ejb-name>
     ...
```

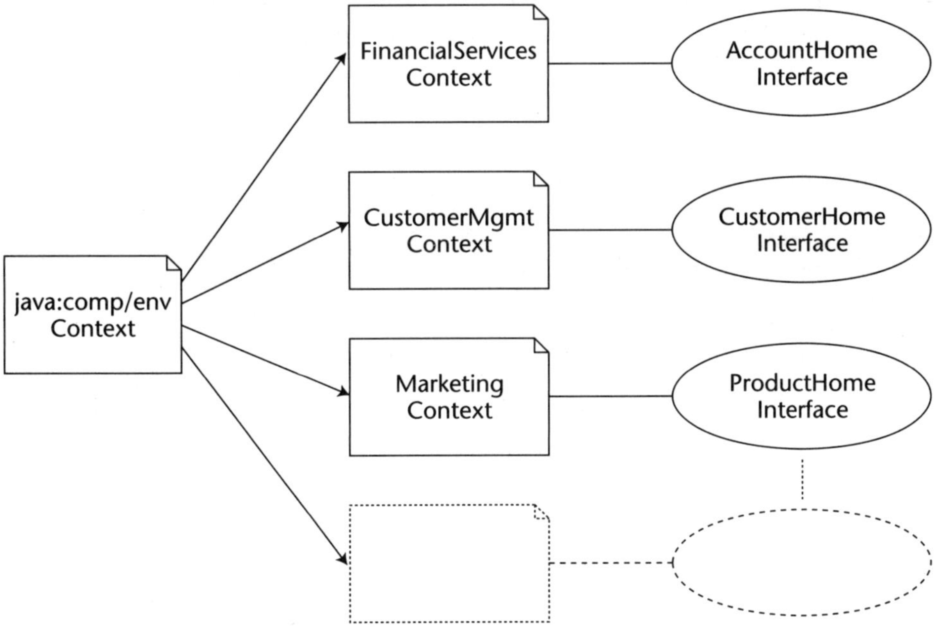

Figure 6.12 Customized EJB-JNDI tree.

Suppose, for example, that the customer component is trying to locate the AccountHome interface. In this case, we will need to modify the customer deployment descriptor to reflect its dependency on the *Accounts* reference as shown below:

```
<ejb-ref>
<ejb-ref-name>FinancialServices/Accounts</ejb-ref-name>
<ejb-ref-type>Entity</ejb-ref-type>
<home>examples.AccountHome</home>
<remote>examples.AccountHome</remote>
<ejb-link>../Accounts/Account.jar#Account</ejb-link>
</ejb-ref>
     ...
</entity>
```

In this example, the Customer and Account beans are deployed in separate .jar files within the same J2EE application (that is, .ear file). An <ejb-ref> stanza is added to the Customer deployment descriptor to indicate a referential dependency on another bean. In this case, the bean is the Account entity, which will be referenced via the *Accounts* alias. In the absence of unique EJB naming requirements across the .jar file of a J2EE application, the EJB specification provides notation for addressing specific beans within specific component files. Thus, the <ejb-link> XML element of the <ejb-ref> stanza references the specific .jar file (that is, Account.jar) and bean (that is, Account) upon which the entire EJB reference depends. Had both beans been deployed in the same .jar file, the specific .jar file (and delimiting the '#' symbol) could have been omitted from the <ejb-link> element. Local interface dependencies can be accommodated by using an <ejb-local-ref> instead of <ejb-ref>, and replacing the <home> and <remote> elements with <local-home> and <local>, respectively, as shown below:

```
...
<entity>
...
     <ejb-name>Customer</ejb-name>
     ...
<ejb-local-ref>
<ejb-ref-name>Accounts</ejb-ref-name>
<ejb-ref-type>Entity</ejb-ref-type>
<local-home>examples.AccountHome</local-home>
<local>examples.AccountHome</local>
<ejb-link>../Accounts/Account.jar#Account</ejb-link>
</ejb-local-ref>
     ...
</entity>
```

EJB references provide a powerful and flexible mechanism for addressing interbean dependencies at the deployment level, regardless of how the application is physically packaged.

Exodus

Entity Beans are held responsible for manipulating view-based, custom data transfer object (DTO) classes

Move DTO manipulations out of the Entity Beans and into special DTO Factory classes, which can operate within the higher-order service layer.

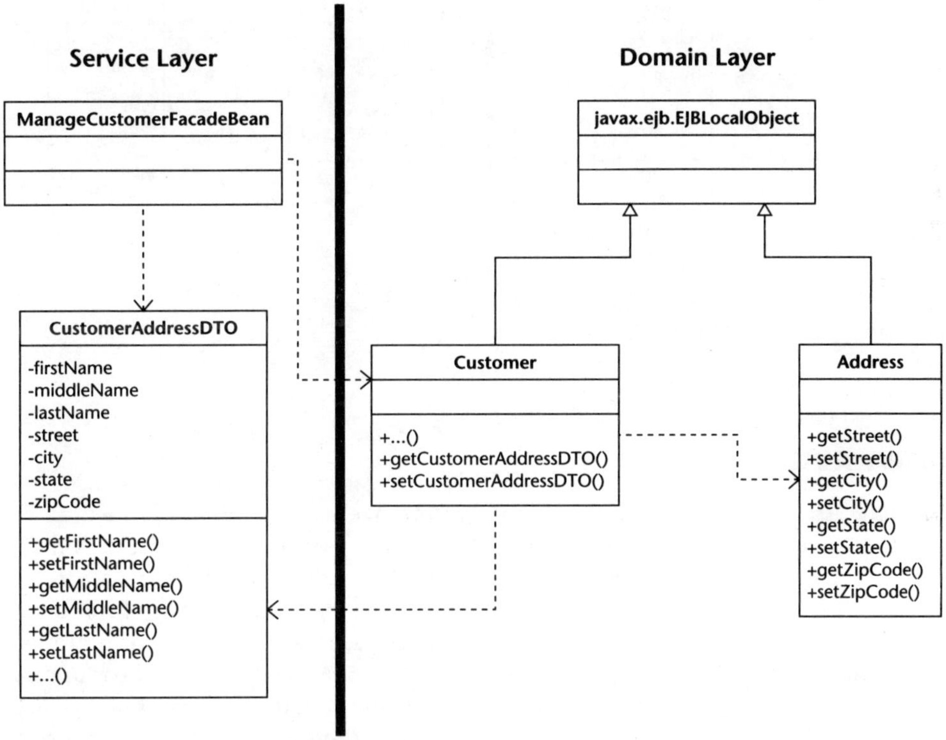

Figure 6.13 Before refactoring.

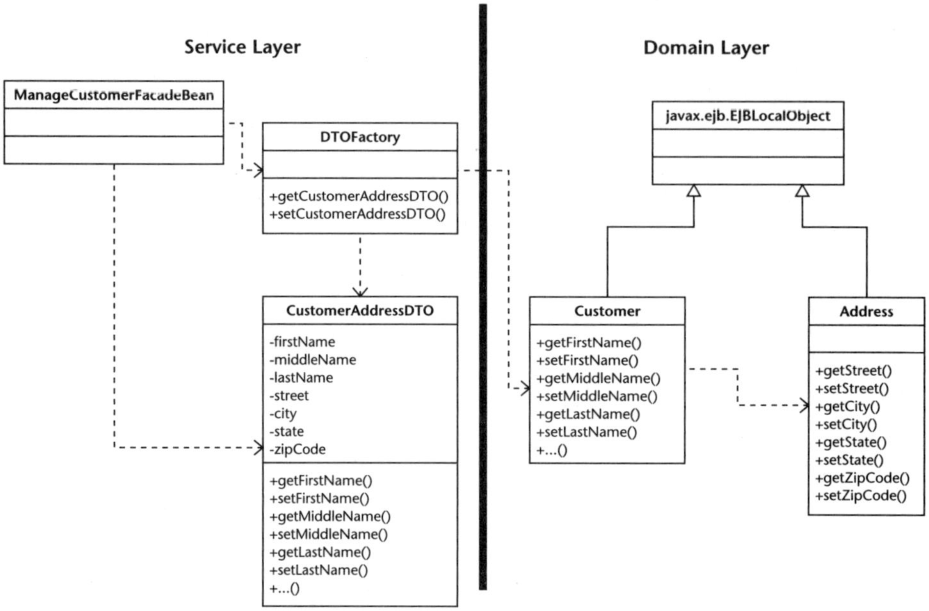

Figure 6.14 After refactoring.

Motivation

DTOs have traditionally been used to combat the overhead of making fine-grained invocations over the network. DTOs generally fall into two broad categories: domain DTOs and custom DTOs. A domain DTO is a bundle of data that represents a specific entity's state. Domain DTOs are typically used to move data across Entity Bean interfaces in bulk. A custom DTO is a bundle of data that is required by one or more use cases. Typically, an application will have one or more screens, which display or update server-side information. Instead of performing this operation using fine-grained remote invocations, a client will typically request and submit a custom DTO that contains all of the information that is required.

Some projects make the mistake of holding Entity Beans responsible for creating these custom DTOs, which actually reside within the application logic layer directly supporting the user interface. When this happens, the reusability of the domain layer suffers because it becomes dependent on the higher-level application logic layer. The domain layer becomes polluted with a specific application's user interface requirements. This makes it difficult to reuse the domain layer in other applications, some of which may not even have a user interface (that is, batch applications, software agents, and so on).

In order to preserve and promote the usability of the domain layer, decouple it from higher-level architectural layers, so that it remains independent.

Mechanics

The following is a list of steps which must be followed in order to apply the Exodus refactoring. These steps outline a strategy for using local interfaces wherever possible in order to improve the performance of EJB invocations.

1. *Create a DTO Factory class or a Session Bean within the service layer.* The choice of implementation depends on how it will be used. If it is more likely to be used by existing Session Beans, then it can be defined as a POJO. Otherwise, it is best to make the factory a Session Bean. The DTO Factory will be responsible for navigating the domain layer in response to requests for custom DTOs from higher-level architectural layers (for example, application logic). Next, move custom DTO import statements and dependent code out of entities and into the factory.
2. *Remove DTO dependencies from the entity layer.* Once a DTOFactory service component has been established it is no longer necessary for Entity Beans to create, accept, or return custom DTOs.
3. *Compile, deploy and test.*

Example

Suppose that we have an application that displays screens which contain information about customers and their accounts. If the customer and account information are represented by separate Entity Beans, it may be possible to make one of the beans responsible for packaging and returning the required information to the client. This information might be returned in a custom DTO class, for example the CustomerAccountDTO class shown below:

```
public class CustomerAccountDTO
{
     private String customerFirstName;
     ...
     private Collection accountIDs;

     public String getCustomerFirstName
          { return customerFirstName; }
     public void setCustomerFirstName(String inValue)
          { customerFirstName = inValue; }
     ...
     public void addAccountID(String inValue)
          { accountIDs.add(inValue); }
     public String getAccountIDs
           { return accountIDs; }
...
}
```

Suppose the CustomerBean entity is responsible for creating and returning instances of CustomerAccountDTO to the client. The Customer entity would query its associated Account entities in order to create the necessary DTO instances, as follows:

```
...
import examples.CustomerAccountDTO;
...
public class CustomerBean implements EntityBean
{
...
      public CustomerAccountDTO
         getCustomerAccountInformation(String customerID)
         {
         // Collect Information from self and subordinate
         // account entities.
         ...
           CustomerAccountDTO returnDTO = new CustomerAccountDTO();
         ...
         return returnDTO;
 }
}
...
```

This is an example of the DTO Explosion AntiPattern in action. Because the CustomerBean is dependent on a higher-level, view-oriented custom DTO, it cannot be easily reused in another application unless the custom DTO is brought long as well—hindering the reusability of the entity layer. This refactoring can solve the problem.

The first step in this refactoring is to create a DTO Factory class that can take full responsibility for creating and manipulating CustomerAccountDTO instances. This will allow the Customer entity to be relieved of these duties, thus breaking the dependency on the custom DTO class.

```
...
public class CustomerDTOFactory
{
...
     public CustomerAccountDTO
getCustomerAccountInformation(String customerID)
{
     // 1: JNDI lookup of CustomerHome. This could be cached
     //    to avoid the expense of future lookups.
     //
     // 2: Call CustomerHome.findByPrimaryKey(), passing In the
     //    customer ID.
     //
     // 3: Under EJB 2.x, Customer can support local Interface.
     //    If so, make fine-grained Invocations to get requested
     //    Information. Otherwise, use domain DTOs for coarse-
     //    grained entity access.
```

```
        ...
        String firstName = customer.getFirstName();
        Collection accounts = cutomer.getAccounts();
        ...
        CustomerAccountDTO returnDTO = new CustomerAccountDTO ();
        returnDTO.setCustomerFirstName(firstName);
        returnDTO.addAccountID(anAccount.getID());
        ...
        return returnDTO;
    }
    ...
}
```

The next step in this refactoring is to remove any dependencies on the custom DTO. It is no longer necessary for CustomerBean to have a *getCustomerAccountInformation(...)* method, because the bean will no longer be responsible for providing this information. That responsibility has moved to the DTOFactory, which resides in the services layer, along with the custom DTO class.

Finally, compile and test the new factory and refactored Entity Beans to make sure that the application behaves as it normally would. For our example, the customer account screens should still be displayed with the right information. The benefits of this refactoring will not be evident from an application usability or performance perspective. Rather, the benefit comes from business components that are more reusable and maintainable.

Flat View

Entity bean and DTO interfaces have large surface areas, which promotes coupling wherever they are used.

Introduce flattened, generic DTOs to eliminate the number of explicit method invocations required to navigate interfaces.

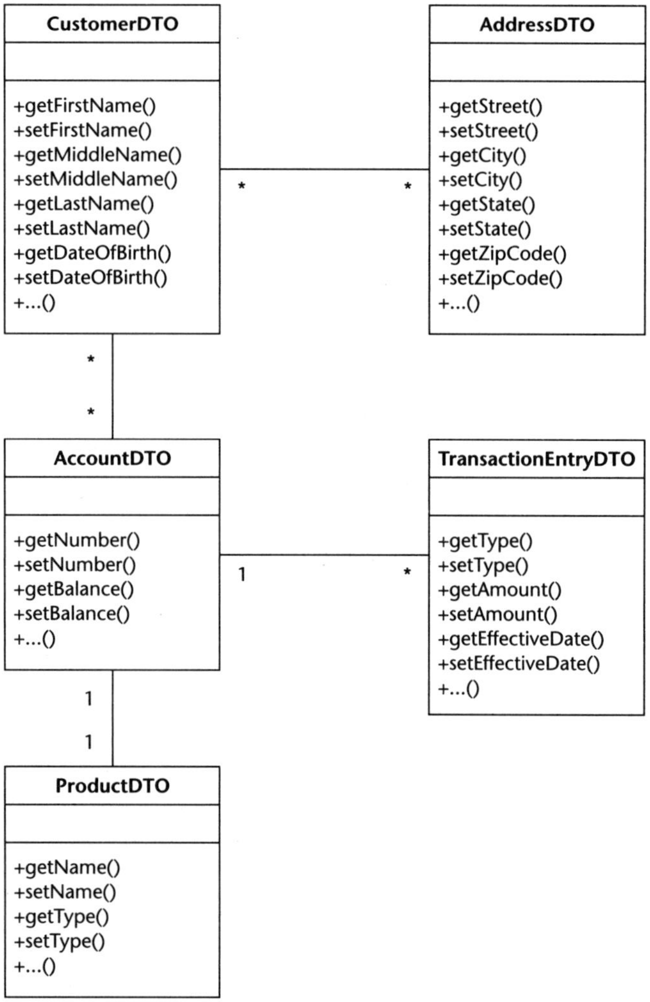

Figure 6.15 Before refactoring.

Key	*Value*
Customer.firstName	John
Customer.middleName	Q.
Customer.lastName	Smith
Customer.Address.street	665 E. 181 Street
Customer.Address.city	Bronx
Customer.Address.state	New York
Customer.Address.zipCode	10457

java.util.HashMap

Figure 6.16 After refactoring.

Motivation

Some systems have Entity Beans and DTOs that have a large number of attributes. In this scenario, it is likely that an unwieldy number of fine-grained getter and setter invocations are required in order to convey data between the service and domain layers (that is, Session and Entity Beans). This same phenomenon is usually echoed between the application logic and service layers, as Web tier components (for example, servlets and JSPs) attempt to extract information from these DTOs.

A flat, generic DTO—as illustrated in Figure 6.16—can be used to alleviate the coupling that can be experienced when manipulating Entity Bean or DTO interfaces with large surface areas. A generic DTO is one that is implemented as a serializeable collection, such as a java.util.HashMap. The HashMap key can contain a moniker that represents the information that is stored in the associated value object. For example, a customer's first name might be keyed as Customer.firstName, while its corresponding object would contain the actual value of the customer's first name, John.

Generic DTOs can help alleviate the compile-time coupling that can be associated with manipulating large Entity Bean and DTO interfaces. An intelligent choice of keys can be particularly helpful because it may be possible to automate the creation and consumption of these generic DTOs using the Java Reflection API. For example, given the Customer.firstName key illustrated in Figure 6.17, it is possible to parse the class name (that is, Customer) and attribute name (that is, firstName), and then use Java reflection to walk a graph of Entity Beans, looking for a Customer bean. Next, Java reflection could be used to dynamically invoke that bean's setFirstName(...) method, setting its firstName attribute to the Customer.firstName key-value specified in the generic DTO (that is, John).

Mechanics

The following is a list of steps which must be followed in order to apply the Flat View refactoring. These steps outline a strategy for collapsing multiple, concrete DTO cases into a single, generic DTO using a keyed Java collection. This helps reduce complexity in applications that have an unwieldy number of concrete DTO classes.

1. *Identify candidate DTO graph.* Find a graph of DTO classes that has become unwieldy in complexity. This may be a graph with too many nodes, or it could be a graph whose DTO classes have an unacceptably long number of getter and setter methods, which must be invoked explicitly. Such graphs become prime candidates for consolidation into a generic DTO structure.
2. *Choose a key-naming scheme.* Pick a key structure that is intuitive and could eventually support automated traversal, such as use of the Java Reflection API described above.
3. *Compile, deploy, and test.*

Example

The first step is to identify a candidate graph for consolidation. For the purposes of our example, let us consider the graph illustrated in Figure 6.16. In this illustration, a single CustomerDTO instance is associated with one or more addresses and accounts. Each account is associated with one product and one or more transaction entries. This graph could conceivably become unwieldy due to a large number of nodes or a potentially large number of getter and setter methods, as hinted at by the ellipses in the class definitions.

The next step in this refactoring is to choose a naming scheme. This can be accomplished by expressing the object hierarchy using class names and dotted notation. For example, the street attribute within an address associated with a customer could be keyed as CustomerDTO.AddressDTO#1.stree, where the "#" and a numeral would indicate the instance number. Figure 6.17 illustrates a potential generic DTO consolidation of the graph shown in Figure 6.16.

The last step in this refactoring is to compile, deploy, and test all of these changes. Keep in mind that any client code of the original customDTO graph will need to be changed to work with the new generic DTO instance. The benefits of all of this consolidation will be realized in reduced complexity and maintenance costs, as the number of explicit class and method implementations is dramatically reduced.

Key	*Value*
CustomerDTO.firstName	John
CustomerDTO.middleName	Q.
CustomerDTO.lastName	Smith
CustomerDTO.dateOfBirth	12/8/1967
CustomerDTO.AddressDTO#1.street	665 E. 181 Street
CustomerDTO.AddressDTO#1.city	Bronx
CustomerDTO.AddressDTO#1.state	NY
CustomerDTO.AddressDTO#1.zipCode	10457
CustomerDTO.AccountDTO#1.number	1122-33
CustomerDTO.AccountDTO#1.balance	$903,000.00
CustomerDTO.AccountDTO#1.ProductDTO.name	ABC
CustomerDTO.AccountDTO#1.ProductDTO.type	Widget
CustomerDTO.AccountDTO#1.TransactionEntryDTO#1.type	Debit
CustomerDTO.AccountDTO#1.TransactionEntryDTO#1.amount	$23,000.00
CustomerDTO.AccountDTO#1.TransactionEntryDTO#1.effectiveDate	3/20/2003

java.util.HashMap

Figure 6.17 Generic DTO.

Strong Bond

You need to persist and relate fine-grained Entity Beans in a portable manner.

Replace bean-managed interbean and bean-to-dependent-object relationships with declarative, container-managed relationships (CMR).

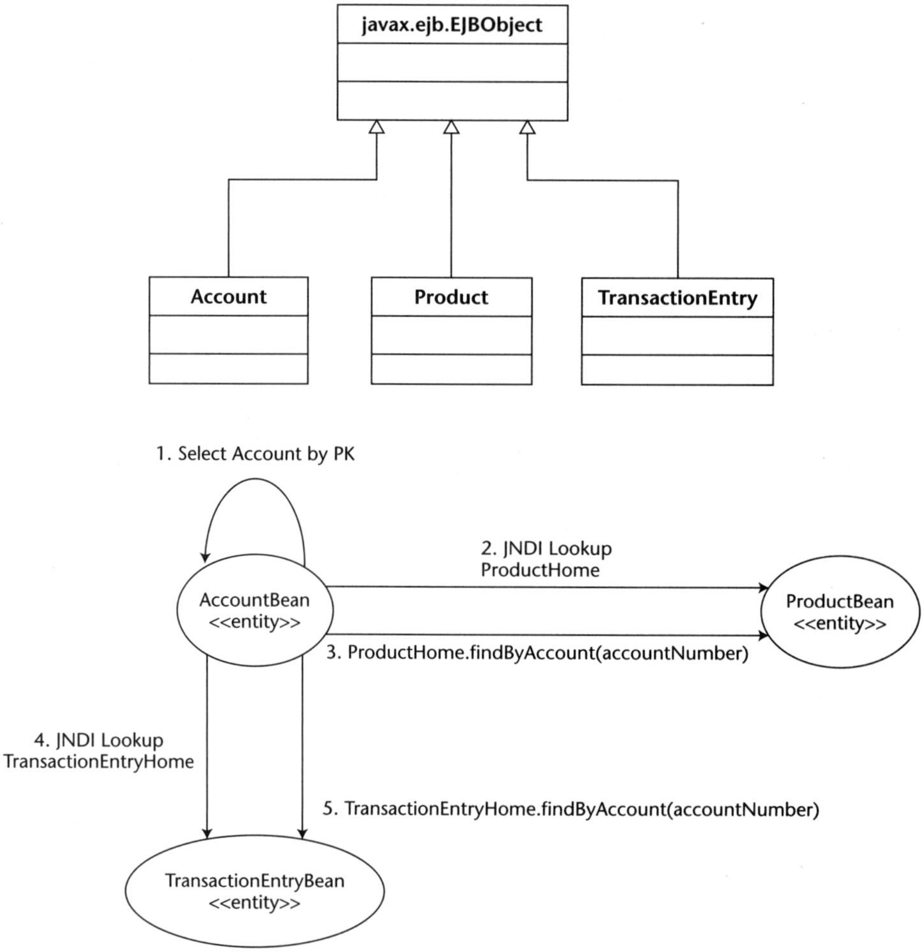

Figure 6.18 Before refactoring.

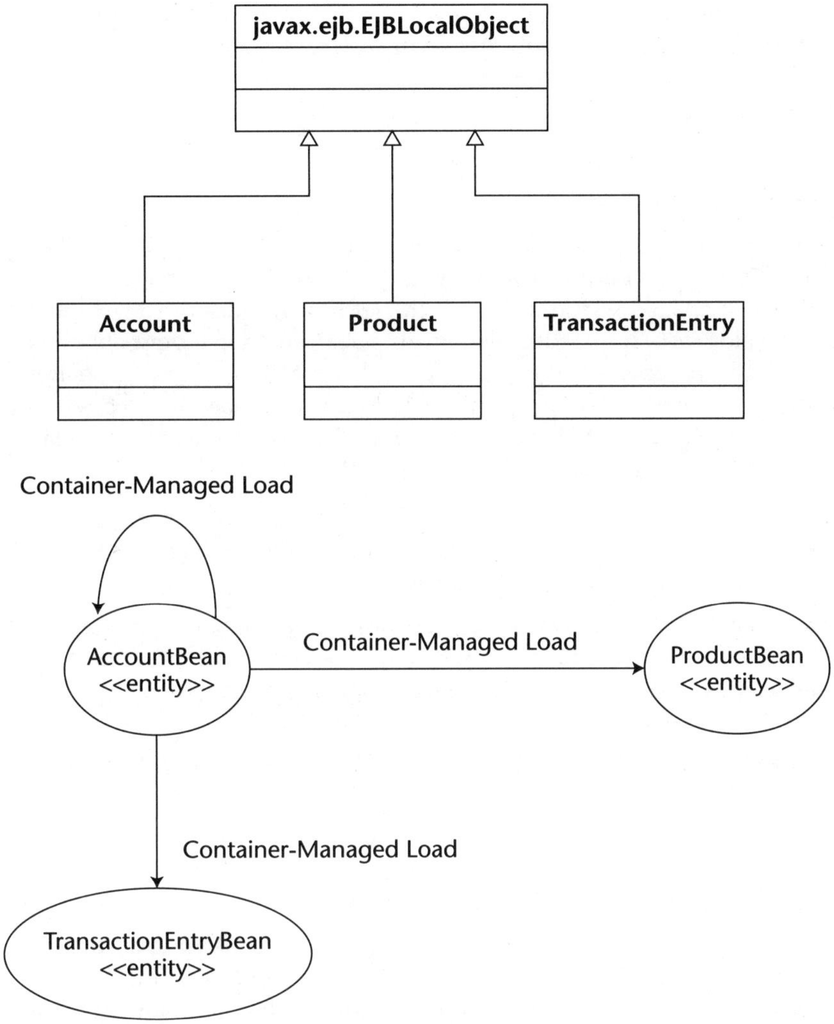

Figure 6.19 After refactoring.

Motivation

EJB 2.x brings considerable advancements in the areas of container-managed persistence. The introduction of local interfaces, along with container-manager relationships, offers a compelling value proposition. There may be cases where we wish to replace bean-managed persistence and relationships with CMP and CMR, respectively. There may be cases where we are creating beans for the first time, and wish to persist and connect them using the very latest capabilities of EJB 2.x. In these situations, we can easily create CMP beans that can be tethered together using the strong bonds of CMR.

Some aspects of deploying CMP and CMR are specific to a particular application server implementation. We will avoid discussion of such topics and will instead focus on the basics, which should be supported by any EJB 2.x–compliant application server environment.

Mechanics

The following is a list of steps which must be followed in order to apply the Strong Bond refactoring. These steps outline a strategy for replacing bean-managed relationships with container-managed relationships (CMR). CMR simplifies the development effort, relieving developers of the burden of managing bean and dependent-object relationships in code. The process starts by identifying bean-managed and dependent-object relationships as candidates for conversion to CMR. Dependent objects are converted into Entity Beans, while local interfaces are introduced across the related Entity Beans to improve performance and support CMR.

1. *Identify bean-managed relationships.* Find bean-managed interbean and bean-to-dependent-object relationships. These relationships can often be simplified and made more efficient once converted to CMR.
2. *Convert dependent objects to Entity Beans.* Dependent objects that can be represented across one or more database tables should be converted into CMP Entity Beans and graphs. CMP support relieves developers of having to manage the persistence of these objects in code.
3. *Introduce Local Interfaces.* Make each interrelated bean provide a local interface in order to support CMR.
4. *Introduce CMR support methods.* Define getter and setter methods on each Entity Bean that will participate in a container-managed relationship. Add a set of getter and setter methods for each CMR relationship.
5. Convert BMP beans to CMP. For each BMP bean, make its interface abstract and replace its attribute definitions with abstract getter and setter method equivalents. The container will invoke these methods when persisting the bean or handling any of its container-managed.
6. *Modify deployment descriptors.* Make the appropriate EJB deployment descriptor modifications in order to support the CMP and CMR mappings.
7. *Compile, deploy, and test.*

Example

Let us revisit the example of the bean-managed Account entity that was introduced in the Coarse Behavior AntiPattern description. The composite Account bean depends upon Product and TransactionEntry POJOs.

The first step of this refactoring is to identify the bean-managed relationships. Because Account explicitly manages its relationships with Product and TransactionEntry POJOs, these relationships must be considered candidates for conversion to CMR.

The next step is to convert these dependent objects into Entity Beans. Thus, ProductBean and TransactionEntryBean classes must be created, along with their respective interfaces and home interfaces.

The next step is to introduce local interfaces, making sure that each bean that must participate in container-managed relationships supports such an interface. The Account, Product, and TransactionEntry Entity Beans must each support local interfaces and home interfaces. The Local Motion refactoring provides specific guidance on how to accomplish this.

The next step in this refactoring is to introduce CMR support methods. This involves defining getter and setter methods on each Entity Bean that will participate in the relationship. Specifically, we will add a set of getter and setter methods for each CMR relationship. For example, we will add to the Account entity getter and setter methods for Product and TransactionEntry relationships:

```
import javax.ejb.EJBLocalObject;
...
public interface Account extends EJBLocalObject
{
     private String id;
     private BigDecimal balance;
     private Product product;
     private Collection transactionEntries;
     ...
     public String getId();
     public BigDecimal getBalance();
     ...
     // Expose CMR relationships so that façade can have
     // easy access

     public Product getProduct();
     public void setProduct(Product InProduct);

     public Collection getTransactionEntries();
     public void setTransactionEntries(Collection InTXEntries);
...
}
```

The next step in this refactoring is to convert BMP beans to CMP. For our example, we will make the Account interface abstract and replace its persistent attributes with abstract getter and setter methods. CMP will use these methods to persist the bean as well as manage its relationships with other beans.

```
abstract public class AccountBean implements EntityBean
{
      ...
      // Container-managed fields...
      abstract public String getNumber();
      abstract public void setNumber(String InNumber);
      abstract public BigDecimal getBalance();
      abstract public void setBalance(BigDecimal Inbalance);
      private BigDecimal balance;

      // Container-managed relationships...
      abstract public Product getProduct();
      abstract public void setProduct(Product InProduct);
      abstract public TransactionEntry getTransactionEntry();
      abstract public void setTransactionEntry(
      TransactionEntry InTransactionEntries);
      ...
      // BMP Implementations no longer necessary under CMP & CMR
      public void ejbActivate() { };
      public void ejbPassivate() { };
      public void ejbLoad() { };
      public void ejbStore() { };
      public void ejbRemove() { };
      ...
}
...
```

The next step in this refactoring is to make the appropriate deployment descriptor definitions to actually enable CMP and CMR. The first section of the deployment descriptor will contain the basic bean declarations and CMP bindings for the Account, Product, and TransactionEntry beans.

```
...
<ejb-jar>
<entity>
<ejb-name>Account</ejb-name>
<local-home>examples.AccountHome</local-home>
<local>examples.Account</local>
<ejb-class>examples.AccountBean</ejb-class>
<persistence-type>Container</persistence-type>
...
<abstract-schema-name>Account</abstract-schema-name>
<cmp-field>
<field-name>number</field-name>
</cmp-field>
<cmp-field>
<field-name>balance</field-name>
</cmp-field>
...
</entity>
<entity>
```

```
<ejb-name>Product</ejb-name>
<local-home>examples.ProductHome</local-home>
<local>examples.Product</local>
...
</entity>
<entity>
<ejb-name>TransactionEntry</ejb-name>
...
</entity>
...
```

The next section of the deployment descriptor contains the CMR definitions required to enforce the 1:1 relationship between Account and Product, and the 1:m relationship between Account and TransactionEntry.

```
...
<relationships>
<ejb-relation>
<ejb-relation-name>Account-Product</ejb-relation-name>
<ejb-relationship-role>
<ejb-relationship-role-name>Account-Has-Product
</ejb-relationship-role-name>
<multiplicity>one</multiplicity>
<relationship-role-source>
<ejb-name>Account</ejb-name>
</relationship-role-source>
<cmr-field>
<cmr-field-name>product</cmr-field-name>
<cmr-field-type>Product</cmr-field-type>
</cmr-field>
</ejb-relationship-role>
</ejb-relation>

<ejb-relation>
<ejb-relation-name>Account-TransactionEntry</ejb-relation-name>
<ejb-relationship-role>
<ejb-relationship-role-name>
Account-Has-TransactionEntry
</ejb-relationship-role-name>
<multiplicity>many</multiplicity>
<relationship-role-source>
<ejb-name>Account</ejb-name>
</relationship-role-source>
<cmr-field>
<cmr-field-name>transactionEntries</cmr-field-name>
<cmr-field-type>java.util.Collection</cmr-field-type>
</cmr-field>
</ejb-relationship-role>
</ejb-relation>
...
</ejb-jar>
```

Finally, these beans must be compiled, deployed, and tested to make sure that all of the modified beans—and added relationships—are persisted to the database properly. If this is the case, then you have successfully replaced a deprecated composite entity with fine-grained container-managed persistence and relationships.

Best of Both Worlds

You want to incrementally introduce CMP into your application.

Provide CMP versions of your beans but subclass existing BMP bean classes to them wherever you wish to maintain BMP.

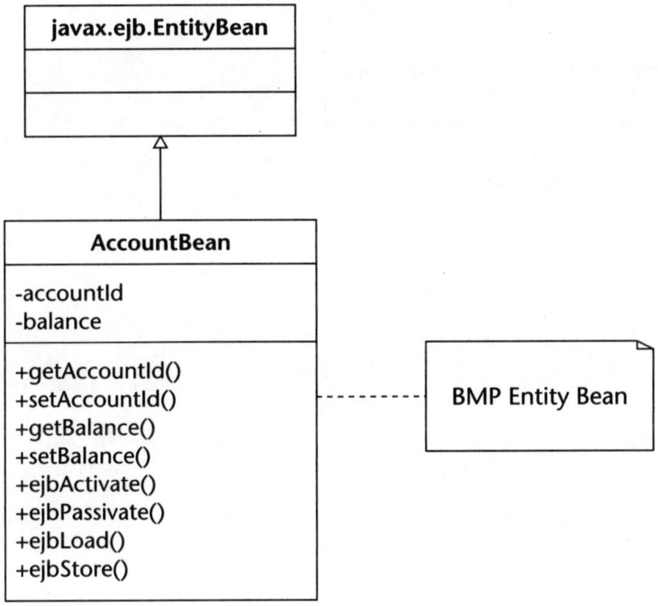

Figure 6.20 Before refactoring.

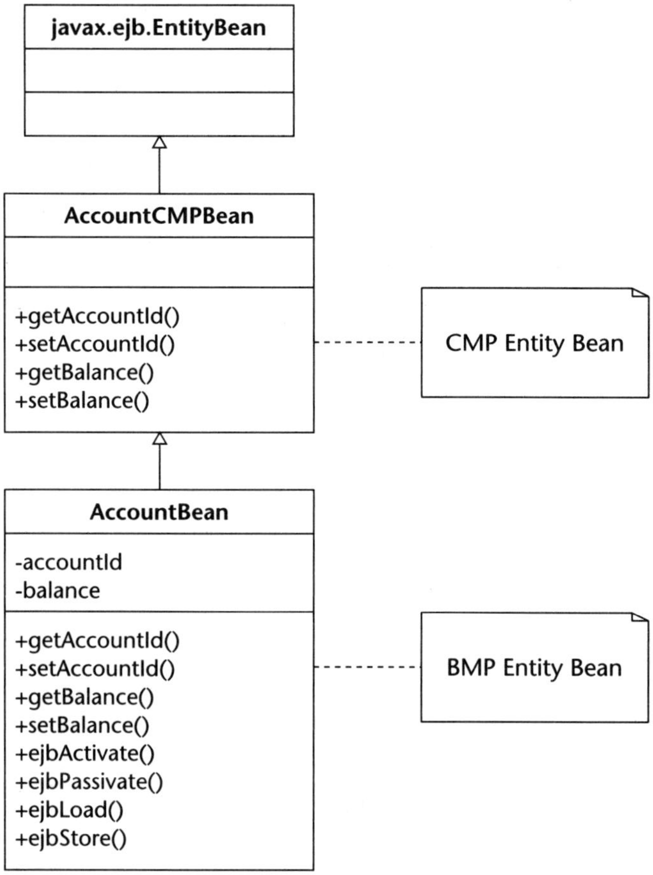

Figure 6.21 After refactoring.

Motivation

The Mirage AntiPattern addressed the often-false notion of using BMP to gain scalability advantages over a comparable CMP solution. Too often, developers end up creating infrastructure code without taking advantage of what is already offered. Developers should design for functionality, while keeping performance in mind. Thus, it makes far more sense to use CMP and only fall back on BMP if this is required.

In modern application servers, the CMP engine will usually be more efficient than a hand-coded BMP solution. In addition, CMP reduces the time spent coding persistence logic, saving valuable development time and related maintenance expense. However, developers are often faced with a system that already makes extensive use of BMP. Converting the entire application at once could be risky and cause errors.

This refactoring can be used to incrementally introduce CMP into an application. The basic concept is to systematically replace BMP beans with CMP bean implementations, and then modify the BMP class to subclass the new CMP implementation class.

The bean is now capable of supporting either CMP or the classic BMP implementation. The decision on which to use can be made by modifying the deployment descriptor as desired. This is an excellent way to try CMP first, before abandoning the BMP implementation entirely.

Mechanics

The following is a list of steps which must be followed in order to apply the Best of Both Worlds refactoring. These steps outline a strategy for incrementally introducing CMP into a BMP application. Specifically, new CMP equivalents to existing BMP beans can be added to the application. The existing BMP beans can be modified to extend their new CMP counterparts. Finally, the EJB deployment descriptor can be modified to select which implementation to use.

1. *Create CMP beans.* Provide a CMP implementation for each BMP bean.
2. *Let BMP beans extend their CMP counterparts.* Modify the BMP bean implementation class so that it extends the new CMP bean implementation class.
3. *Select the implementation in the deployment descriptor.* Modify the bean deployment descriptor, selecting which implementation to use.
4. *Compile, deploy, and test.*

Example

The first step of this refactoring is to create a CMP implementation for a BMP bean that we wish to eventually convert. For the purposes of our example, we will extend the *Strong Bond* refactoring example, which already created a CMP version of the Account bean. To avoid confusion, we will rename the AccountBean CMP implementation to AccountCMPBean.

The next step of this refactoring is to modify our original BMP implementation class so that it extends the new AccountCMPBean as follows:

```
...
public class AccountBean extends AccountCMPBean
{
...
}
```

If the BMP bean is used, then its life-cycle methods (that is, ejbLoad(), ejbStore(), and so on) will override the empty implementations provided by the CMP class. This allows our BMP class to effectively take over the persistence of the entity.

The next step in this refactoring is to specify, in the EJB descriptor, which bean implementation to use upon deployment. For the purposes of our example, we will modify the ejb-jar.xml file that contains the Account descriptor. If you wish to use the CMP version, simply specify the AccountCMPBean implementation in the <ejb-class> descriptor element and Container in the <persistence-type> descriptor element.

```
...
<ejb-jar>
<entity>
<ejb-name>Account</ejb-name>
<local-home>examples.AccountHome</local-home>
<local>examples.Account</local>
<ejb-class>examples.AccountCMPBean</ejb-class>
<persistence-type>Container</persistence-type>
     ...
...
```

However, if you wish to use the BMP version, simply specify the *AccountBean* BMP implementation in the <ejb-class> descriptor element and *Bean* in the <persistence-type> descriptor element.

```
...
<ejb-jar>
<entity>
<ejb-name>Account</ejb-name>
<local-home>examples.AccountHome</local-home>
<local>examples.Account</local>
<ejb-class>examples.AccountBean</ejb-class>
<persistence-type>Bean</persistence-type>
...
```

The last step of this refactoring is to compile, deploy, and test all of these changes to make sure that everything behaves as expected. If this is the case, then you have an excellent mechanism for gradually converting from your application CMP to BMP.

Façade

Your Entity Beans are routinely being accessed remotely.

Wrap these entities with a session or POJO to improve scalability and simplify the application.

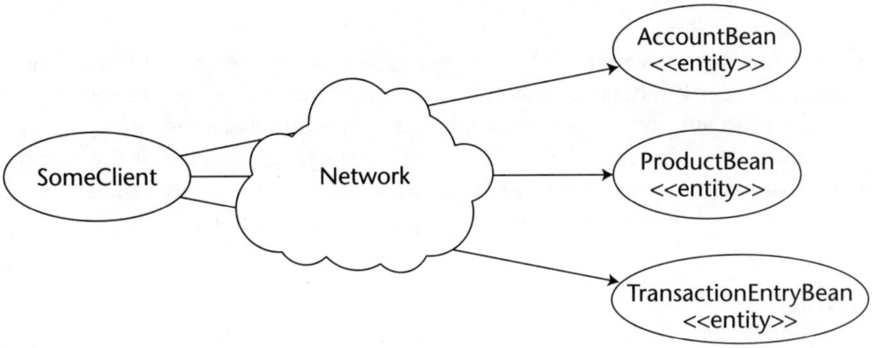

Figure 6.22 Before refactoring.

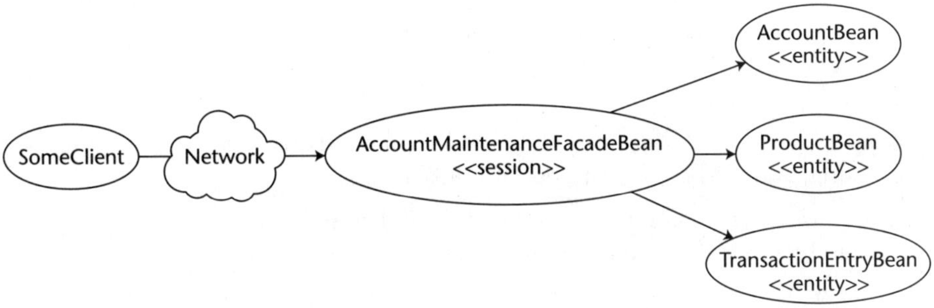

Figure 6.23 After refactoring.

Motivation

Arguably, the most widely recognized J2EE design pattern, the merits of façade are clear. Systems that remotely access their Entity Beans to execute workflows and business processes usually encounter considerable scalability issues. Not only does such usage incur significant network overhead, but it also requires clients to explicitly manage their transactions using the Java Transaction API (JTA). In addition, transactions become distributed across clients and servers, thus further increasing overhead and locking out resources for longer periods. All of this eventually compromises the application's ability to scale.

Clients should use a façade in order to execute a business process or workflow involving Entity Beans. Security and transaction management can be defined at the façade level, and entities can simply support the container-created transactions, using tx_supports. Following this approach will free clients of the burdens of explicit transaction management. Instead, transactions will be managed by the container and will be scoped at the server. This will simplify the application and improve overall performance.

Mechanics

The following is a list of steps which must be followed in order to apply the Façade refactoring. These steps outline a strategy for creating session or POJO-based façades that will provide a simplified invocation interface to its clients.

1. *Introduce session or POJO façade components*. The choice of implementation depends on whether the façade will be invoked remotely. Remote invocation will require a Session Bean implementation. A given façade component should cover a collection of logically related use cases. For example, a MaintainCustomer façade may provide operations to create, update, or bill customers. Each of these operations is a use case; however, they are all related to the maintenance of customers.
2. *Make the façade do all of the work the client once did*. This may involve locating, accessing, and updating a number of Entity Beans.
3. *Define declarative transactions at the façade level*. The session façade method that is invoked by clients should drive the scope of the transaction.
4. *Modify existing transactional clients*. Each applicable, transactional client must be modified so that it no longer manages the transaction, but simply invokes the façade in order to do the work.
5. *Compile, deploy, and test*.

Example

Suppose that our financial services application needs to transfer money from one account to another. The application could accomplish this task by driving the transfer from a Java client program, or from within the Web tier via a servlet or JSP, using JTA.

However, such choices have several negative consequences. First, the client programmer must understand and use the JTA. Although this API is not exceptionally difficult, it does involve additional programming that could have been avoided had the transaction been handled automatically by the application server container. Avoiding this additional programming will reduce development and maintenance costs by simplifying the implementation. Second, coding such business logic in a client makes that business logic far less reusable than if it were extracted and placed in a shared component, such as a Session Bean. Another client program requiring this functionality would probably duplicate the same logic. Of course, if that logic changes, each client program will need to be changed, recompiled, and tested—a potentially expensive and time-consuming endeavor.

An example of JTA use follows, where the SomeClient Java client is using the API to explicitly manage a transactional transfer of funds between two accounts.

```
...
import javax.transaction.RollbackException;
import javax.transaction.UserTransaction;
...
public class SomeClient
{
...
     public void someMethod()
{
...
```

After using the Account home interface to acquire references to the two account EJBs, a JTA UserTransaction must be acquired from the initial context. The UserTransaction provides the JTA interface needed in order to manage transactions explicitly.

```
     try
     {
          // 1: Acquire JTA user transaction
          UserTransaction utx =
              (UserTransaction)getInitialContext().
                   lookup("javax.transaction.UserTransaction");
```

At this point, the UserTransaction's begin() method is invoked in order to start the transaction. After transferring $100 from account2 to account1, the UserTransaction's commit() method is invoked. If anything fails during this process, JTA will throw a RollbackException, indicating that the transfer failed and was rolled back.

```
          // 2: Begin JTA transaction.
          utx.begin();

          account1.deposit(account2.withdraw(100));

          // 3: Commit JTA transaction.
          utx.commit();
```

```
        }
       catch(RollbackException excp)
        {
             // 4: Roll back JTA transaction.
       }
...
```

Although this use of JTA seems relatively straightforward, it does represent additional work and complexity that can be avoided by applying this refactoring. The very first step is to introduce a new Session façade component that can perform the account transfer under a container-managed transaction. For our example, the AccountMaintenanceFacade Session Bean façade will be introduced, in order to handle the transfer of funds between accounts.

```
public class AccountMaintenanceFacade
{
...
public void transfer(String accountID1,
    String accountID2, BigDecimal amount)
    {
```

The next step is to make this façade do the work of the client—transfer funds from one account to another. After using the AccountHome to acquire references to the two accounts, the funds can simply be withdrawn from one and deposited into the other.

```
    // 1: Use AccountHome.findByPrimaryKey to locate each
    //    Account bean.

                account1.deposit(account2.withdraw(100));

    }
}
...
```

Since AccountMaintenanceFacade is a Session Bean, we can make its transfer(...) method transactional without writing any JTA code. Instead, we can proceed to our next step, which is to make the necessary EJB deployment descriptor modifications so that this method runs under transactional control. This change must be made to the ejb-jar.xml file that contains the descriptor definitions for the AccountMaintenanceFacade bean. An extract of this descriptor definition follows.

```
<ejb-jar>
  <enterprise-beans>
    <session>
      <ejb-name>AccountMaintenanceFacade</ejb-name>
      ...
    </session>
  </enterprise-beans>
```

The following <assembly-descriptor> stanza contains embedded XML elements for specifying transactional behavior at an EJB method level. For our purposes, we will specify—via the <trans-attribute> XML element—that AccountMainenanceFacade's *transfer(...)* method will require a container-managed transaction in order to execute. Thus, this method can be executed within another transactional context (managed either explicitly or via the container) or, in the absence of such context, the container will create a new transaction context in order to execute the *transfer(...)* method.

```
    <assembly-descriptor>
      <container-transaction>
        <method>
          <ejb-name>AccountMaintenanceFacade</ejb-name>
       <method-name>transfer</method-name>
        </method>
        <trans-attribute>Required</trans-attribute>
      </container-transaction>
    </assembly-descriptor>
  </ejb-jar>
```

Next, we will modify our SomeClient Java client so that it simply locates the AccountMaintenanceFacade Session Bean and invokes its transfer(...) method instead of performing the transfer itself.

```
public class SomeClient
{
...
     public void someMethod()
{
...

    try
    {
          // 1: Locate AccountMaintenanceFacade Session Bean

          // 2: Invoke the transfer using stringified account
          //    identifiers and the amount to transfer.

          accountFacade.transfer(accountID1, accountID2, amount);
    }
    ...
}
...
}
```

Your last step is to compile, deploy and test all of these changes. Now that this refactoring is in place, you should see reduced complexity throughout the application architecture. Business logic duplication across clients is replaced by shared business components and centralized logic. Unnecessary JTA programming is replaced by container-managed transactions that can be configured at deployment time via descriptors. This deployment-time configuration is another benefit of this approach over explicit JTA programming, which is static after the code has been compiled.

In addition, overall performance will improve, because transactions will be scoped within the application server instead of being potentially distributed across the network.

CHAPTER

7

Session EJBs

This chapter is about some of the issues that arise when architecting, designing, and implementing Session EJBs in a J2EE system. Sessions are middle-tier components that are typically used to implement business or infrastructure logic, independently of client tiers.

The purpose of Session EJBs within a J2EE system is to be components that implement business or technical processes (whereas Entity EJBs are used to support persistent data). Sessions are used specifically where enterprise-level system services are required, such as transaction management, authentication, remote access, and/or failover support through clustered deployment. Session EJBs come in two different varieties, based on the kind of process they are intended to support. Single-step (atomic) processes are supported using *stateless* sessions, while multistep processes are supported using *stateful* sessions (where some process or conversational state is maintained across the steps).

Within the makeup of a typical J2EE system, sessions are obviously an important core element, and the activities regarding when to use sessions and how they should be defined and implemented are crucial to a system's functioning, performance, and maintainability. As stated above, there is specific rationale regarding if and when to use sessions, and the most fundamental of the AntiPatterns discussed later in this chapter involve inappropriately choosing (or not choosing) to implement some process(es) with sessions. Also, sessions are the components within J2EE that are specifically geared toward implementing processes, and the general techniques of mapping application responsibilities into system architecture and design (that is, deciding what specific sessions should be defined, and what methods should go into them) are still important, and their misapplication is the basis for a number of AntiPatterns described later in this chapter. Finally, stateful sessions support some attractive features that have led to their use in unintended ways, to create creative but ultimately problematic solutions to data-caching and performance issues.

One of the core design approaches when using sessions for business applications is to implement a session/entity pair, where the entity implements the data aspects of a business abstraction or document, and the session implements the various business processes and the workflows associated to that entity. This layering of session over entity is done to improve performance (by reducing client-to-Entity-Bean remote invocations), but also, more importantly, to organize and associate processes with data. The different semantics of sessions and entities essentially separate process and data, which is a bit contradictory to basic OO principles. So, coupling the session and entity together in this way allows the abstraction to be used and reused in different contexts.

In this chapter, we will discuss AntiPatterns associated with the use of EJB Session objects, along with refactorings to rectify these issues. Specifically, we will cover the following topics:

Sessions A-Plenty. Using Session EJBs for situations that don't need EJB semantics. This results in unnecessary additional development and performance overhead.

Bloated Session. A session that implements many methods covering multiple abstractions and process areas. This makes the session difficult to develop, test, deploy, and reuse in different contexts.

Thin Session. A session that implements only a part of an abstraction, leading to multiple sessions that need to be used together. This results in additional development and support for many sessions, and makes use and reuse more difficult.

Large Transaction. A transactional session method that implements a long, complicated process, and involves a lot of transactional resources, effectively locking those resources so they can't be used by other threads for a significant period of time. This results in noticeable performance issues and typically results in deadlock when there are many concurrent executions of the method.

Transparent Façade. An attempt at the Session Façade pattern that simply does a direct mapping between the underlying component and the session interface, and does not create subsystem layering and coarser-grained interaction as intended by the Session Façade pattern. This results in additional development and actually worse performance, with no reduction in number of invocations by clients.

Data Cache. Using stateful sessions to implement a distributed memory data cache. There are some specific limitations on sessions that render this an unreliable solution.

Sessions A-Plenty

Also Known As: Golden Hammer

Most Frequent Scale: Architecture

Refactorings: Replace Session with Object, Establish Architecture Guidelines

Refactored Solution Type: Software, Process

Root Causes: Ignorance, pride, narrow-mindedness

Unbalanced Forces: Complexity, performance

Anecdotal Evidence: "Oh, just make another session for that function."

Background

When architects or developers jump onto a new technology such as EJB (or work exclusively with it for some time), they can sometimes get overzealous and use that technology for purposes for which it is not intended or is not optimal, without rationalizing what specific semantics or issues should be handled by the technology and what specific context or conditions suggest its use. EJB is just one of the elements in the J2EE toolkit, and in most applications, a hybrid approach using a combination of EJBs and POJOs (plain old Java objects) is usually the most effective in terms of balancing complexity, performance, reliability, and so on. Specifically with Session EJBs, developers may believe that they are *the* component that is used to implement middle-tier processes, ending up with an explosion of sessions that cover every little processing requirement in the system. This affects development by creating an unnecessarily large and complex set of implementation artifacts, and affects startup and runtime performance by using heavier-weight components in cases where they are not required.

General Form

In this AntiPattern, the overuse of sessions results in a middle tier that is made up of a lot of sessions that vary widely in size (in terms of number of methods), types of requirements supported, and transactional semantics. There are the typical (justified) sessions that implement process logic and workflow for business entities (for example, an Order Management session). However, there are also other sessions that basically support algorithmic processes that are not transactional. These may vary from significant algorithm functions such as complex product-pricing algorithms, to simple procedures like currency conversion. These algorithm-oriented sessions may be accessed exclusively by other sessions or server-side components, and accessed via local interfaces, or they may be remotely accessed by clients as well. Typically, there are no security settings on these sessions, since they are not transactional and are used exclusively within the context of other, authenticated processes. Thus, there are a number of characteristics and usage patterns that appear to be different between the different kinds of sessions in the system.

Symptoms and Consequences

The Sessions A-Plenty AntiPattern is symptomatic of inexperience and/or overzealous use of a particular technology or approach, and is all too common with many different technologies, tools, and so on. The consequences are typically increased time and complexity during development, and suboptimal system functioning. Specific symptoms to look for and consequences that may following include:

- **The middle tier contains a large number of sessions.** There are a large number of sessions defined, for example more than 50. A typical enterprise application can expect at most 20 to 30 sessions.
- **Sessions that support purely algorithmic processes.** Sessions that are purely algorithmic are not transactional and are easily supported by Plain Java classes.

- **There are a number of sessions with one or two public methods.** Sessions that support only a small number of methods *may* indicate trivial or algorithmic sessions, which are better implemented using other approaches. (Note: An exception to this symptom is the appropriate use of the EJB Command pattern, for specific cases desiring pluggable, transactional components.)
- **Application startup is slow.** The application takes a long time to start up because a large of number of sessions are being deployed.
- **Application performance may be poor.** The application may be very slow when running, because more of the functionality is being run through sessions (which means that the EJB container intercepts and processes many more method calls). Also, the application server itself may not perform as well because of the additional resources required to deploy and pool instances for many sessions.
- **Session EJBs are prescribed as the default for processing components.** When mapping system behaviors to implementation artifacts, Session EJBs are prescribed as the target component type, without much or any discussion regarding why, alternatives, and so on.
- **More development effort, due to all the session-related artifacts.** For each EJB session, there are multiple Java artifacts and a deployment descriptor. A large number of sessions means an even larger number of supporting artifacts. Tools that autogenerate EJB artifacts help address this somewhat, but there is still the additional effort of defining the session, incorporating it into the generation tool setup, updating the build process, and so forth.
- **Need to implement a session before implementing or testing any functionality.** If a development team is new to EJB, they will likely spend a lot of time hammering out issues related to EJBs and sessions, and not spend time creating the actual implementation for the process in question. Often, it is a better strategy to implement some process functionality in a non-EJB component first, to validate the logic and algorithm, and *then* use that within a session to give it transactional semantics, reliability, distribution, and so on.

Typical Causes

There are a number of causes of this AntiPattern that are characteristic of the use of new and complex technology, as follows:

- **Lack of understanding of the rationale for choosing sessions.** Session EJBs should be used for process-oriented components that need transactional support (either initiate or join), security checking (either declarative or programmatic), remote accessibility, or high reliability (for example, replication support across a clustered deployment). Note that one reason to choose a stateful session may be to maintain conversational state across a multistep business process, but for Web applications, this information may be maintained within the HttpSession and, at any rate, the business process will still be implemented then in a stateless session.

- **Scheduling pressures don't allow adequate analysis.** If there are significant scheduling pressures, there may be insufficient time to properly define and evaluate the requirements, and make a reasoned choice regarding the appropriate implementation approach.
- **Rigid mechanical analysis and design process.** In some cases, a checklist of analysis/design tasks may be employed to make the process more tractable and, theoretically, remove development risk. However, this also can lead to mechanical execution of tasks.
- **Previous EJB experience concentrated on the implementation of sessions.** A developer new to EJB may be given very specific tasks around implementing and testing predefined Session EJBs, without being involved in the modeling and architecture activities. Thus, the rationale around choosing Session EJBs may not be known to a developer, even though he or she has experience implementing them.
- **Resume booster.** In some cases, a particular technology or approach is chosen for selfish reasons, for example, to gain professional experience. Some requirements simply don't need the development or runtime overhead of sessions, but when you want to use a jeweled hammer, you can make a lot of things look like nails.
- **Academic or prototyping remnant.** If academic exercises or prototyping are done early in a project to gain initial experience, work out ideas, and so forth, there may be remnants of those efforts still hanging around in the implementation. In the face of scheduling pressures, prototypes or exploratory exercises that were intended to be thrown away may instead become the implementation.

Known Exceptions

There are really no meaningful exceptions to this AntiPattern. There isn't a situation that would justify creating an overabundance of sessions when they are not needed, because that will inevitably adversely affect development, performance, and maintainability.

Refactorings

The Replace Session with Object refactoring is the key one to use. In this refactoring, an offending session is replaced with a Java class, and existing clients of the session are refactored to appropriately interact with the class. The easiest approach is to simply convert the Session Bean implementation class to a Java class by removing reference to the SessionBean interface and corresponding implementation methods. Then, the more significant work is refactoring the clients that were using that session to use the Java class instead. The mechanics of getting and using Session Beans and Java classes are different—sessions are located using JNDI and instantiated to interfaces using Home create method, while Java classes are located by the class loader (from the class path), and instantiated through a constructor (Note: purely algorithmic processes may be implemented with static methods, negating the need to instantiate them). Thus, each of the clients needs to be refactored to facilitate these changes.

Another important process-oriented refactoring is performed to establish architectural guidelines. In this approach, concrete guidelines are created and used that define the kinds of requirements and the context that indicates whether or not to use Session EJBs. The mechanics of this approach involve getting more literature regarding J2EE and EJB design, especially documentation and discussions of real-world applications, threaded discussions on Web forums, and so on. Additionally, this information should be translated into guidelines and used during design activities, and also during design review activities.

Variations

There are two main variations on this AntiPattern, the overuse of stateful sessions and not using sessions when you should.

In the first situation, the EJB specification suggests that Stateful Session Beans are the most common type of session to be used. This may stem from the idea that sessions are used to support application processes, and in many cases, those processes will have many discrete steps and associated states. However, Stateful Session Beans consume significantly more resources (memory, processing capacity, disk I/O), and as the number of instances goes up, stateful sessions do not scale well at high volumes.

The second—the converse of the Sessions-A-Plenty AntiPattern—is to not utilize sessions for those specific cases that warrant them. As mentioned earlier, there are specific requirement semantics that justify the choice of Session EJBs, the most important probably being transactional support. Processes that must either initiate or participate in transactional processes, and/or utilize other resources, which themselves are transactional (for example, Entity EJBs, JDBC connections, and so on) should typically be implemented with sessions.

Example

The UML diagram in Figure 7.1 provides an example of this AntiPattern. This diagram depicts a number of Session Beans that vary widely in their purpose and significance. The OrderManagement and AccountManagement Session Beans are the typical business process components that Session Beans are often used for. They require support for transactional business processes and security. The ObjectCreation Session Bean represents a technical component that is responsible for entity instance creation, essentially being a factory object for Entity Beans. Since entity instance creation is usually transactional and likely needs to be invoked locally and remotely, it is justifiable to incorporate this, too, in a Session Bean. However, the DateConversion and CurrencyConversion Session Beans are really just pure algorithmic functions, and don't need the EJB container capabilities because they are not transactional and are accessed locally. What this overall picture communicates is that if Session Beans are used as the default component to implement any kind of processing within a J2EE system, there will inevitably be some Session Beans that are justified, but there will also be others that are not, and in the end, the result will be unnecessary development time and complexity, and reduced performance.

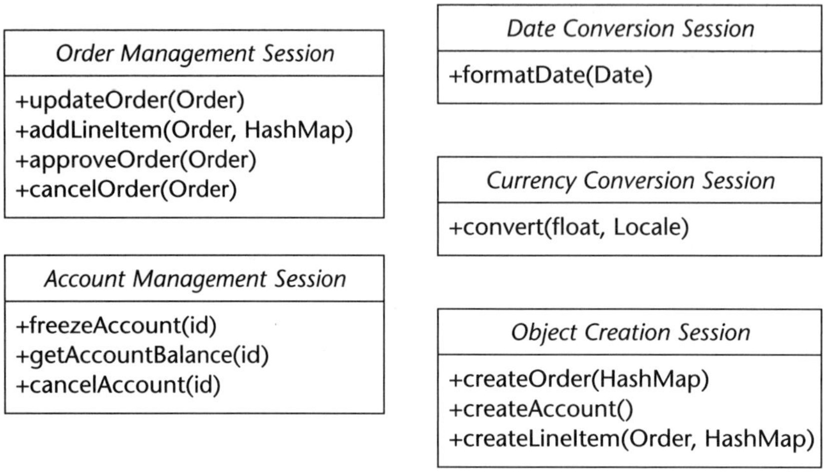

Figure 7.1 Sessions A-Plenty AntiPattern.

Related Solutions

Often in applications, the refactoring of processes reveals certain common process stereotypes, such as object factories and pluggable action objects. These can be reified into generic interfaces and multiple implementations, and then the larger session methods can factor those elements out into specific replaceable implementations. Thus, one of the related solutions is to identify those common, underlying stereotypical process elements and refactor them into interfaces and implementations. These are stereotypical, process-oriented classes (not sessions).

As mentioned above, one of the variants of this AntiPatterns is to overuse Stateful Session Beans, and suffer the performance consequences when the transaction volumes go up. In many cases, stateful session can be refactored so that conversational state is maintained within the client tier (as in within HttpSession), and the stateful session is translated to stateless form. Most Application servers support reasonable support for managing HTTP session state within the Web tier.

AntiPattern

Bloated Session

Also Known As: The God Object, The Blob, Ambiguous Viewpoint

Most Frequent Scale: Application, architecture

Refactorings: Interface Partitioning

Refactored Solution Type: Software

Root Causes: Sloth, haste, ignorance

Unbalanced Forces: Functionality, performance, complexity

Anecdotal Evidence: "Just add that new method to the main session."

Background

Within J2EE, Session Beans are the components that are used to support the processing and workflow requirements of an application. In terms of defining business-oriented sessions, specific business processes described in requirements are usually used to identify the different session methods to implement. However, there are many ways to arrange those methods into sessions. Deciding the set of distinct sessions that are required, and how the methods should be mapped to them, can have a significant effect on development and operation of the system. In general, well-organized sessions should be based on general OO principles of analysis and design. A good approach is to define a session for each core abstraction (for example, entity), and collect together the methods that operate on that abstraction. Such sessions exhibit high cohesion and low coupling, enhancing their understandability, use, and reuse in multiple contexts.

A common AntiPattern in session design, especially among inexperienced EJB designers, is to aggregate a lot of methods into a single bloated session that implements many methods against several different core business entities. These sessions do not represent well-defined abstractions, and are difficult to understand and use, because there are so many methods to review, and it is difficult knowing which subsets of methods should be used with each other to support a particular abstraction or process.

General Form

The Bloated Session AntiPattern is one that implements methods that operate against multiple abstractions. For instance, one method may approve an order, while another method checks the balance of an account, and yet another method applies a payment to an invoice. Typically, the session will be large (in terms of the number of methods), because there are a number of methods supported for each of the abstractions. Also, because multiple abstractions are being supported by a single session, there will typically be just a few sessions, or in some case, only one.

Symptoms and Consequences

There are a number of symptoms of a Bloated Session AntiPattern that center around the core issue of implementing multiple abstractions. The overall consequence is that the session exhibits a broader surface area, resulting in a broader set of clients that want or need to access the session, and leading to problems from multiple, concurrent access and the use of the session artifacts at development time and instances at run time. The specific symptoms and consequences that may arise include:

- **Session methods act on multiple abstractions or entities.** The session has relationships and interacts with many of the core entities within the system. These may be passed in as method parameters, or the session itself may use finders and so on to acquire the entity instances. At any rate, there are probably many Entity Home interfaces accessed across the various methods within the session.

- **Session has a large number of methods.** A session interface that defines a large number of methods, for example, 20 to 30, may be suspect. However, this is only a potential indicator, and the multiple abstractions symptom is still the key one.
- **Few sessions.** When sessions do too much, this will inevitably result in fewer of them. The pathological case is just one, a God Object Session, which implements *all* of the middle-tier processes. This is the ultimate bloated session.
- **Contention or overwrites on session code changes.** Bloated sessions implement a larger percentage of the overall system requirements, so there is a higher likelihood that, in multiple-developer situations, concurrent updates to Java artifacts and deployment descriptors may occur. This can either lead to slower development, causing developers to wait, or clobber changes if there is a less-formal process.
- **Poorer performance, specifically with a bloated stateful session.** Stateful Session Bean instances are held in memory until explicitly removed by the client and consume significant server resources. If a Stateful Bean is used to support a wide set of processes, then there will be more clients using them, holding them in memory, and affecting performance.
- **Unit testing of the session is problematic because there are so many methods.** Testing and validating the unit (in this case, the entire bloated session) means developing and running a large suite of tests against all the methods in the session. A unit test is not complete until *all* of the tests have passed, so the failure of just a single method may hold up release of many other methods that work as they should.
- **The session is harder to understand and use.** When a session implements many abstractions, it appears muddy from the point of view of developers. They find it harder to understand and use because the developers expect the various methods to tie together somehow, but they don't.
- **The session is harder to reuse.** When a number of different abstractions are muddled together into a single component, this inherently creates a tight coupling between all the entities and data types that are used. When some part of the session is desired to be used elsewhere (for example, the credit-checking process) all the other entities and data types are coupled, and must go along for the ride. This creates an unnatural need to include those other types, and in some cases, there may be organizational or economic reasons that preclude leaking all those types and information to the other situation.

Typical Causes

The basic causes behind the Bloated Session AntiPattern are not understanding and applying core OOA/OOD principles to create well-defined abstractions that exhibit low coupling and high cohesion. Specifics include:

- **Nonexistent, thin, or poorly structured requirements.** The identification of distinct abstractions and processes is very dependent on the set of requirements that serve as the starting point. Requirements that are thin, muddy, or poorly structured make it difficult to recognize abstractions and processes.
- **Separation of process and data inherent in EJB.** Part of this may be due to the basic EJB model itself, in that sessions and entities inherently separate process from data. This is somewhat contradictory to pure object-oriented principles (that is, data and its associated operations should be kept together). Novice EJB designers may spend a lot of time concentrating on the entities (because the data, E/R model is so important), and apply less scrutiny and reasoning to deciding what the appropriate sessions should be and what methods should map to them.
- **Technology-oriented process.** When designing and implementing EJBs, the focus may be on the implementation characteristics of EJB as the driving force, and fundamental principles of OO, such as abstraction, subtyping, coupling and cohesion, are not considered enough.
- **Incorrect application of the Session Façade pattern.** When developers define a façade over entities to implement workflow, they may create a single Session façade to contain many (or all) processes/workflows in the system.
- **Purely mechanical creation of session(s) to support a Web Service interface.** In some cases, the guiding principle behind the session delineation may in fact be the need to develop one or more Web Services, to vend new or existing functionality. A purely mechanical approach to defining the Web Service interface (and the interface of an underlying middle-tier session) may lump together all sorts of methods, without regard for any sort of business-related organization.
- **Path of least resistance.** If there is an existing Session Bean that has been implemented and deployed, and is in use, then it is easier to just slip another method in rather than craft a new session, with all the Java artifacts and deployment descriptor details. The underlying cause of this is scheduling pressure, haste, or sloth. When this is done several times, this results in a bloated session.

Known Exceptions

In some cases, a legacy system, legacy chunk of application code, or other element may exist that is best kept intact, in an isolated, encapsulated artifact, so that it has a minimal effect on the rest of the system, and to ensure minimal dependency and use of implementation components. In these cases, a session may be implemented as a façade or adaptor on top of an existing collection of functionality, to sweep it under the rug. This special case may exhibit characteristics of a Bloated Session AntiPattern, but it is an acceptable version because it will actually just be emulating an underlying (legacy, fixed) implementation.

Refactorings

The refactoring required in this case is called Interface Partitioning and seeks to partition the bloated session into multiple sessions that each support a single abstraction. The mechanics involve examining each of the methods defined in the bloated session interface and determining which specific abstraction each one operates against. This can be indicated by the method name itself (for example, approveOrder); in other cases, the abstraction will be one of the key parameters passed in (possibly as an Entity Bean reference or a DTO type). Finally, if generic data structures are used as parameters (for example, HashMap), or if the method implementation itself fetches and operates on the entity data, then the implementation of the method itself can be reviewed to determine the associated abstraction. Once the abstraction is identified for the method, the interface method (and associated implementation) is physically moved to another session. This process will create a number of new sessions and, in the end, the original bloated session itself should only implement one abstraction (or if renamed, may be just a historical artifact).

Refer to the Chapter 3, *Mulitiservice, Refactorings* section for a complete description of the Interface Partitioning refactoring.

Variations

The pathological variation of the Bloated Session AntiPattern is having only one or two Session Beans that implement all processes. This is commonly referred to in OO circles as the God Object AntiPattern. This occurs when there is a purely mechanical approach to defining EJB components, without considering the impact on development or runtime performance of aggregating so much functionality into a single distributed component. From a purely technical perspective, the only real reason to separate functionality into separate sessions is to distinguish Stateful Session Beans from stateless ones. All of the consequences discussed above become magnified when only one or two Session Beans implement all processes.

An especially problematic variation of this AntiPattern is bloated *Stateful* Session Beans, because the instances are retained and consume server resources. Merging a lot of different processes together into a single stateful session can result in many instance variables and lots of retained data. And, if there are many different client instances executing concurrently, then there will be many, large retained instances using up a lot of server resources. The effect will be severely degraded performance.

Another variation occurs when a number of state*less* methods are included within a State*ful* Session Bean. If a lot of methods are thrown together into a few sessions, there is the likelihood that stateless (single-step) methods are implemented on Stateful Session Beans. The result will be reduced performance, because the stateless methods aren't accessed through more scalable Stateless Session Beans. Also, this means that the client always needs to get a handle to a specific Stateful Session Bean instance to execute any of those methods.

Occasionally, a developer may define many variations on the same basic method, taking different numbers of parameters, and so on, resulting in a lot of very similar-looking methods that all support the same basic process. When this is repeated for a number of the processes that the session supports, the result is a Session Bean interface with an apparently large number of methods, and can be confusing and prone to incorrect use. It is better to compact these into just a few, clear methods.

Finally, if someone is unsure about the requirements to be implemented, they may throw a lot of extra functionality, methods, and variations just to cover themselves, again resulting in a Session Bean interface with many methods. The real solution is to get more detailed requirements, validation from users, and business-level prioritization from stakeholders.

Example

The defining characteristic of a bloated session is that it supports several core business or technical abstractions. An example of this is provided in the UML diagram in Figure 7.2. This diagram depicts a Session Bean interface with a number of public methods that operate against a number of different core business entities. The placeOrder(), cancelOrder(), and getOrderStatus() methods all are related to the Order entity, while the reserveInventory() method is related to a Product entity, and the acceptPayment() and validateCredit() methods operate against an Account entity. This illustrates the key concept regarding the Bloated Session AntiPattern, that is, multiple abstractions all supported within one session.

Note that this example is merely illustrative and an actual bloated session would have several methods associated with each abstraction, yielding an overall session interface with many methods.

Related Solutions

In the case of the Swiss Army Knife variation, the issue is that there are many methods that essentially support the same process. The solution variation for this is to aggregate the different method variants into one method that implements the distinct variations depending on what data is passed in (and what values are nulls, and so on). This makes the session interface much smaller and more understandable.

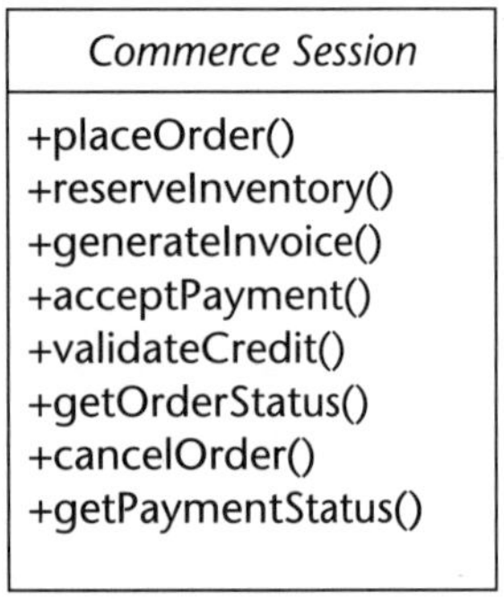

Figure 7.2 Bloated session.

Thin Session

Also Known As: Refactor Mercilessly, Functional Decomposition

Most Frequent Scale: Application, architecture

Refactorings: Interface Consolidation

Refactored Solution Type: Process, software

Root Causes: Ignorance, haste

Unbalanced Forces: Complexity and resources

Anecdotal Evidence: "Just create another new session for that function."

Background

Defining a system's business sessions and associated methods is usually done by reviewing requirements and mapping the various processes described within to separate session methods. As discussed previously, the result ideally is a set of sessions that each implements a specific abstraction. However, if this mapping process is not guided by understanding and experience of OO principles, the result may be far from this ideal.

One such result is the Thin Session AntiPattern, in which there are many sessions that each implement just a few (or one) method, resulting in a large number of very fine-grained sessions. The consequence is that a particular abstraction is implemented by a number of different sessions. This fragmentation causes issues during development because there are multiple artifacts that are coupled to one underlying entity, and changes to that entity then affect many related sessions. Also, client components that support the different processes for that abstraction must instantiate and use several different sessions, requiring the client developer to know about all the different sessions they must use, and requiring many different session instances. This last aspect affects system performance when there are many thin session instances that are instantiated and pooled, because they are all significant components (EJBs) and consume significant server resources.

General Form

The thin session contains a few (or possibly only one) methods related to a particular abstraction (entity). For example, an ApproveOrderService is a thin session that implements just the approval process for the Order abstraction. Other processes for the abstraction are implemented in other thin sessions, resulting in the one abstraction being fragmented across a number of separate implementation artifacts. Since each of those sessions operates against the same entity, they are all ultimately coupled to that one entity, and hence to each other. Thus, the whole collection of thin sessions must be used together wherever that abstraction is to be reused in others. The Thin Session AntiPattern is really manifested as a collection of tightly coupled sessions that implement a few different processes each on the same underlying entity.

Symptoms and Consequences

Many thin sessions place more burden on the developer (to understand and use a collection of components, rather than just one, nicely encapsulated one), and affect runtime performance by creating a lot of server-side components. Some of the specific symptoms and consequences of the Thin Session AntiPattern are as follows:

- **Multiple sessions support methods that operate against the same entity.** Multiple sessions may need to be accessed to perform the set of processes associated to a single abstraction. For example, order processes are supported by OrderCreationSession, OrderApprovalSession, and OrderPaymentSession.
- **Sessions have one or a few methods.** The session interfaces are small (possibly consisting of only one method).

- **There are a large number of sessions.** When the Thin Session AntiPattern is applied to several business entities, this can result in an explosion of sessions.
- **Session name is a verb or verblike.** One of the main reasons for this AntiPattern is having a verb-oriented perspective on sessions, such that the result is session names like ApproveOrderSession or PerformCreditCheck.
- **A single method session has a command-like method.** Another cause of this AntiPattern is using the Command pattern to define sessions. When this is done, each separate session (that represents the command) will have a single public method named something like do or execute.
- **Application clients must always use multiple sessions.** The different process aspects of an abstraction are spread around to multiple client artifacts, and these artifacts all have knowledge and coupling to the core data types, and so on.
- **Changes to the associated entity abstraction force similar changes to multiple sessions.** When developing or evolving a session that supports an abstraction (for example, processes associated with, say, an Order), changes to items which are specific to the abstraction (for example, LineItem-dependent objects, and so on) need to be made to several different session interfaces and implementations, instead of in one place.
- **Harder to understand because processes are spread across artifacts.** Developers looking at sessions will be confused as to how to use them, what other sessions are needed, and so forth.
- **Poorer system performance.** A large number of sessions may result in lower performance, because the EJB container has to deploy more sessions, create more (pooled) instances, and most importantly, route all session invocations through the EJB container to regulate transaction semantics and security.

Typical Causes

The basic cause of the Thin Session AntiPattern is a combination of inexperience with OOA/OOD, and a decidedly verb-oriented leaning when doing the session design. The specific manifestations of this include:

- **Mapping each use case to a separate session.** Deriving sessions and session methods from use cases may be done in a one-to-one way, resulting in separate sessions for every use case. In general, this is not an appropriate approach, because there are typically many use cases that apply to a particular core abstraction (for example, there will likely be multiple use cases that deal with various processes around an Order, like creating, approving, paying, and so on).
- **Inappropriate application of the Command pattern to define sessions.** The Command pattern is applied in situations where verb-type components are desired within an architecture or design to support pluggable or interchangeable behaviors. In some cases, the verb component should be implemented using a session, to provide support for transactions, distribution, and so on.

However, this is a specific kind of design situation, in which the session is supporting an action. In general, this will not be the case, and this results in sessions that support one public operation, resulting in many related sessions being used to cover a single abstraction.

- **Excessive process or subsystem layering.** Subsystem or process layering can be taken too far, to the point of the Thin Session AntiPattern, where each process is essentially its own layer.
- **Stovepipe development.** If developers work in isolation, they may create new sessions when they come across some new requirement or process to implement, rather than check if there is an existing session that should be extended. With multiple developers operating in this manner, there can be many one-off sessions that are created that simply implement one or two methods.

Known Exceptions

If a session is defined for the purpose of encapsulating access to a legacy system, ERP, or even an external Web Service, that access may be thin (for example, only one or two key functions of those systems accessed). This may lead to the session exhibiting a thin, seemingly incomplete interface. If the functionality accessed fits within a larger set of capabilities within the application, then there should be a more complete session, with the implementation accessing those external systems where applicable.

Refactorings

The refactoring required in this case is called Interface Consolidation, and it seeks to consolidate the multiple, related thin sessions into a single one that represents a single cohesive abstraction. The mechanics consist of examining all the sessions, and for each one, determining which specific abstraction it operates against. This will usually be indicated by the session name itself (for example, ApproveOrderSession). In other cases, the abstraction may be indicated by details associated to its method(s), as described in the Bloated Session AntiPattern's *Refactorings* section. Once the thin sessions are merged, client artifacts that referenced any of the original sessions need to be adjusted to interact with the new session.

Refer to Chapter 3, Service-Based Architecture, for a complete discussion of the Interface Consolidation refactoring.

Variations

One of the variations that can crop up is the creation of command-like Session Beans, usually as a result of incorrectly applying the Command pattern. This can yield several Session Beans that have only one method, each of which has the same (command-like) signature. There may be rare cases when making the command object implementations Session Beans is justified (because they are transactional, for example), but in most cases, command objects are implemented as POJOs. In general, Session Beans are intended to support the set of processes associated with an abstraction, whereas a command is essentially the encapsulation of one particular action into an object.

Another variation is that, in some cases, the methods implemented within the Session Bean are purely algorithmic functions, and should not be implemented using a Session Bean at all, but just a Java object (for example, an algorithm object, action object, and so on). Details of this situation are described in more detail in the Sessions A-Plenty AntiPattern earlier in this chapter.

Example

The UML diagram in Figure 7.3 depicts an example of this AntiPattern. This diagram shows the key elements that define this AntiPattern. First, there are multiple Session Beans that implement methods against the same abstraction—in this case, the Order entity. Second, each Session Bean implements a specific process. In some cases, there may be different ways of supporting the same basic process (for example, create or duplicate an Order), but essentially, the Session Bean is still implementing one specific goal. Third, often the Session Bean names will be verb-oriented as shown here. And last, the Session Bean implements one or just a few methods, again, a specific goal or process associated with the abstraction.

Note that this diagram is only an illustration of the concept of the Thin Session AntiPattern, and in a real-world application, there would likely be many more such thin sessions that cover one abstraction.

Related Solutions

There are no related solutions to this AntiPattern.

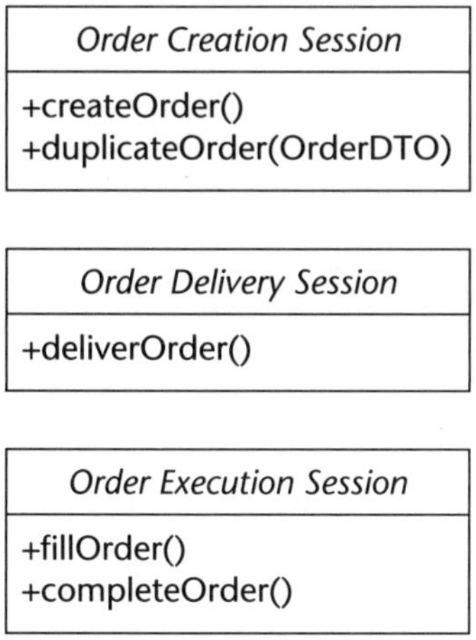

Figure 7.3 Thin sessions.

AntiPattern

Large Transaction

Also Known As: Fat Method, Takes Forever Transaction, Coarse-Grained Process

Most Frequent Scale: Microarchitecture, architecture

Refactorings: Split Large Transaction

Refactored Solution Type: Software

Root Causes: Sloth, ignorance, haste

Unbalanced Forces: Complexity and resources

Anecdotal Evidence: "The whole shopping workflow needs to be in one, transactional process, so I created one overall method to execute all the steps."

Background

Processes that need to be transactional are an important element to weigh in the decision to use sessions to implement business processes. However, transactional methods effectively lock any transactional resources that they use (for example, Entity Beans and JDBC connections) for the duration of the method, excluding other clients from enlisting those resources for their own transactional use. If multiple session instances attempt to access a shared transactional resource (for example, an Account entity), the EJB container will effectively serialize the invocation of those methods and instances. Therefore, it is important to keep transactional methods relatively short, and to keep the granularity of the process small enough that the set of resources involved is not too large.

Unfortunately, a common session AntiPattern involves failing to consider adequately during design these kinds of important transactional aspects, and leads to the Large Transaction AntiPattern. In this AntiPattern, a transactional session method is large, in terms of number of steps within the method and the number of shared transactional resources. Multiple clients invoking the LargeTransaction method on their own session instances are still locked out, waiting for the shared resources to become available. The consequences range from poor performance (when clients eventually acquire the necessary resources), to request failure due to the transaction timing out (when resources don't become available before the transaction times out).

General Form

A Large Transaction Session method is a transactional method whose implementation contains a large number of steps that access shared transactional resources, such as Entity Beans, JDBC connections, and so on. The size and significance of the steps and resources involved mean that the granularity and scope of the process is large, that is, the method implements a very high-level, coarse-grained process, like executing an entire purchase order workflow. Some of the steps may invoke finders that enlist the (many) fetched results into the transaction, while other steps invoke subordinate methods within the session (or other sessions) that themselves enlist further significant transactional resources. Thus, the LargeTransaction method is really just the top-level method of a wide and/or deep graph of transactional method calls. The large transaction will initiate the transaction (for example, a transaction attribute of Requires or RequireNew). The large transaction is usually recognized when performance problems and transaction timeouts occur, initiating a review and refactoring of the large method.

Symptoms and Consequences

The Large Transaction AntiPattern is usually recognized when the system starts to exhibit flakey behavior, with some requests failing randomly due to transaction timeouts. This may not manifest itself at all during internal testing (when there only a few clients); only under realistic loads and load testing does this show up. The following list defines some specific things to look for:

- **Slow execution of application.** The processing time on a Large Transaction will be long, because it acquires many resources and executes many processing steps. This will usually manifest itself as application requests that hang for a period (for example, the browser freezes while waiting several seconds for a response). Even in initial internal testing, processes that seem to take a significant amount of time to complete (for example, 10 seconds or more) should be reviewed for the Large Transaction AntiPattern.
- **Some requests fail due to transaction timeouts.** As the number of concurrent clients increases, the likelihood of transaction timeouts increases, because there are increasing numbers of clients queuing up for the same resources. This is usually the most significant wakeup call that indicates the possibility of a Large Transaction AntiPattern. Although poor performance can be attributed to the DB, query performance, legacy system interactions, and so on, when transactions time out, this indicates that the transaction is either too long (relative to the number of clients, load, and so on), or a deadlock situation is occurring (see the *Variations* section following).
- **Users may complain that a particular atomic feature implements too much.** Large transaction methods or processes may aggregate several distinct processes together into a single, chained sequence, and users may actually prefer to have these used as separate features, where they execute the steps and the sequencing. For instance, an approveOrder process should not (automatically) go through the subsequent steps like getPaymentInfo, createWayBill, and so on. Usually, users want to be allowed to step through those and validate or possibly cancel them.

Typical Causes

Designing sessions and other transactional processes is a complicated affair, and requires a good understanding of the mechanics of EJB, EJB containers, and transactional semantics in general. Some of the specific causes of the Large Transaction AntiPattern include:

- **The process is actually a chained sequence of separate processes.** Often, a LargeTransaction method is really a number of smaller methods and transactions chained together into one, large sequence that can be broken up into separate methods and transactions without violating the transactional integrity of the system. For instance, in a shopping e-commerce sequence, it would be reasonable to perform the different steps in separate transactions (for example, adding items, completing the shopping sequence, validating payment, and so forth). This would typically be supported using a Stateful Session Bean, with each step being a separate transactional method. If a particular step in the sequence fails, the intermediate state and information is still maintained, but only at the actual end of the sequence is data actually written to the DB.

- **Inexperience in modular, layered design.** Novice developers may aggregate a large number of steps into one, coarse-grained process, rather than breaking it up into subsystem layers.
- **Requirements descriptions and use cases are large.** Requirements artifacts that are structured into a few large process descriptions (that is, long, complicated use cases) may lead novice developers to mirror that granularity in their designs.
- **Inexperience implementing significant transactional components within EJBs and the J2EE architecture.** The first time that a situation occurs where clients are locked out due to contention for shared resources, or when a deadlock is discovered, is when developers learn about the complications of transactions, and the need for small, short-lived methods.

Known Exceptions

One exception to the Large Transaction AntiPattern is situations where the resources utilized by the method are not shared, but are specifically dedicated to a single client and thread of execution. For instance, scheduled batch-processing applications sometimes are implemented to execute in a single-threaded, synchronous manner, and will not raise the issue of deadlock. However, the process may still take so long that the transaction timeout interval may have to be adjusted if timeouts occur.

Refactorings

Usually the LargeTransaction method is implemented on the basis that the various steps all need to be coordinated and succeed (or fail) as one transaction. However, if there are timeouts and deadlocks, this approach clearly is not feasible, and so an alternative that yields equivalent semantics and results is required. The Split Large Process refactoring described in detail later in this chapter centers on breaking up the coarse-grained process (and transaction) into separate, finer-grained processes that each execute their own transaction. The overall transactional semantics must be honored, however, so the refactoring also involves implementing transaction-monitoring and corrective actions when subprocess transactions fail.

In terms of implementation, this means that there are basically two core activities in this refactoring: (1) Refactoring the LargeTransaction method into a nontransactional sequence of separate transactions, and (2) implementing transaction-result monitoring across the sequence of separate transactions, catching transaction failures, and implementating compensating actions against completed transactional changes earlier in the sequence after errors occur. The first part may be accomplished by refactoring the LargeTransaction method so that its transaction attribute is set to NotSupported, and ensuring that all subordinate process steps are implemented in separate transactional methods. The most obvious approach is to use session methods with a transaction attribute of Requires or RequiresNew for each of the steps. Often, a LargeTransaction method will invoke subordinate methods on the same session (or other sessions), so this may only require changing the transaction attribute. Alternately, if there are other transactional resources directly accessed in the LargeTransaction method (such as Entity Beans, JDBC connections, and so on), then these should be factored into additional transactional session methods so that, in the end, the refactored LargeTransaction method implementation initiates all of the subordinate transactions by executing transacted session methods.

The second aspect—providing equivalent transactional semantics—requires implementing corrective actions in the cases where process steps fail.

Executing undo functionality is, in many cases, simply not doable when there are concurrent accesses to persistent data, for example. For instance, in the classic banking scenario, an account-transfer transaction may succeed in withdrawing money from the originating account, but fail when depositing the money to the destination account. Thus, when the deposit fails, there is an option to reset the account value in the source account, or perform another *compensating* transaction that corrects the problem by registering a withdrawal or correction. This is similar to an accounting situation in which, if there is an entry error, it is corrected with another entry, but the original entry is left intact. Thus, the implementation of this aspect of the refactoring needs to bracket the overall process sequence in a try/catch block, to catch any offending exception and save the data used within *each* step of the sequence, to use for corrective action later. The implementation of the catch block consists of applying corrective action to each of the completed transaction steps, and returning an overall exception to indicate that the entire process did not succeed.

Another refactoring approach seeks to minimize the resources actually enlisted in the transaction, using nontransactional analogues where possible. In terms of entities, utilizing finders will enlist fetched entities into the transaction. In many cases, however, the entity data is being used in a read-only fashion within the process, and so there is really no need to include it in transactions. One can make the argument that locking entity instances within the transaction ensures that the actual data in the DB doesn't change over the course of executing the method, and there are certain cases where this is important. However, often, the process only needs the data to be current at the time it was first read, so other strategies, such as the Light Query Pattern or JDO approaches to fetching data (described in Chapter 2), should be used to reduce the transactional entity components within the method.

Variations

A particularly troublesome variation of this AntiPattern occurs when there are multiple different LargeTransactions or other transactional components that access a similar set of resources in a different order. This scenario can lead to a deadlock situation. The big issue is that this situation usually manifests itself only under specific situations, such as when there are large volumes of activity or when specific time-oriented processes are run (electronic document exchanges, for example). While deadlock is something to watch out for all the time, it becomes much more likely when LargeTransaction methods exist, simply because there is a greater chance of contention for shared resources, over longer periods of time.

In some cases, a design may result in a very coarse-grained, top-level stateful session, with several layers of successively finer-grained Stateful Session Beans below it in a calling sequence. This is a situation where there is a chain of Stateful Session Beans that can easily tie up many resources in a manner similar to the LargeTransaction method.

Example

The diagram in Figure 7.4 depicts a LargeTransaction method named executeOrder() on the CommerceSession that executes several steps to complete a purchase order process. This scenario can occur when someone attempts to implement a supposedly streamlined user process, whereby hitting the checkout button initiates the completion of the order, and all subsequent process steps as well. This application can also be implemented in this way as an automated purchase process as part of a Web Service or integration process implementation. Regardless of the reason for it, this configuration results in a single, large-grained process being invoked by an outside client, be it a UI component, a Web Service client, or an integration client, and several significant processes are sequenced and executed in this one overall step.

As can be seen from the diagram and sequencing, this method performs a series of steps that call significant transactional session methods, and each of those methods enlists a number of core Entity Bean instances. Because all these steps occur within the same transaction, and each one requires significant processing, this results in a situation in which the method takes a long time to execute and, in the end, has enlisted many shared resources.

Related Solutions

One common solution is to reduce to a minimum the transactional requirements of the method. In many cases, resources like Entity Bean instances are read but never changed through a process, and needn't be accessed in a transactional manner. Also, in many cases, the state of the data at read time is sufficiently current for a process (such as generating a report), and if the data values change soon thereafter, this isn't an issue. The currency of data issue is one of the chief arguments used to justify the inclusion of Entity Bean instances within transactions, but there are many cases where this is really not a requirement. Retrieving read-only data in the form of DTOs or even ResultSets is another approach to removing that part of the process from the overall transaction.

One of the approaches to reducing deadlock is to define a standard order of access to a set of transactional resources. When multiple clients access shared resources, if the resources are accessed in the same order, this can reduce the incidence of deadlock by ensuring that *any* client that accesses the first resource essentially gets a lock on the whole sequence, requiring every other client to wait for all the resources.

Another possible solution approach is to implement a single-threaded, but asynchronous, processing model using JMS. In some cases, one or more of the concurrent clients may not need to synchronously access the shared (contentious) resources, for example, an EAI automation process. In these cases, it is possible to refactor these kinds of client interactions to utilize JMS/MsgBeans so that their accesses can be threaded.

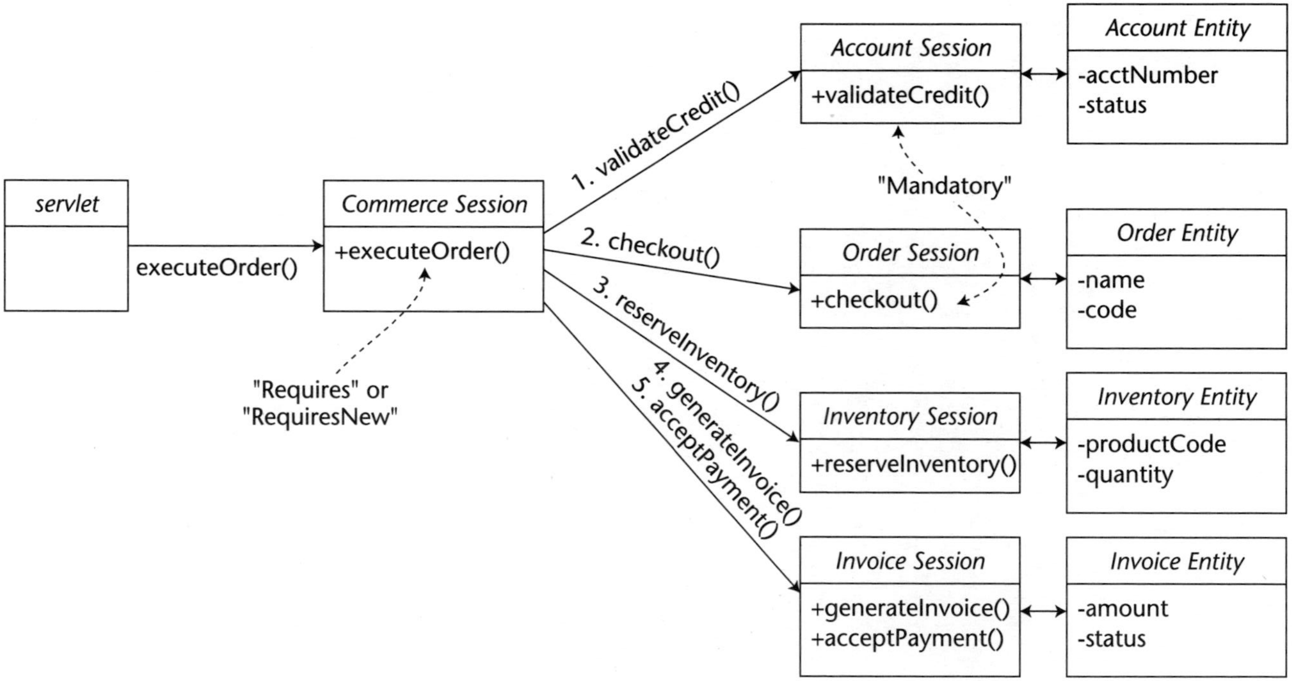

Figure 7.4 Large and long transaction.

Transparent Façade

Also Known As: Direct Mapping

Most Frequent Scale: Application, architecture

Refactorings: Session façade

Refactored Solution Type: Software

Root Causes: Ignorance

Unbalanced Forces: Complexity and resources

Anecdotal Evidence: "I've read somewhere that we should do Session façades."

Background

One of the most common EJB-related patterns is the Session Façade pattern, in which a session is created that wraps one or more Entity EJBs (or other middle-tier components) to eliminate direct remote invocations between clients and entities. However, many newer EJB developers may consider the use of Session facades standard practice, but only have a cursory understanding of the actual pattern and intent. Thus, they do a direct, one-to-one mapping of entity methods to the session methods. The result is not a façade at all, but a direct mapping or transparent façade, where the session replicates the attribute-level accessors and mutators.

One of the original rationales around the Session Façade pattern was to reduce client-to-server network interactions that occurred when performing attribute-level remote method invocations. By interjecting an intervening session (façade) that utilized a data-aggregating pattern such as the Data Transfer Object (DTO) pattern, distributed interactions could be greatly reduced so that all the entities data could be exchanged in a single remote invocation on the session. Thus, the appropriate application of the Session Façade pattern involves aggregating all the individual fine-grained methods of the entity into an equivalent single, coarse-grained method on the enclosing Session façade. Creating façades that directly implement the underlying component interface, at the same level of granularity, doesn't reduce distributed interactions at all, and in fact, introduces an additional layer of EJB machinery that further reduces the poor performance of the chatty interface.

General Form

The Transparent Façade AntiPattern is made up of a Session Bean that is coupled to an underlying Entity Bean, whereby clients interact with the Session Bean to invoke data accessors and mutators on the underlying entity instance. In the correct application of the Session Façade pattern, the Session Bean methods aggregate a number of fine-grained, attribute-level method calls into a single, coarse-grained access, usually passing the set of attribute values as a DTO or equivalent. In this AntiPattern, however, the Session Bean is implemented with the same, fine-grained, attribute-level accessors and mutators as on the underlying Entity Bean, so clients still need to invoke many fine-grained methods against the session to access all the data values. So, the Session Bean that overlays the Entity Bean implements exactly the same methods, which are implemented as simple pass-through calls to similar methods in the associated entity instance. Thus, the Session Bean implements a façade that does not hide anything about the underlying entity, hence the name Transparent façade.

Symptoms and Consequences

The Transparent Façade AntiPattern gives a false impression that the system will perform better and middle-tier components will be more modular and organized. The specific symptoms and consequences that result from the Transparent Façade AntiPattern include:

- **Poorer performance** than **just interacting directly with entity.** A proper application of the Session Façade pattern reduces network interactions, improving performance. But the Transparent façade does nothing to reduce the number of network calls, and adds another layer of EJB calling to the mix, effectively making performance worse than it was before introducing the façade.
- **Tight coupling between the entity interface and session interface and implementation.** Because the Transparent façade directly emulates the entity interface, any changes to the entity (for example, additions of attributes, changes to data types, and so on) must be reflected in lock-step in the session. This effectively increases the development effort required to make any entity changes.

Typical Causes

The main causes of this AntiPattern are inexperience with EJB design and misunderstanding of the Session façade design pattern.

- **Lack of understanding of Session Façade pattern.** Inexperience and lack of understanding of the intentions behind the Session Façade pattern are the most common cause of this AntiPattern.
- **Not understanding the concepts of modular design and subsystem layering.** A fundamental motivation for the Session Façade pattern is to implement subsystem layering, whereby coarse-grained processes are composed of lower-layer, fine-grained processes. Subsystem layering allows processes of different granularity to be used for different contexts as appropriate, and this is a key aspect of flexible, modular design.

Known Exceptions

When client components are strictly server-based (for example, a Servlet container and EJB container in the same J2EE application server), then there really isn't the need to implement the Session façade at all, at least, in order to improve performance. There is still value in creating more coarse-grained subsystem layers through Session facades.

Refactorings

The refactoring of a Transparent façade consists of redoing the Session Façade pattern, albeit in an appropriate way. The result should be a session that has just a few methods and that utilizes the DTO Pattern (for data accessor and mutator) to reduce chatty interactions. The clients that were previously using the Transparent façade are then refactored to interact with the DTO-based accessor and mutator, to exchange DTO objects instead of accessing individual attributes on the entity.

Variations

Transparent Façade over Session is a variation of this AntiPattern. In some cases, a layered set of processes and subprocesses is implemented as a layer of sessions (for example, coarse-grained processes that are composed of a number of finer-grained processes), creating layers of sessions. In some of these cases, the outer sessions may mirror the interfaces of the inner sessions (for example, just flatten the inner session interfaces into one, larger outer session). This may be done to present a single session to a client that is composed of a number of finer-grained sessions. Thus, this AntiPattern is not exclusively about layering on top of an entity; it may also occur when performing layering on top of other sessions or other component types.

Example

The diagram in Figure 7.5 depicts an example of a Transparent façade. The diagram shows a typical multitier J2EE application, in which a remote, thick client component (the OrderView) accesses server-side EJB components to obtain and display information about a specific Order entity instance. The server-side components include the OrderSession, which acts as a façade over an instance of Order Entity Bean. As the diagram indicates, the OrderSession implements the same attribute-level accessors as the associated Entity Bean, resulting in a façade that isn't really a façade. When the client needs to obtain data for a specific entity instance, each attribute value must be obtained by performing a separate remote invocation with the OrderSession, which in turn calls the associated entity instance. Thus, each attribute value access requires one remote call and two EJB method calls, resulting in worse performance than if the client interacted with the entity instance directly.

Related Solutions

Another common pattern employed within *n*-tiered systems is the Business Delegate pattern, whereby a non-EJB class is used to implement process- or workflow-sequencing methods and also to encapsulate EJB interaction semantics.

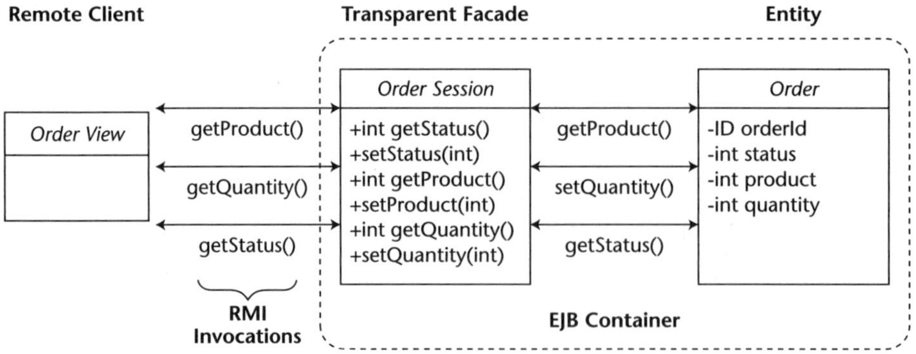

Figure 7.5 Transparent Session façade.

AntiPattern

Data Cache

Also Known As: Runtime Data Store

Most Frequent Scale: Application, architecture

Refactorings: Use Entity Beans for Persistent Data

Refactored Solution Type: Software

Root Causes: Ignorance, pride

Unbalanced Forces: Complexity and resources

Anecdotal Evidence: "Hey, stateful sessions are long-running and stateful, and can be triggered to read from and write to the DB upon transaction boundaries . . . sounds like a perfect cache mechanism!"

Background

Performance aspects of persistence within J2EE systems have been a significant focus of effort since the inception of EJB, and have been a driving force in the evolution of the EJB standard. Vendors have implemented creative solutions within their EJB containers, and developers have utilized various design patterns like the Session façade. Persistence design and performance remain as an important and complex aspect of J2EE system design, and developers continue to attempt new ways to improve performance.

One of the creative solutions has been to use Stateful Session Beans to implement distributed caching. This solution relies on the fact that stateful sessions can provide custom implementation through the transaction life cycle, by implementing the SessionSynchronization interface. This allows the session to invoke its own custom methods just before a transaction is started, just before a transaction is completed, and just after a transaction is completed. These hooks can be used to read (or refresh) data from the DB before the transaction begins, and save updated data (but retain) just before the transaction is completed. The idea is that, because a stateful session maintains state between transactions and is maintained in memory by the EJB container (until it is explicitly removed), this should make a good basis for a reliable cache.

However, there are a couple of key issues regarding stateful sessions that make this approach ultimately unworkable and unreliable. First, sessions are by nature associated with a single client, and by definition they do not support concurrent access by multiple clients. But, in order for a cache to be useful, multiple process threads (and clients) must be able to access and update the same (shared) instance data they use and change, requiring concurrent access. Some EJB containers allow concurrent access, but this may result in dirty reads of intratransaction data values. Also, stateful sessions are not typically replicated across all nodes in a clustered deployment, but usually only one other (backup) node. Thus, it is quite possible for the two nodes that are hosting the stateful session cache instance to fail, while other nodes are still fine. The result is that the cache is lost, but the clustered application server is still running. So, clients attempting to use the cache will fail unexpectedly. This translates to an unreliable caching approach.

General Form

The basic form is a typical Stateful Session Bean that supports a set of business processes, but is extended to support the caching of data that is read, and possibly the persisting of data updates (that is, write through cache).

The stateful session implements the SessionSynchronization interface, so that persistent data used by the sessions methods is cached within the session. The implementation of the SessionSynchronization interface intercepts the start of any of the transactional process methods on the session. For processes and methods that use or provide persistent data to the client, the beforeStart() method is implemented to determine if requested data can be drawn from the cache or needs to be read from the DB. For methods that insert, update, or delete data, the beforeCompletion() and afterCompletion() methods are used to update the sessions cache (if the transaction succeeds), and potentially write updates to the database.

Symptoms and Consequences

The basic approach of utilizing Stateful Session Beans to implement a distributed data cache is outside of the realm of intended use, and leads to a number of symptoms and consequences as follows:

- **Apparent freeze-up for some clients (if deadlock occurs**). Eventually, the response is received, indicating an error (when the transaction timeout occurs).
- **Performance may degrade quickly as the number of clients or users increases.** At large numbers of clients, the performance may be unacceptable.
- **There may be significant performance degradation due to the passivation and activation of large SFSBs.** With this approach, the entire cache for a specific entity is held in one SFSB, and if that is not accessed for a while, the entire cache may be the least used for some time, and passivated to disk. Depending on the amount of data cached within the SFSB, this could consume considerable application server processing to perform the disk I/O.
- **Possibly lost changes to data (updates, deletes) if nodes that SFSBs are deployed on fail.** The overall clustered deployment may still be operational, however, and mechanisms must be in place to recreate the SFSB data cache in this situation.
- **Possible deadlock due to multiple-client concurrent access.** Concurrent access to a single Stateful Session Bean by multiple clients creates the potential for deadlock when those clients concurrently access and lock resources. EJB 2.0 specification allows Session Beans to support concurrent access, although this is not a requirement and is only supported by a subset of vendors. An effective cache requires support for concurrent access, so the use of stateful sessions as a data-caching mechanism can run into deadlock issues when these concurrent accesses occur.

Typical Causes

Knowledge and experience in the fine details of the semantics and limitations of Stateful Session Beans and EJB containers are at the heart of this AntiPattern. Some of the specific causes include:

- **Ignorance or misunderstanding of stateful session semantics.** When utilizing a complex technology such as EJB, it is wise to dig deep, read the specification, and look around at other sources of practical experience (on the Web, and so on) before embarking on a significant undertaking as in implementing a reliable, fault-tolerant caching mechanism.
- **Ignorance of the caching capabilities of entities and EJB containers.** Many major EJB containers provide significant caching capabilities through CMP entity beans. Using CMP and entities often can provide the caching semantics required.

Known Exceptions

EJB Container implementations that do not provide decent caching support through Entity EJBs. In some cases, an EJB container implementation may not provide the needed caching support via Entity Beans. However, in these cases, other third-party caching tools should be evaluated.

Refactorings

One of the big issues with the Data Cache AntiPattern is that stateful sessions do not provide the kind of regulated concurrency control that is necessary for a truly reliable cache mechanism. Entity Beans, however, specifically support the kind of concurrent access controls needed. Thus, one of the refactorings is to utilize Entity Beans with the SFSB as the actual mechanism that holds the data, so that even if there are concurrent accesses to the SFSB, the associated entity will ensure single-threaded access to the actual data.

The most common and supported approach to reliable caching in EJB is the use of CMP Entity Beans. Most major EJB container implementations support caching of CMP Entity Beans, and Entity Beans are inherently designed to support managed concurrent access—the EJB container synchronizes concurrent access across all used instances and the underlying database, across all nodes in the cluster.

Variations

There are no significant variations to this AntiPattern.

Example

The example in Figure 7.6 depicts a typical J2EE application scenario that uses a Stateful Session Bean as a server-side distributed cache mechanism. The central element of this approach is the OrderCache Stateful Session Bean that implements the different CRUD-oriented methods that all clients use to access and update Order data. The implementation of these CRUD methods makes use of the transaction handling capabilities of stateful sessions (when they implement the SessionSynchronization interface) to implement the functionality to access and update the internal state (for example, the cache) to improve the performance of read operations. In this configuration, all clients interact with the singleton instance to read and update Order data in the system. The Session Bean itself retains the state for all Order entity instance data and intercepts requests to read or write data to allow database read or writes to occur, and also to provide cached in-memory data when appropriate. The Stateful Session Bean implements the SessionSynchronization interface so that invocation of any of the CRUD methods has the side effect of executing session code that implements the write-through cache, interacting with the DB at the appropriate points to read new instances and write updates. Note that the implementation of the CRUD operations to and from the database could use JDBC or the entity bean approach. Also, the OrderCache Stateful Session Bean may be replicated across EJB container nodes in a clustered deployment, effectively implementing a distributed caching mechanism.

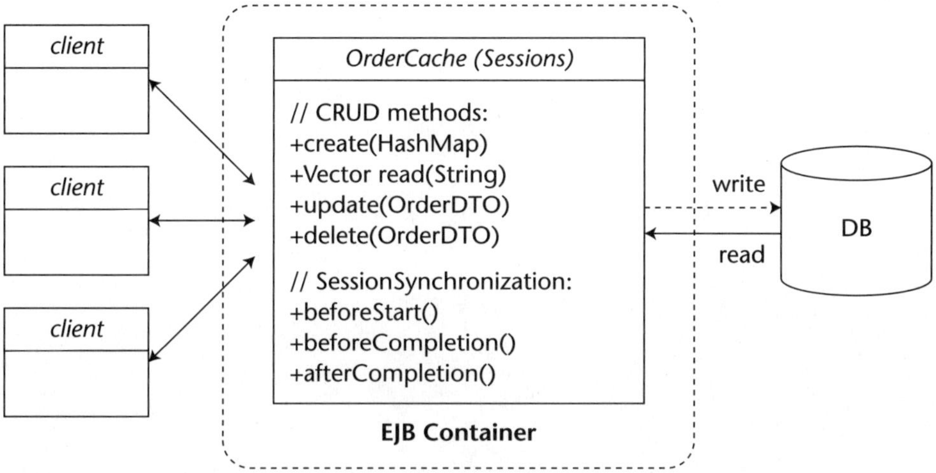

Figure 7.6 Data cache using a Stateful Session Bean.

There are a number of important aspects of this configuration that lead to the problems and result in this being an AntiPattern. First, the implementation of an effective cache means that there needs to be one place where all the cacheable data is accessed, so that accesses and updates all operate on one, synchronized set of data. Typically, the database represents this; the Stateful Session Bean here implements an in-memory singular data source. However, a single Session Bean instance may fail, and replication across clustered deployments usually does not occur across all nodes, so there are definite cases where the cache can be lost. Additionally, since all clients have to concurrently access the same component instance to get at the one in-memory data store, this may actually result in some performance issues and, worse, result in incorrect data reads as a result of concurrent access to the Session Bean.

Related Solutions

Buy before build. If performance is a critical requirement such that caching is deemed to be required, there are third-party tools and frameworks that work within popular J2EE application servers, plugging into container transaction managers, database-connection pools, and so on. As for any significant infrastructure requirement, the goal should usually be to buy before committing significant resources, time, and complexity to building. If your core competency is not complex server-side data caching components, do yourself a favor and buy a caching product.

Refactorings

Java Data Objects (JDO) is emerging as an alternative to Entity Beans, and represents another mechanism that can be used instead of Stateful Session Beans as a way to get reasonable performance for accessing persistent data. The use of JDO may provide good enough performance boost that complicated caching schemes are not required. Session Beans are intended to support application processes, and many of the issues that crop up with poor business processes in the real world are issues with corresponding sessions. For instance, very large process sequences are often problematic in business because they take too long and involve too many resources, and if they take too long, then some potential customers just give up and go away. Also, when an external party has to do many, very specific tasks to get anything done, it takes a long time. These are the kinds of issues that crop up with sessions—large and long processes, chatty interfaces, and so on. The most common refactoring for many of these problems is a form of process or subsystem layering.

Session Façade. This refactoring is the EJB session variant of the well-known Gang of Four (Gamma, Helm, Johnson, Vlissides, 1996) pattern, in which a set of fine-grained operations are aggregated together into a larger, coarse-grained operation.

Split Large Transaction. This refactoring breaks up a large, long transactionally intense process into separate transactional parts when possible.

Session Façade

A client remotely invokes many attribute-level accessors and mutators on an Entity Bean, resulting in a chatty interaction that exhibits poor performance.

Introduce a session as a façade over the entity, and aggregate the fine-grained attribute accessors into a single, coarse-grained method, reducing the network interactions and improving performance.

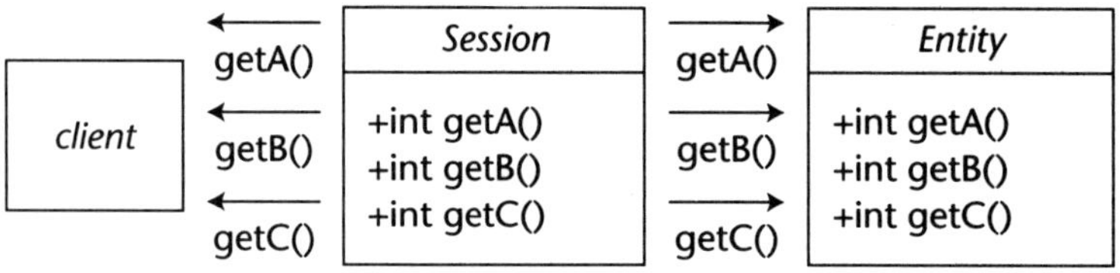

Figure 7.7 Before refactoring.

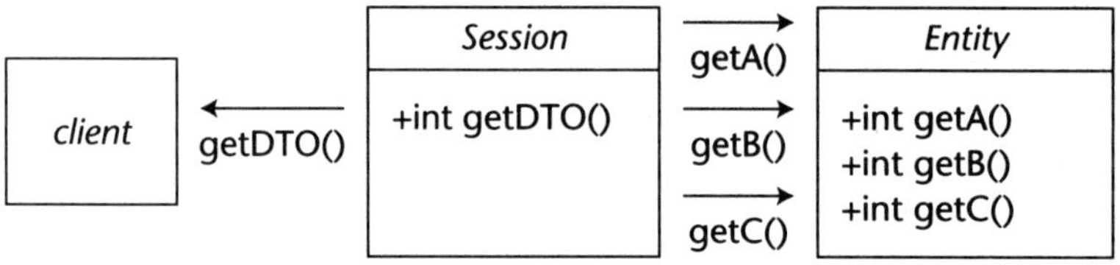

Figure 7.8 After refactoring.

Motivation

One of the original motivations for using the Session Façade pattern within distributed J2EE systems was to reduce the number of remote method invocations between remote clients and server-side components, improving performance. This is still a very common application of the Session façade, and is implemented by aggregating many fine-grained, attribute-level interactions between remote clients and server-side Entity Bean components into a single remote call that passes many attributes within a bulk DTO.

The Session Façade pattern can also be used to create subsystem layering, implementing coarse-grained methods that aggregate and coordinate interactions with finer-grained process components (sessions, entities, or POJOs) to implement business logic and workflow. This creates simpler interfaces for clients to use, and encapsulates the sequencing and workflow steps associated with a business process within a session method, instead of requiring the client to have knowledge and implement that. Also, subsystem layering can allow various granularities of process to be more easily reused by encapsulating distinct processes and subprocesses within well-defined session methods.

The Session Façade pattern is discussed in greater length in Alur, Crupi, and Malks' *Core J2EE Patterns* (Alur, Crupi, and Malks 2001).

Mechanics

The mechanics of this refactoring apply specifically to the situation of the Transparent Façade AntiPattern, in which the Session façade component exposes the same granularity methods as the underlying components. The result should be an appropriate Session façade that actually does create more granular methods and subsystem layering. The different steps in this refactoring are as follows:

1. *Determine the coarse-grained process(es) that the Session façade should implement.* The first step is to decide what subsystem layering the Transparent Façade session should implement, that is, what it was originally intended for. Session facades are typically used to implement bulk access to Entity Beans, and/or to implement coarse-grained processes that are themselves made up of process steps and workflow. If there are existing clients that use the Transparent façade, they can usually be examined to decide what the usage context is, and indicate which of these was intended. Also, since the Transparent façade doesn't implement the coarse-grained processing that it should, this implementation usually finds its way into the clients, so this may also be helpful in deciding what implementation should be put into the Session façade.

2. *Refactor the Session façade to implement the coarse-grained process.* This step consists of creating the coarse-grained method(s) on the Session façade. As mentioned in the previous step, this will usually consist of bulk accessor and mutator methods (when providing coarser-grained access to entity beans), or process steps, workflow, and sequencing. Also, when current clients of the session have needed to implement the coarser-grained interactions to use it in context, this client implementation can be refactored down into the session. Note

that, in the previous step, there may have been multiple client components that were implementing analogous process code to interact with the Transparent façade, so one task that may be involved here is merging the (possibly different) implementations of the process into one before putting it into the Session façade.

3. *Refactor the client(s) to use the new, coarse-grained Session façade method.* Client components identified in step one are refactored to remove the process implementation code that was found there, and replace it with calls to the new Session façade.
4. *Remove the fine-grained methods from the Session façade.* Fine-grained methods in the session that were the manifestation of the Transparent façade are removed as a final step.

Example

The following provides an example of this refactoring, as applied to the previously presented Transparent façade example.

In the first step, we need to decide what coarse-grained process was intended for the Session façade. As can be seen from the diagram, the interactions are directly with an Entity Bean, accessing individual attributes. This indicates that the intention is to access data from the Entity Bean, and thus, the methods on the Session façade *should* be basic bulk data accessor and mutator for the Order entity. Thus, we can introduce the new bulk method signatures to the session, and add an OrderDTO class to serve as the bulk access object type. Both of these are indicated in the following code fragments:

```
// Additional method signatures on session:
     public OrderDTO getOrder() throws RemoteException;
     public void setOrder(OrderDTO value) throws RemoteException;

// New DTO type:
public class OrderDTO {
     public int status;
     public int productId;
     public int quantity;
}
```

The next step is to add the implementation of the new coarse-grained methods to the session:

```
// New implementations on session:
    public OrderDTO getOrder() throws RemoteException {
          OrderDTO value = new OrderDTO();

          // Assume Order entity instance 'order' acquired elsewhere
          value.status = order.getStatus();
          value.productId = order.getProductId();
```

```
        value.quantity = order.getQuantity();

        return value;
    }

    public void setOrder(OrderDTO value) throws RemoteException {

        // Assume Order entity instance 'order' acquired elsewhere
        order.setStatus(value.status);
        order.setProductId(value.productId);
        order.setQuantity(value.quantity);
    }
```

The next step involves refactoring the client to utilize the new, coarse-grained methods. This is shown below in Figure 7.9. The original, fine-grained methods that were present in the Transparent façade are removed.

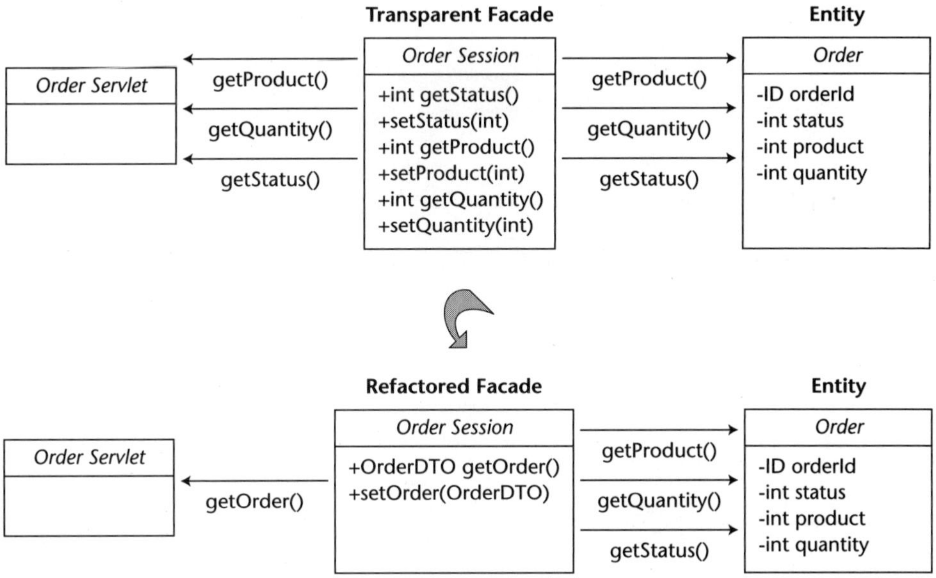

Figure 7.9 Refactored transparent Session façade.

Split Large Transaction

A transactional session method enlists many other transactional resources, and executes a lengthy, coarse-grained process, resulting in poor performance and transaction timeouts at higher loads.

Split the large transactional method into a number of smaller transactions, and refactor clients to invoke these methods separately. Thus, each of the methods is then a much smaller transaction, with fewer resources locked in at any one time.

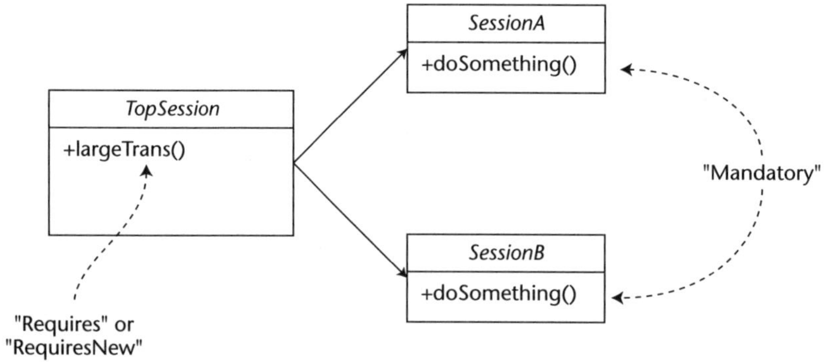

Figure 7.10 Before refactoring.

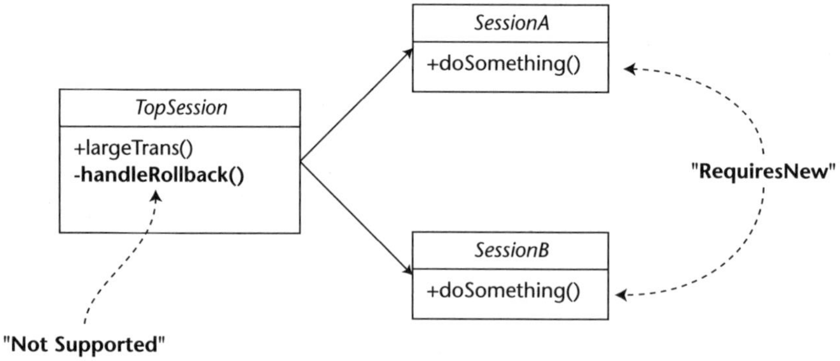

Figure 7.11 After refactoring.

Motivation

The most important motivation of this refactoring is to reduce issues of performance and deadlock that result from having large transactions that lock many shared resources over significant amounts of time. Obviously, when significant performance issues occur, or worse, deadlock becomes an issue, then this becomes a critical motivation to refactor the Large Transaction AntiPattern.

A secondary motivation for this refactoring is to create smaller, more manageable and encapsulated processes that each can be executed in a single invocation step, and allow reimplementation using Stateless Session Beans, which are more scalable.

Mechanics

The following describes the sequence of steps to perform this refactoring:

1. *Refactor the LargeTransaction method into a nontransactional equivalent.* Typically, the large transaction will be in a session method. Making this nontransactional amounts to changing the transactional attribute value to NotSupported.
2. *Refactor all the subordinate transactional steps into transactional session methods, for example, using a transactional attribute value of Required or RequiresNew.* In many cases, the implementation with a LargeTransaction method will include invocations of other session methods, so in these cases, all that may be needed is to ensure that the transactional attribute on those methods is the necessary value. There may also be interactions with nonsession transactional resources (for example, Entity Beans and JDBC connections); these interactions should be factored into other, transactional session methods so that in the end, the nontransactional session method only consists of nontransactional code and invocations to other, transactional session methods.
3. *Add code to handle transaction monitoring to catch failures and rollbacks emitted from individual steps.* The entire sequence of calls to the lower-level transactional methods needs to be wrapped in a try/catch block to be able to detect and handle problems when any of the transactional methods fails.
4. *Add code to implement compensating actions when transactional subprocesses fail.* If the try/catch block described above catches a transaction failure from one of the steps in the calling sequence, the response needs to be to apply a compensating action to each of the previous steps that was completed. The actual compensating action is dependent on the business process being executed. In most cases, it involves recording information about before and after values, utilizing a set of business rules to determine what the compensating action should be, and computing the compensating value to use based on those previously recorded values.

Example

The following provides a step-by-step walkthrough of this refactoring, as applied to the Large Transaction AntiPattern example presented previously.

The first step in this refactoring is to change the transaction attribute setting for the top-level session method to NotSupported, making it nontransactional. This ultimately is done by editing the deployment descriptor for the session, but in most EJB developments today, other tools are used to generate that artifact, with the various deployment details embedded into the Session Bean class as javadoc tags. Thus, the typical situation here is to add or change a javadoc tag that defines the transaction attribute setting for the LargeTransaction method.

The next step sets the transaction attribute settings on each of the subordinate sessions to Required or RequiresNew. This is accomplished in the same way.

The implementation of the executeOrder() method in the CommerceSession is enhanced to monitor the status of transactional steps and catch cases where a transactional step in the sequence fails. The following code shows the executeOrder() method with the monitoring block added:

```
public boolean executeOrder(OrderDTO order,
int custId, PaymentDTO payment) {
     boolean success = false;
int invoiceId;

// Note: assume accessed sessions have been acquired...

     // Validate that customer can place order:
     if (accountSess.validateCredit(custId, order.getTotal())) {

          // Try/catch process steps to catch transaction failure:
          try {
               orderSess.checkout(order.getOrderId());

               inventorySess.reserveInventory(order);

               int invoiceId = invoiceSess.generateInvoice(order);
               invoiceSess.acceptPayment(payment, invoiceId);
               success = true;
           } catch (Exception e) {
               // One of the transaction steps failed;
          }
     }

     return success;
}
```

Finally, the catch block has implementation added that executes appropriate compensating actions to effectively negate the previous successful transactions that occurred within the sequence. This code is shown here:

```
// Add process state indicators:
boolean checkout = false;
boolean inventory = false;
boolean invoice = false;
// Try/catch process steps to catch transaction failure:
try {
     orderSess.checkout(order.getOrderId());
     checkout = true;

     inventorySess.reserveInventory(order);
     inventory = true;

     int invoiceId = invoiceSess.generateInvoice(order);
     invoice = true;

     invoiceSess.acceptPayment(payment, invoiceId);
     success = true;
} catch (Exception e) {
       // Determine which stage this failed at,
      // and compensate accordingly:
      if (invoice)
           invoiceSess.removeInvoice(invoiceId);

           if (inventory)
           inventorySess.returnInventory(order);

      if (checkout)
           orderSess.reopenOrder(order);
}
```

CHAPTER 8

Message-Driven Beans

Messaging, as a formal construct, has been around for a while. JMS, the Java Messaging Service, was the first official entrée for Java developers into the messaging world. At first, JMS was slow to take root. But as developers discovered the incredible usefulness of guaranteed messaging, they began to adopt the technology more quickly.

In response to the growing adoption of JMS for remote programming, Sun introduced the concept of a message-driven Enterprise JavaBean, or a message-driven bean. Message-driven beans themselves are pretty straightforward to write. Usually, the issues surrounding them are standard EJB issues, like those discussed in the previous EJB chapters, or messaging related. As a result, this chapter is more of a focus on messaging in the J2EE world than on the message-driven beans that implement it. The relationship between the bean and its environment is fundamentally important when creating these message beans.

The following AntiPatterns focus on the problems and mistakes that many developers make when using message-driven beans, as well as common mistakes that people make when designing and deploying message-driven architectures. We'll cover them all in this chapter. All of these AntiPatterns represent common problems in message-driven architectures and, in particular, using message-driven beans. This chapter will first discuss these three AntiPatterns and then discuss the refactorings that can be used to fix and avoid them.

Misunderstanding JMS. JMS offers a number of messaging choices. It is easy to confuse these, or choose the wrong one. This can work both ways. An architect might not use a topic when he or she really needs to distribute messages, or might use topics everywhere even though it is overkill for some applications. This section will primarily discuss the JMS concepts, where they should be used, and where they might be misused.

Overloading Destinations. One of the more confusing things that people can do is create a destination that will be used for numerous message types. For example, you can send text- and map-based messages on the same queue, which requires the receiver to distinguish them. But you can also send two different maps on the same queue, or two different XML schemas. This can also lead to problems.

Overimplementing Reliability. JMS provides reliability in messaging, including the option of once and only once messaging. Given this support, it is not necessary, in most cases, for the message beans to recheck if something is a repeat. Only in very rare cases does the JMS server need to be second-guessed on every message. This section will discuss how this pattern comes into play, often when iterating solutions or building a replacement of an old solution, such as RMI, where code was necessary to check for uniqueness in messages.

AntiPattern

Misunderstanding JMS

Also Known As: Choosing the Wrong Options

Most Frequent Scale: Programmer

Refactorings: Architect the Solution

Refactored Solution Type: Process, education

Root Causes: Lack of education or experience

Unbalanced Forces: Time to market, scaling a smaller solution, performance

Anecdotal Evidence: "Why is the financial code getting messages sent to the customer service code?"

Background

JMS provides two models for messaging. The first, point-to-point, is like TCP/IP to the hard-core network developers. There is one program sending messages to another program, one sender, and one receiver. The second type is public-subscribe. The publish-subscribe method is more like UDP/IP for the hard-core network folks. In the publish-subscribe method numerous receivers can receive one sender's messages—one sender and many receivers. These two models are pictured in Figures 8.1 and 8.2.

If that were it to JMS, things would be pretty easy. But JMS, like most messaging infrastructures, also has the concept of persistence and durability. Persistence makes sure that each message is received. In the case of point-to-point messaging JMS uses the concept of a persistent queue. The queue is created in the server, usually by an administrator or programmatically. Messages to the queue are stored until they are read. Once read, in the simplest case, they are removed. In more complex settings, you may group messages into a transaction to ensure that a group of messages is read before deleting any of them. JMS says that queues are supposed to be persistent, so they are pretty easy to understand. Although you can make nonpersistent queues and messages with expiration dates, that is not the default.

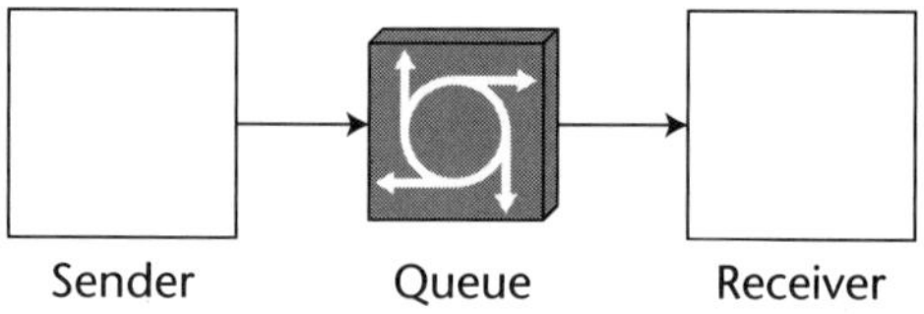

Figure 8.1 Point-to-point messaging.

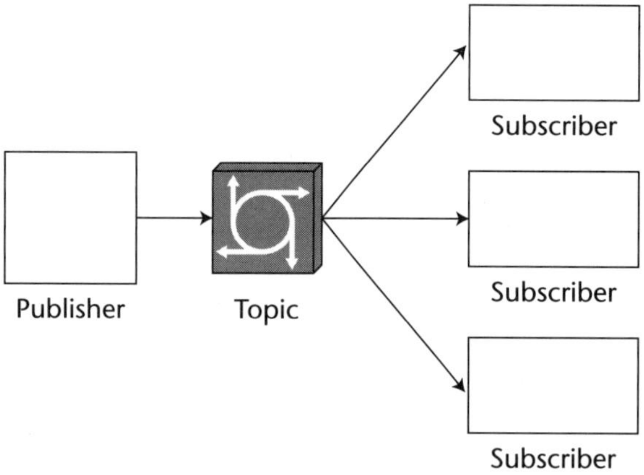

Figure 8.2 Publish-subscribe messaging.

Publish-subscribe messaging in JMS is accomplished via something called a topic. Topics can have multiple subscribers or receivers. Unlike queues, topics are not, by definition, persistent. Instead, the subscriber might want to be treated persistently, so it can create a durable subscription. This difference in persistence between subscribers is one of the tricky JMS implementation details. The other is that, until you register the durable subscriber, the server won't know to save its messages. So you might have to register a subscriber before turning the clients on.

The last thing to note about the basic JMS landscape is that the sender in both cases does not have to be a single application. Point-to-point really means one or more points to one point, and publish-subscribe means one or more publishers and one or more subscribers. Sometimes the multiplicity of senders confuses implementers into thinking they need to use multiple subscribers.

Both queues and topics are called "destinations" in the JMS world. So, we will continue that terminology here.

The problem that many developers encounter when creating JMS-based applications is knowing which type of messaging to use and the associated details of that messaging choice.

General Form

There are a number of forms that misunderstanding JMS can take. First, you might use a queue with multiple receivers. Some JMS systems might prevent this, but others might allow it, so you can't be sure that the JMS provider will prevent you from "breaking" the conceptual model of a queue. Conceptually, a queue guarantees once and only once delivery, but with two receivers you can get the situation pictured in Figure 8.3, where each subscriber is missing messages.

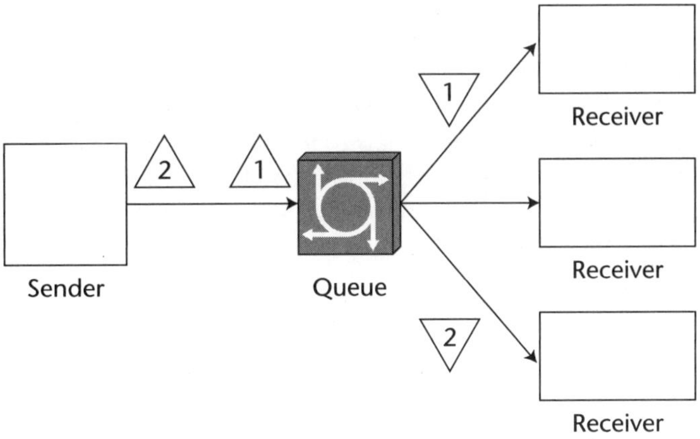

Figure 8.3 Too many queue receivers.

The converse of this problem occurs when you have one receiver but you use a topic. This isn't a big problem on most systems, but it requires that you use a durable subscriber to get the expected behavior.

The second form of this AntiPattern is misusing persistence. Suppose that you register a number of durable subscribers, and one of them is never told to process messages. The JMS provider will have to store those messages in anticipation of the broken subscriber's return. This can affect disk usage and possibly performance if the messages are large enough. In the worst case, the messages could overflow the disk.

Another problem occurs when you don't preregister durable subscribers and they miss messages. For example, suppose that you have a publisher listening for changes to a database, and you want the subscribers to be notified of these changes, as in the scenario pictured in Figure 8.4. If the publishers start publishing before the receivers start subscribing, the subscribers will miss messages, even if they have durable subscriptions. You must make sure the subscriptions are registered before you start sending.

Symptoms and Consequences

The primary symptom of this AntiPattern is that you use the wrong JMS construct for the solution you are creating. This results in side effects such as lost messages or the system overflowing. A discussion of symptoms follows:

- **A queue is used instead of a topic.** When a queue is used instead of a topic, the receivers will miss messages. Depending on the messaging system, this can result in anything from minor to devastating effects.
- **A topic is used instead of a queue.** Generally there is little harm in using a topic instead of a queue. The one gotcha is that queues are implicitly persistent and topics aren't, so you have to use a durable subscriber for the topic to get the same behavior as a queue.
- **Durable subscribers are registered late.** Most JMS providers won't hold messages in a topic if there are no durable subscribers. So, you can lose messages if the publishers start before the subscribers are registered.
- **Registering too many durable subscribers.** The provider will hold messages for durable subscribers until they are read or expire. If you have extra subscribers that aren't reading messages and acknowledging those reads, you can create a storage problem for the JMS provider.
- **Using the wrong subscribers.** If you want guaranteed messaging for the publish-subscribe method, you have to use durable subscribers. Otherwise, some subscribers may lose messages.

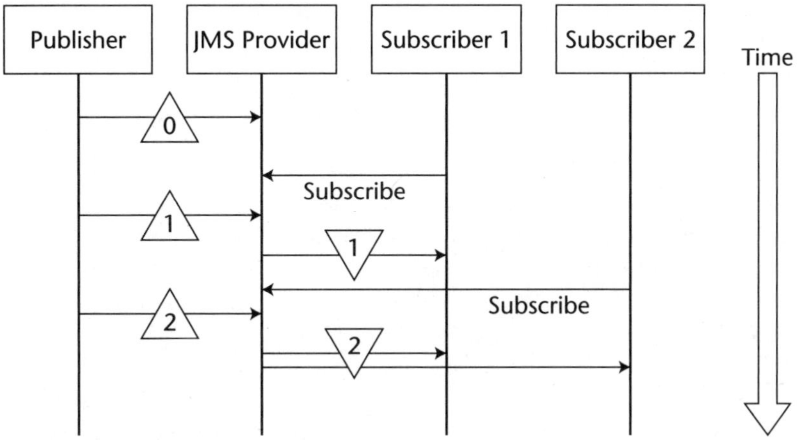

Figure 8.4 Missing subscriptions.

Typical Causes

Like many J2EE AntiPatterns, this one is often driven by lack of time or changing requirements:

- **The solution is built over time.** Requirements change. Where once there was one subscriber, now there are two. Where once messages didn't need persistence, now they do.
- **Subscriptions that were being used aren't any more.** Suppose that you used to have a custom application that notified the marketing group when a new customer was added to the database. Recently, the company reorganized, and marketing and sales were combined. You remember to take down the custom application, because everyone was complaining about the double emails, but you forget to remove the subscription. Now, there is a "dead" durable subscription in the JMS provider's configuration.
- **There was just one listener and now there are several.** Take the same example as above, only now your company has realized that marketing and sales should be separate. You have just converted the notification code to use a queue, so you add another receiver for it. Now, the sales group gets some notifications and marketing gets others. Neither group is happy.
- **Inexperienced developers.** If you don't know a technology, you are bound to make mistakes. JMS and messaging in general have some fundamental concepts, such as queues and topics, that can't be interchanged without possibly creating bizarre results. You have to know both what to do and why problems occur to be successful at avoiding the Misunderstanding JMS AntiPattern as well as the others in this chapter.
- **Applications are launched manually.** When applications are launched manually, it is possible to forget to launch the subscribers for a topic before the publishers, resulting in missed messages.

Known Exceptions

There are no known exceptions to breaking the JMS conceptual models. However, you may find specific cases where you want to have multiple receivers on a queue for load balancing or some other design. This will require specific testing on your JMS provider to see what happens. In particular, before choosing this architecture, create some test cases to ensure that your provider will behave the way that you expect when there are multiple clients on the queue. For example, are the messages still once and only once? Are they in order? You may find other unforeseen cases, as well, where you "break" the standard patterns, but all will be exceptions to the rules.

Refactorings

The solution to the Misusing JMS AntiPattern is to rethink your design by applying all of the refactorings from this chapter, especially Architect the Solution. Draw a diagram with each element involved in a JMS relationship and establish which things require queues and which require topics. Then, determine your persistence needs. Configure your destinations and code appropriately from this design. You may find that you have unused durable subscriptions that you need to clear. Or you may find that you are using a queue when you need a topic. In all cases, you want to figure out the ideal solution and then either build it or move your existing solution in that direction.

If your group is new to JMS, it is worth spending some time on education, with books, classes, or both. You might also implement a few prototypes to test out your designs. Messaging requires a different mindset than other network models. The ability to rely on the messaging provider for delivery changes the way you build applications and frees you from some of the monotonous tasks of ensuring message delivery. But the price of this freedom is a new set of concepts that you have to internalize before you can build great JMS applications.

Variations

The two main misunderstandings with JMS can be inverted. For example, you can use durable subscribers everywhere, even though you don't need the persistence. Or you can use topics everywhere just to "be safe." But this is overkill as well. Keep in mind that anywhere you could underleverage JMS you might also overleverage JMS. Specifically, you may use persistence when you don't need to. You might also encounter this AntiPattern when you plan destinations at deployment, as discussed with the next AntiPattern, Overloading Destinations.

Example

Let's take a look at how this AntiPattern often comes into being. Imagine that you are building an application to synchronize two of your company's databases. You have created timer-based beans for pooling the databases for changes, and two matching message beans for handling updates. This gives you a design like the one pictured in Figure 8.5. Since you have one sender and one receiver for each message, and the messages must be persistent to ensure that none are lost, you use queues.

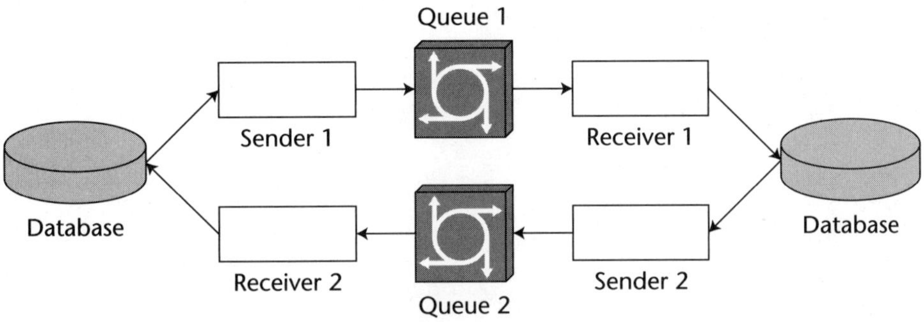

Figure 8.5 Database synchronizer design.

Now, the boss wants to add some business monitoring to the application. First, you add a new receiver to each queue, but messages are lost. This is the result of the first form of the AntiPattern, using queues when you need topics. So you turn the queues into topics. Now, if you launch the applications in the wrong order, messages are still lost. Again, the AntiPattern is at work; you aren't setting up persistence or it is initialized in the wrong order. Finally, you create durable subscribers, as pictured in Figure 8.6, for the two message beans, and you are working and monitoring at the same time.

In reality, the three steps to upgrade the application could be very painful, because the durable subscriber issue requires timing mismatches to happen and they may not happen every time, making the application hard to debug. Luckily, you have just read about it and won't make that mistake yourself.

One thing to note before we switch gears, when you change from queue to topic you want to be sure that all of your messages were processed and that none are left in the queues. This means that the publishers must be shut down first, then the subscribers. This sort of timing is discussed more thoroughly in Chapter 1 in the refactoring called Plan Ahead.

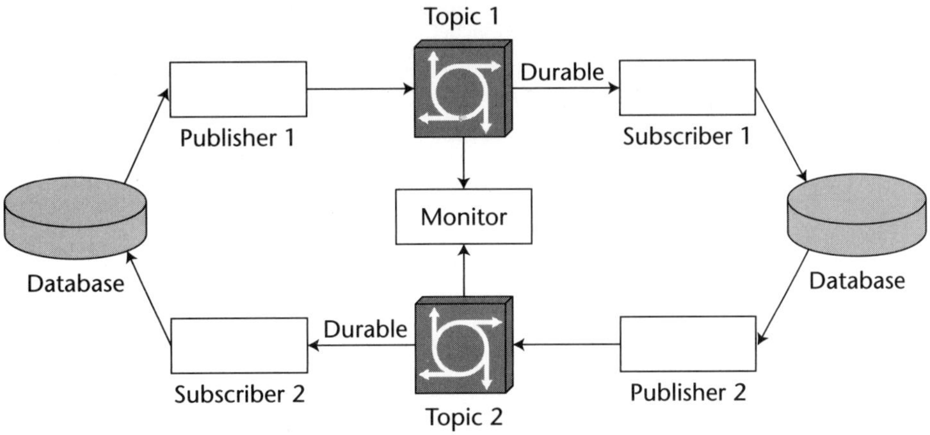

Figure 8.6 Database synchronizer with monitoring.

Related Solutions

The solution for misusing JMS is to learn as much as you can and plan your solutions ahead of time. This is tightly related to the planning discussed in Chapter 1, "Distribution and Scaling."

AntiPattern

Overloading Destinations

Also Known As: Which Message Is This?

Most Frequent Scale: Application

Refactorings: Architect the Solution, Plan Your Network Data Model

Refactored Solution Type: Process

Root Causes: Overloading destinations, feature creep, lack of experience, building over time

Unbalanced Forces: Constantly changing requirements, time to market, design time

Anecdotal Evidence: "Why do we have to switch statements in onMessage?" "Why are there so many destinations?" "Which destination should I use?"

Background

One of the core elements in a JMS solution is the collection of destinations. Each destination represents two things: First, a destination provides a rendezvous point for senders to find receivers. Second, the destination has an implicit, according to JMS, job of associating a data format with the communications.

We discussed some of the problems that can arise from a destination's first role in the previous AntiPattern, Misunderstanding JMS. Although these problems can be troublesome, they are generally identified quickly and solved accordingly. When the second role of a destination, that of data controller, is misused, there are potentially worse problems that may grow over time. Misusing the destination's data role is subject to this AntiPattern.

The JMS API provides a number of message types, including messages that store a HashMap, messages that store an object, and messages that store text. This last type has become a popular means of sending XML via JMS. One of the major problems that can arise with message-driven beans, and messaging in general, occurs when the client and server have a disconnect about what one is sending and the other is planning to receive. In other words, the sender and receiver need an agreed-upon data model.

Messaging existed before JMS and still exists in non-JMS forms. Many of these messaging infrastructure products provide explicit data mappings for each destination to prevent this AntiPattern. However, because not all systems require explicit data mappings, and there are certainly examples where you may not want it, JMS doesn't place that burden on the provider. Instead, it is up to the developer to handle message validation and the underlying data model.

It is also worth noting that not all JMS providers support all message types, or they may support some extensions to the standard types. Therefore, in a cross-JMS provider situation, the issue of a data model can be even more critical.

Overloading the data model for a message is not the same as parameterization. For example, a message-driven bean that takes an XML message with an email address, subject, and content and uses JavaMail to send an email to that address with that subject and content isn't overloaded just because the bean supports arbitrary XML or HTML in the content. On the other hand, if the same bean also accepted messages with XML content for logging it and its destination, the bean would probably qualify as overloaded and thus match the general form of this AntiPattern.

General Form

The basic form of this pattern is simply that one destination is receiving multiple message types or formats. When this happens, as pictured in Figure 8.7, the receiver has to perform a check before it can respond to the message. This means that the receiver's code will contain if or switch statements that key off of data in the message to determine what to do with it.

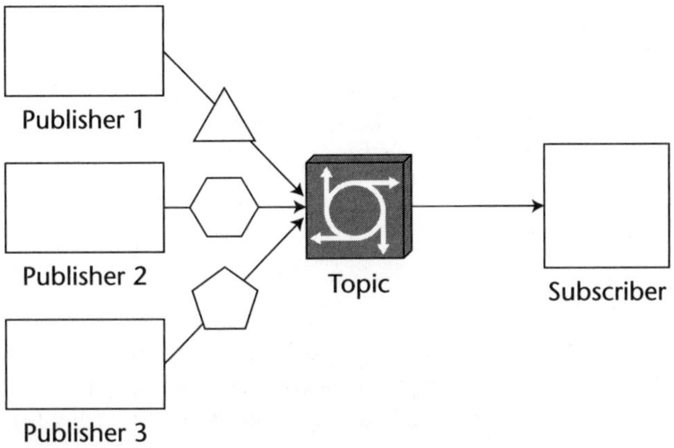

Figure 8.7 Destination overload.

Depending on the client, this check may have a minimal impact on performance. However, in the more degenerate cases, the client may be receiving numerous different formats that require a lot of work to evaluate. For example, the messages could require the client to parse XML to distinguish the type before processing. With large XML messages, or complex decisions required to distinguish the type, performance can be degraded significantly.

Symptoms and Consequences

The issues with destination overloading don't occur just at the implementation level. Perhaps the bigger concern is the effects at an architectural and conceptual level. When developers get used to overloading destinations, the result is similar to that of the object-oriented design problem of creating classes with too many methods. A single message-driven bean is being asked to perform a separate behavior for each message; lots of behaviors can easily lead to a very complex bean implementation. Just as object designers don't want a class overloaded with behaviors, a JMS designer should not want a destination overloaded with behaviors. In other words, overloaded destinations lead to both implementation and design consequences.

- **Overloaded destinations require the message-driven beans and custom JMS code to perform checks for each message type and handle it appropriately.** This means that every subscriber must understand the different messages, or at least know to ignore the ones it doesn't understand. This places a much higher requirement on you than if you have limited data models for your destination.
- **Once developers get in the habit of destinations with multiple message types they will not hesitate to add new types.** This can lead to problems in the case where you have a topic with multiple subscribers and not all of them are updated to the new message types. In short, the developers can break other subscribers too easily. The entire system is fragile.

- **Depending on the messages and how they can be identified, overloading can create performance problems.** This is particularly true when some form of serialization or deserialization has to occur before the message type is known. For example, if two XML messages are sent to the same destination, the receiver may have to parse the entire XML to determine which type each message belongs to.

Typical Causes

Overloaded destinations are an easy path. If you keep overloading one queue between a sender and receiver, or between multiple senders and one receiver, then you have less administrative work setting up your destinations and fewer class files. So, it is easy for people to fall into this trap, much as it is easy for UI developers to hard-code strings into the UI code instead of using ResourceBundles.

- **Inexperience.** It is easy to fall into the habit of thinking of the client as the destination rather than the destination as a conceptual entity. When you make this assumption, destination overloading is an obvious outgrowth, because you want to send all messages to the "client" and therefore send all messages to the same destination.
- **Message-driven beans themselves.** The idea behind a message-driven bean is that the application server, or bean container, manages the JMS connection for the developer. This generally associates a single destination with each bean. In other words, the bean and destination become somewhat synonymous. If the developer of the bean thought it would be easy to provide some extra functionality with a different message format, he or she is implicitly overloading the destination.
- **Planning destinations at deployment.** Most JMS providers use JNDI as an indirect mechanism for loading destinations. JNDI allows the developers of the message beans, or sometimes the deployer of the message bean, to refer to the destinations as named entities. If the destinations aren't well documented, the deployer may simply fill in the different destinations without considering their associated data model. In this case, the problem was really caused by the designers that didn't plan ahead and was implemented by the developers and deployers.

Known Exceptions

There may be times when you want to support multiple message formats on a single destination. A great example of this is the administrative message architecture mentioned in the refactoring called Plan Ahead in Chapter 1. In that case, one message may be used to tell the receiver to stop listening for messages, or at least stop processing them, so that the system can be shut down cleanly.

The other acceptable use of destination overloading is in a generic service such as a message hospital or monitoring application. In these situations, the listener that is getting the messages is not looking at the content, it is just processing it as generic information. As long as the JMS code can handle the various JMS message types, there is no architectural issue with this type of overloading.

When you do need to overload a destination, you should use message selectors or headers to identify the various types. This will allow the receivers to filter on message type without looking at the contents. If your JMS provider doesn't support arbitrary message headers and properties, you should make sure to minimize the code necessary to distinguish types.

Refactorings

There is one simple solution to destination overload: Don't do it. In order to avoid overloading your destinations, you have to use the Plan Ahead and Design your Data Model refactorings from Chapter 1 along with the Plan Your Network Data Model refactoring from this chapter. You can't wait until the last minute to plan one on top of the other. There are two main refactorings that come into play when planning. One is simply to architect the solution at the beginning, as in the Plan Ahead refactoring from Chapter 1. This means figuring out the components, the types of destinations you need and, moreover, the messages that will be sent to those destinations. This second refactoring is Plan Your Network Data Model. Essentially, the solution to destination overloading is to start with a reasonable plan for your destinations and their data models. Then, move forward with this plan, revising it as necessary, but always watching out for overloading.

Variations

In the same way that you might overload destinations too much, you could potentially go the other way and not use overloading when it is appropriate. If you have a lot of administrative messages, you could imagine creating separate destinations for each one. This is probably overkill. Rather, you might create one library for managing and handling these administrative messages in standard ways that beans can call as necessary.

Example

Let's take a look at an example where overloading is encountered and removed. Suppose that you are writing a system to manage the flow of documents through a manufacturing process. You have a number of steps that are automated, such as verifying the document format and assigning a tracking number. You also have steps for checking the document in and out of the database. A common use case for this system would be to add a new document. This use case might entail a flow of events like the ones pictured in Figure 8.8.

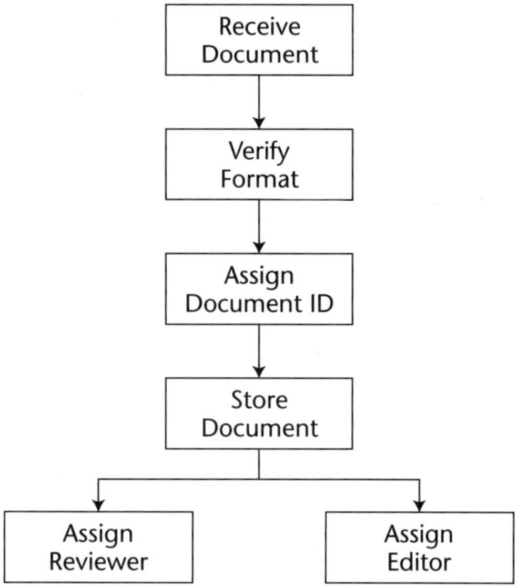

Figure 8.8 Adding a document.

In this process, some of the steps are handled by message-driven beans, so the question is which ones. The easy implementation for a simple solution is to put all the automation in one bean. Each client would send messages to the bean asking for or submitting a document. This solution, pictured in Figure 8.9, will work great if there are only a few steps.

But if there are a lot of steps, as in our example, the code for this one bean will be overwhelming and hard to manage. Instead, you might break the code into multiple message-driven beans. These beans might leverage Session Beans or libraries for some of the common tasks. This tiered approach might look like the one pictured in Figure 8.10.

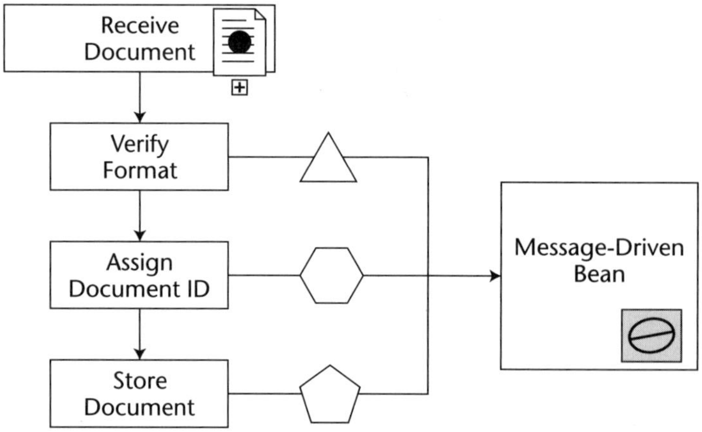

Figure 8.9 Simple solution.

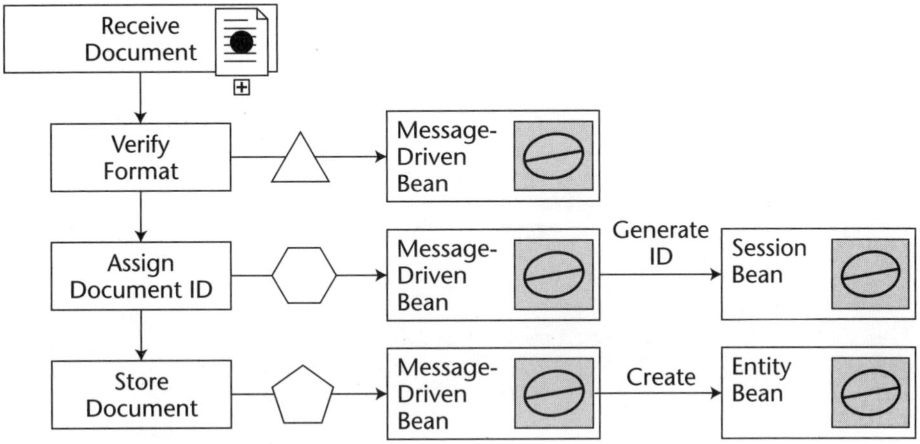

Figure 8.10 Tiered solution.

The other element of a refactored solution is the inclusion of administrative messages. Although these messages might be sent to the same destinations as the application messages, the message beans can use a library, an administrative API if you will, to handle checking to see if a message is an administrative message and possibly help determine how to respond.

The administrative API might also rely on message selectors, or other headers, to filter out administrative messages.

Related Solutions

Many of the issues brought up in Chapter 1 regarding distribution and scaling apply to this chapter. In particular, if you want to plan your bandwidth requirements, you need to know the destinations, their types, and their data models. So, good planning and design, whether upfront or iterative, is the key to a successful J2EE deployment because it forces you to look at destinations as logical entities and tie down their data models appropriately.

AntiPattern

Overimplementing Reliability

Also Known As: Too Much Persistence

Most Frequent Scale: Application

Refactorings: Architect the Solution

Refactored Solution Type: Architecture

Root Causes: Solutions grown over time, lack of experience

Unbalanced Forces: New requirements, performance, transactional requirements, reliability

Anecdotal Evidence: "Why are we getting multiple copies of messages?" "Why do we save the data three times?"

Background

I am sure the idea that something is too reliable is not commonly heard in software development circles. Developers are all too often accused of not creating reliable code. But there is a time in JMS when you can go too far. In order to understand how and why you can go too far, you first have to understand how JMS deals with reliability.

One of the primary benefits of messaging over other networking technologies is the availability of persistence and reliability. When you send a message from a Web browser to the Web server, the message is transient—it exists for the time of the request and no longer. The same is true of RMI, CORBA, and other networking technologies. Messaging, on the other hand, encapsulates the idea of a message into a physical unit that can be stored to disk. Messaging providers can save messages for later delivery or guaranteed delivery.

JMS provides several levels of persistence and reliability. First, messages sent to a JMS destination can be marked persistent, using DeliveryMode.PERSISTENT, or not persistent using DeliveryMode.NON_PERSISTENT. These flags allow the server to determine if the message should be stored to disk. For queues, this is sufficient to gain persistence. For topics, you also need to use durable subscribers. But either case is relatively simple, and with little work you can create a solution that can rely on the JMS provider to save the messages in route.

The teammate of persistence is acknowledgement. When a client receives a message, it has to tell the provider that the message was received and no longer requires storage. JMS supports three levels of acknowledgement. First, sessions can be set to automatically acknowledge each message as it is read. Second, sessions can be set to only acknowledge messages when the developer does it manually. Third, the sessions can be set to acknowledge lazily. This may result in duplicate messages, but still allows the provider to clean them up from the disk at some point and may save some network bandwidth.

JMS also provides the idea of transactional acknowledgement and transaction send, as pictured in Figure 8.11. In this case, a group of messages are sent or acknowledged atomically. This style of acknowledgement can be very useful for multimessage conversations.

Problems arise when a solution fails to leverage the basic concepts of persistence and acknowledgement. Although it may seem odd, you can actually create too much reliability, in the sense that you are doing work that doesn't actually add reliability to the final solution.

General Form

This AntiPattern can take three primary forms. The first form occurs when the client underuses the JMS server by storing information from messages before sending them. For example, a client might save the data for a new customer entry in a file, then send a message containing the same data to a message-driven bean that will put the data in a database. This is overkill. The message itself is persistent so there is no reason to also store it in a file.

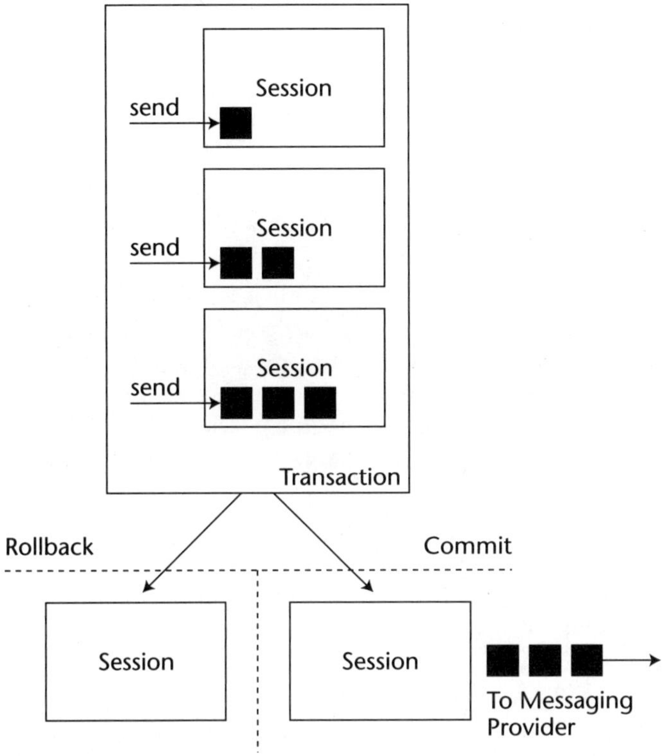

Figure 8.11 Transactional acknowledgements.

The second form of overpersistence is to fail to acknowledge, or delay acknowledgement of, messages. This will result in their storage on the server, and possible duplicate delivery, even though they are already handled. The same thing can happen when you wrap acknowledgements into a transaction. If the transaction scope is too big, it may be easy to have it fail and leave messages in the persistent store. Missed acknowledgements not only affect the persistent store, they also require the client to handle duplicate messages.

The final form of this AntiPattern is one that can take effect over time. That is the lack of expirations on messages. Some messages shouldn't expire, like ones that indicate deposits or withdrawals into a bank account. But some can expire, perhaps after a long time period. By leveraging the expiration settings on messages in JMS you can ensure that old messages are cleaned up when they lack usefulness. An example of this might be a stock price update. After a day, or in some cases a few minutes, this value is no longer important and has been replaced by another message with a new price. Therefore, those messages can be expired quickly and cleared from the system.

Symptoms and Consequences

Overreliability can take place at the clients, when they implement their own reliability mechanisms, or at the provider, when the client doesn't tell it to clean up messages after they are used:

- **Duplicate messages will often indicate some form of overreliability.** The major cause of duplicate messages is a failure of the handler to acknowledge messages because of an exception, but overreliability can also be a cause.
- **JMS senders that store data in a persistent store before sending the message are often overpersisting the data.** Depending on how this persistence is implemented, it may actually add no real reliability improvement. In particular, if you send the message before persisting the data, you are rarely adding value. If you persist the data before sending it you do handle the possible issues between save and send, but may have to have a lot of code to handle a system restart in that case.
- **Failure to acknowledge messages can result in duplicate messages.** This requires the receiver to handle duplicate messages. In the case of a financial transaction, failure to handle the duplicate message might result in double withdrawals or deposits, neither of which is a good thing for a bank.
- **If messages are all set to persist without expiration, it is possible to create a topic or queue with numerous messages.** In the worst case, these messages might fill up the disk or effect performance in some other way. Whenever expiration is not used, the designer should validate that infinite life is required for that message.

Typical Causes

Perhaps the key conceptual change when moving from standard network programming models to JMS is the addition of persistence. Not recognizing or leveraging this change is what leads to overpersistence and overreliability.

- **Converting a network technology to messaging.** When nonmessaging protocols, such as RMI, are converted to messaging, you may have already built in a persistence mechanism to ensure delivery. Once the JMS solution is put in place, this mechanism can generally be removed. One common situation in which this would happen occurs when a session bean is converted into a message-driven bean.
- **Exceptions in the message-handling code.** Uncaught or miscaught exceptions in your message-driven beans, or other JMS receivers, can lead to serious problems. One of the common problems occurs when a message is handled but not acknowledged. In this case, you will get duplicate messages that require checks in the code to handle. For example, if the data from a message is inserted in the database, the message-driven bean may have to check if the data is already

there before inserting code to handle duplicates. In some situations, the code for handling duplicates could get very complex, especially when the data that the bean has to check could be updated after the first message, which is subsequently duplicated, was received.

- **Failure to acknowledge manually.** When a session is set to manual acknowledgement, you need to be sure to perform the acknowledgement. Otherwise the messages will build up. The same applies to transactions that must be committed to guarantee acknowledgement.
- **Including more information than necessary in a message.** In Chapter 1, we discussed a number of standard architectures. Misusing these architectures can lead to overreliability—for example, if you have a central database with information used by all clients, or perhaps entity beans storing the information, and your messages pass that information around to clients that use the database directly the messages are overly large. In this case, the JMS provider is guilty of storing more than it has to. You might replace big messages with small notifications that trigger database or entity bean calls on the other side.

Known Exceptions

In cases where you are moving information from one persistent store to another you may intentionally duplicate the data into the message for transport. For example, if you are synchronizing two databases with JMS, the data will be in the first database, then in the first database and the message, then in the first and second database. This isn't overreliability; it is just a simple and clean design. Of course, you wouldn't delete the data from the first database to send the message because you want it there as well. But, what you are doing is trusting the message with the copy of the data that belongs to the second database.

You might also encounter situations where you are doing work with data before sending a message and expecting some form of reply. This is common in a session bean or servlet where, for example, you are using data about a customer, then send some of that data in a message, but keep a copy for continued use in the bean or servlet. Or you may be doing work between the send and reply. In these cases, you may save data persistently, even though it is in the message, to ensure that the sender has a valid copy.

Refactorings

The first step in avoiding unnecessary reliability or persistence is to architect your solution, as discussed in the Architect the Solution refactoring in this chapter. By starting with a clear picture of the messaging participants and their requirements, you can avoid adding too much reliability into code. In cases where you are evolving a solution, you can still create this design and use it to update existing code to the new requirements.

A couple of ways to help manage reliability are to use transactions where possible to group messages and to rely on expiration dates to clean up unnecessary messages. Transactions can be particularly useful when you want to deal with messages that deal with other transacted elements, such as a database. By using the XA functionality in JMS, you can link message acknowledgement with database interactions or with other JMS code.

Variations

A similar problem that can occur with JMS is unprioritized messages. This problem is similar to that of thread scheduling and overreliability. When messages don't have a priority, it is possible that important messages, such as administrative messages, won't be received until after a message that they should affect. However, priorities can create unusual situations and should be used sparingly and carefully. Keep in mind that the JMS specification doesn't require the providers to deliver messages by priority; it merely provides that mechanism as a hint to the delivery code.

Example

Imagine that you are automating a business process. Perhaps you are even using a process-automation tool or rules engine. In many cases, these engines will store some data persistently. If each step in the process is resulting in a JMS message and its response, you may be storing more data than necessary in either the message or the engine. For example, if the message will include the customer ID, as pictured in Figure 8.12, and the process only needs this information for each transition, then you don't need to store the customer ID in the process engine. The ID will be persisted by the JMS provider for you. In the case of custom code, this means that you don't have to remember which message went with which instance of the business process. Each step can figure that out from the message that triggers it.

Using the same example, we might also be able to mark some messages as nonpersistent. In particular, if the process engine has to store information between steps, and has the logic to handle a failure at each step, then it isn't necessary for the messages to be stored to disk, only that they be acknowledged appropriately to ensure once, and only once, delivery.

Related Solutions

One of the first steps in building a reliable, but not overly reliable, solution is to choose the right data architecture, as described in Chapter 1. The other refactorings in Chapter 1 will also help you avoid redundant reliability code and overloaded messages by helping you streamline your overall network architecture.

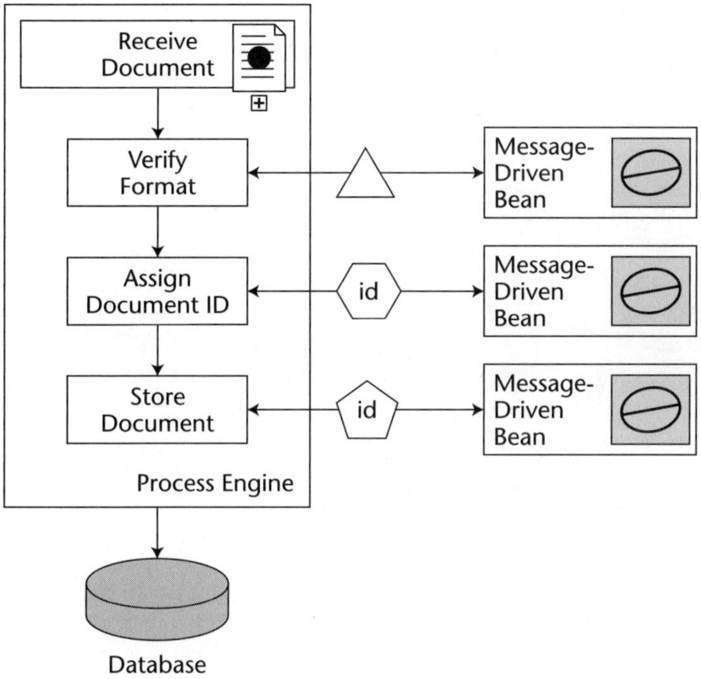

Figure 8.12 Automated process.

Refactorings

On one level, building good message-driven beans is easy. Message-driven beans have very few required methods and are purely reactionary. But the context in which you build and deploy them can lead to problems with overreliability, lost messages, and the other consequences of the AntiPatterns discussed above. The following refactorings help to fix these AntiPatterns through planning and design.

By applying these refactorings to the following AntiPatterns, you should be able to fix and avoid a lot of common problems that people have with their message-driven beans and other JMS applications.

The main lesson for message-driven bean writers, and all JMS developers, is to think about the context for their code. JMS code isn't like a simple application, or even a complex application, such as an email client or word processor. JMS applications are inherently networked. Moreover, they have built-in services such as persistence, priorities, and guaranteed delivery. These services must play a role in the design of each JMS client.

Architect the Solution. Developers working at the endpoints of a distributed application build many J2EE solutions. You have to think globally and work locally to build successful J2EE implementations.

Plan Your Network Data Model. There are a lot of books about patterns and designs for application. Distributed applications require the same techniques. In particular, the data that you are sending to your JMS applications and message-driven beans must be planned and documented to avoid complexity and performance degradation.

Leverage All Forms of EJBs. Obviously, message-driven beans aren't the only type of Enterprise JavaBean, so don't treat them that way. Session and entity beans can play an important role in a JMS-based solution.

Architect the Solution

JMS decouples the sender and receiver, but this can lead to poor planning.

You can't think just of the endpoints of a JMS solution, you have to think about the entire solution, including the network and JMS provider.

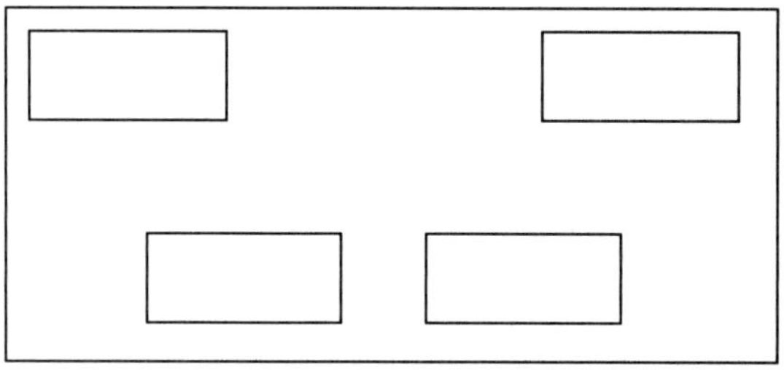

Figure 8.13 Before refactoring.

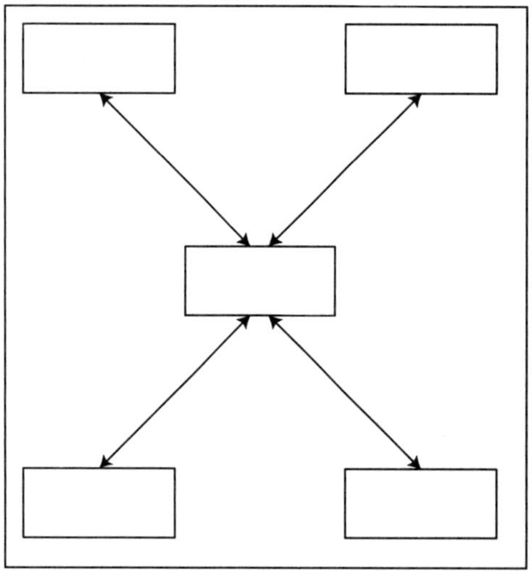

Figure 8.14 After refactoring.

Motivation

When developers think about individual components in a J2EE solution, they often ignore the supporting roles played by JMS providers, application servers, databases, and other middleware. In doing so, it is easy for the developer to overimplement or underimplement their code. This leads to the Overreliability AntiPattern as well as the others in this chapter.

Mechanics

Architecting a JMS solution starts at the network and works outward. Key aspects of the design process include the J2EE providers that you pick as well as the design choices you make, such as using beans versus custom code. The following steps outline the work that should go into a design before development starts. This work may be repeated during iterative development.

1. *Draw a network map*. The first step in building a network solution is to draw a map. If you are extending an existing solution, start with the elements you already have. Include in the map all of the endpoints, all of the edges, and all of the middleware that gets you from one endpoint to another.
2. *Analyze reliability requirements*. For each edge in the system, think about what kind of persistence it needs. If this is a new solution, you might just assign a level of persistence. If you are tying together existing code, you should take into account what the code already does. If the code is already handling transactional messaging, you might use minimal persistence and reliability in your messaging to improve performance. If the endpoint has minimal reliability, then the messaging infrastructure should provide more.
3. *Evaluate technology features*. Depending on the middleware you use, you may have certain features, but you may also have constraints. For example, JMS is not a truly synchronous communication scheme. While JMS supports request-reply semantics, many of the providers are not implemented in such a way that request-reply uses an open connection. Rather, request-reply is just a simple way of waiting for the other side of a message to send a different message back. This means that there are problems that can arise while the message is in the middle or at either end. With synchronous calls, such as HTTP, the sender can get a very clear and immediate failure response.
4. *Select technology features*. JMS offers queues and topics, subscribers, and durable subscribers, as well as other technology choices. Assign this information to the edges appropriately.
5. *Feed information about the edges into the nodes*. If you mark all of the edges in your network map persistence and say that they all use JMS, then you need to take this into account at the endpoints. The endpoints shouldn't need much persistence code or reliability. They should, however, handle duplicate messages and acknowledge messages appropriately. If you are using JMS and you send a request-reply style message, you may wait a while for the response. JMS doesn't require the receiver to be online, so the sender could have to wait for

the sender to be launched, process other messages, and finally process and respond to its message.

6. *Look at the data model.* Messages have a format; the data model will drive this format and can help with other planning discussed in Chapter 1.
7. *Document the results.* Now that you have a map, document that information. Include information such as destination names and data models. This documentation provides the design and details for the implementers and deployers.

Example

Many of the first-generation enterprise application integration products used messaging as a fundamental technology. Messaging enabled the creation of dumber endpoints, which led to the idea of adapters to map from messages to external systems. In this case, dumb just means that the endpoints, or adapters, didn't need to know how they would be used or much about the greater application they would play a part in. This is similar to the idea of Web Services, which simply exist without a context.

One drawback of these early systems was that when you configured the endpoints, or adapters, you would often assign a destination-like value to them. Then, when you configured another adapter, or wrote code, you had to remember this destination. J2EE solves part of this problem with JNDI, which allows you to create one level of indirection with the destinations, but you still need this map. While tools are beginning to help make these connections automatically, they aren't all the way there yet. So, for now, you need to document these destination identifiers, which are a logical outcome of the design process.

Failure to document destination identifiers in these older systems could lead to funny bugs, where one endpoint gets too many or too few messages. Depending on the implementation, you might even find a group of adapters performing updates with completely invalid data. In other words, many people building the systems didn't follow the necessary steps to create the solution.

For example, many people treat the choice of technology as the first step in the process. They spend a lot of time and money evaluating and then purchasing the J2EE or other provider that they want to use. Looking at our steps, you can see that this is backwards. Let's go through the steps and see why.

First, you need to figure out what you are doing by drawing a network map. How are you using the network? If you aren't using the network, then why buy some expensive J2EE or other technology? Step 2 is thinking about your reliability requirements. Do you need reliability? If so, to what level? Vendors have messaging products with differing levels of reliability. If you need strong reliability guarantees, don't pay for the weak products.

Given your network and reliability requirements, you can look at other technology requirements, which is Step 3. These might include ease-of-use, preferred APIs, platform support, and more. With this information, you are ready to evaluate and purchase a specific vendor's tools, which is Step 4. You may have noticed that we waited until Step 4 to pick a vendor, when most people do that at Step 1. From there, you can build the data model and work on the endpoints, Steps 5 and 6. But you have to do your homework in order to make the right choices later in the process.

Plan Your Network Data Model

Your network is overrun with data from your JMS.

Plan for the actual use cases.

```
<customer>
     <name>John Doe</name>
</customer>
```

Listing 8.1 Before data-model refactoring.

```
<customer>
     <name>John Doe</name>
     <address>444 East West St. Hollywood CA 90210</address>
     <account>1100111</account>
     <!-- Real Customer data -->
<customer>
```

Listing 8.2 After data-model refactoring.

Motivation

One of the key elements of your architecture will be the set of messages you will be sending. These messages are so important that they deserve a discussion all to themselves. Messages for message-driven beans are the primary data-transfer mechanism. Once you install a solution built with one data model, it may be very hard to change it. Messages may exist in the persistent queues and topics that can't be updated, or endpoints may be too fragile or important to replace. In any case, you want to get the model as right as possible at the beginning. Getting it right means building a set of messages that can be extended and improved, and that also have room for new endpoints and messages to be added easily and reliably. It also means avoiding the Destination Overloading AntiPattern discussed previously.

Mechanics

Creating your messages is a bigger process than you might think. There are a number of issues that can be planned in from the beginning easily but are very hard to add once you have a solution running. The following steps outline the basic issues that you need to resolve before putting code on paper:

1. *Consider a common data model.* In applications like EAI, there will be data models for the external application that you are dealing with. This may also apply when you use Web Services, existing EJBs, or legacy applications via CORBA. When you are in a situation where there are multiple representations of the same data, such as a customer or invoice, you should consider making a common data model to use on the network. This common model would represent a greatest common denominator of the other data models. Any message would use the common model instead of a local model. Endpoints would convert to and from the common model as needed.

2. *Think about administrative messages.* Many solutions will require upgrades, logging, error handling, and other approaches that may work better if you can tell the various message beans that they need to shut down or stop message processing. You might even want to set configuration parameters at run time using messages. In order to perform this type of operation, you have to plan for administrative messages. These messages will likely be sent to the same destinations as other messages, so you need to keep them in mind in the implementation.

3. *Plan for filtering.* JMS provides the concept of message selectors to perform filtering. If you are using messages that contain XML or another format that requires deserializing, you might want to use headers to provide an easy filtering mechanism. You might also provide selectors to help identify administrative messages.

4. *Think about bandwidth.* The data model is intricately tied to bandwidth usage. While creating the data model, think about example data sets and data sizes. Also, when overloading a destination, think about how hard it would be to filter on type.

5. *Build tools.* Techniques such as administrative messages and filtering can be added with libraries. Other tools, such as the message hospital described in "*Developing Enterprise Java Applications*" are also a useful element of a complete solution. This hospital is designed to fix or handle bad messages. You might also build tools to monitor and log information about messages on the network. Hopefully, your vendor will provide some of these tools.

6. *Analyze security concerns.* Data may be encrypted, obfuscated, signed, or marked in some other way for security reasons. Document these requirements early, because they may play a key role in other decisions, including the data formats themselves. For example, you may have to use headers to send security information to decrypt a message.

7. *Think about your JMS provider.* Does your provider support the message types you want to send? If not, you might need to change them. You might also be able to leverage features that your JMS provider implements that aren't standard such as message compression for text messages, or encryption.

Example

Recently Siebel started marketing a solution called the Universal Application Network (UAN). The idea behind this solution was to create a set of standard business processes. In order to do that, Siebel had to create a data model for the processes to use. This common data model is a great example of how you can standardize the data on your network, even though the message receivers might have to map it before they can store the data in an external system such as one from SAP, PeopleSoft, or Oracle.

So, what should you do if you are evaluating UAN as a solution for your business? Step 1 is to ask the vendor enough questions to feel comfortable that their solution was planned with the issues listed above in mind. Step 2 is to find out if the solution has a support for administrative messages. A key element would be a message that would act as a trigger that stopped all the senders so that the system could be shut down cleanly for upgrading. Upgrading plans, in general, are a great area for asking questions.

Step 3 is to find out if the vender provides a good way to filter messages. Do you have to read an entire message to filter it or are there shortcuts?

Step 4 is to find out how the messages are. What type of bandwidth will the product require to accommodate your particular solutions?

Steps 5 and 6 require you to find out what tools and security the vender provides, or whether that is left to another vendor. Step 7 is to find out what vendors are supported.

In other words, if you buy a solution, you want to ensure that it was created with all of these issues in mind so that it doesn't build in any of the AntiPatterns from this chapter.

Leverage All Forms of EJBs

You only use session beans.

Use all types of beans appropriate for the problem you are trying to solve.

```
public class NewCustomer implements MessageDrivenBean
public class GetCustomerInfo implements MessageDrivenBean
public class ValidateCustomerNumber implements MessageDrivenBean
```

Listing 8.3 Before leverage refactoring.

```
public class InsertCustomer implements MessageDrivenBean
public class Customer implements EntityBean
public class ValidateCustomerNumber implements SessionBean
```

Listing 8.4 After leverage refactoring.

Motivation

Message-driven beans are a great addition to the J2EE family and provide a guaranteed delivery infrastructure, via JMS, that the other enterprise JavaBeans don't have. However, there are some constraints. Message-driven beans are generally restricted to a single destination. While this is not bad, it can limit you when you have multiple message formats. Message-driven beans require a JMS provider. This is a potential problem when you need to communicate with an enterprise bean from a non-Java application. Message-driven beans are also nonpersistent, unlike entity beans that represent application data.

Of course, there are other advantages and disadvantages. But the important point is that a great J2EE solution probably can't restrict itself to one type of Enterprise Bean. Moreover, by designing message-driven beans that rely on the other types of beans, you can handle very simple and very complex situations.

If you always use message beans, you may end up with a lot of misused JMS concepts as discussed in the Misunderstanding JMS AntiPattern. You might also create a lot of overreliable code, as described in the Overimplementing Reliability AntiPattern.

Mechanics

Before you use message-driven beans, perform the following three tests:

1. *Consider why you are using message-driven beans.* When you build your network map, if you want to rely on the messaging infrastructure for reliability, then message-driven beans are the ideal endpoints. However, if you start from scratch and just need to make requests from a custom client to an EJB, you may be better off with a Session Bean that relies on a more synchronous, less heavy protocol. Message beans require the JMS provider, while Session Beans do not.
2. *Look for overloaded destinations.* One good place to use Session and Entity beans with message beans is when you have multiple messages that need to use the same business logic. You can implement the messaging with message-driven beans that call Session and Entity Beans to perform the logic. This allows each message bean a unique destination with a simple data model, without duplicating code.
3. *Look for data persistence.* Beans that represent or store data are often best implemented as Entity Beans rather than message-driven beans with custom persistence code.

Example

Imagine that you have a number of connectors or adapters that take information from external systems and feed it through a standard set of business rules. Moreover, imagine that you can't implement a common data model because these applications are a combination of legacy and new code. Step 1 is to look at the types of beans you want to use. In this case, you might want to use message-driven beans as the access points for the business rules, but Entity and Session Beans as the implementations of those rules. Figure 8.15 shows an example of how you might mix beans like this.

Within the same system, you might also add new code that does rely on a common data model. In this case, you could reuse the Session Beans to provide transformation logic to map to and from the common model.

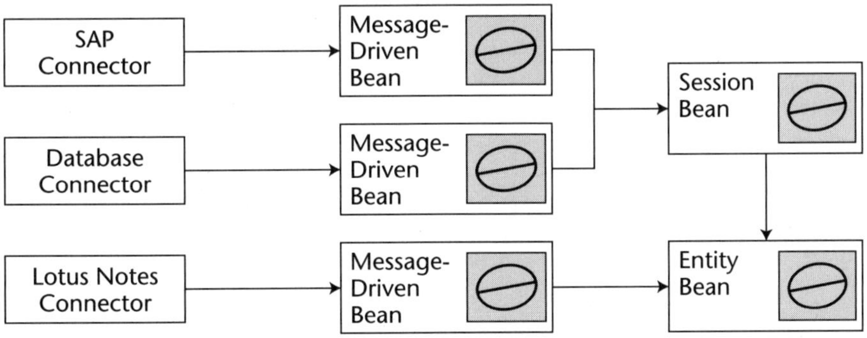

Figure 8.15 Mixing beans to create a solution.

The trick is to use messaging where it is appropriate and Session Beans where they are appropriate. In Step 2, you want to be sure that your message-driven beans deal with a narrow scope of work so that their destinations are not overloaded. Finally, you want to evaluate the persistence constraints, which is Step 3. If you don't need any persistence and you are using a queue, you may be able to use a Session Bean instead and reduce the overall load on your messaging server.

CHAPTER

9

Web Services

In this chapter, we will discuss AntiPatterns associated with the implementation of Web Services in a J2EE environment, along with refactorings to rectify the issues resulting from these AntiPatterns.

Web Services technology is a relatively new aspect within the J2EE standards. The Web Services Developer Pack (WSDP) from Sun combines a number of APIs to support various approaches to Java-based Web Services development. The Java API for XML-based RPC (JAX-RPC) is emerging as a popular choice for RPC-based interactions because it handles manipulation of SOAP and XML internally, allowing developers to implement client and server elements with standard, familiar Java interfaces, data types, and so on. The Java API for XML Messaging (JAXM) is geared toward XML document exchange and messaging (as opposed to RPC), and its API presents more of an explicit approach to SOAP and XML document handling, manipulation, and so forth. JAXP provides standard APIs for programmatic XML parsing and XSL-based transformations. Also included is SOAP Attachments API for Java (SAAJ) and Java API for XML Registries (JAXR). EJB 2.1 has added support for Web Services by allowing Stateless Session Beans to serve as Web Service endpoints.

Because the real-world application of Web Services is relatively new, there hasn't been a lot of time for commonly repeated AntiPatterns to emerge. However, there are commonalities in terms of goals and mechanics with other J2EE technologies. One important capability that J2EE and EJB support is the notion of location-transparent, distributed access to remote functions. In J2EE, this is accomplished using RMI/IIOP or JRMP protocols, and serialized Java objects are the message format. In Web Services, similar goals are supported by HTTP and SOAP 1.1/XML. Therefore, a number of the issues and AntiPatterns that arise with the use of EJBs (especially Session EJBs) are (and will) emerging within the Web Services area. Additionally, some of the emerging issues are related to Web Service semantics, technologies, tools, and development issues. For many, the development of Web Services is their first exposure to the concept of service-oriented architecture (SOA), and hence, some issues and AntiPatterns emerge from that.

A significant aspect of Web Services is that a Web Service represents an abstract interface described by Web Services Description Language (WSDL). Abstract notions of what constitutes a good interface have impact on the development and maintenance of the service itself, and clients that are bound to that interface. Interfaces that are well-defined abstractions, with cohesive collections on operations, experience less frequent changes, and hence, cause less breakage to clients. Also, Web-Service-specific aspects of the interface (in terms of data types, RPC versus document-style interface, synchronous versus asynchronous interface, and so on) have impact on development and runtime characteristics.

In this chapter, we will discuss AntiPatterns associated with the use of Web Services in J2EE systems, along with refactorings to rectify the issues raised. Specifically, we will cover the following AntiPatterns:

Web Services Will Fix Our Problems. Adopting Web Services to fix some major problems in an existing J2EE application. Issues with extensibility and reuse are usually due to poor architecture and design, and implementing Web Services over a bad architecture only makes it worse by re-creating the bad structure with even more technology, artifacts, and issues.

When in Doubt, Make It a Web Service. You can go overboard on the use of Web Services, implementing and vending processes and functionality for applications that do not need Web Services and do not benefit from them. The result is lower performance than native J2EE approaches, and additional development time being required to understand, implement, and deploy additional Web Service artifacts.

The God Object Web Service. This consists of implementing a single Web Service that supports a lot of different operations. At the extreme, the result is a single large Web Service that vends all external functions, and with which all clients interact. This is problematic because the interface details of the Web Service inevitably change over time, and when a single Web Service implements a lot of operations, many clients will be affected by the change.

Fine-Grained/Chatty Web Service. This is the Web Service analogue of the "chatty interface" issue with Entity EJBs. The Web Service is defined with many fine-grained operations, and clients end up invoking many operations in sequence to perform an overall process. The operations may be supporting CRUD-type requirements and be manifested as attribute-level accessors or mutators. Alternately, the operations may each represent a very fine-grained step within an overall process sequence.

Maybe It's Not RPC. This consists of using an RPC-style Web Service to support document-style operations. Operations that implement Create, Read, Update, and Delete (CRUD) operations on business entities or documents are more suited to document-style, asynchronous interactions.

Single-Schema Dream. This is an attempt to use a single XML schema for the one, shared definition of a business document to be exchanged among multiple customers and partners. Ultimately, this doesn't work, because each organization still has its own specific definition of the document, in terms of attributes, data formats, and so on. Thus, the initial architecture has to be refactored to accommodate partner- or customer-specific schema variants, and do transforms to and from the various formats.

SOAPY Business Logic. A Web Service endpoint component implements business logic, but is also coupled specifically to Web Service data types and/or contains an implementation that explicitly deals with SOAP/XML processing, severely reducing the reuse potential of the business logic. The most typical case occurs when a Session Bean is used for the endpoint.

AntiPattern

Web Services Will Fix Our Problems

Also Known As: Silver Bullet

Most Frequent Scale: System, architecture

Refactorings: Service-Oriented Architecture, Servlet/JSP Refactorings

Refactored Solution Type: Process, software

Root Causes: Ignorance, haste

Unbalanced Forces: Complexity, performance

Anecdotal Evidence: "I've just read an article where companies are saving a lot of money by implementing Web Services to solve their current integration problems."

Background

The introduction of any significant new technology is often heralded as the silver bullet that will (finally) solve all those systems problems that were due to shortcomings in existing technology. Web Services are that next big thing, and there is a common perception that, when used, they will solve a lot of existing problems as well as increase the ease and speed of application development. Interoperability between heterogeneous systems is certainly one of the key benefits. A secondary, but still very important, benefit is reuse and rapid application development, enhanced by Web Services' support for platform-neutral, loosely coupled, and self-contained services.

A key Web Services concept that aims to facilitate greater reuse and speed development is service-oriented architecture (SOA). SOA defines an architecture that is structured as a set of application-independent Web Services that each implement a specific business or technical function. This allows applications to be more rapidly created by enabling a compositional style of development, whereby loosely coupled services can be selected, extended, and aggregated in various ways to form unique applications. Thus, to really reap many of the reuse and rapid application development benefits of Web Services, an architecture organized around services (or at least, reasonably cohesive abstractions) is important. However, much of the hype and marketing discussions around Web Services focuses on the benefits and the specific technology aspects (SOAP, XML, and so on), and the impression is that all one has to do is slap a Web Service on top of an existing system and all those benefits will ensue.

The Web Services Will Fix Our Problems AntiPattern consists of adopting Web Services to fix some major problems in an existing application. Issues with extensibility and reuse in current J2EE applications are usually due to poor architecture and design (as described in many of the other chapters in this book). The main ones have to do with a poorly abstracted business or technical middle tier, and having business logic bound up in non-middle-tier components (for example, JSPs, servlets, and so on). Even though there are many tools available today that support building and even autogenerating Web Service interfaces on top of existing applications, the resulting structure of the Web Services and SOA will be a reflection of the underlying architecture. So, poor maintainability, extensibility, and reuse cannot be fixed by just implementing Web Services, because the underlying implementation behind the Web Services is really the problem.

General Form

The form this AntiPattern takes is a number of Web Service interfaces are implemented on top of an existing, poorly architected or structured system. Given the architecture of the underlying system (or lack thereof), the Web Services interfaces exhibit the same structure for example, a bloated Web Service that sits upon a bloated session (see Chapter 7, "Session EJBs"). Another example is business logic that is bound up in existing JSPs that needs to be significantly refactored (or duplicated) to be accessed and used through a Web Service. Thus, the form this AntiPattern takes will be a number of Web Services that emulate AntiPatterns seen in other areas of J2EE systems. Most commonly, this will be manifested as bloated Web Services (that support multiple entities or documents and a large number of operations), or many thin Web Services, that collectively implement a single abstraction.

The basis of this AntiPattern is a decision by high-level technical managers and decision makers to put Web Services interfaces on their existing J2EE systems, as an attempt to improve poor maintainability and extensibility, without understanding that Web Services are really just an interface mechanism on top of another implementation, and it is the structure, modularity, and so on of that implementation that chiefly affects development.

Symptoms and Consequences

The main symptom of this AntiPattern is Web Services that have been implemented on top of an existing J2EE system that just don't seem to improve development times. In fact, they make them longer, by introducing more technology, tools, artifacts to manage, and so on. Some of the specific symptoms and consequences are as follows:

- **Decision to implement Web Services is made by high-level managers, not by project architects.** Discussions and decisions to use the Web Services approach are based on idealized information, marketing hype, and so on. People outside of a project team (for example, a high-level group manager) see the external issues of long development times, difficulties extending existing applications, and reusing an existing implementation for new applications, without understanding what the real causes of these issues are.
- **Implementing Web Service interfaces causes a major refactoring in the underlying system.** The actual implementation of the Web Services requires either significant refactoring of the existing business logic implementation or, more commonly, business logic is copied and pasted into Web Service implementation artifacts, creating a maintenance nightmare.
- **The resulting Web Services are highly coupled to each other, limiting reusability for other applications.** The Web Services created are difficult to use outside of their original purpose, that is, for creating other applications. The ideal of composing applications from a collection of loosely coupled Web Services is never realized, because the Web Services are instead tightly coupled.
- **Long development time.** The implementation of a Web Service takes a long time (reimplementing existing functionality, refactoring, and so on).
- **Copied and pasted business logic creates a maintenance issue.** If time isn't taken to refactor business logic, then copied and pasted code becomes problematic to maintain.
- **Everything else suffers due to time crunches.** When architects and developers spend a lot of time getting trained, experimenting, reimplementing things multiple times, and dealing with new technology in general, this takes away a lot of time from implementing real application functionality. This is a typical effect of getting into new technology for the wrong reasons, too early, and so on, so the implementation of actual business functionality suffers greatly.

Typical Causes

The most fundamental cause of this AntiPattern is not understanding the influence that underlying system architecture has on the quality and usefulness of Web Services interfaces for that system. The specific causes include:

- **Two-tier application architecture.** Two-tier applications are fine on their own, but when reusing or repurposing business logic into new uses (for example, Web Services, integration, and so on) is necessary, the shortcomings of this approach become readily apparent.
- **Poor middle tier architecture and design.** If a system was poorly architected and structured, slapping Web Services on top of it will not resolve basic issues (see the Bloated Session and Thin Session AntiPatterns in Chapter 7, "Session EJBs"). A middle tier that is not at least somewhat structured as a set of service abstractions will be harder to attempt to fit a services orientation on top of.
- **Technology-focused downplaying of process, architecture, OO principles.** When architects and developers look to technology for the substance of the problems or solutions, they neglect other important factors such as architecture (which at a certain level, isn't about technology at all), process (well-defined and structured requirements), and so on.
- **Believing all the hype, combined with being an early adopter.** Web Services has received a lot of hype, and currently there is a lot of material out there that suggests that Web Services are an ideal solution, a better way than present approaches. In some situations, people continue to see new technology as the solution to current problems, and are quick to jump onto it and adopt new approaches.

Known Exceptions

In some cases, there will be legacy systems that are basically quite aged, but are still in use and provide business value. Often, these types of systems are integration targets within larger organizations, and therefore, a Web Services approach is attractive in terms of supporting (better) integration and interoperability. However, these systems may be implemented in a more monolithic way, and rearchitecting them may not be cost-effective in terms of their remaining lifetime.

Packaged applications may provide native APIs that can be wrapped with Web Services, or, in some cases, the application itself may provide those capabilities or tools. In either case, the Web Service(s) operations, structure, and so forth will be a function of the application's API, and there is no possibility of changing that.

Refactorings

The big issue in this AntiPattern is that the existing system architecture is not structured to accommodate Web Services to produce the desired benefits. Thus, a major software refactoring is required to rework and fix the underlying system architecture, which is ultimately what needs to be refactored, to provide a more modular, service-oriented structure for Web Services. The refactorings described in Chapter 3, "Service-Based Architecture," and Chapter 7, "Session EJBs," describe some of the specific issues with poorly structured middle-tier components, and their associated refactorings. Also, the situation of business logic bound up in JSPs or servlets is the other major refactoring that may need to occur. These AntiPatterns and refactorings are described in Chapters 4 and 5.

An alternate process-oriented refactoring is to decide not to use Web Services at all. If the real goal of using Web Services is to ultimately implement a services-oriented architecture, and heterogeneous interoperability is not a requirement, then there really is no justification for using Web Services at all. A service-based architecture approach can be built entirely within J2EE technology and lead to the same benefits of accelerated development and improved reuse.

Variations

This AntiPattern is just a specific application of a very typical AntiPattern that occurs whenever any significantly new technology emerges. It happened when Java appeared (If we switch from C++ to Java, things will be better . . .). In general, new technology doesn't fix fundamental problems in software architecture or design.

Example

The diagram in Figure 9.1 is a small example of this AntiPattern. What we see is a Bloated Session AntiPattern (which is an AntiPattern described in Chapter 7) that implements many different methods across a lot of different abstractions, with a similarly structured Web Service endpoint implementation layered on top of it.

The bloated session creates a situation of tight coupling to many different application data types and client components, making development more complex and severely limiting reuse. In this case, a Web Service is slapped on top of this poorly structured session, with the expectation that the external, client view of the system will be usable, be scalable, and allow the reuse of the Web Service in multiple applications. However, the same issues will hamper the use of the Web Service, including many Web Service clients being coupled to one large Web Service interface, coupling to many data types, and limited reuse.

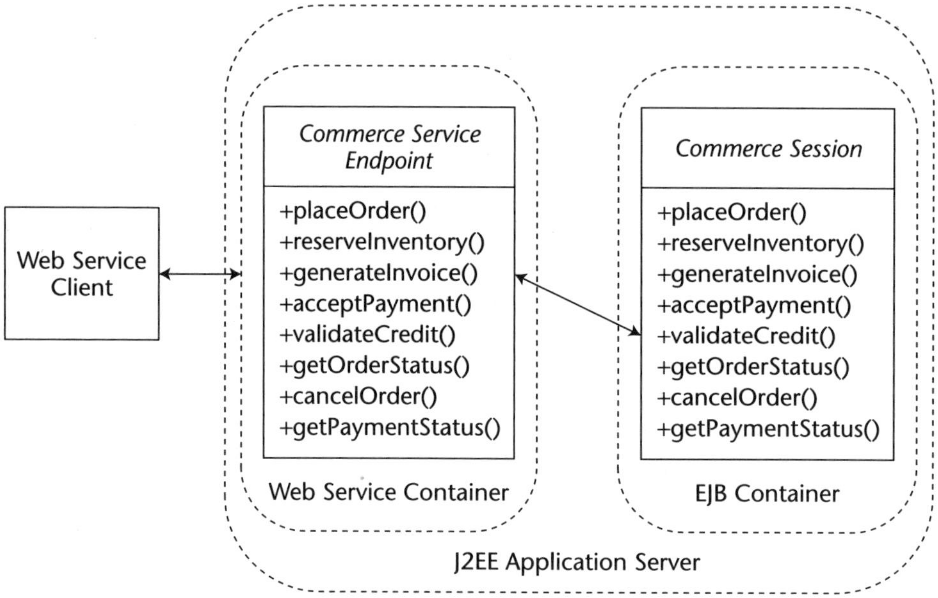

Figure 9.1 Bloated Web Service over bloated session.

Related Solutions

One of the best ways to uncover issues and mitigate risk in software development is to implement a prototype or thin slice. By taking a modest, measured approach to implementing a very specific, non-mission-critical bit of functionality, many of the issues pointed out here should become apparent very quickly. This allows the different refactoring approaches to be attempted, and, in some cases, this may initiate a significant rearchitecting effort, to prepare for (later) wider-spread adoption of Web Services. The prototype shows in miniature many of the issues that will arise, and allows for refactoring and rearchitecting techniques to be applied before major Web Services developments get underway.

AntiPattern

When in Doubt, Make It a Web Service

Also Known As: Golden Hammer

Most Frequent Scale: Application, architecture

Refactorings: Web Service to J2EE Component, Vend Data Instead of Algorithm

Refactored Solution Type: Software

Root Causes: Avarice

Unbalanced Forces: Complexity, performance

Anecdotal Evidence: "Let's implement that as a Web Service!"

Background

Typical uses today of Web Services center around enterprise application integration (EAI) and business-to-business (B2B) scenarios. However, in a broader sense, Web Services are intended to be ubiquitously accessible, encapsulated units of functionality, accessible anywhere on the Internet. These qualities can lead some architects and developers to envision much more diverse uses for Web Services. For example, there are algorithmic or command-type functions like a spell checker that utilize a set of reference data like a dictionary that changes over time; encapsulating the algorithm and the data with updates behind a Web Service ensure that any client always gets up-to-date operations.

In other cases, some may reason that if a Web Services approach provides a better way to support distributed functionality, then middle-tier functions and services which are currently implemented in a distributed way using Session EJBs (like an order management session) would be better if implemented with Web Services.

However, a Web Service interchange involves significant runtime performance. XML is certainly not a compact data format, and the transmission, marshaling, and unmarshaling of XML can take considerable time, certainly more time than serialized Java objects transmitted over RMI. Development effort and complexity are greater, too, because implementing a Web Service involves a number of processes, including XML parsing and validation, binding to Java objects, invocation to business logic components, and so on. In cases where there are many small interactions that happen frequently (such as the spell checker), using a Web Service is probably going to be prohibitive in terms of performance. Thus, a Web Services approach should usually be done when it *has* to be done, such as when services or functions are being accessed by heterogeneous client platforms, or when there are firewall restrictions in which interchanges are restricted to HTTP.

As with many new, hyped technologies, a Web Services AntiPattern that arises is the When in Doubt, Make It a Web Service approach, which goes overboard and uses a Web Services approach for implementing and vending processes and functionality that do not need Web Services and do not benefit from them. The result is lower performance than would have been achieved with native J2EE approaches, and additional development time being spent to understand, implement, and deploy additional Web Services artifacts. This is the Golden Hammer AntiPattern, which in this case means that everything looks like it should be implemented as a Web Service (the nail).

General Form

This AntiPattern takes the form of a J2EE system with many Web Services implemented, for all sorts of different functionality, including services used exclusively by internal application clients. In many of these services, there is no justification for implementing them as Web Services, and doing so just adds development complexity and time, additional development artifacts to deal with, and reduced performance in some cases.

Systems that only interact with other Java components have no need for Web Services at all, and so any Web Services existing in these cases is an example of the AntiPattern. Also, J2EE server-side services or functions that are used purely by other

Java components can be accessed in Java-specific ways, and Web Service implementations on these represent an example of this AntiPattern. Also, fine-grained, frequently accessed algorithmic type functions that are implemented as Web Services may represent a form of this AntiPattern, when the frequency and data exchanges are large and yield unacceptable performance.

Symptoms and Consequences

Functionality that is inappropriately implemented as a Web Service will manifest some visible symptoms and consequences in terms of development impact and runtime performance. Some of the specific items to look for include:

- **Intrasystem communication only.** Functionality behind a Web Service that is only accessed by other J2EE system components doesn't get any benefit from a Web Services interface, and is better accessed via standard J2EE mechanisms, such as EJB interfaces, RMI, or local interfaces.
- **Many Web Services**. If there are many Web Services within one J2EE system, this *may* indicate that there are some that are really not necessary.
- **Algorithm-type Web Services.** A Web Service that implements a frequently accessed algorithmic function will likely be prohibitive in terms of performance.
- **Poorer system performance in general.** Web Service interfaces and communication generally are less efficient than more direct methods, for example, RMI or serialized Java objects. Marshaling and unmarshaling of XML and the transmission of the SOAP/XML all take more time than direct Java methods. For larger documents, the performance effect could be significant.
- **More development, testing, and debugging time.** In order to implement a Web Service, there are additional development artifacts, development time, and so on. Dealing with SOAP, XML, data type formats, and other Web Service components means that additional effort is required to completely implement functionality as a Web Service.
- **More time is used up learning new technologies and tools**. In cases where a Web Service approach is not warranted at all, obviously, this can eat up a lot of time, while adding no real value to the project.

Typical Causes

This AntiPattern is basically caused by overzealous interest in implementing Web Services. Specific details of this include:

- **Excessive interest in using a new technology.** Some architects and developers go looking for situations that may lend themselves to a Web Service implementation. Everything looks like a nail when you want to use a hammer. . . .

- **Incomplete understanding of functional and operational requirements.** Another cause of this is not doing the necessary evaluation of the true requirements to decide if a Web Services approach really is appropriate. One of the key reasons for using Web Services is to support heterogeneous interoperability, and if that situation or requirement doesn't exist, then there is certainly a lot less justification for using it.
- **Building for unspecified future requirements.** Another common justification for a Web Services approach is to facilitate future interoperability requirements. So, Web Service interfaces are implemented when there isn't actually a concrete need to support heterogeneous interoperability, but it is felt that there is likely to be such a need someday. Building for future, fuzzy requirements is usually a bad idea, and especially so for Web Services, because there is a high likelihood that changes will occur to the technology and tools, which will require changes to the Web Services.

Known Exceptions

A potential exception to the rule of not using Web Services to do intrasystem communication is to get at business logic implemented in a client tier (for example, the Web tier) from the middle tier. Middle-tier components should not usually interact with a client tier, but if there is some business logic bound into a servlet, for instance, a Web Service interface can facilitate a loosely coupled way of executing that interaction. Note that this is a quick-and-dirty approach, and should probably only be undertaken when performing the correct methodology (for example, refactoring the business logic down into the middle tier) is unfeasible due to time constraints or other factors.

Refactorings

The basic issue described by this AntiPattern is the inappropriate use of Web Services in situations and with requirements that do not warrant it, or when it is simply not a feasible approach. Thus, the basic refactoring approach is to remove the Web Service interaction and use a more appropriate mechanism, or refactor the Web Service design so that it becomes feasible to use in terms of performance.

One of the main rationales for using a Web Service approach is to support heterogeneous interactions between clients and server-based functionality. In cases where the client and Web Service are both implemented strictly within the J2EE platform, using a Web Services approach is not needed because the endpoints are homogeneous within the J2EE platform, and performance is usually better using standard J2EE mechanisms for vending and interacting with server-based functionality. Thus, the refactoring for this is Replace Web Service with J2EE Component, in terms of what the client interacts with. This usually amounts to just changing the way the client interacts with the server-based components, utilizing RMI or HTTP to interact directly with the existing implementation component, for instance, a Session Bean or servlet. The Web Service interface may be retained for possible future, heterogeneous clients.

Another major rationale for deciding against a Web Service approach is that it is prohibitive in terms of performance. In cases where client-to-Web Service interactions have a high frequency, and/or the message payload is large, performance testing and real-world use may indicate that a Web Service interface approach is just not efficient enough.

In the case of algorithmic Web Services, the real issue is the frequent remote requests made to a distributed component every time the algorithm is used. However, one of the values of the distributed algorithm is that it can utilize current data and the client does not need to worry about any of that. The significant requirement here is that the data changes over time, but the algorithm does not. Thus, a potential refactoring for this is to rearchitect the Web Service to supply the data for the algorithm, but provide clients with an (unchanging) implementation of the algorithm. In terms of J2EE, a locally loaded Java class implements the appropriate algorithm and makes use of data that is downloaded and updated via a Web site that delivers the data. This is better than a strictly non-Web-Service approach, which usually involves shipping physical data updates and so on. In order to move the code from your algorithmic Web Service, apply Fowler's Extract Class refactoring from *Refactoring: Improving the Design of Existing Code* (Fowler, 2000).

Variations

One variant of this AntiPattern is to use as many Web Service technology elements as possible. Web Services encompass many different technologies that accommodate different usage scenarios. In any particular scenario, there will typically be a subset of technologies needed, and it is important to understand what each technology and mechanism provides and why it is needed (or not).

There are many tools that support the autogeneration of Web Services from existing components (for example, EJBs). It may be tempting to simply use these tools on many (or all!) of the components within an existing system, to expose them as Web Services, and possibly even to access them locally (for example, within the system). However, as stated previously, there should be a specific rationale applied to establish which bits of functionality really should be exposed.

Example

The diagram in Figure 9.2 depicts an example of a J2EE system that implements a number of different processes and functions as Web Services. The scenario depicts a couple of business Web Services that provide an interface for external clients to perform key business functions with the system, such as receiving new orders and canceling accounts. However, there are also some internal, algorithmic-oriented functions shown on the right side of the diagram that are exclusively used by the other Web Service implementations within the J2EE application server context. These internal functions are implemented as Web Services under the rationale that it would simply be better to allow for some future requirements and deployment options. In use, it turns out that these internal Web Services are frequently accessed whenever there are interactions with the external Web Service (for example, date conversion occurs for many elements within the exchanged document), and the performance as seen by the external client is terrible. Upon doing some analysis, it is determined that these internal Web Services are using a lot of processing time to marshal and unmarshal data, to make the calls, and to bind XML to and from Java objects. When these functions are refactored as POJOs and called directly within the implementations of the main business Web Services, performance improves dramatically.

Related Solutions

There are no related solutions for this AntiPattern.

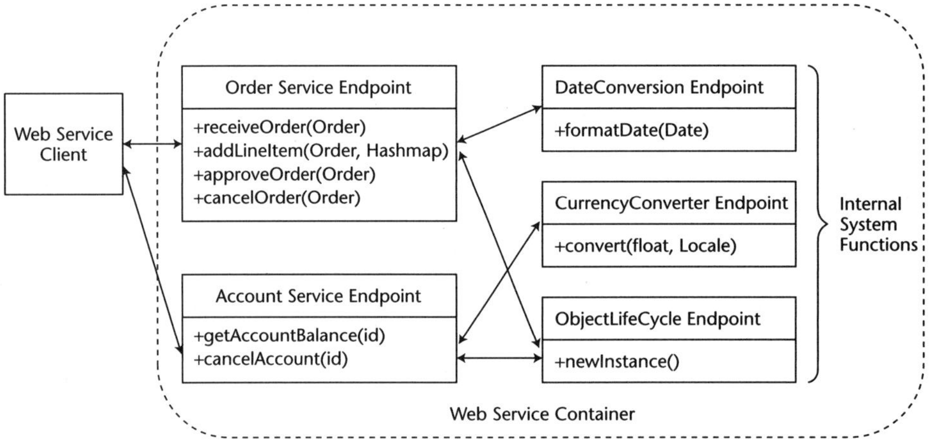

Figure 9.2 Web Services everywhere.

God Object Web Service

Also Known As: The Blob

Most Frequent Scale: System, architecture

Refactorings: Interface Partitioning

Refactored Solution Type: Software

Root Causes: Ignorance, sloth

Unbalanced Forces: Complexity, performance

Anecdotal Evidence: "Just add that new operation to *the* Web Service."

Background

Developers may see Web Services as simply a better mechanism to enable interoperation between clients and server-based functions, and not really consider the concept of services, SOA, and other elements. Such a mechanism-focused view ignores the general structuring principles regarding well-defined services, abstractions, and more, and can lead to a hodge-podge of unrelated operations in a single Web Service. At the extreme, the result will be a single Web Service that vends all external functions and with which all clients interact. From a pure runtime implementation point of view, this will work. And, it may be reasoned that this is a good approach, because only a single WSDL has to be created and maintained, and only a single URL must be maintained. However, the interface details of the Web Service inevitably change over time, and when a single Web Service implements a lot of operations, many clients will be affected by the change. In some cases, this means that dynamic invocation code has to change to accommodate the new operational signature, parameters, and so on. In the case of statically generated client stubs, those stubs have to be regenerated whenever the WSDL changes.

The God Object Web Service AntiPattern is the Web Services version of putting too much into a single component and not creating separate, distinct abstractions. This creates a broad coupling between a wide range of server functions and all the many clients that use the different parts, severely limiting reuse.

When many clients are utilizing one interface, and several developers work on one underlying implementation, there are bound to be issues of breakage in clients and developer contention for changes to server-side implementation artifacts.

General Form

The general form of the God Object AntiPattern is a single Web Service that vends a large number of operations, and those operations exchange different core business abstractions or documents. This is similar to the Bloated Session AntiPattern (see Chapter 7), but in a Web Services vein. The WSDL that represents the Web Service will be large, and the number of underlying implementation components (for example, servlets, sessions) may be many. In some cases, the underlying system architecture may be reasonably structured and tiered, but many of those underlying components are then vended out through a single Web Service.

Symptoms and Consequences

The God Object Web Service will usually be recognized by a large, complicated WSDL, indicating a broad set of functionality vended through the Web Service. Some of the specific symptoms and consequences are:

- **Multiple types of documents exchanged.** A Web Service that is not a clear abstraction will support operations on many different document types, for example, orders, invoices, and payments.

- **A large number of operations in the Web Service, as defined in the WSDL.** The WSDL for the Web Service defines a lot of operations (for example, 20–30). (Note: This may also be a symptom of fine-grained Web Services.)
- **Higher likelihood of blocked developers and clobbered code changes.** If there are many operations aggregated into the same Web Service, there may be multiple developers implementing, testing, and maintaining different sets of those operations. And thus, when concurrent development or maintenance is occurring, there is a high likelihood of contention when they attempt to update the Web Service implementation artifacts (WSDL, implementation classes, and deployment descriptors), and possible clobbering of changes if the code repository is not managed very well.
- **Client interactions fail more often, due to frequent changes in the Web Service definition.** Client implementation code may have to change frequently. For clients who use a static invocation approach, changes to the Web Service interface must be accompanied by the regeneration of client stub code.
- **Reuse is more difficult.** If a Web Service exposes a broad range of operations, this implies considerable dependency and coupling to the variety of data types and implementations for each of those operations. Hence, reusing the Web Service in other contexts requires all those dependencies to come along for the ride, when all that is wanted is to use a particular operation. Also, successful reuse is predicated on well-defined, well-understood components. When a Web Service has a muddy interface, it will be confusing and appear less credible and reliable, and most developers will opt to look elsewhere or reimplement it, rather than counting on a potentially flakey implementation.

Typical Causes

A God Object Web Service usually occurs from lack of knowledge and inexperience within the overall area of OO software development. Some of the specific cases of this include:

- **Inexperience with object-oriented and/or services-based architecture.** The concepts behind objects and services are still important with Web Services, and a lack of knowledge of them can have a significant affect on the development, maintenance, and reuse of the code.
- **Purely technical perspective on Web Services.** If architects and developers see Web Services as simply a different set of remote method invocation technologies, then the interface between external clients and the internal system may be implemented with the Web Service.
- **The underlying system architecture is monolithic.** The services that are vended to external clients are implemented with internal components, and if the internal system architecture is monolithic, or if there are a few, large sessions that implement a myriad of business logic functions, then this perspective will likely influence the overlying Web Services. The Web Service structure is often a reflection of the underlying architecture (or lack thereof).

- **Continuous, mechanical additions to an initially small Web Service.** An initial, modest Web Service is implemented, and serves as the basis for subsequent additional external operations. However, developers may follow a somewhat mechanical process to create the new operations (for example, mechanically repeat the same development process) and simply extend the Web Service. Without an initial or refactored idea of what distinct Web Service abstractions should be produced, a mechanical approach may simply extend the Web Service.

Known Exceptions

There are no significant exceptions to this AntiPattern.

Refactorings

Similarly to the Bloated Session AntiPattern in Chapter 7, the God Object Web Service should be partitioned on the basis of cohesive abstraction. The Interface Partitioning refactoring in Chapter 3 can be applied to this situation in a similar way to subdivide the God Object Web Service into multiple Web Services that are more self-contained, standalone, and specific to a purpose or abstraction. In the case of Web Services, partitioning should be based on the specific document that the operations deal with or operate on—for example, all the operations that deal with a Purchase Order entity, or a document, should be cohesively aggregated into one Web Service. Thus, CRUD-type operations, and possibly other related operations, such as status changes, should all be placed together. This process of partitioning should be followed for any other entities, documents, or target data items that the operations deal with.

Variations

Tools that autogenerate Web Service interfaces and other elements can autogenerate a big, ugly Web Service from a big, ugly application. If a Web Service is generated from a God Object Session EJB, then the resulting Web Service will reflect that. Autogeneration tools will simple resurface the underlying architecture of a system, good or bad. Hence, a well-architected set of Web Services will ultimately be easiest to implement and maintain on a well-architected underlying system.

Example

In Figure 9.3, you can see a Web Service that implements a wide range of significant business operations, dealing with several core business abstractions. Various external clients interact with this one single Web Service to exchange Order, Payment, and Invoice business entities (as XML documents). This is a typical representation of a God Object Web Service, because it implements many different kinds of operations for many different purposes, and there is only one Web Service that all external clients interact with for all of the vended operations. In reality, there are usually many more operations implemented on a God Object Web Service, because there are usually several different operations that relate to one specific business entity, and when this is multiplied by all the different entities that may be exchanged with external parties, this can lead to a Web Service interface that implements a lot of operations.

Related Solutions

The basic principles behind the Session Façade pattern described by the Gang of Four (Gamma, Helm, Johnson, and Vlissides, 1996) center on the concept of subsystem layering, to create high-level façades that have coarse-grained operations, layered over a number of finer-grained process components that implement successively finer-grained subprocesses. Thus, a layering of processes results. In a similar fashion, Web Services may also be layered, especially if the lower-level subprocesses are themselves operations that external clients should have access to. Thus, some clients will access higher-level Web Services, with coarse-grained process operations, while others will utilize the lower-level, finer-grained processes. (See Chapter 7 for a discussion of the Session Façade refactoring.)

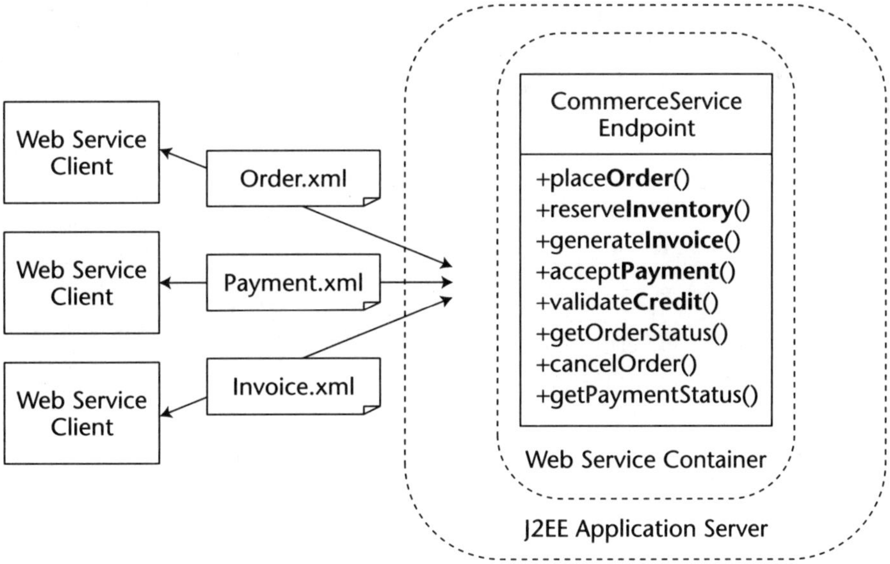

Figure 9.3 The God Object Web Service.

AntiPattern

Fine-Grained/Chatty Web Service

Also Known As: Chatty Interface

Most Frequent Scale: Application, architecture

Refactorings: Operation Aggregation (Interface Aggregation), Document Transfer Object (Data Transfer Object), RPC to Document Style

Refactored Solution Type: Software

Root Causes: Ignorance

Unbalanced Forces: Complexity, performance

Anecdotal Evidence: "Let's make every Session method as a Web Service operation."

Background

A common problem with developers new to Web Services is that they create operations and messages that are too fine-grained. You shouldn't create an operation for every Java method. Instead, each operation should clearly represent an action or business process. The granularity of operations and messages should be such that clients get perceived value out of executing *an* operation, and the situation where a client must interact with multiple operations to do anything meaningful needs to be avoided.

A Web Service exposes application functionality to heterogeneous clients in a manner that is similar to the way that Session EJBs expose operations to Java-based clients. Thus, many of the same performance and granularity considerations apply. Fine-grained Web Services lead to the familiar chatty interface problem, and the performance issues will likely be more pronounced due to the additional bandwidth and processing requirements for XML-based messages, and the larger size of the data passed when doing document-style exchanges.

In some cases, developers may be more familiar with two-tier-oriented models (or two-and-a-half tier), and impart more responsibility on the client to execute the overall business process logic. Thus, clients must implement the sequencing and workflow coordination, invoking multiple Web Service interactions to complete one overall process. In one sense, this may be seen as beneficial, because the client can then maintain conversational state across steps within a process, which isn't supported in any standardized way by Web Services. However, this also means that the sequencing and coordination of the business process workflow lies within the client, instead of behind the Web Service—for example, implemented in the middle tier of the underlying system.

General Form

Fine-grained Web Services exhibit the same kind of situation as the chatty interface with Entity EJBs. For example, they have many fine-grained operations. These operations may be attribute-level accessors or mutators, or operations that implement very fine-grained steps within an overall process sequence. In either of these cases, a client ultimately needs to execute multiple interactions with the Web Service to complete a meaningful process. This has a few significant consequences. First, performance is poor because each interaction takes significant time (to marshal and unmarshal XML documents at each endpoint, and transmit XML over the wire), and when there are many interactions, this results in poor performance. Second, this requires clients to have too much knowledge of the Web Services' details, which they have to coordinate in the proper way.

Symptoms and Consequences

The symptoms and consequences of this AntiPattern are similar to those that occur with other interface-based components such as sessions and entities. The specific symptoms and consequences include:

- **Multiple different Web Service operations are required to execute one overall process.** If a client *must* interact with multiple Web Service operations to achieve a particular goal, then this is a sign that those operations could be aggregated into a single, more coarse-grained operation. This is similar to the chatty interface issue when non-EJB clients interact directly with Entity Beans.
- **Web Service operations are basically attribute-level setters or getters.** If a Web Service interface looks like an EJB Entity interface, for example, and basically consists of getter and possibly setter for different attributes or properties of a core entity, then this is too fine-grained.
- **A Web Service may have many operations defined on it.** When there are many fine-grained operations, there will typically be a larger number of operations, because they cover a lot of the subprocesses (and not the larger, subsystem façade-type processes).
- **A Web Service interface may be similar to the interface or implementation methods of underlying component(s) implementing the Web Service.** In some cases, a Web Service is created that is essentially a Transparent façade over some other components (EJB Session, Java object). Thus, the methods of the underlying component bleed through to the Web Service interface, and this can result in many fine-grained (implementation-oriented) methods surfacing through the Web Service.
- **Business logic is implemented in the client, limiting reuse.** If the implementation of a particular business process is implemented in a client of the Web Service, then other clients must redundantly implement the same logic.
- **Confusing interface.** A Web Service interface with many operations becomes confusing because it is not known in what order to invoke them. If these lower-level methods are aggregated into a few coarse-grained methods, then typically, any of those (few) methods can be invoked in their own right, without any prior setup, for example, so, the Web Service interface is easier to understand and use.
- **Poor performance.** This is a Web Services variant of the chatty interface, whereby clients need to interact multiple times with a remotely accessed service, to perform one, overall process. Depending on the granularity of the operations, many interactions can be required, and each one has a penalty in terms of performance.
- **Bloated client implementation.** The onus is on the implementer of the client to put together all the client interactions, data setup, response handling, and so on.
- **Nontransactional processes.** Because Web Services do not inherently support transactions that span operations, implementing an overall process this way will generally not have transactional integrity. There are vendor-specific solutions that involve maintaining transaction IDs within the SOAP header, but then these approaches are nonportable. If some subset of operations succeeds, followed by operations that fail, there isn't any way to roll back the changes that have already been done within the process or workflow.

Typical Causes

The main cause of this AntiPattern is insufficient structuring and layering of Web Services and operations. Specific causes include:

- **Direct generation of Web Services from sessions or Java classes.** If Web Services are generated from existing sessions with fine-grained, chatty interfaces, the result can be Web Services that implement a similar interface style.
- **Inexperience with process layering, Session façade, and other aspects.** As in the application of the Session Façade pattern, Web Service operations should generally be coarse-grained processes. Ideally, they should be stateless as well, so that an entire, complete process is executed and completed through one Web Service operation. This implies that the implementation of the Web Service operation may perform a number of steps to sequence and coordinate resources for the process. However, this is desirable, in that it pushes knowledge of the steps, sequencing, and conversational state into the Web Service implementation (and out of the clients), and also removes the need in many cases for clients to maintain conversational state.
- **Inexperience with *n*-tier architecture.** Web Services force more stringent separation between tiers. Even when using a modern, multitier, supportive infrastructure (for example, J2EE application servers), there are cases where the application is built in a two-tier manner, for example, servlets and JDBC. And even if EJBs are used, there are many cases where the granularity of operations defined on sessions, for example, is too fine-grained, and more business logic is imparted to the client artifacts.
- **Only being familiar with two-tier, client-centered design.** In some cases, the default approach may be to embed more business logic in the client, simply because that's what was done using other technologies and application approaches. However, the Web Services model forces business logic to be specifically implemented within the Web Service, which is effectively the server side of a client-server arrangement.

Known Exceptions

In some cases, Web Services are used to wrap legacy systems or packaged applications. If the system interface itself has a very fine-grained interface, that will lead to this situation. However, the solution to this is to introduce another subsystem façade layer on top of it, that is, create another Web Service layer over the top. This upper Web Service layer then implements the important business process logic, workflow, or sequencing (within the implementation components for that upper-layer Web Service). In cases where the legacy system is internal, it will probably be more appropriate to use a more direct integration approach (rather than a Web Service), for example, a JCA connector (if available).

Refactorings

A similar approach to the Session Façade AntiPattern (found in Chapter 7) can be applied to a fine-grained Web Service to produce a coarser-grained, more efficient interface. The façade pattern aggregates a set of fine-grained operations into a larger, coarse-grained business goal, introducing an effective subsystem layering. Clients are then refactored to reduce their interactions down to the one, coarser-grained operation. Note that this is specifically applicable to workflow and action-oriented processes and operations, for example, executing a purchase order. Operations that are more CRUD-specific (when the operation is more centered on sending or receiving significant data) can also be combined with the DTO and Document Style refactorings described below.

The data transfer object (DTO) core J2EE patterns (Alur, Crupi, and Malks 2001) have been used widely to improve performance of CRUD-type interactions between clients and EJBs. A similar approach can be used in conjunction with Web Services. In this case, however, the DTO is manifested as an XML document (or document fragment) that aggregates many attributes and related objects to allow exchange in a single interaction. The introduction of local interfaces in EJB has reduced the importance of the DTO pattern with EJBs; with Web Services, there is no such equivalent communication shortcut, so this approach is very relevant to Web Services.

Extending to the principle behind the DTO refactoring, the RPC to Document Style refactoring takes a more significant approach to refactoring the entire RPC interaction type into a document-style exchange. The SOAP envelope contains an XML document representing the entire entity, and additionally includes action-oriented information to facilitate content-based processing by the Web Service. This approach means that the same *kind* of document is always sent to a single Web Service operation, and the content of the document dictates different types of processing. This is applicable when many of the required operations need to send a lot of attributes and relationship objects; thus, the DTO would probably end up being quite like an entity instance.

Variations

There are no significant variations of this AntiPattern.

Example

The diagram in Figure 9.4 depicts an example of the Fine-Grained Web Service AntiPattern. The client here is interacting with the Web Service to get information about a specific Order entity. The Web Service presents a fine-grained interface, requiring the client to make several calls to the Web Service to get the complete set of data for one Order instance. This results in poor performance, and requires that the client itself have knowledge of the different attributes and relationship elements for the Order entity and be able to reconstruct those on the client side. This puts too much knowledge into the client regarding the structure and relationships of the Order entity.

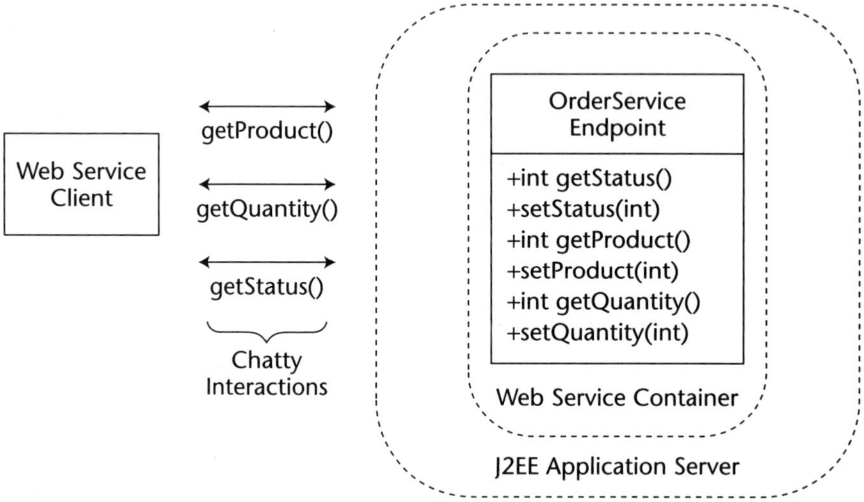

Figure 9.4 Fine-Grained/Chatty Web Service.

Related Solutions

There are no related solutions for this AntiPattern.

AntiPattern

Maybe It's Not RPC

Also Known As: Procedural Programming

Most Frequent Scale: Application, architecture

Refactorings: RPC to Document Style, Synchronous to Asynchronous Messaging

Refactored Solution Type: Software

Root Causes: Ignorance, inexperience

Unbalanced Forces: Complexity, performance

Anecdotal Evidence: "Web Services are an RPC mechanism, right?"

Background

Web Services are fundamentally about distributed exchanges between heterogeneous platforms. There are basically two flavors of exchange that can be done: RPC-style interactions (remote method call), and document-style interactions (electronic document interchange). However, many beginning discussions and tutorials for Web Services concentrate specifically on Web Services as an RPC mechanism, implementing simple remote functions, to provide key learning regarding data type mappings and serialization, client invocation methods (static and dynamic approaches), and more. Also, tools like JAX-RPC tend to focus on RPC-style semantics, allowing developers to interact with Web Services through familiar Java interfaces and operations, and concentrating on details regarding parameter and return value data-type translations. However, there are specific situations in which the document-style approach is called for. Also, there may be some interactions that may be more function and procedure oriented, but that may still benefit from a document-style interaction approach.

This AntiPattern occurs when attempting to shoehorn an RPC approach into something that is inherently document-oriented. Document-oriented interactions exchange instances of significant business entities, such as Purchase Orders, Invoices, and more. In these cases, the action or goal around the exchange is essentially a create, read, update, and delete (CRUD) operation such as creating an entity (for example, on a partner system), updating data (sending updated information about a shared entity), or deleting data. Using an RPC approach to implementing CRUD operations on entities or business documents results in operations that have a lot of parameters with custom types, SOAP document fragments, and so on. Clients interacting with the Web Service need to do significant work to create the appropriate separate data elements before invoking the Web Service, and Web Service implementation components need to reconstitute those data parts into an overall document for request processing.

Note also that in general, RPC-style interactions are synchronous request and response invocations, emulating a method call with return value. Document-style interactions are often asynchronous, because clients usually do not need an immediate response (the response is usually that it simply succeeded or failed), and document exchanges typically involve mission-critical transactions between parties, utilizing message-oriented middleware (for example, JMS) to provide reliable delivery. Part of this AntiPattern then, too, is unnecessary or unsuitable use of a synchronous messaging style (associated with RPC) when CRUD operation semantics really dictate an asynchronous approach used with document-style interactions.

General Form

In this AntiPattern, a Web Service implements one or more RPC-style operations that essentially support CRUD-type actions for significant business entities, for example, createOrder or updateInvoice. These operations will likely need to specify a significant number of parameters and/or complexity in those parameters (for example, custom types) to facilitate the passing of the necessary attributes of a business entity.

Alternately, a document exchange process may be implemented through RPC by attaching the document as a SOAP attachment. Essentially, the approach is still RPC, but all the operation-specific data is being passed as an XML attachment.

Symptoms and Consequences

This AntiPattern is usually recognized when it seems that there is a lot of work to implement and evolve the XML documents and data types associated to the Web Services operation. The following lists some specific symptoms and consequences:

- **The Web Service operation implements CRUD operations.** Web Services that primarily perform CRUD operations are essentially exchanging entity instance data in most cases, and using a document-style approach is much more natural than relying on a fragmented collection of entity attribute values.
- **A Web Service operation has a large number of parameters that are derived from a single object.** Many of the parameter values are obtained from a single root object or a set of objects related together through some root object. For instance, transmitting LineItems, tax components, payment details, and so forth is associated with an instance of an Order entity.
- **A number of the parameters may be custom types or SOAP document fragments, reflecting that they are document components or subdocument parts.** When a complex business document is communicated using an RPC-style approach, often the various subparts of the document (such as a tax component on an order) are communicated as separate data elements. Conversely, if an RPC operation includes many custom data types and SOAP document fragments, this may be an indicator that the interaction really should be document style.
- **The client may have significant implementation associated with creating or consuming the parameter values**. For example, the client may need to construct instances of complex Java types or document fragments, essentially retrieving and constructing various data parts that (in hindsight) would probably be better represented as a document.
- **Poor system performance.** This occurs because clients or client threads are stuck waiting for synchronous responses. Clients may experience the system freezing while this occurs, or degraded system performance when thread(s) are waiting for responses.
- **Significant client implementation.** When there are a few parameters to a procedural-oriented Web Service, the client code needed to obtain the appropriate parameter values and do the stub-based invocation will usually be modest. Coding all the necessary queries, object factories, and possible transformations to fit into an RPC-style interface will likely take more time than defining a suitable document (for example, an XML Schema), and coding the client to perform document-oriented queries and transformation of data (using DTO-like objects, JDBC result sets, and so on). Also, if reliable transmission is required (which is

usually the case when doing updates to documents), there will likely be additional implementation to support this (for example, responding to transmission timeouts, or error responses).

- **Significant Web Service/server implementation.** As in the case of the client, the server side of the service has to repackage together the different parts. This usually means either creating an instance of a document (for example, some potentially complex persistent object, with relationships) or updating various parts of an existing document.
- **There is breakage to clients when business entities change, propagating equivalent changes to the operational signature.** If and when there are even subtle changes to the underlying business document (which is represented virtually by all those parameters as parts), this means changes to the WSDL, regeneration of any static invocation stubs, and changes to the client implementation to interface correctly with the new parameters, types, and so on.

Typical Causes

Programmers tend or want to think of Web Service invocations as another kind of method invocation, and this may skew their perspective so they do not consider when and where the document-style approach should be used. Some of the typical causes include:

- **Focusing on RPC aspects of Web Services.** As stated earlier, a lot of discussion of Web Services, especially tutorials and Hello World exercises, focus on RPC semantics—implementing and invoking a remote function. However, Web Services are also used for B2B applications, document exchanges, serious systems development, and data exchanges between clients; it is important to understand the relevance of the document style and asynchronous messaging, JMS, and more.
- **Haste.** When embarking on a Web Service operation interface, a key determination should be whether the operation is supporting CRUD-type operations on a specific document or entity instance, or whether it is instead just an invocation of an operation, algorithm, or so on.

Known Exceptions

In cases where a Web Service wraps an existing legacy system, such as an ERP, that system may not support document-style Web Service interactions. In some cases, a proprietary interface mechanism on the legacy side is mapped (or generated) directly to a Web Service, breaking out a large number of parameters and data values. In some cases, there also may be issues with complex types, XML Schema support, and other elements. In these cases, there really is no alternative to doing an RPC-styled interface.

Third-party Web Services that supply an RPC-styled operational interface dictate the style of interaction, and in some cases, there's nothing that can be done about it. If the Web Service provider is a partner, then there is the possibility of refactoring the service (and your client implementation) into a document-styled approach.

Refactorings

The main refactoring here is RPC to Document Style, found later in this chapter, which changes the WSDL details and associated client and server implementations to utilize a Document-style model. The WSDL definition is changed so that either all operations within the service are set with style=document or this is done on a per operation basis. Also, the document approach will involve the definition of an XML schema to define the document structure and semantics, and this is used by either endpoint to create or process the document's content. Finally, the messaging approach is refactored to be asynchronous. This may involve a JMS-based implementation on the client side (for example, publishing to a JMS destination that asynchronously receives messages from and interacts with the Web Service). JAXM is the other commonly used API that supports these requirements, because it directly supports a model of documents and messaging (as opposed to procedures and synchronous method calls).

Variations

A variation of this AntiPattern is using an RPC style in cases where one or more of the endpoints has limited support for complex data types. The implementation of custom data types varies among tools. In some cases, custom serializers/deserializers are required, or (in the case of legacy or packaged applications) custom data types support may be limited, hampering interoperability. The use of custom data types as RPC parameters thus can be an issue in some cases.

Example

Listing 9.1 presents a Web Service WSDL that supports a CRUD-type operation (for example, createOrder). This operation is declared as an RPC-styled, synchronous, Web Service interaction. The items in bold indicate the operation, the parameters, and the response type. Note that the exchange style is indicated as rpc.

This is representative of the AntiPattern because the interchange requires several different arguments to carry different parts of one entity instance—in this case, an Order instance. This is merely illustrative, and in a real-world case, an Order would be a large entity with several simple and complex type attributes and document fragments to represent subordinate parts of the document. Thus, the <input> section of the SOAP operation would be very large.

In a document-style interaction, the WSDL itself would not describe every little detail of the entity; those would instead be described in the XML schema for the entity.

```
<definitions
     targetNamespace="urn:order"
     xmlns="http://schemas.xmlsoap.org/wsdl/"
     xmlns:xsd="http://www.w3.org/2001/XMLSchema"
     xmlns:soap="http://schemas.xmlsoap.org/wsdl/soap"
     xmlns:soapenc="http://schemas.xmlsoap.org/soap/encoding/"
     xmlns:tns="urn:order" >
<types>
</types>
<message name="order">
     <part type="xsd:string" name="product" />
     <part type="xsd:int" name="quantity"/>
     <part type="xsd:int" name="customer"/>
</message>
<message name="response">
     <part type="xsd:bool" name="response"/>
</message>
<portType name="orderManager">
     <!-- request-response messages -->
     <operation name="createOrder">
          <input message="order"/>
          <output message="response"/>
     </operation>
</portType>
<binding name="orderBinding" type="tns:orderManager">
  <soap:binding style="rpc"
transport="http://schemas.xmlsoap.org/soap/http"/>
  <operation name="createOrder">
<soap:operation soapAction=""/>
       <input>
          <soap:header message="order" part="product" use="encoded"
             encodingStyle="http://schemas.xmlsoap.org/soap/encoding/"/>
          <soap:header message="order" part="quantity" use="encoded"
             encodingStyle="http://schemas.xmlsoap.org/soap/encoding/"/>
          <soap:header message="order" part="customer" use="encoded"
             encodingStyle="http://schemas.xmlsoap.org/soap/encoding/"/>
          <soap:body use="encoded"
             encodingStyle="http://schemas.xmlsoap.org/soap/encoding/"/>
       </input>
      <output>
          <soap:header message="response" part="response" use="encoded"
             encodingStyle="http://schemas.xmlsoap.org/soap/encoding/"/>
          <soap:body use="encoded"
             encodingStyle="http://schemas.xmlsoap.org/soap/encoding/"/>
      </output>
   </operation>
</binding>
</definitions>
```

Listing 9.1 RPC style for CRUD operation (WSDL).

Related Solutions

One related solution is to send all the information as a MIME attachment and not as separate RPC arguments. In some cases, the data may be transmitted as just an attachment, if it is just going to be directly inserted (not updated).

Another similar approach is to send one whole business document as a SOAP document fragment. JAX-RPC supports SOAP document fragments as parameter types in RPC-style invocations. If the overall semantic really isn't purely a CRUD of an entity, it may still be useful to consider transmitting SOAP document fragments for specific parameters when they represent essentially documents of related objects (for example, a LineItem associated to an Order).

Another alternative is to implement a hybrid-style Web Services with document-style operations to support CRUD functions and RPC-style operations for the non-CRUD operations. A Web Service can have some operations that are RPC-style, and others that are document-style. For the CRUD/entity type operations, where most of the entity information is being exchanged, these can be implemented using the document style. For other operations, where only a few attributes (for example, a document status) are being obtained or changed, it may still be suitable to implement these in RPC style.

AntiPattern

Single-Schema Dream

Also Known As: Ubiquitous Standard

Most Frequent Scale: Application, architecture

Refactorings: Bridging Schemas or Transforms

Refactored Solution Type: Software

Root Causes: Inexperience, avarice

Unbalanced Forces: Complexity

Anecdotal Evidence: "We'll all work off the same, standardized document schema, so integrating new partners will be seamless."

Background

One of the important applications of Web Services is the standardized, platform-neutral exchange of business documents electronically between organizations. A significant aspect of this involves the shared access to and use of metadata descriptions for the documents themselves—in the form of a DTD or XML schema. One of the ultimate goals of the B2B approach is to define standard formats for various business documents, akin to those used in EDI.

Web Services is envisioned as enabling greatly expanded interoperability between trading partners, suppliers, and so on. One classic example is a product manufacturer who needs to interact with multiple suppliers to exchange information on raw materials and parts. The manufacturer is the central party, exchanging availability and inventory information from partners in a hub-and-spoke configuration. The hub is essentially a composition of the various participants.

Note that in this scenario, the partners need to engage in significant discussions and eventually reach consensus regarding document content, format, and even exchange schedules or approaches. At the end of all that process, there should result an XML schema that represents the format of the document that is used when exchanging data with that partner. If this *can* be the selected standard, all the better.

Thus, the result may be that there is an internal schema and a separate bridging schema used for each different partner. Ideally, all partner interactions utilize the internal schema, meaning that there is only one used. Realistically, the result will be something in between, with most partners having at least some specific format, interpretation, or other details.

This is really a B2B, electronic document interchange AntiPattern, but since this is a major use of Web Services, it is presented here.

General Form

This AntiPattern takes the form of a single XML schema that is selected to be the one, shared definition of a business document to be exchanged among multiple customers and partners. There are many standards groups, such as the Organization for the Advancement of Structered Information Standards (OASIS) and Electronic Business using XML (ebXML), and industry-specific groups, such as the Petroleum Industry Data Exchange (PIDX), that are attempting to define standardized business documents to support various core business processes and workflows. The AntiPattern is doing all the work of selecting one of these standards, but in the real world, this doesn't work, because each organization still ultimately has its own specific definition of the business document in terms of its attributes, data formats, and other elements. Thus, the initial architecture and design operates on the basis of utilizing a single XML schema, but some time into the implementation, the realization will occur that the system has to accommodate partner- or customer-specific schema variants, and it will be necessary to do transformations to and from their format.

Symptoms and Consequences

Issues that arise when collaborating on document formats and mechanisms are clues that the single schema approach may need adjusting. The specific symptoms and consequences of this approach include:

- **Most exchange partners or customers need their own specific schema.** What becomes apparent quickly in this sort of scenario is that most parties that will participate in the exchange will have their own definition of the business entity, although it may be very similar. As new partners are engaged, they have specific needs that require changes to the provided schema.
- **In order to deal with partner-specific differences, the Web Service implementation may have if-then-else type statements in the code.** When party-specific processing becomes necessary, the quick-and-dirty approach is to put branching statements in code, which branch on the parties' ID, and so on, and perform the distinct processing, mapping, and other functions. This ends up requiring the hard-coding of references to party ID and multiple similar code blocks, and as the number of parties increases, this becomes unmanageable from a maintenance perspective.
- **Some clients break.** If there are not bridging schemas for each of the other partners, then changes to the one schema will break existing partners (note that even if a partner doesn't use some element within the document, they still need to produce and consume documents against the current schema).
- **Data is sent in an incorrect format**. If a partner receives a generated document that does not conform to its format, the document handling may not work properly. There can also be more insidious errors when there are subtle differences in data formats, enumeration values used, and other details, such that the processing is completed, but slightly incorrect data is saved.
- **Additional, unplanned development is required.** There may be considerable refactoring and expansion of the Web Service implementation to support multiple schemas and transformations (such as using XSL). Recognizing this upfront will save time by building these requirements into the architecture and design from the outset.

Typical Causes

Conceptually, the idea of having a standardized document format applied across many parties is a good one. However, not understanding or putting enough importance on exposing differences between different parties' views and needs usually leads to this AntiPattern late in the process. Some of the reasons this occurs are:

- **Naivety, inexperience.** People who have any amount of B2B document interchanges with multiple partners (as the central participant) have experienced the reality of the standard document theory.

- **Early adopter of standards (or de facto, emerging standards).** The principles behind Web Services are sound, including the idea of standardized business documents. There are several bodies exerting a lot of effort in this regard, in various industries and for many important document types. However, the reality of this kind of effort is that it takes years to achieve some sort of standard that many participants are willing to accept (for example, EDI), and even in those cases, the kitchen sink approach usually ends up occurring, whereby there are a lot of optional elements. Thus, even with standards, it is very common to use specific processing to decide what optional elements are of interest.

Known Exceptions

The main exception to this AntiPattern occurs when the exchanges are all within a single organization. If all participating parties have basically identical schemas (for example, they are different departments or branch plants) then having one common document format can be enforced.

Refactorings

A refactoring solution takes an approach described by the Adaptor Design Pattern put forth by the Gang of Four (Gamma, Helm, Johnson, and Vlissides 1996), which involves injecting an adaptor component to let classes work together that couldn't do so otherwise because of incompatible interfaces. The Schema Adaptor refactoring, described later in this chapter, is an approach that introduces a format adaptor component within the overall processing flow to transform documents between external and internal formats. In this scheme, the external parties are allowed to have slightly different schemas and formats, and XSL transforms are defined for each external interaction, and are then used by the SchemaAdaptor to facilitate the transformations. XSL transformations are the most common and effective way to transform XML documents, so the basic function of the Schema Adaptor is to programmatically execute an appropriate XSL transformation. For each exchange partner that needs to retain its own document format, an XSL transform is defined to adapt the schema to the internal schema of the receiving J2EE application. This approach implies that there is an additional XML schema introduced here—one that represents the partner's format. The Web Service implementation must have access to this XML schema to allow parsing and transformation to the internal, standard XML schema for the business document. Note that if the exchanges are two-way with a particular partner, then there need to be two XSL transforms defined, one for each direction of the exchange.

Variations

There are no significant variations of this AntiPattern.

Example

Figure 9.5 depicts a miniexample of a typical application service provider (ASP) scenario, whereby the ASP exposes an important exchange function to its partners, allowing them to send in electronic orders. The diagram shows two different external clients, but in reality, there are usually more, and there could be many. This is typically referred to as a hub-and-spoke B2B document exchange situation, the ASP being the hub of exchanges to and from multiple parties.

As the diagram shows, each client is exchanging Order XML documents that are based on the same common document schema. This schema is also used by the ASP to parse and process the documents.

The AntiPattern situation here is that the external partners usually have their own variation of the Order schema, and, thus, would prefer (or sometimes demand) to send a document that conforms to their schema and require the ASP to handle any of the differences. Thus, this diagram might represent an initial model, but as the design and deployment progresses, it would become apparent that each partner would potentially want to utilize its own schema and force the architecture and design to change to accommodate that.

Related Solutions

There are no related solutions for this AntiPattern.

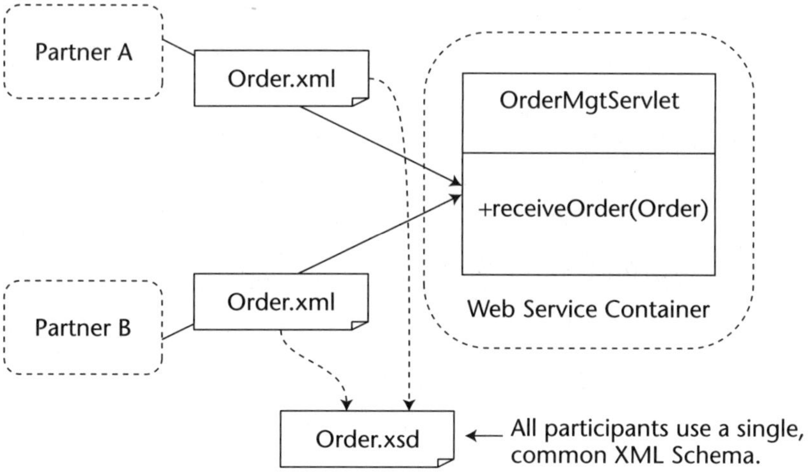

Figure 9.5 Single schema.

SOAPY Business Logic

Also Known As: Muddy Tiers

Most Frequent Scale: Application, architecture

Refactorings: Web Service Business Delegate

Refactored Solution Type: Software

Root Causes: Ignorance, sloth, apathy

Unbalanced Forces: Complexity, performance

Anecdotal Evidence: "Why should I care about multitier architecture when I'm just implementing a set of Web Services?"

Background

Incorporating Web Service interfaces into J2EE applications involves architectural and design decisions similar to those faced with other client interfaces such as servlets and JSPs. In this regard, some of the AntiPatterns that arise from those components may also manifest themselves in similar ways in Web Services. Specifically, implementing core business logic within a servlet (or a Web Service endpoint component) is usually a bad idea for any kind of significant enterprise application. This severely limits reuse by binding the business logic to tier-specific interfaces, classes, and data types. If a J2EE system has to support interactive end-user access (through Web-tier components) and automated client access (through Web Services), the common core business logic that supports both of these is typically factored out into a decoupled middle tier. In many cases, additional components are used to translate client-specific data and types (such as HttpRequest) into more neutral types (such as HashMap) to facilitate the separation and decoupling of the business logic components from overlying tiers.

Specifically in the area of Web Services, there are a number of tools now that automatically generate implementation artifacts from WSDLs or, conversely, allow an appropriately implemented J2EE component to serve as the implementation behind a Web Service interface. And for the most part, the interface and data types involved are not Web-specific. However, there are a few cases where, depending on the semantics and definition of the Web Service, there may still be some coupling to the Web tier. For instance, in JAX-RPC, built-in SOAP-Java data bindings will produce some Web-Service-specific Java types for the specified SOAP parts, such as XXHolder classes (for instance, FloatHolder), DataHandler (for MIME type data), and Source (for XML data within the MIME attachment).

EJB 2.1 specifies that Stateless Session Beans may be used to implement Web Service endpoints; however, if the SOAP envelope contains some of the elements mentioned above, a JAX-RPC supportive session interface *will* be coupled to Web Service usage because the associated Web-service-specific Java types will show up as method parameters. If the session operation implements important business logic, the coupling to Web Service types will limit the reuse of this business logic.

The basic gist of this AntiPattern is letting Web-Service-specific implementation types bleed into business logic components, limiting their reuse for other client types and contexts.

General Form

In this AntiPattern, a Web Service endpoint implements business logic, but is also coupled specifically to Web Service data types and/or contains an implementation that explicitly deals with SOAP/XML processing, severely reducing the reuse potential for the business logic.

This takes the form of either a servlet or Session Bean that has business logic implementation, but is also defined specifically as a Web Service endpoint. Depending on the additional infrastructure used (for example, JAX-RPC), this may just be the use of some Web-Service-specific data types; in other cases, the servlet or session may actually contain a number of processing steps that perform actions such as parsing and possibly transforming XML, binding XML to Java objects.

The litmus test for this AntiPattern is whether there are Web Services data types and/or processing tasks coupled together with core business logic of the J2EE system; if so, this undesirably couples together the Web Service implementation with business logic, and it will severely limit reuse.

Symptoms and Consequences

Web Services represent yet another client interaction approach in a J2EE system, and many of the symptoms and consequences around close coupling between the client tier and the middle tier emerge here. Some of the specific symptoms and consequences include:

- **Web-Service-specific data types are passed to business logic components.** Underlying business logic component interfaces and methods have arguments that are specific to the Web Service implementation, tools, and so on—for instance, passing a javax.activation.DataHandler type, that is, the JAX-RPC Java binding for a MIME type, to EJB.
- **Middle-tier business logic components perform XML-based processing.** This may include XML parsing, XSL transformation, or the construction of XML documents from application data, among other things.
- **Nonreusable business logic.** If the business logic components include an implementation that is specific to Web Services, Web Service APIs or tools, XML, and so on, then these will really not be usable for other client types. Most applications will have at least one other client tier (for example, a Web application client tier or Java thick client tier).
- **Redundant implementations of business logic.** If the reuse of business logic is difficult, a response may be to copy, paste, and modify the logic into a different component, effectively creating a different, redundant implementation.

Typical Causes

Web Services are yet another client interfacing mechanism, and many of the causes of poor separation between other client components (such as servlets and JSPs) and the middle tier are echoed here. The specific causes and details to watch for include:

- **Inexperience in architecting *n*-tier solutions.** Web Services are just another interface mechanism to get at business process logic. Experience developing multitier applications, especially when there is more than one client type involved, drives home the need to have clear separation between tiers and ensure that business process logic in the middle tier is not coupled in any way to any of the client or other overlying tiers.
- **Web Services-centric view.** When the immediate goal is specifically to implement a Web Service, then there may be insufficient consideration given to the potential of other types of clients that may eventually want or need to access the same business logic. Business logic that is closely coupled to a Web Service usage will be harder to reuse for other client types such as servlets, EJBs, and so on.

Known Exceptions

The only exception to this AntiPattern occurs when the system being developed is only to be specifically accessed via Web Services, and no other client tier is used (or going to be used). In this case, having poor separation between the Web Services components and business logic is not a big issue, because there are no other components attempting to access the same business logic. However, this determination is tricky, and a lot of one-off, quick-and-dirty systems have ended up being used for a long time, for multiple purposes. So, be wary of deciding that this is your situation.

Refactorings

The Business Delegate pattern as described by Alur, Crupi, and Malks (2001) has been commonly applied to decouple Web-client and middle-tier components. A variant of this, the Web Service Business Delegate found later in this chapter in the *Refactorings* section, can also be applied to Web Services to achieve a similar separation. In EJB 2.1, Web Service endpoints may be implemented using Stateless Session Beans or Java classes. The actual dispatching of Web Service requests is handled by the respective J2EE containers and JAX-RPC runtime, translating SOAP envelopes to appropriate Java data types and calling the appropriate operations. However, in effect, these components should then dispatch their requests to underlying business logic components, translating the information to and from Web-Service-specific data types in the process. Thus, the Web Service endpoint implementation class implements the appropriate data type conversions and coordinates calling down to business logic components.

Variations

A variation to this AntiPattern is Web-Service-specific JMS message handling. Web Service implementations may, in some cases, deliver their payload to JMS destinations. Some JMS vendors provide API extensions that allow the JMS message to be the SOAP envelope itself, and allow SOAP/XML-specific APIs on the message, for example, DOM interface, JAXM APIs, or Apache SOAP APIs. Using these elements couples the implementation of the JMS destination specifically to SOAP and more.

Another bad variation on this AntiPattern is actually including XML-based processing code within business logic components. Processing Web Service requests and returning responses ultimately involves a translation from Web-Services-specific data types, such as XML, to neutral forms (for example, Java objects, JavaBeans, or references to entity beans). XML usually needs to be parsed and translated, and in some cases, XSL-based transformation of XML is required before translation, or before sending responses back to client. This sort of processing should not be done in the sessions.

The sessions should be completely independent of Web Service semantics. This sort of adaptation is best handled through an intermediate processing class (for example, the Web Services Business Delegate described later in this chapter).

Another variation of this approach is implementing XML marshaling and unmarshaling within JavaBean implementations. JAX-RPC supports the XML-to-Java binding between complex XML schema types and JavaBean classes, but the JavaBean classes are required to be able to marshal and unmarshal themselves to and from XML; therefore, the implementations of these classes will have some dependency on XML parsing components.

Example

The diagram in Figure 9.6 shows an example of a Stateless Session Bean that is used as the implementation component for a Web Service. The Stateless Session Bean is used to directly receive the Web Services request as dispatched by the JAX-RPC runtime in the Web Services container. Because of the direct dispatching, the Session Bean interface operation has parameter types that are specifically coupled to JAX-RPC binding types for MIME attachments, effectively creating an operational signature that is Web Services-specific. This limits the Session Bean to being used only as a Web Service implementation component, limiting its reuse.

Related Solutions

There are no related solutions for this AntiPattern.

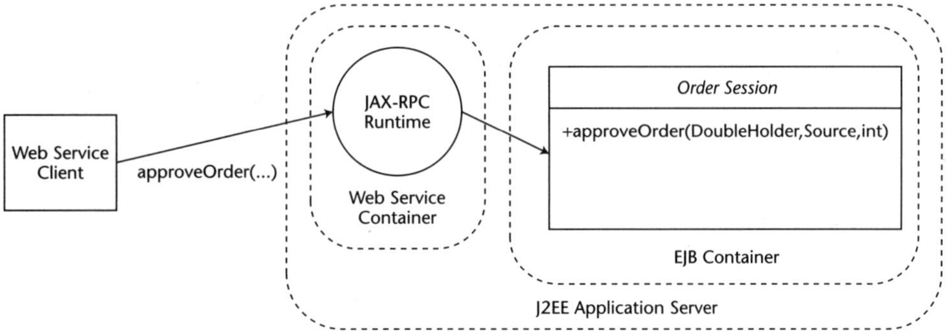

Figure 9.6 SOAPY business logic.

Refactorings

Web Services represent another way to execute the functionality within a J2EE system, essentially representing another kind of client tier. For this reason, a number of the AntiPatterns that arise in client components, such as JSPs and servlets, are also manifested in the Web Services tier. In general, many of the client-tier related AntiPatterns have to do with embedding business logic in the client tier, and tight coupling between client and middle tier. The refactorings for these issues are similar as well, focusing on creating adaptors and intermediary components to decouple the tiers and push core business logic and process down into the middle tier, where they can be most flexibly used and reused. The takeaway here is that AntiPatterns and refactorings that deal with client-tier issues will show up with Web Services, and so solutions in those areas are useful to consider when doing Web Services design and refactoring.

Another significant aspect of Web Service AntiPatterns is the fact that they are another interface mechanism, and a number of AntiPatterns and refactorings that have emerged in the usage of distributed components, for example, EJBs, are also germane to Web Services. For instance, the chatty interface problem with Entity beans and the use of Session façade used to solve it have relevance to Web Services. Again, some of the problems and solutions for effective distributed object design are also applicable to Web Services.

The following refactorings provide solutions to some of the AntiPatterns described earlier in this chapter:

RPC to Document Style. This refactors a CRUD-style Web Service interaction that is implemented as a synchronous, RPC-styled approach into a document style, asynchronous approach, which is more natural and appropriate for CRUD operations on business documents.

Schema Adaptor. This refactoring introduces an adaptor component within the handling of electronic document exchanges with multiple parties, to adapt differences between business document formats.

Web Service Business Delegate. This refactoring interjects an intervening Java component between a Web Service endpoint receiver (usually a servlet) and an underlying business logic component, such as a Session Bean, to remove WebService-specific handling code from the business logic component and/ or to remove WebService-specific data types and coupling from the component to facilitate easier reuse.

RPC to Document Style

A synchronous RPC-style Web Service operation implements a CRUD-type operation with a lot of parameters, custom types, and/or SOAP document fragments, leading to significant implementation effort, problems related to unmarshaling of complex types, and poor performance due to heavy synchronous interactions.

Change the Web Service definition to document style, and translate the data exchange to an XML document and asynchronous message delivery.

```
  <soap:binding style="rpc"
transport="http://schemas.xmlsoap.org/soap/http"/>
  <operation name="createEntity">
<soap:operation soapAction=""/>
       <input>
          <soap:header message="entity" part="attribute1" use="encoded"
             encodingStyle="http://schemas.xmlsoap.org/soap/encoding/"/>
          <soap:header message="entity" part="relation1" use="encoded"
             encodingStyle="http://schemas.xmlsoap.org/soap/encoding/"/>
          <!-- more attributes and complex relationships -->
        </input>
     </operation>
```

Listing 9.2 Before RPC to Document Style refactoring.

```
  <soap:binding style="document"
transport="http://schemas.xmlsoap.org/soap/http"/>
  <operation name="createEntity">
<soap:operation soapAction=""/>
       <input>
          <soap:body parts="body" use="literal"/>
       </input>
   </operation>
```

Listing 9.3 After RPC to Document Style refactoring.

Motivation

This refactoring provides a solution to the Maybe It's Not RPC AntiPattern described in this chapter. There are two basic types of invocation styles that are supported with Web Services: RPC and Document. RPC style is intended for method invocation, whereas document style is intended for B2B document exchanges. However, the line between these two isn't exactly crisp. Method calls can and are used to update various attributes associated with an entity, and documents can contain process or action directives to enable content-based processing, effectively executing a specific method with the remaining document content as the parameter.

The use of the document-style exchange model is motivated by several issues. First, the RPC-style model defines a specific interface with arguments, types, and so on. As changes occur, this interface changes, and clients that are coupled to it need to be updated or they break. Document style always just passes a document, so the actual mechanical interface doesn't change, just the content of the document itself. Second, validation of the data being sent or received is easier with XML documents, because a validating XML parser can quickly attempt to parse them and determine where any parts of the document violate the associated XML schema. RPC-style validations require much more of an element-by-element approach. Finally, actions can be included in the document itself, enabling content-based processing, and removing the specific action or handling indicator from the SOAP header itself. When actions are added or changed, only the content of the document and the back-end handlers change, not the mechanisms that generate or parse the SOAP headers.

Mechanics

The basic mechanics of this refactoring are to convert a calling style that has separate data elements and actions that are related to each other so that, instead, a single XML document is created or received. The RPC approach is a traditional method using a synchronous invocation style with an action, parameters, and a return type. The Document approach is more of an asynchronous, message-passing approach, which uses bulk operations to generate a document (for example, out of a database or Java instance) and conversely to receive and handle whole documents in a coarser-grained fashion. The following list describes the various steps for refactoring an RPC-style approach to a document style:

1. *Define an XML schema for the document*. The first change is to establish and use an external document schema to refer to the document (instead of an included type definition within the WSDL: Define XML Schema for Document). This needs to include all the attributes that were being passed as parameters. Publish the XML schema to a network-accessible location.

2. *Make WSDL changes*. Then, a few specific changes are needed to the Web Service definition to define a document-oriented, one-way invocation: Be sure to include a namespace declaration for the external XML schema representing the document, then change the message element so that it indicates a body part, and set the element attribute to the type of the root type within the XML

schema. Change the operational definition so that it only indicates an input message (for example, define it as a one-way message), and change the style attribute value for the operation to document. Note that this can be done at the soap:binding level (applying it to all operations) or at the specific operation to affect it only. Change the soap:operation binding definition to define the soap:body element so that it refers to the parts to be included, and set encoding = literal to include the document without any further encoding.

3. *Make service endpoint changes.* The Web Service endpoint implementation may need to change (depending on the specific tools used) to support handling an XML document instead of unmarshaled, separate parameters. JAXB may need to be introduced to support the binding of the XML document to a root entity instance, related objects, and other elements.
4. *Make service client changes (for each client).* Client implementations will need to change to create an XML document conformant to the XML schema and use it in the invocation of the Web Service. Note that the JAXM API provides more explicit support for asynchronous messaging through the use of providers. JAXM client and provider combinations may be deployed to a J2EE Web container or J2EE EJB container to facilitate the asynchronous message style.

Example

The following walkthrough applies this refactoring to the example presented earlier in the Maybe It's Not RPC AntiPattern description.

First, an XML schema is defined for the Order entity. In our small example in Listing 9.4, the Order entity is a very simple set of attributes, but the following example shows you what the XML schema looks like:

```
<xs:schema
     xmlns:xs=http://www.w3.org/2001/XMLSchema
     elementFormDefault="qualified" attributeFormDefault="unqualified">
     <xs:element name="Order" type="OrderType"/>
     <xs:complexType name="OrderType">
            <xs:complexContent>
                  <xs:sequence>
                    <xs:element name="product" type="xs:string"/>
                      <xs:element name="quantity" type="xs:double"/>
                    <xs:element name="customer" type="xs:string"/>
            </xs:sequence>
          </xs:complexContent>
      </xs:complexType>
</xs:schema>
```

Listing 9.4 Order XML schema.

The XML schema declares a complex type called OrderType, which includes three elements to hold the product, quantity, and customer name.

Next, you need to make a number of changes to the WSDL so that it describes the operation as a document-oriented operation (these are indicated by boldface in Listing 9.5). First, the Order schema reference is included in the definitions section, so that the WSDL can locate the schema. Note that the URL of the schema is a specific, network-accessible HTTP location. Next, the message definition is changed to declare that the body is a part of type Order, based on the imported XML schema. Also, the operation definition is changed to a one-way message (for example, an asynchronous message), and the style attribute is changed to *document*. Finally, the SOAP binding of the operation is changed so that the parts attribute refers to *body* (for example, the message declared earlier in the WSDL), and the encoding is changed to *literal*.

```
<definitions
     targetNamespace="urn:order"
     xmlns="http://schemas.xmlsoap.org/wsdl/"
     xmlns:xsd="http://www.w3.org/2001/XMLSchema"
     xmlns:orderNS="http://www.myStuff.org/Order.xsd"
     xmlns:soap="http://schemas.xmlsoap.org/wsdl/soap"
     xmlns:soapenc="http://schemas.xmlsoap.org/soap/encoding/"
     xmlns:tns="urn:order" >
<types>
</types>
<message name="order">
     <part name="body" element="orderNS:Order" />
</message>
<portType name="orderManager">
     <!--one-way operations (client initiated) -->
     <operation name="createOrder">
          <input message="order"/>
     </operation>
</portType>
<binding name="orderBinding" type="tns:orderManager">
  <soap:binding style="document"
transport="http://schemas.xmlsoap.org/soap/http"/>
  <operation name="createOrder">
<soap:operation soapAction=""/>
        <input>
            <soap:body parts="body" use="literal"/>
        </input>
   </operation>
</binding>
</definitions>
```

Listing 9.5 RPC refactored to document style.

The next steps in this refactoring are to make any necessary changes in the Web Service endpoint and client implementations to support doing a document-style, asynchronous interaction. This is dependent on the Web Service implementation tools used, either JAX-RPC, JAXM, or something else, so the detail of these changes will be specific to those tools. However, in general, the change to a document-style approach means that the client will utilize some tool to generate an entire XML document, based on the XML schema, usually by gathering data from user input or a database query, or by fetching an instance of an Entity Bean.

Schema Adaptor

A single XML schema is used as the common XML document definition for exchanges between multiple business parties. However, many of the parties need some unique attributes or data formats, rendering the single-schema approach unworkable.

Introduce an adaptor component in the Web Service implementation to transform partner-specific XML format to an internal format when receiving messages, and transform the internal format to a partner format for outgoing ones.

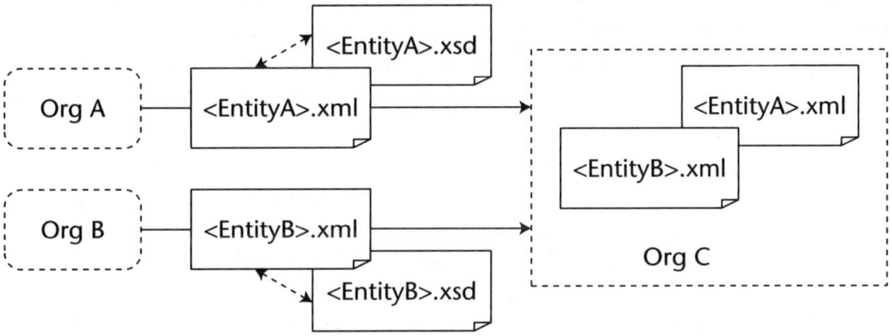

Figure 9.7 Before refactoring.

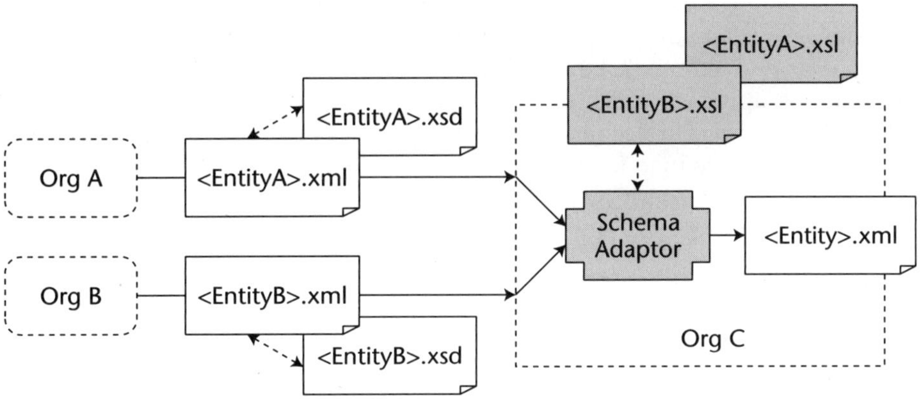

Figure 9.8 After refactoring.

Motivation

In many B2B scenarios, there are significant business entities that are exchanged between parties as XML documents. Often, the partners have already defined their own electronic document formats and schemas, and wish to continue to use them. However, the receipt of the documents should ideally be handled in the same way, regardless of the actual source. Also, if a particular partner decides to make a change to the format, this should not have any effect on other partners. Thus, the ideal situation is to be able to allow partners to transmit documents in their own format (and change the format when they need to), but to transform those documents into a single, standard, internal format that is used in the actual processing.

In order to facilitate document interchange on a practical level among many parties, a document exchange Web Service needs to be able to consume a document encoded with a foreign schema, and process and transform that document into an internal schema.

Note that this refactoring approach is suitable for those situations where there are only small differences between partner and internal formats, that is, a few additional fields required, possibly one not used, and so on. The SchemaAdaptor must be able to transform a document from a partner format to an internal format, so this implies that all mandatory data in the internal format must be represented in the partner format *or* that the XSL transform itself must be able to generate suitable values. So, each of the partner schemas should be similar, differing only in the inclusion of nonmandatory fields, data format variations, and similar aspects. This refactoring provides a solution to the Single-Schema Dream AntiPattern, described previously.

Mechanics

This refactoring solution amounts to introducing a transformer component within the XML document processing flow, and programmatically utilizing partner-specific XSL transforms to transform the document from an external partner format to an internal, partner-independent format. The key steps and details involved in implementing this refactoring are included in the following list.

Note that this approach relies on the concept that, when multiple parties are exchanging the same *kind* of document, such as a purchase order, *most* of the elements will be similar enough to map to one, common form (for example, PONumber in one schema is equivalent to OrderID in another).

1. *Implement the SchemaAdaptor Java component*. The SchemaAdaptor is simply a Java class that programmatically implements an XSL transform against an XML document. JAXP actually supplies an API to do the transformation itself, so all this class really has to do is locate the appropriate partner-specific transform and use the JAXP transformation method. The internal implementation needs to be able to locate the appropriate partner-specific XSL transform (.xsl file), based on a passed-in partner ID and the document type. The XSL documents themselves must be organized in a way that is keyed to a partner identifier [for instance, by a Data Universal Numbering System (DUNS) number] to enable

locating and fetching the appropriate transform. So, the SchemaAdaptor API must take a partner identifier as a parameter, supplied by the caller. This implies that the initial recipient of the document (for example, the Web Service servlet) must be able to identify the sending client partner, usually by extracting the required information from the SOAP header. Thus, the effort associated with adding a new partner amounts to defining a new XSL transform for it and storing it in the standard, retrievable location.

2. *Define and organize partner-specific XSL transforms*. Each exchange partner will need an XSL transform document (for example, an .xsl file) to facilitate transforming the document from its format to the one, internal format. The organization and retrieval of the partner-specific XSL transforms may be done by storing the information in a DB or in some structured file-system location that the SchemaAdaptor can read, keyed to the partner ID.

3. *Define or use partner-specific XML schemas*. In order to receive and transform the partner-formatted documents, the SchemaAdaptor must have access to the partner-specific XML schema. As mentioned previously, in many cases, these schemas are already in place, so the task is to simply ensure that they are network accessible (so that the partner-format XSD reference can be resolved by the Web Service). In other cases, the partner may be just adopting EDI, so completing the implementation will require that it define the XML schema for its own document format.

4. *Update the Web Service implementation to use the SchemaAdaptor*. The implementation of the actual document-receiving Web Service is updated so that it calls the SchemaAdaptor to render a uniform document format for subsequent processing as before. This should replace any if-then-else, partner-specific code that may have crept in. As mentioned previously, the Web Service itself also has to be able to pass on an identifier for the partner. This may be contained within the SOAP envelope or within the enclosed business document, or it may even be determined by getting that information directly from a certificate if certificate-based, X.509 interactions are supported.

Example

The following example provides a walkthrough of the way that this refactoring is applied. First, the SchemaAdaptor component is required to facilitate the programmatic transformations between the external and internal schemas. This component is simply a POJO that utilizes the XSL transformation capabilities of JAXP to take an input XML document, locate the appropriate XSL transform, and apply it to produce a transformed XML document. The key elements here include the location of a customer-specific XSL file (keyed to the customerId) and the actual transformation of the input document (passed in as an instance of type Reader), to return a transformed XML document. The code for the SchemaAdaptor is shown as follows in Listing 9.6:

```
import javax.xml.transform.Transformer;
import javax.xml.transform.TransformerFactory;
public class SchemaAdaptor {
     public static Reader transform(int customerId, Reader in) {

          // First, locate applicable XSL transform
          // This is unique to the customer:
          // (Note: getTransform impl assumed...)
          String fName = getTransform(customerId);
          FileReader file = new FileReader(fName);
          StreamSource src = new StreamSource(file);

          // Set up the transformation stuff:
          TransformerFactory fact = TransformerFactory.newInstance();
          Transformer trans = fact.newTransformer(src);

          // Perform the transformation:
          StringWriter out = new StringWriter();
          StreamResult res = new StreamResult(out);
          trans.transform(new StreamSource(in), res);

          StringReader result = new StringReader(out.toString());

          return result;
     }
}
```

Listing 9.6 SchemaAdaptor listing.

The next step in implementing this process is to establish a location for the partner-specific XSL transform files so that the SchemaAdaptor can locate them based on the identified customer that is executing the exchange. This process is often implemented by using a file structure that is keyed to the customer ID, for example. At a predefined base location, there will be one folder for each customer, named for its customer ID and containing XSL documents. Note that there may be several XSL documents within a folder for each distinct business type to be exchanged.

The next step is simply to ensure that the incoming XML documents reference accessible XML schemas, so that when they are processed by the Web Service, the parser can validate using the schema. Usually, the external party will expose these schemas at an HTTP-accessible location by itself. But, this step is necessary to ensure that those partners understand that their schemas have to be publicly accessible for this whole process to work.

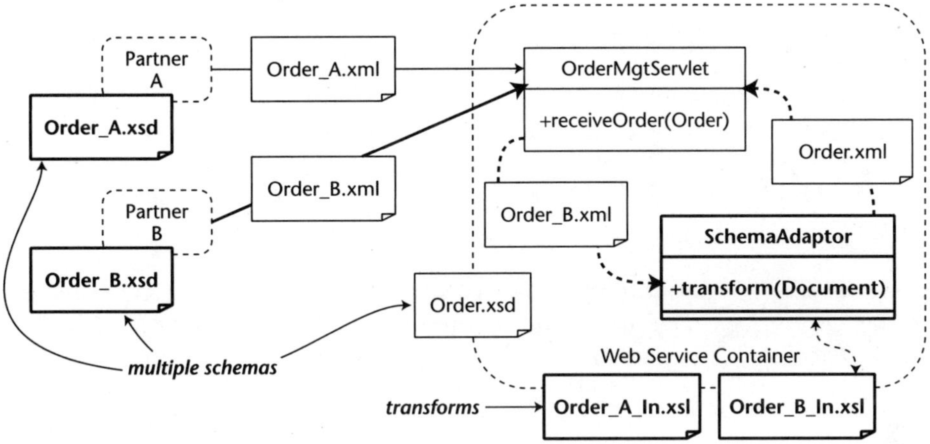

Figure 9.9 Schema adaptor refactoring example.

The final step is to update the Web Service endpoint implementation so that it uses the SchemaAdaptor to transform the incoming documents to the internal format *before* passing on to other processing steps or components. Given the implementation above, there are three steps necessary to add into your existing Web Service implementation. First, a customer identifier of some kind needs to be obtained so that it can be passed into the SchemaAdaptor and be used to locate the correct XSL. Usually, the SOAP header includes some type of caller identification. Alternately, in many cases, these kinds of important B2B document exchanges occur over HTTPS using certificate-based authentication, so the certificate can be examined to provide the caller's identity. Next, the received XML document must be provided as an instance of Reader; there are a number of types of Readers, including StringReader and FileReader, that can be instantiated from the input to pass to the SchemaAdaptor. Finally, the output comes back as a Reader, but this can be converted to a String, File, and so on, if need be.

The diagram in Figure 9.9 depicts the refactoring of the single schema to use the SchemaAdaptor and party-specific schemas and transforms.

Web Service Business Delegate

J2EE system components (servlets, Session EJBs) are used as the underlying implementation for a Web Service, containing the core business logic of the system. However, those components are coupled to Web-Service-specific tasks and data types (for example, SOAP, XML, JAX-RPC), severely limiting the reuse of that business logic by other clients.

Interject an adaptor component between the Web Service container handler servlet and the underlying business logic component to decouple the business logic component from the Web Service tier and allow it to be reused by a variety of clients.

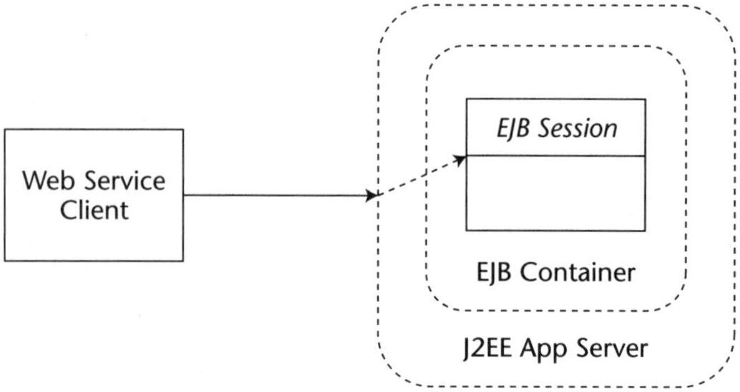

Figure 9.10 Before refactoring.

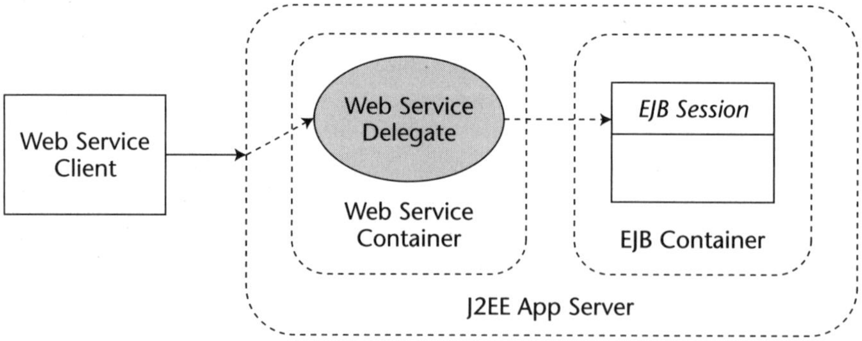

Figure 9.11 After refactoring.

Motivation

Business process logic should generally not be coupled to any particular client-tier mechanism, because of the concrete or likely future goal of utilizing that logic for different client types, and so on. There are many J2EE applications that support an interactive, Web-based way of creating or updating business objects *and* support Web Service access to do the same thing in an automated way. It is therefore important for these kinds of processes to be completely decoupled and independent of a specific client tier.

Also, when handling and processing requests to Web Services, a number of specific actions may need to occur before the actual business process logic can be executed, such as parsing and validating the incoming XML document, possibly performing a transformation to other document formats (as in the SchemaAdaptor refactoring above), and binding the document to Java objects from XML. If the business logic is bound up with these Web-Service-specific actions, that business logic will only be usable in that context. This refactoring provides a solution to the SOAPY Business Logic AntiPattern described previously.

One additional motivation for this refactoring is to support content-based processing and dispatching. In this approach, some part of the content (for example, the SOAP header field) is used to indicate what specific component should be dispatched to satisfy the request. Having an intermediary delegate class provides a convenient place to implement general-purpose content-based dispatching.

Mechanics

As in the Business Delegate Pattern, this refactoring involves introducing an intervening Java delegate class between a client and the actual back-end process component, along with performing the following steps:

1. *Define a new servlet class to be the handler for the Web Service.* This class will become the Web Service delegate.
2. *Create a servlet implementation to perform Web Service-related processing.* The implementation of the servlet service() method should be implemented to contain any of the steps from the existing implementation component that pertain specifically to Web Service, SOAP, and XML handling (such as XML parsing, XSL transformation, XML-to-Java binding operations, or reading SOAP headers to perform dispatching). In the case of a Session endpoint (as handled through JAX-RPC), this is unnecessary, because the session will not include any implementations of this nature.
3. *Create a servlet implementation to convert Web-Services-specific data types to types applicable for middle-tier Session Beans.* For Session endpoints handled by JAX-RPC, the Web Service delegate still may need to include an implementation to transform or convert Web Services-specific data types to standard Java data types or application types like entity DTOs. The extent to which this will be

needed is dependent on the specifics of the data being passed down to the session. The general rule to follow here is that the session interface and implementation should not include any references to JAX-RPC data types. If it does, then the implementation should be included in the Web Service delegate to perform the appropriate conversion.

Example

The diagram in Figure 9.12 shows the refactoring of the direct interaction with a Session bean to insert the Web Service Delegate (shown in bold) in front of the bean.

To apply this refactoring, first a servlet class has been introduced called the OrderDelegate, which is configured to be the handler for the Web Service operation. This servlet implements the same approveOrder() method as the session previously did, because the JAX-RPC framework is invoking it in exactly the same way when a request is received.

Finally, the approveOrder() method is implemented to extract the relevant data from the Web Services data types of DoubleHolder, Source, and int, and instantiates an instance of OrderDTO. Then, it invokes the underlying Session method with the OrderDTO instance.

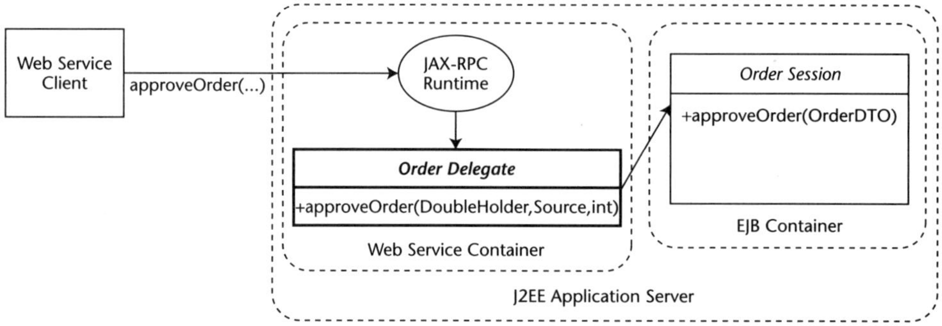

Figure 9.12 Web Service business delegate example.

CHAPTER 10

J2EE Services

J2EE has grown into a large package of development libraries and technology standards. The other chapters in this book focus on some of the more popular technologies in detail. This chapter focuses on J2EE in general and the mistakes that can be made at this more fundamental level. In particular, developers need to watch out for underleveraging J2EE or overleveraging native code.

The following AntiPatterns focus on the problems and mistakes that many developers make with some of the more fundamental J2EE technologies, such as JNDI, JNI, and WebStart, and with J2EE development in general. These AntiPatterns cross the boundaries between other chapters, like servlets and JSPs, and focus on the technologies like JNDI, which are used in numerous places within J2EE.

As with most things, J2EE programming requires knowledge to avoid mistakes. Many of the common problems that people have are caused by not understanding the alternatives that J2EE offers. Topics covered include the following:

Hard-Coded Location Identifiers. JNDI provides a simple means of looking up contact, connection, and location information. However, even the JNDI connection information should be configurable so that developers don't have to recompile code every time a network change occurs.

Web = HTML. Many people, not just J2EE developers, associate the Web with HTML. This is simply not the case. There are a number of ways to leverage J2EE and the Web that don't require the developer to use HTML or Web page user interfaces.

Requiring Local Native Code. Native code, code that isn't written in Java, is a fact of life. Some systems can only be accessed from code in native libraries. Legacy systems may have core algorithms in native code that must be reused. However, using native code via the Java Native Interface, JNI, is not the only choice. It can, in fact, be the worst choice in many cases.

Overworking JNI. When you use the JNI, there are some particular issues when interfacing with J2EE applications. Many simple JNI implementations overwork the JNI interface and cause performance degradation as a result.

Choosing the Wrong Level of Detail. J2EE provides several layers of technology. For example, you can write an application that uses RMI directly or use a Session Bean that you access with RMI. Choosing the wrong level to work at will affect the reliability and overall performance of your final solution.

Not Leveraging EJB Containers. The EJB concept has been improved with every update to the J2EE standards. These beans represent a great programming model for leveraging existing services such as load balancing, fault tolerance, and data storage. When possible, developers should leverage the bean containers' services to improve their application without additional work on their part.

Hard-Coded Location Identifiers

Also Known As: String Constants, Hard-Coded Strings

Most Frequent Scale: Application

Refactorings: Parameterize Your Solution

Refactored Solution Type: Process, code

Root Causes: Sloth

Unbalanced Forces: Time versus design

Anecdotal Evidence: "Why do I have to recompile the code to change the database user login?"

Background

In GUI programming, Java developers who are not used to the localization process will often put strings for menu names and buttons in their code. This technique is easy. It puts the string where you need it. But, when a translator tries to translate the program to Spanish or Japanese, these hard-coded strings are terrible to deal with. The solution is to use resource bundles and property files to store strings that the user sees. Then the programmer loads the strings from the correct bundle.

This same concept applies to enterprise applications. In particular, this idea of externalizing strings, or parameterizing the application, is extremely important as J2EE applications move through the testing and production stages. Often testing is performed against a different machine or database than the production system. Storing the connection information for a database in the code itself will result in recompiles during staging. Recompiling is an opportunity to introduce errors and should be avoided whenever a system is being moved from test to production. Therefore, hard-coding location identifiers, while easy to do and commonplace, can lead to instability, making it a prime example of an AntiPattern.

General Form

Hard-coded location identifiers generally occur in applications that are built from prototypes or built quickly. Perhaps a JSP developer needs to access a database and so includes the connection information on the page, as shown below.

```
Connection con =
DriverManager.getConnection("jdbc:cloudscape:rmi:CloudscapeDB",
                            "stephen","stephen");
```

Perhaps a JMS developer builds the JNDI connection information right into the application code. In all cases, the strings that define the information required to connect to other elements in a J2EE solution are included in the program instead of in separate configuration files.

Symptoms and Consequences

The primary indicator of hard-coded location identifiers is that they are in the Java code. The primary consequence is that you have to recompile the code to change them. Thus, you should look for the following symptoms in your code:

- **You are storing location identifiers in Java code.** It is easy to build identifiers into your code. This may be accomplished in a number of ways, all with the same result. First, you can just include connection information as strings in the code where you connect. Second, you can use static variables to hold connection information. Finally, you can put connection information in ListResourceBundles. This last technique is not as bad as the first two, because the bundles can be recompiled separately from other code, but it still requires compilation and Java programming knowledge to make a change.

- **Identifiers are in JNDI but JNDI connection information is hard-coded.** Sometimes JNDI provides a false sense of flexibility. Just because the JMS connection information is in JNDI doesn't mean that you can hard-code the JNDI information safely. What it means is that you have less connection information to load dynamically.
- **Changes to connection information require a recompile.** When connection information is hard-coded, you have to recompile the code to change it.
- **Configurations can't be resold.** In a consulting or resale situation, you might have a solution that uses J2EE configurations. If the code you provide hard-codes connection information, such as a database name in a JSP, the user has to open these files to reconfigure them.

Typical Causes

Hard-coded identifiers are generally caused by a shortage of time or experience. Developers hard-code things because they are in a hurry and it is faster, or they don't know any better and it is easy. So the question is, "Why do developers rush over the location identifiers?" There are a number of reasons:

- **The solution is built over time.** As with any other problem, you may create hard-coded identifiers when you build a solution over time. Perhaps you start with a prototype under hard time constraints and build that into a real application. Old implementations can get left inside the final solution.
- **JNDI is seen as a buffer.** Sometimes people think of JNDI as a buffer against hard-coding locations. While this is true, JNDI itself involves location identifiers that should be parameterized.
- **Lack of education or experience.** New developers may not realize the consequences of using hard-coded location identifiers and include them without understanding the inevitable results.
- **Marginalizing locations.** Every location that you hard-code could result in a problem. This includes JNDI servers, database servers, and URLs on Web pages. You can't say one kind isn't important just because of the type of location you are storing.

Known Exceptions

In most cases, the URLs on Web pages don't need to be parameterized. This is true of HTML and JSPs. In the cases where you do think the link might change, the easiest way to handle that is a redirect script on the server so that the pages don't have to change for the ultimate target to change.

Refactorings

The primary solution to hard-coded location identifiers is to use the Parameterize Your Application refactoring, as discussed in the refactoring section of this chapter. This can mean using configuration parameters in an .ear file deployment, or creating property files for loading information. You might also look at creating configuration pages that set the values for important information by messaging with the application that is making connections.

Variations

There are a lot of possible locations in an application. JNDI servers, database servers, usernames, passwords, URLs, and so on all provide location and connection information. All of these can be hard-coded or parameterized in most cases.

Example

Imagine that you are creating an application like the one in Figure 10.1. In this case, a set of JSPs are communicating with a set of session EJBs, which in turn send messages to a custom application that does JDBC calls to a database.

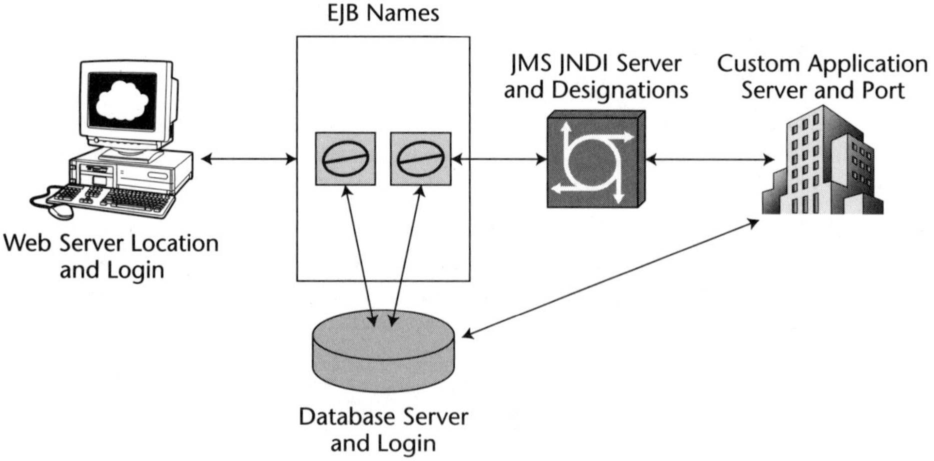

Figure 10.1 Sample locations.

There are a lot of location identifiers in this example, including the JNDI connection information for the JSPs and the EJBs, the names of the EJBs, the name of the JMS queue, the database server, username and password, and possibly some of the database table names. The AntiPattern will exist if these values are hard-coded, for example, if the JSPs hard-code the JNDI connection information, or the EJBs hard-code the JMS queue names.

A better solution, after the refactoring, will use deployment-level configuration for the JNDI connection information, the names of the queue, and the names of the EJBs. The custom application won't have these configuration parameters available to it, so you might use command-line arguments to configure the database connection information, or a properties file.

Related Solutions

Handling location identifiers correctly is a part of the planning ahead and general design work that goes into a good distributed application, as discussed in Chapter 1. Like this chapter, Chapter 1 is focused on general concepts in J2EE and solutions such as network applications, and provides a lot of useful refactorings, including Plan Ahead and Choose the Right Data Architecture. The refactorings in Chapter 1 aren't specific to J2EE technologies, but will help prepare you and your application for the refactorings in this chapter.

Web = HTML

Also Known As: Web Applications Mean Web Pages

Most Frequent Scale: Application

Refactorings: Match the Client to the Customer

Refactored Solution Type: Process, architecture

Root Causes: Marketing fever, underplanning, lack of design

Unbalanced Forces: Customer requests, elegance, design

Anecdotal Evidence: "This application is hard to use." "Why do we have to wait every time we click a button?"

Background

As the Web became popularized, many companies realized what a powerful application platform it represented. But there were some issues with the responsiveness of HTML-based user interfaces. With the introduction of Java, people thought that they could use applets as the necessary addition to Web applications that would allow full-featured programs to be loaded seamlessly on every client machine. Unfortunately, the reality wasn't the same as the marketing.

Instead, people discovered that applets ran into version issues, and that large applets had numerous load-time constraints. Moreover, the addition of JavaScript, Flash, and other client-side technologies seemed to make HTML a sufficient user interface platform. But that isn't always the case. Some applications require a richer interface than the one a Web page can provide. Also, there are applications that can be implemented either as Web pages or full-blown applications, but work better in an application than a Web page. To make the right decisions, application developers have to look at their users' needs, not just at the available technology. Put bluntly, always using HTML for your application user interface is wrong, and doing so is caused by assuming that using the Web means using HTML, making that assumption an AntiPattern.

General Form

J2EE applications that fall victim to the Web = HTML AntiPattern will have a browser-based interface that uses HTML. But this interface is likely to require extensive use of dynamic HTML, Flash, applets, or ActiveX controls. As a whole, the interface will probably be hard to use for some tasks and rough around the edges in general. The reason for these difficulties is that the designer will have pushed the tools beyond what they are designed to support. Put simply, the developers assumed that to use the Web they had to use a browser and HTML and ended up creating a complex solution when an easier one was available.

Symptoms and Consequences

Problems with Web = HTML applications range from user difficulties to poor performance. Although performance is one possible metric for determining if you suffer from this AntiPattern, it is not a true litmus test. Rather, you have to look at the choices that led up to using HTML. Did you have an alternative, and was HTML the best choice? In order to make this determination, you must look deeper at the solution you created to see if it matches one of the following symptoms. A match may indicate that you are using HTML when it isn't the best choice.

- **You are using a lot of dynamic HTML.** Web sites that have extensive dynamic HTML and lots of client-side scripting, such as JavaScript, can easily push the limits of truly portable, well-coded Web interfaces and cross into the realm of browser-specific applications.

- **Your application relies on custom browser plug-ins like ActiveX controls.** The real value of Web-based applications is in their ease of deployment. They place few requirements on the user. By using specific browser plug-ins, you are limiting your clients. This may look okay in the short term but becomes a real problem over time.
- **User experience problems with your application.** Web applications are great for displaying catalogs of information, accepting simple form input, and performing some basic user interactions. But complex user interactions, such as using drag-and-drop and menus, can be klunky when implemented with dynamic HTML. This can reduce the user experience and, as a result, the efficiency with which people perform their work.
- **Your application doesn't support all of the major browsers.** When you rely on HTML as the primary interface framework, you can accidentally make the interface browser specific. Over time, if you add users, your original assumptions about browsers can prove faulty.

Typical Causes

Generally, the Web = HTML AntiPattern is caused by managers, architects, developers, or some other member of the project team's desire to mark off a check box that they think exists for J2EE applications. This check box says that Web applications are HTML applications. This isn't true, but it is a common misconception caused by one of three things.

- **A mental check box.** Often people think that enterprise applications should be Web applications, which have to use HTML as the interface vehicle. This attitude and misunderstanding can lead to a check-box mentality whereby HTML is not a choice but a perceived requirement. This check-box mentality comes from a lot of marketing hype that surrounds the Web.
- **User interface design inexperience.** People graduating from computer science programs around the country and developers moving from a mainframe background into the J2EE development environment will often have little experience with designing for a good user experience. This can result in compromises and poor design chooses that allow an HTML interface where one shouldn't be used.
- **Management design.** Managers in today's IT departments have heard a lot of talk about the value of Web applications over the old-style client server programs. Some of the praise for Web programs is completely justified, and Web applications based on HTML are a great solution for many problems. But they are just one tool, not the only tool in a great designer's toolbox.

Known Exceptions

There are a number of great applications that use HTML as their primary vehicle. Companies like Amazon, Yahoo, Google, and the now defunct WebVan all provide powerful HTML front ends to the services they market. HTML isn't the problem, having an HTML-only attitude is. These companies don't try to reach beyond the capabilities of HTML, so it provides all of its benefits with few restrictions. Essentially, they choose to create applications that fit in the HTML world well, and as a result they have not really encountered the AntiPattern.

In one sense, there really aren't exceptions to a faulty assumption. The Web isn't just about HTML, but that doesn't mean you can't create great HTML applications. It means you can't force applications into HTML just because they will be used on the Web.

Refactorings

The solution to a Web = HTML AntiPattern is to do some good old user interface design. Talk to users; find out what they need to do. Build prototypes and work with users to see if you have captured their requirements. See what type of user interface works best. Try applets for small dynamic areas in a Web page. Try dynamic HTML, as long as it doesn't go so far that it becomes browser specific or hard to maintain. Try out a full-blown Java client. Swing provides a powerful framework for building a full-featured application for the user; if you don't like Swing, there are alternatives available on the Web. If you need to deal with deployment and updates, you can leverage WebStart to perform automated deployments and caching of your client applications. WebStart is a great compromise between applets that load every time the user launches them and clients that require installation.

The bottom line is that you have to refactor your application to match the client to the customer, as discussed in the refactoring section. You have to keep an open mind and avoid the Web = HTML trap that is so easy to fall into.

Variations

In the same way that companies can latch onto HTML as the one right Web technology, they can do the same thing with other J2EE technologies. Some companies may see RMI as the one true messaging protocol and miss a solution that would be easier to implement with CORBA or JMS. With the advent of Web Services, there has been a move to make everything a Web Service. But JMS offers a number of advantages over the current Web Service standards like HTTP and SOAP, primarily guaranteed delivery. The bottom line for this AntiPattern is that you want to pick the best choice, not focus on the most common or most hyped choice as the only one.

Example

A great example of how this AntiPattern can come into play is email. A lot of people get their email using a browser. This solution allows them to check their email anywhere without placing a lot of requirements on their computer. So many people would say that these email programs are a good idea. Most people would say that Eudora, Outlook, or Evolution—all standalone applications for reading email—are also good ideas. So, we have two approaches to the same problem from different angles. As a result, both types of email provide a great example of the kind of design decisions that a J2EE developer faces when creating a user interface.

Most standalone email applications provide some form of spell checking. A spell checker, like the one pictured in Figure 10.2, is generally implemented as a dialog box that lets the user pick the right word to replace a wrong one. After the user picks a new word, the email is updated and the search for misspelled words continues. If the user has a word that he or she often uses and that isn't in the program's dictionary, the user can usually teach the word to the dictionary so that future spell check sessions will include the new word as a valid choice.

Really fancy email programs may provide real-time spell checking using the underline decorator found most commonly in Microsoft Word.

HTML-based email solutions don't have the same options. One of the more ingenious spell check solutions I have seen is to allow the user to submit a message for checking. The result is a page with choice boxes wherever a misspelled word was found, pictured in the small in Figure 10.3. The user chooses the right word and submits the corrected message. In order to support custom values, the HTML page must either include text areas with the choice boxes, or provide a choice for replacing the box with a field. In any case, the user will do some submitting and waiting in order to complete the spell check session. Moreover, the concept of learning new words has to be separated from the spell check UI in the simplest case.

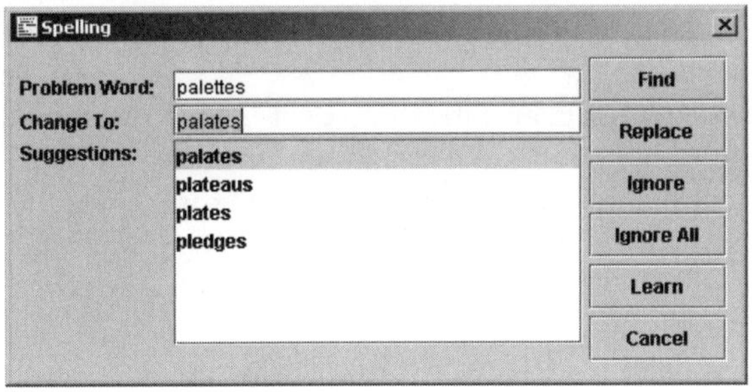

Figure 10.2 Basic spell check dialog box.

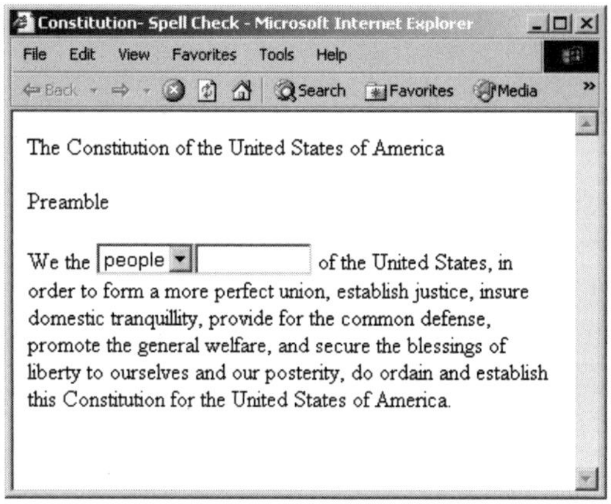

Figure 10.3 HTML spell check solution.

Of course, HTML developers can rely on DHTML to create a solution that is much closer to Figure 10.2. But in order to do so, they are adding a lot of code to the HTML client that may have portability or maintainability issues.

So, if the user wants all of the benefits of a full application, like the one in Figure 10.2, and the developer stuffs it into the interface for Figure 10.3, we have the AntiPattern. But if the HTML-based solution recognizes its limitations, we don't.

HTML isn't the wrong solution for email. But the developers of a Web-based email application must decide to take the disadvantages of the HTML UI with the advantages.

Related Solutions

A number of companies are offering libraries and frameworks for keeping applications up-to-date on the user's machine. These products give you the full freedom of installed applications with the added benefit of easy upgrades, giving you the benefits of the Web without the restrictions.

Because this book is primarily focused on J2EE, and the main user interface options within J2EE are HTML pages, that is what you will see throughout the book. We have included this AntiPattern to open your eyes to other options. To learn more about the basic issues in user interface design, take a look at *The Humane Interface: New Directions for Designing Interactive Systems* (Raskin 2000), *About Face 2.0: The Essentials of Interaction Design* (Cooper 1995), or another UI design book. You might also be interested in *Programming with JFC* (Wiener and Asbury 1998) for an introduction to Swing.

Requiring Local Native Code

Also Known As: JNI

Most Frequent Scale: Application

Refactorings: Control the JNI Boundary

Refactored Solution Type: Code

Root Causes: Legacy code, inexperience

Unbalanced Forces: Experience, code constraints

Anecdotal Evidence: "This program only runs on the AIX/Solaris/Windows system." "Why are we running an old version of Java on the HP-UX box?"

Background

Many enterprise applications will, at some point, want to link to legacy data or applications. This data might be contained on a mainframe or stored on another old computer system. The applications or libraries that you need to use might reside on an older system of some sort. You might also encounter situations where the library or application you want to talk to isn't old; it just doesn't provide a Java interface. In all of these cases, you may be forced to rely on the Java Native Interface (JNI) to access your data or functionality. It is in this scenario that Requiring Local Native Code creeps in.

General Form

JNI, by definition, invokes code that runs natively on a specific system. You can identify this in library form by the use of the native keyword, as shown below in a clip from the java.lang.System class.

```
public static native long currentTimeMillis();
```

If you need to use JNI, you will therefore need to run it on the appropriate system. However, this does not mean that you have to run the JNI code from within your J2EE solution. For example, you don't have to run JNI code from a JSP just because you need to run it. Forcing this connection between native code behind JNI and other J2EE components such as JSPs is at the heart of this AntiPattern. Keep in mind that the AntiPattern isn't the JNI itself, it is requiring it to be local with the J2EE code.

Symptoms and Consequences

Local native code is easy to spot; you just look for the use of the native keyword or the loadLibrary call. It is equally easy to identify the consequences of native code, because the primary one is that you can't run your code anywhere you want to.

- **Your J2EE code contains calls to native methods.** This is the obvious tip-off that you are using JNI code directly.
- **You have to run your J2EE code on a specific machine.** In general, J2EE code is portable and can be run on different J2EE servers and on different operating systems and Java Virtual Machines (JVMs). JNI can create severe limits on the type of machine as well as the JVM. It may also place constraints on your J2EE server indirectly.
- **You have to ship native libraries with your code.** This is a dead giveaway that you use JNI and is also one of the major hassles that results. Keeping native libraries up-to-date can be a maintenance nightmare.

Typical Causes

Generally, JNI is used for one of two reasons. First, the developers don't have another way of accessing a required library, or second, the developers think that they need it for performance. But once the choice is made to use native code, the next question is, "Do you need it locally?" This is where experience comes into play.

- **Your solution requires JNI.** Just the fact that you need to use JNI can lead to thinking that the JNI has to be local.
- **Inexperienced architects.** Developers new to J2EE may not feel comfortable with all of the tools and, as a result, think that there isn't an alternative to calling JNI code directly.
- **Project deadlines.** Calling and writing JNI methods is pretty simple. So it is easy to fall into the trap of using JNI methods directly in a J2EE application when project deadlines are looming.

Known Exceptions

If you need to access native libraries, you may need to use JNI. Using JNI isn't the AntiPattern. The AntiPattern is requiring that the JNI run locally with your other J2EE code. In general, the solution to local JNI code will rely on some form of network communication. In some extreme cases, where you can't network, or can't deal with errors well, this network code may not be permissible to the design, in which case you may want to co-locate the JNI code with full knowledge of the ramifications. A couple examples of acceptable co-location are JDBC drivers and JCE connectors. In both cases, you may need native code to reach the database or external system. In both cases, you may have performance constraints that require the driver to speak directly from the J2EE platform to the external system. Therefore, you would want to co-locate the native code in these limited cases.

Refactorings

The solution to local JNI code is to use a distributed technology instead, as described in the Control the JNI Boundary refactoring later in this chapter. There are a number of ways to do this. The basic pattern is to move the native code to a separate Java application. Then provide a distributed API for this application using JRMI, CORBA, JMS, or some other networking technology. The JNI code is logically separated from the other J2EE code and acts like a standard component of a distributed solution.

Variations

There are two variations of this AntiPattern worth noting. The first is the AntiPattern in disguise. In this case, you use a Java library in your application that itself depends on JNI code. Perhaps this library is a JCA connector or JDBC driver. If you don't recognize the native implementation early on, you can fall into the AntiPattern. The 100 percent Java certification can help you avoid this variation of the pattern.

The second variation occurs when you jump to a new version of the J2EE before its availability is widespread. In this case, you will be limited in where you can deploy your solution and which service providers can support you. So, as with the Local JNI AntiPattern, you limit your solution by the choice of implementation. A simple example of this variation would have been to use the JDBC 2.0 APIs before any JDBC 2.0 drivers existed. This would have locked you into the JDBC/ODBC bridge, which might have been an unreasonable restriction.

Example

Imagine that you have a library written for HP-UX that you use to access a legacy flat file database. You want this data available to your J2EE application, but the work to convert the data is overwhelming and potentially prone to errors. So you decide to wrap the library in JNI. At this point you haven't created the AntiPattern.

Now the question is, "How do you access the JNI?" If you create a library with JNI calls and use it in your EJBs or servlets, then you have created the AntiPattern by requiring that the local code be co-located with the J2EE code. A better alternative is to create a CORBA server that wraps the JNI calls into an object model. This gives you a solution like the one in Figure 10.4.

But then you read the rest of this chapter and realize that you aren't leveraging EJBs where you might be able to. So you decide to wrap the JNI inside EJBs instead of custom CORBA objects. This solution would look like the one pictured in Figure 10.5. The problem is that you are placing incredible constraints on the EJB and its environment. If you can resolve those constraint issues and run the EJB, then you have completed step one to making the database available.

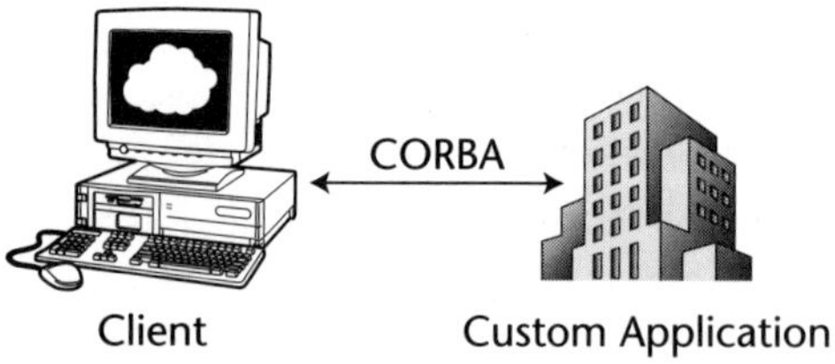

Figure 10.4 JNI behind CORBA.

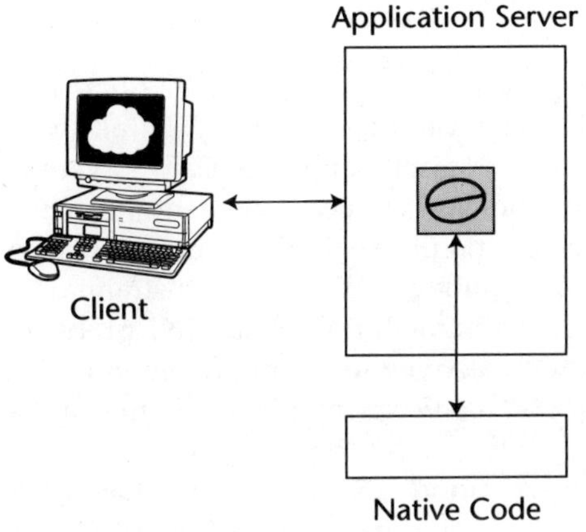

Figure 10.5 JNI from an EJB.

The next step is to make sure that the EJB you created is just a wrapper for the JNI. Move all other code into separate EJBs, creating a solution like the one in Figure 10.6. In this solution, you have a constrained EJB, but the other EJBs that make up your solution can be placed anywhere that a J2EE server is available.

The key point is that you don't tie your JNI too tightly to your application. You want to separate it out.

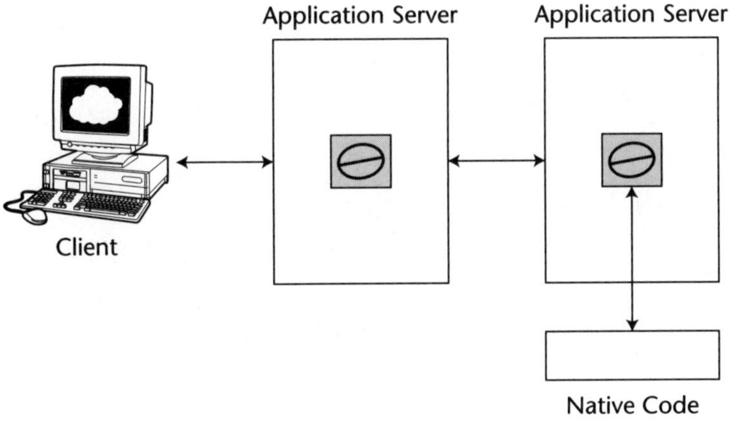

Figure 10.6 Multiple EJBs.

Related Solutions

Depending on how you choose to implement your JNI wrappers, you may find that you can leverage an application server as a wrapper for your wrapper. Basically, you may want to take advantage of the EJB containers as discussed in the Fully Leverage Your J2EE Technologies refactoring. In this situation, you would implement the native code in an EJB, knowing that the application server and EJB are highly limited, but also knowing that the other users of this EJB will not be subject to the same constraints.

CORBA, especially IIOP, provides another possible solution to the JNI problem. Rather than writing any JNI code, you can create a native wrapper around your library that provides accesses via CORBA. Then, your J2EE code can simply access the native code via standard Java-CORBA libraries.

Some JMS providers, such as TIBCO Software, provide C libraries for their JMS servers. If you are using one of these providers, you could use JMS instead of CORBA to wrap your native code.

Overworking JNI

Also Known As: The JNI Barrier

Most Frequent Scale: Application

Refactorings: Control the JNI Boundary

Refactored Solution Type: Architecture

Root Causes: Inexperience with JNI

Unbalanced Forces: Ease of implementation versus performance

Anecdotal Evidence: "We use C code but the application is still slow."

Background

JNI is a powerful tool. But, like any tool it has some limitations. One major limitation in current JVMs is that making JNI calls can require a fair amount of overhead. This overhead takes the form of time within the method call. For example, while calling a Java method might take 1 millisecond, calling a native method might take 2 milliseconds. The actual times are highly dependent on the virtual machine. But in most cases, the native code is actually inducing a performance cost.

General Form

Given that calling a JNI method can take additional time, the AntiPattern is pretty straightforward; making a lot of JNI calls can be a performance problem. When you use JNI, you want to minimize the number of times that you cross the Java-to-native border. Put another way, Overworking JNI is an AntiPattern because it reduces performance. The form that the Overworking JNI AntiPattern takes is simply to make enough JNI calls to reduce your performance in a detrimental way.

Symptoms and Consequences

The primary symptom of this AntiPattern is degraded performance, which results in a failure to meet performance requirements. Therefore, either of the following two symptoms can indicate the AntiPattern:

- **You are making a lot of JNI calls.** Making a lot of JNI calls is likely to overwork the JNI boundary.
- **You use native code but don't see performance improvements.** When you use JNI incorrectly you can actually see a performance degradation instead of a performance boost.

Typical Causes

The basic causes of JNI overload are inexperience and lack of knowledge. Lack of knowledge can take a number of forms. In some cases, the developer may just not know the issues with JNI. In the worst case, the developer knows the issue but isn't aware of the JNI because it is hidden somehow.

- **The JNI calls are hidden.** Some libraries may use JNI without telling you; others might use it but not directly. For example, the Java File object ends up making a number of JNI calls to get information from the File system. This isn't really hidden but it is also not a directly visible issue. Other libraries I have encountered use native code to leverage legacy implementations, even though they could be pure Java. In these cases, the users may not even realize what is happening or when the JNI calls are made.

- **The JNI calls are too fine-grained.** If JNI isn't bad, but too much JNI is, it is easy to see how you might design yourself into a corner. When you make a JNI call, it should do as much work as possible to minimize the actual cost of the call's overhead. So rather than doing 10 JNI calls, it is better to make one that calls the 10 native functions.
- **Developers have little experience with JNI.** JNI has an assumed performance boost, because it uses natively compiled and optimized code, which leads the inexperienced developer to think that just by using JNI he or she will improve performance. This is simply not true in all cases.

Known Exceptions

There is no real exception to this AntiPattern. If you are using JNI, minimize the times that you cross the border; in other words, minimize the number of JNI calls.

Refactorings

The solution to overworking JNI is to minimize the times you make native calls. There are a number of ways to do this, as discussed in detail in the Control the JNI Boundary refactoring later in this chapter. The two simplest solutions are to remove the JNI or write high-level JNI calls. Replacing JNI code with pure Java code solves the JNI problem. It may introduce other issues, so it isn't the solution for all cases, but for many situations, the latest JVMs can run Java at speeds close to the average developer's JNI implementations. The second solution, writing high-level JNI calls, is a minimal design requirement. You just want to wrap your native code in a way that minimizes the number of native method calls you make.

Variations

The overhead for JNI is similar to the overhead for a network call. Both RMI and JNI make it easy to call code in another environment, but at the price of some time spent on overhead. You can think about how you design distributed applications, and the AntiPatterns in Chapter 1, as similar to the issues with JNI because both can result in unexpected situations controlled by code outside of the JVM.

Example

One of the networking libraries we have worked with was originally written in C. We leave out the name because it is a good example of this AntiPattern, and we don't want to get into trouble with the vendor. Suffice to say that it is a real product that has plenty of customers. When Java came out, the vendor wrapped the C libraries with Java libraries using JNI. The problem was that their very fast solution in C became a slow solution for Java. Other technologies such as JMS were faster, even though they were slower on the network. The problem was that the developers thought they could just wrap C with Java and everything would be okay. In the process, they created a situation in which a single message could result in hundreds of JNI calls, slowing the overall performance tremendously. Essentially, the developers overworked JNI.

Another example, that we encountered recently, occurred when we were writing a library to watch the file system for changes. To do this in Java, you simply need to walk the file system looking for changes. The problem is that each call to get the files in a directory, or the last modification time for a file, results in a JNI call. While the underlying system call is probably very fast, the JNI overhead adds to it, making the solution a bit slower than we would like. Our initial solution made numerous calls to File objects. To improve performance, we couldn't change the File object, but we were able to remove many of the unnecessary calls by changing our algorithms. This resulted in a 50 percent improvement in speed without changing the library itself. In other words, we reduced the JNI calls without removing them.

Related Solutions

Many of the solutions from Chapter 1 can be models for solving your JNI boundary issues. For example, in the same way that you look for network hubs and bandwidth requirements in Chapter 1, look at your JNI calls and try to minimize their number and maximize their value. In the same way that JNI represents a boundary between the JVM and other code, network protocols, as described in Chapter 1, have the same boundary. So, the application of the Choose the Right Data Architecture refactoring in Chapter 1 also applies to JNI. When you have to make JNI calls, you want them to do maximum work.

AntiPattern

Choosing the Wrong Level of Detail

Also Known As: Writing Lots of Custom Code. Not Invented Here.

Most Frequent Scale: System

Refactorings: Fully Leverage J2EE Technologies

Refactored Solution Type: Code, architecture

Root Causes: Programming habits, lack of architectural direction, mistrust in products

Unbalanced Forces: Time to market, performance, available technology

Anecdotal Evidence: "How come we don't use EJBs anywhere?" "Why do we still have so many servlets instead of JSPs?"

Background

J2EE and the standard Java libraries provide a lot of options to developers. When connecting two programs, you can use HTTP, JRMI, CORBA, sockets, email, datagram sockets, or JMS, just to name the major options. Given all of these options, it is easy for a developer to become reliant on one technology or another out of habit, preference, or external pressure. But not every technology is necessarily the best for each situation. Moreover, many of the technologies provided by J2EE are layered, with more functionality and value as you move up the technology chain. By sticking to the lower levels of the Java pyramid, developers can lose out on a lot of useful and powerful choices. The bottom line is that by choosing the wrong technology, you work at the wrong level of detail and lose out on the full benefits of J2EE.

General Form

The general form of this AntiPattern is using one technology when another would be better. For example, imagine that you have two applications that need to talk to each other. You could write two custom applications and a TCP/IP-based protocol for them to communicate with. Or you could use RMI to hide the TCP/IP code. Or you could use JMS to add reliability to your messaging. Or you could build message-driven Enterprise JavaBeans that leverage the application server to provide a context and features like load balancing and fault tolerance. Or you could put a bunch of strings in a servlet to define an HTML page instead of using a JSP. In all cases, you are using one technology when another provides better support for the problem you are trying to solve. Depending on the level of detail, you are losing value and gaining flexibility.

Symptoms and Consequences

Applications written at too low a level will generally be harder to maintain than the alternative implementations. However, applications written at too high a level will be less flexible in general. There are design choices to make. The symptoms of this AntiPattern will be that you have to do too much code to get the work done, or are unable to do your work because you don't have access to the functionality you need.

- **You use raw sockets.** If your application is built to use very low-level communication mechanisms, such as TCP/IP or UDP/IP, you will have to implement the protocol and design it to support the various error messages and exceptional conditions that might occur. Moreover, you will be writing code that uses if-statement-like implementations to choose a path based on the requests that it receives. This implementation will scale with the size of the problem; the bigger the problem, the bigger the solution. As a result, large problems can result in hard-to-maintain code bases. Similarly, new developers will have to learn the protocols and the code in order to maintain or add to it.
- **Low-level programs have to implement the hard features themselves.** JMS provides once-and-only-once semantics with guaranteed delivery. Sockets do

not. With sockets, you have to solve the hard problems yourself. Moreover, you will often have to solve them every time you implement a new application.

- **Your client choices are limited.** Applications that use a very high-level communication mechanism, such as JMS, are limiting the clients that they can support. Although most programming languages have support for sockets, they don't support JMS. This can lead to a problem if clients written in other applications need to access your JMS-based application.
- **Higher-level communication mechanisms often rely on servers.** JMS generally requires a server; JRMI requires a name server or JNDI. These external servers add to the overall deployment requirements for your finished solution.

Typical Causes

The choice to use a specific technology is often based on habit. Developers use what they know works, and may avoid things they don't know about or haven't used before. By using what they know, the developers may end up using the wrong level of detail.

- **Developer habits.** Developers use what they know, as do most people, when solving a problem. If you know a hammer works, you use it. If you know a screwdriver works, you use it. You don't switch to the power screwdriver "just because." You need a motivating reason.
- **Lack of experience.** Java has a wide range of developers with extremely varied experience. The developers that came out of the Unix world are used to writing socket-based applications. They know the issues and are good at solving them. Developers who have just started programming in college using Java may have used RMI for their courses and don't know about sockets or JMS. As with their habits, the developers' experiences can drive design choices toward one technology or another.
- **Misunderstandings.** Sometimes developers learn a lesson on one system, or on one version of Java, and think that it applies to their current project. This isn't always the case. Although synchronized methods were slow in the first JDK release, they are not now. So, people that still write really complex code to avoid them are wasting time. Similarly, people avoiding JMS because they think it has to use JRMI and that JRMI is slow are missing the boat.

Known Exceptions

While there are not really exceptions to this AntiPattern, this is not a black-and-white issue. You have to pick the right level of detail for your J2EE solutions; you can go too high- or too low-level.

Refactorings

The solution to picking the wrong level of detail is to pick a more appropriate one, in other words, to fully leverage J2EE technology, as discussed in the refactoring of that name at the end of this chapter. In order to find the right level of detail, you have to look at your requirements. If you need the flexibility of a custom sockets application, then use that. But if you are performing simple network communications, you should certainly move up to one of the higher-level APIs. Likewise, if you are working really hard to fit your application into the JMS or JRMI mold, then you might want to drop down a level and do more of the work yourself.

Variations

In the same way that you can pick the wrong level of detail with networking technologies, you can do so with data storage options. For example, you could write a custom file format. Or you could write an application that uses XML. Or you could leverage a database that writes the files for you. Each level has advantages and disadvantages. Picking the wrong level could paint you into a corner that takes a lot of time and effort to get out of. For example, suppose that you store everything in files, and then realize that your solution is getting too hard to maintain, so you switch to a database. You will have to write programs to migrate your data, and other programs to deal with data in the interim. At the heart of this AntiPattern is the decision to use an API that provides too little or too much detail compared to the problem you are trying to solve.

Example

Let's take a look at one example in detail. Suppose that you want to write an application with an HTML interface. You decide to use servlets and end up writing code like this:

```
public void service(HttpServletRequest request,
                   HttpServletResponse response)
      throws ServletException, IOException
    {
        PrintWriter    out;
        Enumeration headers;
        String curHeader;

        response.setContentType("text/html");

        out = response.getWriter();
```

Listing 10.1 Sample servlet HTML code.

```
out.println("<HTML><HEAD><TITLE>");
out.println("Print Environment");
out.println("</TITLE></HEAD><BODY>");


out.println("<H1>Requested URL</H1>");
out.println(HttpUtils.getRequestURL(request).toString());
out.println("<BR>");

out.println("<H1>Headers</H1>");
headers = request.getHeaderNames();

while(headers.hasMoreElements())
{
    curHeader = (String) headers.nextElement();
    out.println(curHeader+"="+request.getHeader(curHeader)+
              "<BR>");
}

out.println("<BR>");
out.println("<H1>Request Information</H1>");

try
{
    out.println("AuthType="+request.getAuthType()+"<BR>");
    out.println("Scheme="+request.getScheme()+"<BR>");
    out.println("Method="+request.getMethod()+"<BR>");
```

Listing 10.1 *(continued)*

You have a lot of hard-coded strings. Could there be a better way to handle this using a different J2EE technology? Yes. JSPs were created to solve this problem. Therefore, you have the AntiPattern; you chose the wrong level of detail. In this case, the servlet is the wrong level of detail because it has to hard-code strings as Java strings instead of using a JSP to output the HTML, where possible, as straight HTML, thus, hiding the complexity of the printing code and making the solution easier to maintain.

Related Solutions

In Chapter 1, we discussed the Plan Ahead refactoring for building distributed scalable applications. The same is true on a finer-grained level. If you don't plan ahead, you won't end up with the right technology to grow your solution over time. When you plan your overall architecture, take the time to think about the specific technology you will use for the endpoints and the network protocols. The design time allows you to think about the constraints and advantages of each choice.

AntiPattern

Not Leveraging EJB Containers

Also Known As: Writing Custom Servers

Most Frequent Scale: Application

Refactorings: Fully Leverage J2EE Technologies

Refactored Solution Type: Architecture

Root Causes: Developer habits, legacy code

Unbalanced Forces: Architecture versus developer preference

Anecdotal Evidence: "Check out the new load-balancing code I wrote."

Background

Before EJBs were standardized, several companies had already started to create something now called application servers. The idea was to write the hard part of an enterprise-grade server application and allow their customers to plug in the custom parts. EJBs are really a formalization of the customization part more than a concept all their own. Perhaps the big question is not how these servers came to exist, but why.

In the early nineties, the workstation vendors were trying to move corporate developers into a model called client-server. In this model, the server does most of the work, while clients provide the user interface. The client-server model is a fine one, but it has one problem. Servers need to be powerful, fast, reliable, and lots of other things that are hard to do. Moreover, when everyone has to write his or her own servers, it means that the industry needs lots of developers that have the skills and experience necessary to create these robust applications. Worse yet, the knowledge and code that went into each server was not always reusable because it might belong to one company or another.

Application servers changed all that. The application server is the hard-code. Companies can buy an application server built with years of experience and testing and plug in their code without even understanding all of the hard-coded algorithms that go into making the server reliable and robust. When developers don't leverage the code that the application server developers wrote, they are falling into an AntiPattern.

General Form

Some developers still like to write their code themselves. This "not invented here" attitude leads to custom server implementations. When developers bypass application servers, they are missing out on a lot of great implementations, features, and functionality that they could be leveraging. In its most fundamental form, this AntiPattern occurs when the developers implement code that they could leverage. Put simply, underleveraging the available J2EE technology is an AntiPattern.

Symptoms and Consequences

If you write a main method anywhere in your J2EE solution, you may be shortchanging yourself. The same is true if you implement your own load balancing or fault tolerance. This type of code should be leveraged when possible.

- **You have custom distribution in your applications.** When you write applications that run in a standalone environment, you are duplicating work that the application server vendors already did.
- **Custom servers require more maintenance.** If your company writes the server, your company maintains it. If a server vendor writes the code, they maintain it. They fix the bugs, saving you time and money in the long run.

Typical Causes

Failure to leverage the application server is generally caused by cultural issues within a development group. Leveraging tools has historically been a hard pill for developers to swallow and it leads to overimplemented and re-implemented features.

- **The solution is built over time.** Older applications were written before EJB was an available option. These applications may still provide value to your J2EE solution.
- **"Not invented here attitude."** Managers and architects all have to watch out for the "not invented here" attitude. Leveraging existing code can be a great business decision.
- **Hard problems are fun to solve.** Developers like to solve hard problems. Servers are hard to write well, so it is easy for developers to want to write them just to see if they can.

Known Exceptions

If you have an application that already exists and you are performing little or no maintenance, then it is probably okay as is and not worth the cost to rewrite as an EJB. Likewise, if you are writing a very small server, without all of the robustness requirements that an application server provides, then you might implement it manually.

Refactorings

The solution to lots of custom servers is to rewrite them as EJBs. Just as you might rewrite applications that use the wrong level of detail to use higher-level networking technologies, you can rewrite your custom applications to leverage all of the power in a J2EE server. These fixes are summarized in the Fully Leverage J2EE Technologies refactoring discussed later in the chapter.

Example

A lot of EAI vendors are starting to sell both process automation engines and application servers. This is a great benefit for their customers, but because they generally didn't write the two servers at the same time, they are based on different code bases. This means that the company has two load-balancing libraries, two fault-tolerance implementations, and two of everything else their servers need. In other words, by building over time, they forced a higher level of work than if they had planned from the start better.

Of course, in this example, the vendors didn't always know what the future would hold, so we can't really blame them. But it is a great example of how you can fall into a situation where you aren't leveraging the tools you have.

In a similar vein, J2EE developers can implement code that they don't have to, like fault tolerance or guaranteed message delivery. For example, suppose that you write a JMS-based application that has load-balancing code to handle messages on the same topic, and fault-tolerance code to handle one copy of the application going down. This code is already available in an application server. You aren't leveraging J2EE and have created the AntiPattern. J2EE developers should leverage the application server and use it as much as possible.

Refactorings

Since the AntiPatterns in this chapter cover a wide range of issues, the refactorings are equally broad in nature. However, they all represent basic proven design and development strategies. You must plan for change by including parameters to applications. You must build appropriate user interfaces. You must leverage the tools you have in an optimal way. You must do at least these things to create the best possible solutions for yourself and your users.

Solving the problems discussed in this chapter is mainly a process of designing your solution to meet your needs. Although designing a solution before you build it is not a new idea, these refactorings should help you focus on some of the major issues that J2EE developers run into.

By combining these refactorings with the others in this book, you will be able to improve the maintainability, scalability, and reliability of your J2EE solutions.

Parameterize Your Solution. Whenever your application requires configuration information that might change, such as a server name or user login, treat that information like a parameter. Pass it into the application rather than hard-coding it.

Match the Client to the Customer. Java provides numerous implementation choices for your client code; pick the one that best suits your needs, not the one that a marketing person said had a lot of neat bullet points.

Control the JNI Boundary. JNI is a powerful tool with real side effects. Focus your time on the boundary between JNI and Java to ensure that you minimize these side effects in your applications.

Fully Leverage J2EE Technologies. J2EE incorporates a lot of technologies and is implemented by a wide range of servers and services. Use what you can instead of reinventing the wheel to maximize your value and minimize your cost.

Parameterize Your Solution

Your application has hard-coded location identifiers.

Use parameters and JNI to make your solution more dynamic.

```
logFile="c:\temp\foo";
```

Listing 10.2 Before refactoring.

```
try
{
    logFile = (String)
      initCtx.lookup("java:comp/env/logfile");
}
catch(Exception exp)
{
}
```

Listing 10.3 After refactoring.

Motivation

Most J2EE projects are developed in one environment and deployed in a different one. This means that something about the code will change between the two environments. Possibly the change will be the name of an LDAP server or a JNDI server, but there is almost certainly some kind of change that will be required. Changing code is hazardous because it opens up an opportunity for the introduction of errors. Parameterization removes the need to change the code by allowing developers to just change the parameters without recompiling the code. This refactoring is in direct response to the Hard-Coded Location Identifiers AntiPattern.

Mechanics

Parameterization of a J2EE solution is similar to the localization process for a client application. You want to find strings and replace them with parameters of some sort. Then, you want to make these parameters available to your code using as flexible a mechanism as possible, as outlined in the following steps:

1. *Identify strings that are hard-coded.* Hard-coded strings are often an indicator that you should build a parameter.
2. *Use JNDI.* Most J2EE technologies exhibit a preference for using JNDI to find things. Use this preference. JNDI creates an implicit parameterization.
3. *Leverage existing parameter-passing schemes.* The .ear file format, along with other J2EE deployment standards, provides ways to pass parameters. Leverage these whenever possible.
4. *Build custom schemes when necessary.* As a last resort, you might need to create custom schemes to pass parameters. For a custom application, this might include a configuration file or command-line arguments.

Example

Some of the common things to parameterize are: database login information, JNDI server and login information, queue or topic names, server URLs, and names.

Step 1 in applying this refactoring is to look for these values. Basically, anything used to identify something that you would normally include as a string should probably be a parameter. Second, make sure that you are using JNDI when possible. Third, leverage existing schemes. Specifically, to define the parameters, you might use EJB deployment parameters, as in the following example:

```
    <session>
      <display-name>statelesssessionprint</display-name>
      <ejb-name>statelesssessionprint</ejb-name>
      <home>statelesssessionprint.StatelessSessionPrintHome</home>
      <remote>statelesssessionprint.StatelessSessionPrint</remote>
      <ejb-class>statelesssessionprint.StatelessSessionPrintBean</ejb-
class>
      <session-type>Stateless</session-type>
      <transaction-type>Container</transaction-type>
      <reentrant>False</reentrant>
      <env-entry>
          <env-entry-name>logserver</env-entry-name>
          <env-entry-type>java.lang.String</env-entry-type>
          <env-entry-value>localhost</env-entry-value>
      </env-entry>
    </session>
```

Then, you would access them as follows:

```
try
{
    logFile = (String) initCtx.lookup("java:comp/env/logfile");
}
```

```
catch(Exception exp)
{
}
```

Also, these parameters should use standard technology as much as possible. So in this case, we used the standard environment mechanism in EJB 1.2. In the worst case, Step 4 is to create your own schema using command-line values or property files.

Match the Client to the Customer

All of your applications use HTML interfaces, including highly customized DHTML.

Leverage WebStart to provide full-blown applications when they work best.

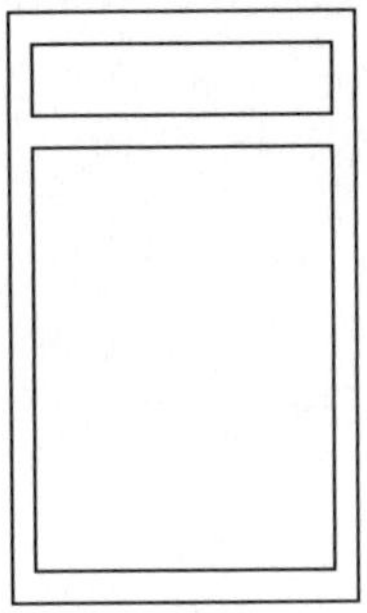

Figure 10.7 Before refactoring.

Figure 10.8 After refactoring.

Motivation

The user interface for your application is where the rubber meets the road. Creating a bad user interface can make your application hard to use. Hard-to-use applications aren't used unless necessary. So, the obvious conclusion is that a good user interface will keep people using your application. Of course, that is just User Experience Design 101. But it is true. With the advent of the Web and the Web = HTML AntiPattern, it is easy to create a bad user interface in response to a faulty assumption rather than addressing the customers' true goals.

Mechanics

User interface design is a giant topic and has numerous books, courses, degree programs, and consultants dedicated to it. We don't want to downplay the importance or complexity of good design, but here are some of the basic steps:

1. *Talk to users.* Find out what the users want to do with the application. Don't focus on what you want them to do, but on what they really want to do.
2. *Build prototypes.* Whether on paper or in code, prototypes provide a great way to speed user feedback. It is a lot cheaper to draw some pictures and find out about a problem than to find out about the problem halfway through the project.
3. *Don't make decisions too early.* Figure out what you need to do before you pick the technology. If you say HTML from the start, you are limiting your options.
4. *Respect the complexity of interface design.* Building a great user interface is not easy. For some reason, enterprise developers fall into a trap where they think that the interface is easy. It's just HTML. But interfaces are a hard business. Interface developers have to deal with serious constraints and user concerns. Rich client interfaces have complex threading semantics and performance algorithms.
5. *Rely on experts.* Use experts to help you through the process.

Example

In one of my past lives, I worked for a company that built training solutions for corporations. One of the products we started working on was a curriculum-development tool for online classes. The online classes were going to be simple HTML pages with links. But we decided, after Step 1, talking to users, that the application for building the classes would be a Java application. We figured that we needed that level of interaction with the user to handle spell checking and other features. But once we had a prototype, Step 2, we realized that we could redo the application as a set of JSPs. So, we ended up with an HTML-based application that created very clean HTML-based courses. Overall, the solution was vastly better, considering the audience. The prototype, and a willingness to change, Step 3, led to a better solution.

On the other hand, we did limit our feature set to make this choice. The spell checking was reduced, and the general interactivity was minimized to prevent server round trips. But with the addition of JavaScript and some DHTML, we created a great solution. I think this is a great example because it could have gone the other way. I have been involved with other projects that started as "Web" applications and turned into full-blown applications. Throughout the process, we respected the process and the complexity, Step 4.

The bottom line is that you want to match the interface to the clients' needs. If wide accessibility is a need, then the Web is a great solution. But if a highly interactive interface is the need, then a full application is likely the best solution.

Control the JNI Boundary

You have lots of JNI calls.

Minimize your JNI calls and have each do the maximum work possible.

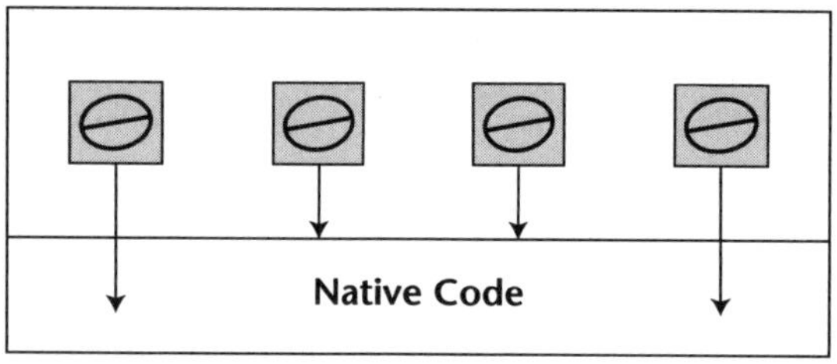

Figure 10.9 Before refactoring.

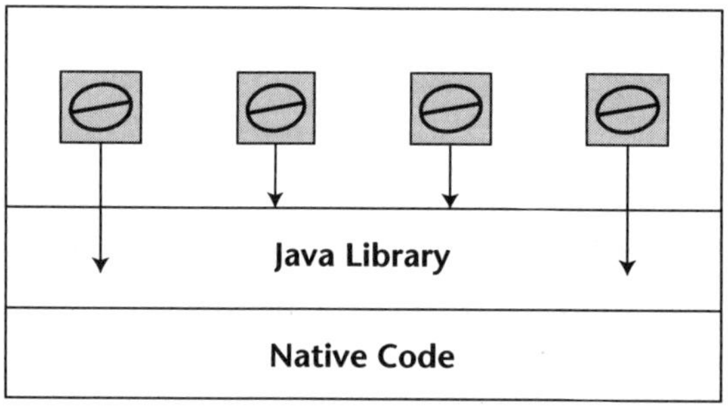

Figure 10.10 After refactoring

Motivation

JNI calls cross a virtual boundary that has performance implications. By watching how JNI is used and minimizing the border between Java and native code, you can improve performance. Similarly, the way you implement or use JNI has implications for the code that you run and where you can run it. So, controlling the JNI border provides you with a built-in check for JNI usage itself and helps you avoid the Overworking JNI AntiPattern and the Requiring Local Native Code AntiPattern.

Mechanics

In order to control the JNI boundary, you need to control JNI usage. That means taking a close look at were you use JNI and determining if that is the best choice, as covered in the following steps:

1. *Question all native methods.* The first step to controlling the JNI border is to try to avoid JNI in the first place. Look for places you use JNI and make sure that it is necessary. Use performance testing if necessary to squelch naysayers who think that JNI is always faster.
2. *Use network technology instead of JNI when possible.* Network technologies such as CORBA provide a mechanism for linking Java to other languages. Moreover, they don't put limits on the Java code the way that JNI does.
3. *Use high-level JNI semantics.* If you have to use JNI, try to do a lot with each call. Minimize the number of calls by making high-level calls with more complete semantics.
4. *Think in two directions.* JNI can also be used to call into your Java code. We mentioned earlier the example of a file watcher that looked for changes to a given directory. This code takes a lot of time to check a large directory. But, some operating systems have a mechanism to notify programs of a file system change. On these systems, we could use JNI to push notifications from the native code to the Java code instead of polling and save a lot of time.

Example

Imagine that you have a compression algorithm that is written in C. Perhaps this algorithm reads a video file format or some other data. You want to use the algorithm in a Java application. What do you do? Well, you could use CORBA, but the requirements in this example don't lend themselves to networking. You would have to do something like turn the data from one format into another and then reinterpret it in the Java application. Instead, you decide to use JNI directly. So you write the code to decompress the data and pass the formatted data to the Java code in a single method call. Further, suppose this implementation works great, as mine always do. So, you did Steps 1 and 2 to decide on JNI. You also did Step 3 to minimize the number of calls.

Now, you get a new set of files that are really collections of the compressed files. You could write a loop to call the native method multiple times. Or, you could write a new native method that takes an array of filenames and returns an array of data. Assuming that there are no memory constraints brought on by the data, this second method, which will reduce the JNI boundary, is likely to be superior to using multiple native calls. In other words, apply Step 3 again, in the new situation. The goal is to control the boundary. It is often reasonable to use JNI, but how you use it is the question. Finally, don't forget that you can call into your Java code from C with JNI.

Fully Leverage J2EE Technologies

You have code to handle load balancing and fault tolerance.

Leverage application servers for the hard-coding.

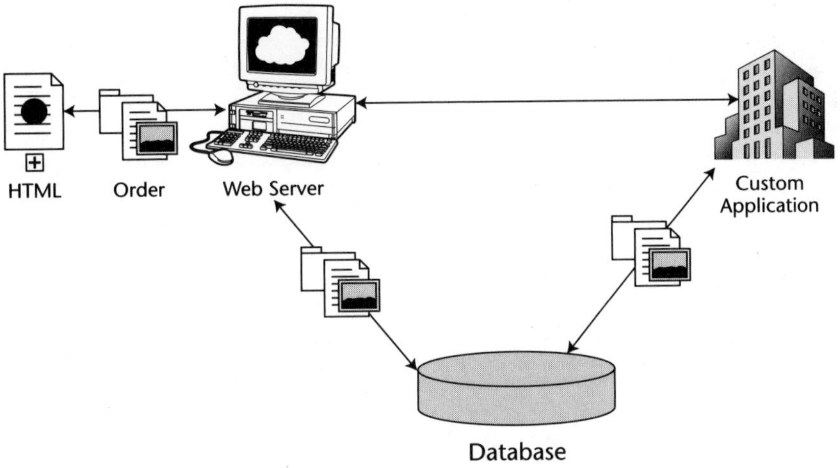

Figure 10.11 Before refactoring.

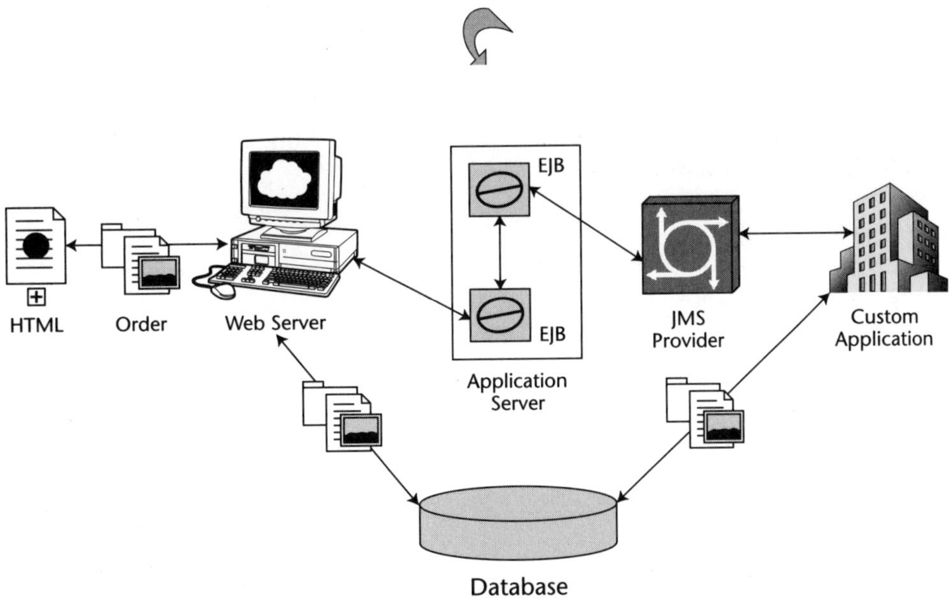

Figure 10.12 After refactoring.

Motivation

Writing enterprise-quality code can be hard. Transactionality, reliability, and scalability are hard problems. Many of the J2EE vendors have teams with hundreds of years of cumulative experience solving these problems. When you use their products, you gain the benefits of that experience. When you write custom code to handle something you could use off-the-shelf, you are throwing away a lot of work, and you are falling into the Choosing the Wrong Level of Detail and Not Leveraging EJB Containers AntiPatterns.

Mechanics

Leveraging J2EE is a two-part process. First, you have to make a decision to trust your J2EE vendor's code. Then, you have to decide how to leverage their code. The trust issue requires research and investigation. The decision on how to leverage the server is really architectural and involves answering some simple questions, such as the following:

1. *Can your server be an EJB or a set of EJBs?* Many applications that act like servers could be implemented as a set of EJBs.
2. *Can your server be implemented as a servlet?* Other servers can be implemented as servlets that run within a servlet engine.
3. *Can your server be load balanced?* Many application servers support load balancing. You can leverage this feature if your server logically supports load balancing and you convert it to an EJB or servlet.

Example

Some prime examples of underleveraging J2EE include: writing JMS clients instead of message-driven beans, writing custom servers instead of EJBs, writing servlets instead of JSPs, and writing JDBC code instead of using container-managed persistence and Entity Beans.

Basically, the higher up the "food chain" you go, the more you are leveraging the existing technology. So for example, if you could write several hundred or thousand lines of code to build a JMS client application, or you could write your onMessage method and leverage the J2EE server for the rest, which is Step 1. You could write a custom server, or just a servlet, which is Step 2. J2EE is a powerful collection of technology and experience that should be leveraged whenever possible.

Summary

We have covered a lot of ground in this book. You are hopefully now equipped to not only recognize the AntiPatterns in your code but also see your way out of the AntiPatterns through the refactorings provided. Armed with the knowledge of what can go wrong while developing enterprise applications with J2EE, as well as how to fix the problems, it is our hope that you will be able to write better applications to power your enterprise into the future.

APPENDIX

A

AntiPatterns Catalog

Overworked Hubs 23

Hubs are rendezvous points in your J2EE application. These hubs may be database servers, JMS servers, EJB servers, and other applications that host or implement specific features you need. When a hub is overworked, it will begin to slow down and possibly fail.

The Man with the Axe 31

Failure is a part of life. Planning for failure is a key part of building a robust J2EE application, but failing to plan results in The Man with the Axe.

Persistence AntiPatterns 63

Dredge 67

Applications must frequently retrieve data from databases in order to drive query screens and reports. Applications that do not properly distinguish between shallow and deep information tend to load all of this information at once, leading to applications that outstrip available processing and memory resources and cannot scale to meet user demands.

Crush 75

Shared access to data in a multiuser environment must be carefully coordinated to avoid data corruption. A *pessimistic* locking strategy can ensure such coordination—at the expense of performance—by allowing only one user to read and update a given data record at a time. An optimistic strategy can offer better performance by allowing multiple users to view a given data record simultaneously. Great care must be taken to avoid data corruption and overwrites in a multiuser environment.

DataVision 81

Application component models should drive their underlying database schema—not the other way around. This AntiPattern shows the dysfunctional application model that can result from not heeding this advice.

Stifle 87

Most J2EE applications that deal with persistent data act as database clients, which converse with database servers over a network connection. These J2EE applications must make optimal use of network bandwidth in order to achieve the greatest levels of database scalability. Such applications can be bottlenecked by not optimizing the network pipeline for database communications.

Service-Based Architecture AntiPatterns 111

Multiservice 115

A multiservice is a service with a large number of public interface methods that implement processes related to many different key abstractions or entities. The result is a service that is coupling to many underlying business or technical components, and also is utilized by many clients, making development and maintenance difficult, and reducing flexibility and reuse.

Tiny Service 121

A tiny service is a service that incompletely represents an abstraction, implementing only a subset of the necessary methods, resulting in the need for multiple services to completely implement the abstraction. The result is that clients have to utilize several services to implement a significant business process, and need to implement the sequencing and workflow.

Stovepipe Service 127

Stovepipe services are a set of business services that are implemented in isolation, producing a duplicated implementation of nonfunctional, technical requirements that are common to all or many of the business services. The result is a duplicated, inconsistent implementation of technical functions and large, difficult-to-maintain service implementations.

Client Completes Service 133

In this AntiPattern, important functionality, such as the validation of input data, security checking, and event auditing, is implemented in client components instead of within the service, resulting in an incomplete service that does not perform some aspects necessary for it to be truly standalone and usable in other contexts.

JSP Use and Misuse AntiPatterns 155

Ignoring Reality 159

This AntiPattern is about the tendency of developers to ignore the reality that errors do happen. All too often users are served Java stack traces, which causes them to lose confidence in the application, and if the problem is not dealt with, this can eventually lead to the project being canceled.

Template Text in Servlet 243

The Template Text in Servlet AntiPattern refers to the tendency of some developers to put hard-coded strings of HTML into their servlets. Developers whose applications are stuck in this AntiPattern will have a hard time fixing bugs in the HTML that is generated because the HTML is imbedded in Java code instead of being in an HTML file.

Using Strings for Content Generation 249

In many cases, a servlet will have HTML embedded in it and it will not be possible to remove the content. When strings are used to generate the content, the servlet and the HTML that it generates are much harder to maintain than they could be.

Not Pooling Connections 255

Database connections are expensive to open and keep open in terms of time and resources. Applications stuck in this AntiPattern will suffer from performance problems in all aspects that relate to accessing the database.

Accessing Entities Directly 261

A servlet should not remotely access an EJB entity via a fine-grained API. The overhead of marshaling and unmarshaling the data involved in the remote call will cause the application to slow to a crawl.

Entity Bean AntiPatterns 283

Fragile Links 287

Developers often hard-code JNDI lookups of Entity Beans in their applications. However, this practice can cause a system to become brittle and resistant to change.

DTO Explosion 293

A common mistake is to make the entity layer responsible for accepting and returning view-oriented DTO instances. This reduces the reusability of the entity layer, because it is wedded to a particular application's user interface or reporting requirements.

Surface Tension 301

Sometimes the sheer number of explicit custom DTO classes, and the complexity of their interrelationships and interfaces, can make an application very difficult to maintain.

Large Transaction 383

This AntiPattern is a transactional session method that implements a long, complicated process, and involves a lot of transactional resources, effectively locking out those resources to other threads for a significant period of time. This results in noticeable performance issues and deadlock when there are many concurrent executions of the method.

Transparent Façade 391

The Transparent façade is an attempt at the Session façade pattern in which the Sessions interface directly matches the underlying component (usually an Entity Bean). This creates a façade that does not create subsystem layering and coarser-grained interaction as intended by the Session façade pattern. This results in additional development and actually worse performance, with no reduction in number of invocations by clients.

Data Cache 395

This AntiPattern uses Stateful Session Beans to implement a distributed, in-memory data cache. However, an effective cache must support a certain set of requirements, and while Stateful Session Beans may look like they should do the trick, there are limitations in concurrency support, reliability, and failover which ultimately render this an unworkable approach.

Message-Driven Bean AntiPatterns 411

Misunderstanding JMS 413

JMS offers a number of messaging choices. It is easy to confuse these or choose the wrong one. An architect might not use a topic when it's really necessary to distribute messages, or might use topics everywhere even though it is overkill for some applications.

Overloading Destinations 421

One of the more confusing things that people can do is create a destination that will be used for numerous message types. For example, you can send text- and map-based messages on the same queue, which requires the receiver to distinguish them. But you can also send two different maps on the same queue or two different XML schemas. This can also lead to problems.

Overimplementing Reliability 429

JMS provides reliability in messaging, so it is not necessary, in most cases, for the message beans to check if something is a repeat. Only in very rare cases does the JMS server need to be second-guessed on every message. This AntiPattern comes into play when iterating solutions or building a replacement for an old solution, like RMI, where code was necessary to check for uniqueness in messages.

Web Services AntiPatterns 447

Web Services Will Fix Our Problems 451

This AntiPattern is choosing to adopt Web Services with the idea that they will fix some major problems in an existing J2EE application. Issues with extensibility and reuse are usually due to poor architecture and design, and implementing Web Services over a bad architecture only makes it worse by recreating the bad structure with even more technology, artifacts, and issues.

When in Doubt, Make It a Web Service 457

Architects and developers go overboard and use a Web Services approach for implementing and vending processes and functionality that do not need Web Services and do not benefit from it. The result is lower performance than J2EE-native approaches, and additional development time being required to understand, implement, and deploy additional Web Service artifacts. This is the "Golden Hammer" AntiPattern, which in this case means everything looks like it should be implemented as a Web Service (the nail).

God Object Web Service 463

This AntiPattern involves putting many operations within a single Web Service that operates against different abstractions, entities, or business documents. At the extreme, the result is a single large Web service that vends all external functions, and with which all clients interact.

Fine-Grained/Chatty Web Service 469

This is the analogue of the "chatty interface" issue with Entity EJBs. The Web Service is defined with many fine-grained operations, and clients end up invoking many operations in sequence to perform an overall process. This requires many invocations to perform an overall process, resulting in poorer performance, and requires each client to implement sequencing and workflow for a process.

Maybe It's Not RPC 475

This AntiPattern consists of forcing a synchronous RPC-style implementation for Web Service operations that implements Create, Read, Update, and Delete (CRUD) operations on a major business entity, where an asynchronous, document-style approach is more appropriate. CRUD-oriented business document operations implemented using the RPC approach often end up with a lot of parameters that are custom types and SOAP document fragments.

Single-Schema Dream 483

This AntiPattern results from choosing a single XML schema to serve as the one business document definition for a specific business entity (such as Order) to be used in a multiparty electronic document exchange. This doesn't work, because each party has its own, slightly different document definition and requirements, in terms of attributes and data formats. Thus, the initial architecture and design operates on the basis of utilizing a single XML schema, but ultimately has to be refactored to accommodate partner- or customer-specific schema variants, and to do transforms to and from their format.

SOAPY Business Logic 489

In this AntiPattern, a Web Service endpoint component implements business logic, but is also coupled specifically to Web Service data types and/or contains implementation that explicitly deals with SOAP/XML processing, tying the business logic implementation explicitly to a Web Service's context. This severely reduces the reuse potential of the business logic. The most typical case occurs when a Session Bean is used for the endpoint.

J2EE Service AntiPatterns 509

Hard-Coded Location Identifiers 511

JNDI provides a simple means of looking up contact, connection, or location information. However, even the JNDI connection information should be configurable so that developers don't have to recompile the code every time a network change occurs.

Web = HTML 517

Many people, not just J2EE developers, associate the Web with HTML. This is simply not the case. There are a number of ways to leverage J2EE and the Web that don't require the developer to use HTML or Web page user interfaces.

Requiring Local Native Code 523

Native code, code that isn't written in Java, is a fact of life. Some systems can only be accessed from code in native libraries. Legacy systems may have core algorithms in native code that must be reused. However, using native code via the Java Native Interface, JNI, is not the only choice. It can, in fact, be the worst choice in many cases.

Overworking JNI 529

When using JNI there are some particular issues related to interfacing with J2EE applications. Many simple JNI implementations overwork the JNI interface and cause performance degradations as a result.

Choosing the Wrong Level of Detail 533

J2EE provides several layers of technology. For example, you can write an application that uses RMI directly or a Session Bean that you access with RMI. Choosing the wrong level to work at will affect the reliability and overall performance of your final solution.

Not Leveraging EJB Containers 539

The EJB concept has been improved with every update to the J2EE standards. These beans represent a great programming model for leveraging existing services such as load balancing, fault tolerance, and data storage. When possible, developers should leverage the bean containers' services to improve their application without additional work.

APPENDIX

B

Refactorings Catalog

Distribution and Scaling Refactorings 1

Plan Ahead 37

When building a J2EE solution, think about issues in distribution before they come up. One way to help with this is to plan for some standard life-cycle issues from the start. These life-cycle issues include how you are going to fix bugs and upgrade software.

Choose the Right Data Architecture 41

There are different data designs. You can build hub-and-spoke designs, random distributions, centralized data stores, distributed data stores, and all sorts of combinations of these. Pick the right one for each job.

Partition Data and Work 46

When there is too much data, sometimes you need to organize it. Generally, data is organized along a particular axis, such as time or location. In very large data sets, you might organize data several ways or on multiple axes.

Plan for Scaling (Enterprise-Scale OO) 51

Encapsulation, abstraction, inheritance, and polymorphism are the key components of object-oriented programming. J2EE is about taking these concepts to a larger scale. Where objects encapsulate data and the implementation, EJBs encapsulate data and the implementation into Session and Entity Beans. Both Enterprise Beans and other objects abstract concepts. JMS creates a polymorphic relationship between sender and receiver, whereby one sender may talk to many receivers that are not well known to the sender.

Plan Realistic Network Requirements 54

When you plan the network requirements for an application, you have to look at realistic data requirements and realistic traffic patterns. Not planning accurately can result in unexpected network performance consequences.

Use Specialized Networks 56

Add bandwidth by adding networks. Using small, specialized networks allows you to add bandwidth inexpensively and control bandwidth interactions between network applications.

Be Paranoid 58

If there is one good thing you can say about paranoid people, it is that they are always ready for the worst. When planning a distributed application, you have to be paranoid. You have to think about possible failures far more than you do in single-computer applications.

Throw Hardware at the Problem 60

When all else fails, throw hardware at the problem. Some problems are easily solved with bigger hardware. Some are only solved with more hardware or an expensive redesign. Throwing hardware at problems is a tried-and-true solution to many scaling problems.

Persistence Refactorings 63

Light Query 92

Applications can retrieve much larger volumes of shallow information more efficiently if lightweight JDBC queries are used in lieu of heavyweight Entity Beans.

Version 98

An application can support multiple, simultaneous logical transactions involving user think-time if the right versioning mechanisms and checks are put into place. Introduce versioning mechanisms into the entity and DTO layers, and check versions in the Session Façade layer.

Component View 103

Use proper object-oriented analysis and design to refactor pseudocomponents, which were originally conceived from an existing database schema or a data-centric mindset.

Pack 107

Use the batch-processing capabilities of JDBC 2.x (or greater) to optimize intensive database operations.

Service-Based Architecture Refactorings 111

Interface Partitioning 140

This refactoring is used to rectify the situation of a large, multiabstraction service (the Multiservice AntiPattern). Interface partitioning rectifies this AntiPattern by segregating the service into multiple services that each represents a distinct abstraction.

Interface Consolidation 144

This refactoring is used to rectify the situation of many, fine-grained services (the Tiny Service AntiPattern). Interface consolidation rectifies this by aggregating a set of services together that collectively implement a complete, single abstraction. Different service interfaces that operate against the same abstraction are consolidated (along with their implementations) into one service that represents a single cohesive abstraction.

Technical Services Layer 147

This refactoring introduces layering to stovepipe services to create an underlying layer of common technical services, splitting the middle tier into business and technical service layers. The Technical Services Layer refactoring works to extract the duplicated technical functions and define a single interface and implementation as a technical service. This occurs for each of the distinct technical process areas and abstractions, resulting in a technical services layer that the business services use.

Cross-Tier Refactoring 151

This refactoring addresses the Client Completes Service AntiPattern, moving the client-based functionality back into the underlying services so that they are truly standalone and not coupled to any particular client type. This may involve retaining the implementation in both the client and service (for performance reasons), but in either case, the necessary business or technical functions are refactored into the services so that they implement the necessary functionality and operational aspects to be usable in a variety of client contexts.

JSP Use and Misuse Refactorings 155

Beanify 201

That data should be encapsulated with its functionality is one of the fundamental tenants of object-oriented programming. Beanify provides the mechanics for you to get unorganized data out of your session and organize it into a bean. Having your data encapsulated in a bean will improve the reliability and maintainability of your application.

Introduce Traffic Cop 204

An application that has all the navigational information hard-coded into the servlets and JSPs will be much harder to change than it should be. The Introduce Traffic Cop refactoring will help you to move all that navigational information out of the individual servlets and JSPs and place it into a central servlet.

Introduce Delegate Controller 210

When a single controller is responsible for all the application logic, the controller will be very hard to change or update. For any reasonably sized application, the class will become almost impossible to follow because it is so big. The Introduce Delegate Controller refactoring will help you to pull small, interrelated pieces of functionality out of the overly big controller and place them into smaller controller classes. The big controller can then delegate that functionality to the smaller controllers.

Introduce Template 216

JSP code is very hard to maintain when it is copied and pasted into several different JSPs. As with any other programming technology, copying and pasting leads to hard-to-change code. The Introduce Template refactoring provides practical help in getting the common parts of your JSP ready to be reused in a template.

Use JSPs 278

Instead of having HTML in your servlets, use JSPs to capture the plain HTML and include the JSP from within your servlet. Having the plain HTML for your application embedded in your servlet will cause maintenance headaches; HTML code embedded in Java code is very hard to debug. This refactoring takes you step-by-step through the process of removing the HTML from your Servlet and replacing it with a JSP import.

Entity Bean Refactorings 283

Local Motion 326

Most applications do not invoke their entity beans remotely. Instead, they are invoked by co-located Session Façade Beans, which, in turn, are invoked by remote application clients. In this scenario, the Entity Bean invocations can be far more efficient if those beans support a local interface. Session façades can use the local interface instead of the slower, more heavyweight remote interface.

Alias 331

Application code that references the actual JNDI locations of EJBs and services could break if those components are relocated at deployment time. Use EJB references to add a layer of abstraction that insulates the application from such deployment-time changes.

Exodus 335

Entity Beans are often stuck with the responsibility for creating and returning custom DTOs to support screens and reports. This limits the reusability and maintainability of the entity layer, because the entity layer becomes dependent on higher-order, view-oriented DTOs that may be specific to a particular application. Add a DTOFactory component to the services layer. This component will be responsible for creating and manipulating custom DTO instances. This decouples the entity from the custom DTOs, which ultimately improves reusability.

Flat View 340

Entity beans and DTOs that have a large number of getters and setters tend to increase coupling with client components. In addition, exceptionally large numbers of DTO classes can be difficult to maintain. Use a flat generic DTO to reduce the number of explicit DTO classes and DTO getters and setters within an application.

Strong Bond 344

Bean-managed interbean and bean-to-dependent object relationships are no longer necessary under EJB 2.x (or greater). Use container-managed relationships (CMR) to implement these relationships without writing a single line of code.

Best of Both Worlds 351

Moving from BMP to CMP can be done incrementally. Simply introduce CMP implementations and modify existing BMP implementations to extend their CMP counterparts. Now, the choice of implementation can be specified at deployment time.

Façade 355

Java can do database-intensive operations. Simply use the batch-processing capabilities of JDBC 2.x (or greater) to the optimize network pipeline between database clients and servers.

Session EJBs Refactorings 361

Session Façade 402

This refactoring introduces a session as a façade over another EJB component that aggregates a number of fine-grained methods into fewer, coarse-grained methods and effectively creates subsystem layering. This may be done over a specific entity to aggregate individual attribute accessors or mutators into coarse-grained bulk accessor or mutator methods, or over multiple sessions and/or entities to implement a sequenced workflow process by aggregating the various fine-grained steps into a coarser-grained process.

Split Large Transaction 406

This refactoring splits a large transactional method into a number of smaller transactions, and refactors clients to invoke these methods separately. Transaction monitoring and compensating actions are implemented to produce an equivalent overall transactional result. Thus, each of the methods is then a much smaller transaction, with fewer resources locked in at any one time.

Message-Driven Bean Refactorings 411

Architect the Solution 438

Developers working at the endpoints of a distributed application build many J2EE solutions. When doing so, you have to think globally and work locally to build successful J2EE implementations.

Plan Your Network Data Model 441

There are a lot of books about patterns and designing for applications. Distributed applications require the same techniques. In particular, the data that you are sending to your JMS applications and message-driven beans must be planned and documented to avoid too much complexity and performance degradation.

Leverage All Forms of EJBs 444

Obviously, message-driven beans aren't the only type of EJB, so don't treat them that way. Session and Entity Beans can play an important role in a JMS-based solution.

Web Service Refactorings 447

RPC to Document Style 496

This refactors a CRUD-style Web Service interaction that is implemented as a synchronous, RPC-styled approach into a document-style, asynchronous approach, which is more natural and appropriate for CRUD operations on business documents.

Schema Adaptor 501

This refactoring introduces XML document transformations into the document-handling flow into an electronic document exchange process, to enable participants with moderately different formats for a business document to interoperate. This introduces a SchemaAdaptor component within the handling flow that utilizes XSL transforms to transform the external schemas to the single, internal format for consistent processing within the J2EE system.

Web Service Business Delegate 506

This refactoring decouples the Web Service endpoint implementation from underlying business logic, enabling the business logic to be reused for any kind of client. This approach interjects an intervening Java component between a Web Service endpoint receiver and an underlying business logic component, such as a Session bean, to remove Web Services-specific handling code from the business logic component and/or to remove Web Service-specific data types and coupling from the component to facilitate easier reuse.

J2EE Service Refactorings 509

Parameterize Your Solution 544

Whenever your application requires configuration information that might change, such as a server name or user login, treat that information like a parameter. Pass it into the application rather than hard-coding it.

Match the Client to the Customer 547

Java provides numerous implementation choices for your client code; pick the one that best suits your needs, not the one that a marketing person said had a lot of neat bullet points.

Control the JNI Boundary 550

JNI is a powerful tool with real side effects. Focus your time on the boundary between JNI and Java to ensure the minimization of these side effects in your applications.

Fully Leverage J2EE Technologies 553

J2EE has a lot of technologies and is implemented by a wide range of servers and services. Use what you can instead of reinventing the wheel, to maximize your value and minimize your cost.

APPENDIX

C

What's on the Web Site

This appendix provides you with information on the contents of the Web site that accompanies this book. Here is what you will find:

- System Requirements
  - JDK 1.3.1 or higher
  - JBoss (www.jboss.org), or:
  - Sun's J2EE Reference Implementation (java.sun.com), or:
  - JBoss 3.0.x or greater (www.jboss.org)
- What's in the Web site
  - Source code for many of the examples in the book

System Requirements

Make sure that your computer meets the minimum system requirements listed in this section. If your computer doesn't match up to most of these requirements, you may have a problem using the Web site.

For Windows 9*x*, Windows 2000, Windows NT4 (with SP 4 or later), Windows Me, or Windows XP:

- PC with a Pentium processor running at 600 Mhz or faster
- At least 128 MB of total RAM installed on your computer; for best performance, we recommend at least 256 MB
- Ethernet network interface card (NIC) or modem with a speed of at least 28,800 bps
  - A CD-ROM drive
  - JDK 1.3.1 or higher (tested with Sun's JDK)

For Linux:

- PC with a Pentium processor running at 600 Mhz or faster
- At least 64 MB of total RAM installed on your computer; for best performance, we recommend at least 128 MB
- Ethernet network interface card (NIC) or modem with a speed of at least 28,800 bps
  - A CD-ROM drive
  - JDK 1.3.1 or higher

For Macintosh:

- Mac OS X computer with a G3 or faster processor running OS 10.1 or later
  - At least 64 MB of total RAM installed on your computer; for best performance, we recommend at least 128 MB
  - JDK 1.3.1 or higher

What's on the Web Site

The following sections provide a summary of the software and other materials you'll find on the Web site. The companion Web site for this title can be found at http://www.wiley.com/compbooks/dudney.

Author-created materials

All author-created material from the book, including code listings and samples, are on the Web.

If you still have trouble with the Web site, please call the Wiley Product Technical Support phone number: 1-800-762-2974. Outside the United States, call 1-317-572-3994.

You can also contact Wiley Product Technical Support at www.wiley.com/techsupport. Wiley will provide technical support only for installation and other general quality control items; for technical support on the applications themselves, consult the program's vendor or author.

References

Alur, Deepak, John Crupi, and Dan Malks. *Core J2EE Patterns: Best Practices and Design Strategies*. Upper Saddle River, NJ: Prentice Hall PTR, 2001.

Cooper, Alan and Robert M. Reimann. *About Face 2.0: The Essentials of Interaction Design*. Indianapolis, Indiana: Wiley Technology Publishing, 2003.

Fowler, Martin. *Refactoring: Improving the Design of Existing Code.* Reading, MA: Addison Wesley, 2000.

Gamma, Erich, Richard Helm, Ralph Johnson, and John Vlissides. *Design Patterns, Elements of Reusable Object-Oriented Software*. Reading, MA: Addison-Wesley, 1996.

Marinescu, Floyd. *EJB Design Patterns: Advanced Patterns, Processes, and Idioms*. Indianapolis, Indiana: Wiley Technology Publishing, 2002.

Monson-Haefel, Richard. *Enterprise JavaBeans (3rd Edition)*. Sebastopol, CA: O'Reilly & Associates, 2001.

Raskin, Jef. *The Humane Interface: New Directions for Designing Interactive Systems*. Reading, MA: Addison-Wesley, 2000.

Roman, Ed, Scott Ambler, and Tyler Jewell. *JavaBeans (2nd Edition).* Indianapolis, Indiana: Wiley Technology Publishing, 2001.

Schneier, Bruce. *Secrets and Lies: Digital Security in a Networked World.* Indianapolis, Indiana: Wiley Technology Publishing, 2000.

Wiener, Scott R. and Stephen Asbury. *Programming with JFC.* New York, NY: John Wiley & Sons, 1998.

Index

Numbers

A

M

N

O

P

T

W